Farming in the First Millennium AD

Frontispiece: The production and marketing of grain as depicted in the Harley Psalter *c* AD 1000, British Library MS 603, fol. 21.

Farming in the First Millennium AD

British Agriculture between Julius Caesar
and William the Conqueror

PETER FOWLER

 CAMBRIDGE
UNIVERSITY PRESS

PUBLISHED BY THE PRESS SYNDICATE OF THE UNIVERSITY OF CAMBRIDGE
The Pitt Building, Trumpington Street, Cambridge, United Kingdom

CAMBRIDGE UNIVERSITY PRESS
The Edinburgh Building, Cambridge CB2 2RU, UK
40 West 20th Street, New York, NY 10011-4211, USA
477 Williamstown Road, Port Melbourne, VIC 3207, Australia
Ruiz de Alarcón 13, 28014 Madrid, Spain
Dock House, The Waterfront, Cape Town 8001, South Africa

http://www.cambridge.org

First published 2002

Printed in the United Kingdom at the University Press, Cambridge

Typeface Erhardt MT 10.5/14 pt   *System* LaTeX 2_ε [TB]

A catalogue record for this book is available from the British Library

Library of Congress Cataloguing in Publication data

Fowler, P. J.
Farming in the first millennium AD: British agriculture between Julius Caesar and
William the Conqueror / P. J. Fowler.
    p. cm.
Includes bibliographical references (p.).
ISBN 0 521 81364 6 – ISBN 0 521 89056 X (pb.)
1. Agriculture – Great Britain – History – To 1500.   I. Title.
S455 .F639   2002
630′.941′0902 – dc21   2001043847

ISBN 0 521 81364 6 hardback
ISBN 0 521 89056 X paperback

To Charles in friendship,
many a field and forty years on since
Fowler and Thomas 1962

MASTER: 'What do your friends do?'

MONK: 'Some are ploughmen, some shepherds, some oxherds; some again, huntsmen, some fishermen, some fowlers, some merchants, some shoe-makers, salters, bakers.'

AELFRIC'S *COLLOQUY*,
trans. Swanton 1993, 169

Contents

Illustrations

FIGURES

Preface

'What do you say, fowler?'

THE 'MASTER' IN AELFRIC'S *COLLOQUY* TRANS. SWANTON 1993, 172

My title is indicative rather than precise. Broadly, the book is about farming in Britain from the Roman invasion of AD 43 until about AD 1000. It is not intent on discussing farming in either the century or so before the birth of Christ or the eleventh century AD in detail. Narrow, however, would be a perspective which did not take cognisance of Julius Caesar's description of the island he invaded or of *Domesday Book*, William I's great survey of the land he too invaded and, unlike Caesar, successfully conquered.

This book is the sequel to my *The Farming of Prehistoric Britain* (Fowler 1983a, now O.P.). That paperback was itself spawned from *The Agrarian History of England and Wales* I.1 *Prehistory* (Piggott 1981; Fowler 1981a). *Farming in the First Millennium AD* is stimulated by the second part, volume I.2, of that same *Cambridge Agrarian History* (Finberg 1972a), in which I was privileged, as a young beginner, to be marginally involved (Finberg 1972a, 4, 385). My brush with great historians then has remained the inspiration of an ambition to write an up-to-date complement to their work. This essay is conceived as a preliminary step to that end. Relative to that, and to what can now be discussed compared to the state of knowledge when Finberg *et al.* were writing, the scale and size of this *Farming in the First Millennium AD* allow scope to do little more than to illustrate by example and discuss a few general points.

Yet this text steadfastly follows one very important precept in our three progenitors. Just as those works were not conceived in time-periods (Bronze Age, Early Iron Age, etc.) so neither is this essay on the first millennium AD conceived in terms of 'Roman Britain' and 'Anglo-Saxon England'. My aim is to try to look at agrarian history during a particular thousand years consciously seeking a neutrality in terms of periodisation and cultural ascription. Dark (2000, viii), also most helpfully reviewing the whole of the millennium, nevertheless bases her work on the main archaeological and text-defined historical periods, remarking that this approach 'faces the problem that such periods do not necessarily apply to the whole of Britain at the same time, if at all'. A wider problem lies in those last three words, for historians' and archaeologists' period and cultural labels are not necessarily relevant to agrarian history at all. They may even – and indeed probably – obscure significance in the consciously agrarian perspective adopted here. So I start by trying to assume only, on fairly good evidence, that farming was indeed practised throughout Britain between the first and the eleventh centuries AD. The obvious thought that such practice is likely to have retained elements of continuity, within perhaps rather than always throughout the millennium, is clearly a candidate for testing.

Farming in Britain throughout the first millennium is now demonstrated by a huge amount of primary evidence, mainly non-documentary. In that respect, the situation is fundamentally different from a generation ago. Agrarian material from the early centuries AD, for example, is probably at least thrice the quantity, and immeasurably both better in quality and wider in range, than when Applebaum (1972) produced his learned overview; and likewise, for the mid-millennium onwards, the settlement and agrarian archaeology of much of Britain has virtually been created since Finberg (1972b) in particular was trying to fit, too neatly, his farming story of Anglo-Saxon England into an historical framework. Nevertheless, my essay is highly, even painfully, selective: for one thing, too much relevant information across a considerable range of academic disciplines now exists for one individual to absorb even-handedly. So it is neither comprehensive nor inclusive; it cannot be, and makes no attempt to be so. I can but hope that my personal selection is interesting to others.

Among notable omissions in this survey is Ireland. I had intended to include it but Fergus Kelly's *Early Irish Farming* (1998), produced at an enviable level of scholarly excellence while I was writing, makes such intention redundant. His work has, however, reinforced the view from across the Irish Sea that much exists in field and library in Ireland of relevance to the whole of Britain. In a continuation of the great two-way tradition in the middle centuries of the first millennium AD, therefore, I have raided Kelly as and when I have thought it useful to lift Irish material, not to attempt to tell Ireland's agrarian history but to use Irish material to illumine land and practices further east. This is meant as homage, not pillage.

Similarly, but more generally, I am deeply influenced by the works, freely made use of here, of a few others in a select band of scholars

in early historical *agraria* whose pioneering achievements I can but ad-
mire: Margaret Gelling, Della Hooke, Joan Thirsk and K.D. White. I also
overtly acknowledge my dependence on others with respect to documentary sources. I am no linguist and use others' translations from Latin and
Anglo-Saxon; but dependence on others' work, its accuracy and interpretation, is a hallmark of any attempted overview, so in a sense language is
not particularly different from other evidence.

The chapter sequence goes from the general through the evidential
and down a scale to greater detail within a functional framework before
emerging with the outcomes of farming as witnessed by its edible product,
the sort of societies it sustained, and a modern historical view of the process
of farming in the first millennium. I have written with two audiences
specially in mind. First, since the topic is of interest to people outside
academia, the book tries to be fair both to current ideas and to the huge
amount of evidence. It also attempts to present both in a way which
could also be a reasonably good read for anyone with an interest in any
or all of the countryside, history and farming. My text is an exercise in
attempted communication. To that end, risking appearing unscholarly,
I have removed to Appendix 1 most of the in-text references of earlier
drafts, keeping in the published text only those references essential to
underpin its academic generality and key specifics. I hope they are not too
obtrusive for any general reader.

Second, I have in mind students of all ages. I have tried to provide
second- and third-year University Honours undergraduates with a reasonably modern review incorporating both generalisation and a hard
selection of detail. I have also indicated in Appendix 1 a good series of
entry points into various fields of enquiry for the individual wishing to
take an interest further. It has been structured to be useful, for example,
in preparing an essay for 'continuous assessment', in starting a project
during coursework, and even at the start of post-graduate work on an MA
or higher research. Bibliographically, it should prove reasonably useful up
to late 2000, even if some of the later references are not absorbed into the
text and appear only in Appendix 1.

Questions about the past may or may not be interesting in themselves,
but collectively they raise another: is there anything of relevance here to
Britain as the twenty-first century begins? This question became particularly apposite in the summer of 1999 as much of this presentation was
revised. Then, as 'big questions' continued to be asked about national
identity and the nature of the British countryside, its history, its ownership and its 'traditional' ways of life, public debate was fired by suggestions
that Anglo-Saxons were no longer 'politically correct' because they 'lost'

(cf. Sellar and Yeatman 1930). Public (and ministerial) consideration was also given to the suggestion that they should in any case be dropped from examination syllabuses because there was no longer room for such marginal persons. Whatever the Irish, Scottish and Welsh responses, what price English ethnogenesis? Romans, on the other hand, apparently continue to be acceptable, presumably because they were civilised and winners, two characteristics which brought about one of the supposedly 'great' periods in British history.

Yet, in the days either side of 1 January 2000, Anglo-Saxons (but not any other sort of Briton) were suddenly flavour of the moment in numerous public assessments of what life was like a thousand years ago. *The Observer*, following the chronological misconception perpetuated from on high, contained the lovely thought that 'the millennial moment came and went and people scarcely noticed . . . it is a safe bet that at midnight on December 31, 999, virtually every one of the million or so souls living in England was asleep' – a nice thought from the very end of our time-span with which to begin at the beginning.

Acknowledgements

I would first thank my personal, albeit unknowing, mentors, Professors H.P.R. Finberg, Glanville Jones and Shimon Applebaum, authors of the *Cambridge Agrarian History* I.2. Over forty years, Collin Bowen and Charles Thomas have been inspirational and helpful; the latter has in particular given authority to my linguistic observations and read the penultimate version of this text critically. I thank two anonymous readers of the same version for their knowledgeable, justifiably hard and constructive critiques, largely adopted. I benefited much from early comments from Professor David Austin, and have also enjoyed personal help from Professor Richard Bailey, David Breeze, Dave Cowley (Scotland), Christopher Loveluck (Flixholme), David Miles (Thames valley), Susan Mills and Bridget Boyd (Bede's World, academic and culinary matters respectively), Peter Murphy (environment) and Robert Sheil (soils).

Key photographs of farming scenes about a century ago were copied from images on display (Pls. XXIII, XXX, XXXII) at the Musée de la Ferme d'Autrefois at Hyelzas on the Causse Méjean, Languedoc, France. Permission to photograph ards, ploughs and wooden tools there was also gladly accorded (Pls. XXI, XXII, XXVIIa, XXVIII). Similar material from Galicia, Spain, was collected in joint fieldwork with Peter Reynolds in 1974 (Pls. XXVIIb, XXXI). I acknowledge material and permissions from, and willing help from the staffs of, the British Museum (Pl. XXVa) and British Library (Pl. XXVb and cover); and Cambridge University Air Photographic Collection (Pls. IV, XVIII), and the NMR (Crown Copyright) (Pls. III, VIII, XX: the last also with the permission of the photographer, Tim Gates). Pl. XXXVIII is by Jean Williams, and Pls. II, V, VI, IX, XII, XV, XVI, XVII, XXIX, XXXIV and XXXVIII are unmistakably the work of Mick Sharp. It is a pleasure, and entirely to this book's benefit, to be associated with him and Graeme Stobbs once more in a publishing endeavour. The latter prepared all the line-drawings, often working from graphics published by numerous colleagues whose original work is gratefully acknowledged. Framework (Gill Andrews and John Barrett) allowed me to use their unpublished plan of the Heathrow field system (Fig. 7.5). Similarly, Fig. 7.7 is based on recent field survey by RCAHMS.

Particularly seminal occasions were conferences in London in 1993 and San Marino in 1994 (Rackham 1994; Hines 1997). I could not have started without a corpus of scholarly work, highlighted in Appendix 1, and the detailed work of many people listed in the Bibliography. Among them, I owe a particular debt to the later twentieth-century generation of publishing scholars: Katherine Barker, Dr Martin Bell, Dr John Blair, Professor Wendy Davies, Dr Margaret Faull, Dr Margaret Gelling, Dr Della Hooke, Dr F. Kelly, Professor Martin Jones, Professor Henry Loyn, Professor William Manning, Professor Peter Salway, Professor Peter Sawyer, Professor Pauline Stafford, Dr Christopher Taylor, Professor K.D. White and Dr Tom Williamson. My dependence on them is overt, and obvious throughout the text; I acknowledge it with gratitude.

Much of the then available basic material was assembled and a first draft written (and subsequently scrapped) during a two-term study leave in 1991–92 granted by the University of Newcastle upon Tyne. Help was unconsciously provided by a decade of first-year undergraduates there who sat through my course *Britain in the First Millennium AD*. Some carried out neat pieces of specific work which I have drawn on here. Among them, Anne Larison assembled bibliographical data which I have relied on absolutely. The Vice-Chancellor, James Wright, also amicably agreed to my early resignation from an established Chair, creating in lieu a personal research post. Simultaneously, I held a Leverhulme Emeritus Fellowship to complete this book and I am most grateful to the Trustees for their Award and their patience. Their patience is, however, nothing as compared to that of a succession of editors at Cambridge University Press: I thank them all.

Editorial note

The following words are used only in the following senses:

agrarian to do with agriculture

agriculture synonymous with 'farming'; not meaning only arable farming

Anglo-Saxon pertaining to something which is specifically of the Anglo-Saxon people and their doings, e.g. Anglo-Saxon kingdom or as in 'Anglo-Saxon settlement pattern' where it means only the pattern of settlements of Anglo-Saxons; but not 'Anglo-Saxon period' or 'Anglo-Saxon climate' (much of the book being directed towards trying to identify whether there was a characteristic 'Anglo-Saxon agriculture', although this is not assumed)

arable (as a noun) land cultivated for crop production; (as an adjective) produced by cultivation, as in 'arable crop'

British as in 'the British' or 'British people', meaning all those who inhabited Britain before the Anglo-Saxons, or were descended from such inhabitants in the second half of the first millennium AD; or more generally meaning 'of Britain' as a geographical space consisting of what is now England, Scotland and Wales, with adjacent islands as appropriate (but not Ireland or Northern Ireland)

Conquest a term eschewed as far as possible but referring either to Romans and AD 43 when used by Romanists or to Normans and 1066 when used by early medieval historians

farming everything to do with the production of food from the land by people and therefore to do with the management of land

millennium unless otherwise indicated, the first millennium AD, AD 1-1000

pastoral based on pasturage, non-arable, as in 'pastoral landscape'

Roman pertaining to something which is specifically Roman as in 'Roman Britain' meaning only Britain as a province of the Roman Empire, but not 'Roman period', or as in 'Romano-British' people, period, culture, etc.

Abbreviations

ADS   Archaeological Data Service, York

ASC   *Anglo-Saxon Chronicle* (the translation used here is in *EHD*)

BAR   British Archaeological Reports, Oxford

BG   Handford, S.A. and Gardner, J.F. (1982, 2nd edn), *Caesar. The Conquest of Gaul*, Penguin, Harmondsworth

CBA   Council for British Archaeology

EASE   *Encyclopedia of Anglo-Saxon England* = Lapidge *et al.* (1999)

EHD   *English Historical Documents* = Whitelock 1955

HE   Bede, *Historia Ecclesiastica* (AD 731) = *Ecclesiastical History of the English People* = McClure and Collins 1999

HMSO   Her Majesty's Stationery Office

NMR   National Monuments Record (English Heritage, Swindon)

RCAHMS   Royal Commission on the Ancient and Historical Monuments of Scotland

RCHME   Royal Commission on the Historical Monuments of England

1 | The first millennium AD

> Agriculture (including pastoralism) is central to societies because it feeds people. Thus most human groups at some time make attempts to extend their area, either to feed more people or to feed some of them better.
>
> SIMMONS 1997, 161

Agriculture was the economic basis of Britain throughout the first millennium AD. In that respect, it continued a 4000-year-old prehistoric tradition there. By the time of the birth of Christ, farming was a well-established way of life in Britain. With reasonable success, it supported a sizeable population, a viable economy and a variegated landscape. Such was also the case a thousand years later.

In a global perspective such a situation is not especially remarkable, either in time or in space (Grigg 1974). Self-sufficient agrarian communities, some of much greater complexity and achievement compared to those of late prehistoric Britain, had already existed many times around the world. And just across the Channel (as yet unnamed as 'English'), much of Europe had enjoyed a reasonably successful way of life based on cereal farming for at least five millennia (Barker 1985; Thorpe 1996). This was a phenomenon, emergent from the post-glacial temperate deciduous forests, which had flourished in particular habitats, as beside the Swiss Lakes and along the Danube; likewise widely around the Mediterranean where specialist forms of crop production had developed, notably with olives and vines.

Elsewhere in the world, humans had long colonised most biomes such as temperate grasslands and different types of tropical forests, their various agrarian developments especially favouring habitat interfaces such as desert edges and montane foothills. In such zones, communities adapted opportunistically, for survival and more. Their farming systems involved other specialist crops, such as legumes in Mesoamerica and sweet potatoes in Polynesia in the first millennium, and the adaptation of particular species as main crops such as rice, yams, maize and squashes (Simmons 1997, 70–87, Fig. 4.4). Britain was a long way from the early heartlands of such processes which had already provided the bases of numerous

1

economically successful human societies, for example in south-east Asia, eastern China and India, and in the Americas the south-central Andes and Mexico (Smith 1995; Harris 1996). Nor were such developmental processes only in the past; they continued in many parts of the world in the first millennium AD. Agriculture in Britain at that time was, therefore, but one facet of a global phenomenon. In that it was based on thousands of years of farming tradition, it and its socio-economic outcomes shared characteristics with, for example, large parts of the Asian subcontinent (cf. Harris 1996); though a subsequent stasis there, still apparent in aspects of at least technology, is not reflected in the present state of British agriculture. In contrast, elsewhere agrarian societies were newly developing, in eastern North America (Smith 1992; 1995, chapter 8) for example, a situation which was very definitely not the case in Britain. Nevertheless, a broad perspective allows the minutiae of British insular *agraria* with which we concern ourselves here to be seen as generally of no great external significance at the time.

Exceptions to such a generalisation may well be sought, in the century between Caesar and Claudius perhaps, and in the tenth century AD too. In the same sort of time-frame, more or less as Claudius arrived in the heavily farmed lands of south-eastern Britain, maize arrived in the vast eastern deciduous woodlands of North America between the mid-Western prairie and the Atlantic coast. Thereafter, however, while in Britain we tend to look with the passing centuries for nuances in crop types and at changing relationships between arable and pasture among developed agrarian societies, development was different on the west side of the Atlantic. There, it took most of the first millennium before societies from northern Florida to southern Ontario finally became 'maize-centred' in the century between the Peace of Tiddingford (906) and Ethelred's midwinter in Shropshire (1016) (Hill 1981, maps 82, 162; Gartner 1999).

Lest we imagine we are dealing on either side of the Atlantic with arcadian nostalgia, it is as well to remember that, throughout the first millennium, our topic was, for most people, the prime matter of concern each day. This remained so throughout life: farming was literally a matter of life and death, and was always, beneath the realities of agricultural labour, an issue of deep passions involving status and tenure, gender and sex, ritual and religious belief, self and eternity. This rawness at the core of agrarian communities, which can be detected without too much difficulty in Britain in the first millennium AD, is dramatically expressed in a poetic fragment from the ancient Near East with which a native Briton, indigenous American or Saxon colonist could well have empathised:

> She seizes the Godly Mot –
> With the sword she doth cleave him
> With the fan she doth winnow him –
> With fire she doth burn him
> With hand-mill she grinds him –
> In the field she doth sow him.
>   (trans. Pritchard 1969, 112–13)

British farming over the ten centuries between Julius Caesar and William the Conqueror can, indeed should, be seen against a broad background and as part of a long-term process. In this essay, we are merely isolating one facet of that process in one small part of the world during one short period of time. In AD 1 our subject was what it was because of what had already happened, and its nature throughout the next thousand years was as much preconditioned by that experience as it was by environmental variables, like climate, and cultural changes like new farmers and practices. Creating a historical view of farming in first-millennium Britain, then, very much involves judgements about different emphases to be given to different balances through time between the traditional and the innovative. Much of the reality of farming – the geology of its stage, for example, and the seasonality of its practice – was unchanging, and so from one point of view there is no story to be told: 'Farming is as farming was', an idea still manifesting itself in rural attitudes at the beginning of the twenty-first century. But things did change from time to time, albeit neither regularly nor even progressively, and so, in truth, a story is there for the telling. Such as it is in a chronological sense will emerge in chapter 14.

Our task is to discern, if possible, how Britain was farmed during the first millennium AD, and why it was farmed in the way that it was. A whole series of questions follows, for example: What sorts of farming were practised? What kinds of life-style did they both require and support? What were the major changes, if any, over that millennium in farming and society? What did the countryside look like? Who owned it and how was it arranged? Who farmed it and how? More prosaically, perhaps, can we describe with conviction a plough, a field, or a day in the life of a farmer, generally during the millennium or at any one point in time within it?

History and farming in the first millennium AD

Another basic question is how we know what we know. We discuss this in general with some detail in chapter 2. Here we summarise how scholars arrived at the state of knowledge by about the mid-1990s.

'[T]he way to it lies through the Norman record' (Maitland 1960, 5). Maitland was, a century ago, and remains still, the great historical scholar of late Anglo-Saxon and Norman England; his 'it' in this quotation was the former, and it comes from his seminal book *Domesday Book and Beyond*, originally published in 1897. He was explaining his use of the retrogressive method, 'from the known to the unknown'. Domesday Book was the 'knowable' rather than the known; but through it, 'the Norman record', nevertheless lay the way to the 'Beyond' of his title, that is old English history before 1086. This attitude has dominated the historical study of the Anglo-Saxon period, reaching its apotheosis probably in Hodgkin (1935), Stenton (1943) and Blair (1956).

Coming at the earlier part of the millennium also primarily from a documentary point of view, Classical scholars have in contrast tended to think forwards and also outwards: Roman Britain, relatively small beer in Imperial terms, came towards the end of Classical civilisation chronologically and was marginal geographically. So the story of Roman Britain, cast in a documentary frame, has tended to be told from beginning to end in military and political terms, with non-narrative matters like farming and art treated thematically and somewhat awkwardly if at all (e.g. Collingwood and Myres 1937; Richmond 1955; Frere 1967). No wonder then that, with Classicists moving forwards in time ever less enthusiastically as Classicism fades, and historians probing backwards from the knowable familiarities of *Domesday* to the dark *Beyond*, a non-meeting of dissimilarities rather than a gap in time has occurred somewhere in between (cf. Holdsworth and Wiseman 1986). Many have consequently taken refuge either or both in the rich mythic and legendary heritage about the period or in the concept of the 'Dark Ages'. The former has often led to fantasy; the latter, originally a literary conceit (Ker 1958), has tended to be used as a convenient excuse to say nothing on the implicit grounds of the historian that if there is virtually no documentary evidence then there is nothing to be said. Fortunately Morris (1973), somewhat controversially but with scholarly panache, exploded the 'read nothing, say nothing' school of diplomatic negativism, while throughout the first half of the twentieth century a suite of archaeologists with a 'see something, say something' approach to material culture proposed a series of interpretations for the period essentially AD 400–700, e.g. Leeds 1913; Harden 1956.

That is all now history, so in a sense does not matter except as contributory to an academic horizon *c*.1970 from which we attempt to take up the story. Probably, however, the most influential book of all had already been published for fifteen years by then. From Hoskins' *Making of the English Landscape* (1955) developed among many in a new generation of students a different, more comprehensive approach, especially to landscape, from which developed different ways of asking questions other than primarily in a chronological template, and new perspectives and interpretations. The process continues. The titles of some recent books nevertheless indicate that historiographical divisions persist, for example *The Landscape of Roman Britain* (Dark and Dark 1997) and *Landscape and Settlement in Britain AD 400–1066* (Hooke and Burnell 1995). One of the interesting enquiries (to the author anyway) to try to answer in this book is whether such a division is justified in terms of agrarian history as well as being explicable in terms of first-millennium historiography.

The setting

By the last centuries BC, much of the landscape of the British Isles had already been used several times over, and a lot of it farmed during the preceding 4000 years (Pl. I; Mercer 1981; Piggott 1981; Fowler 1983; Pryor 1998). Some of it had reverted; other parts were at one stage or another in a repeating pattern of abandonment and reclamation (Pl. II). Most of it was under agrarian use, ranging from intensive arable to extensive pasture, from managed woodland (Pl. III) to 'no-man's lands' (chapter 4). Very little of the land was in any sense 'wildscape', though some of it doubtless looked like unkempt wilderness even if it was quietly but critically being 'farmed' for perhaps its poisons and medicinal plants (chapter 12). Successful conventional farming, producing mainly cereals and animals for many purposes, including war, was the predominant characteristic of a British countryside in which many of the agrarian and technological challenges of a pre-mechanical, pre-industrial economy had been met (chapter 8). By and large, such a generalisation holds good for the next millennium too; our challenge is to spot the significant variations.

One base-line is clearly defined: Caesar's description of Britain (*BG* V.12–14) as perceived in 54 BC based on his interpretation of information acquired by what we would call techniques of field reconnaissance and questioning of a non-systematic sample of the population. He remarks that: 'By far the most civilized inhabitants are those living in Kent (a purely maritime district), whose way of life differs little from that of the Gauls. Most of the tribes in the interior do not grow corn but live on milk and meat, and wear skins' (*BG* V.14).

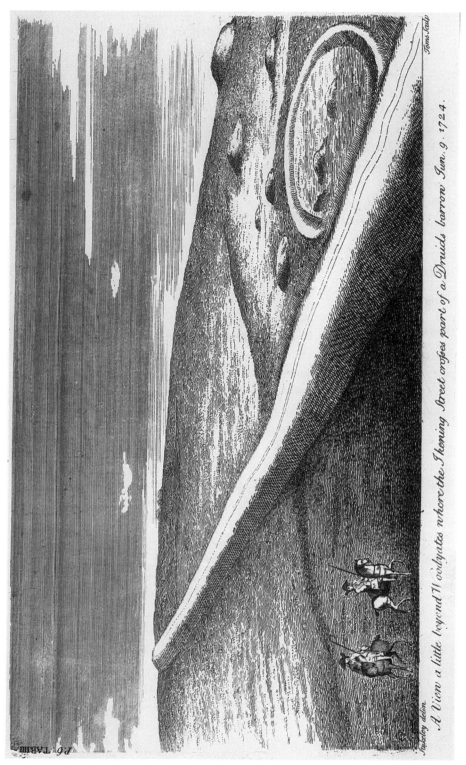

A View a little beyond Woodyates where the Ikening Street crosses part of a Druids barrow Jun. 9. 1724.

Plate I An ancient landscape: Ackling Dyke (a Roman road) cutting part of a disc barrow in the Bronze Age barrow cemetery on treeless Oakley Down, Dorset, as depicted by William Stukeley on 9 June 1724.

Farming probably intensified during the early decades of the new millennium, fuelled by demand from a growing domestic market, more affluent in the south-east than hitherto, and from abroad where Roman expansion in Europe required more and more grain to sustain empire. British agricultural success, as recorded by Tacitus telling of exports to Gaul, may well have reinforced the reasons for Imperial invasion in AD 43. Over the next century, the impact of that military and political event on farming in Britain was, as in so much else, considerable. It added to a landscape already littered with the cultural and environmental debris of its predecessors a further four centuries of characteristically Roman features, all with agrarian implications, notably military establishments, towns, villas and communication structures like roads, canals and harbour facilities (Pls. I, VIII; Fig. 4.2; see Bede on twenty-eight cities in chapter 3; and generally Dark and Dark 1997). Villas as centres of agrarian estates rather than as Classical buildings in foreign parts may well represent one of the most significant agrarian developments of the millennium, with an increasingly significant influence from the later first century AD onwards and then, less obviously, long after the fourth century; and a similar claim can be argued for the facilitation of civil and commercial transport around at least the southern parts of Britain. Such at one and the same time enabled and demanded greater agrarian production and, while neither the villa nor transport systems continued to function as intended as the Roman economy collapsed, parts remained recognisably in place, even in use in the case of some roads and fortifications along them.

Between the fifth and seventh centuries AD, nevertheless, agrarian history becomes very uncertain, with few documentary sources and only fragmentary, largely ambiguous archaeological evidence. Most of the limited mechanical technology of the Roman period had lapsed by the mid-fifth century if not earlier, yet it seems highly likely that much of the agriculture being practised in England by indigenous communities when Anglo-Saxons were arriving was at least on a par in technological terms with the husbandry of later pre-Roman Britain. That of the immigrants was, at best, probably similar. With it they found space to farm in a mosaic of well-farmed and derelict areas. By AD 600 most areas of south and eastern England, like the Vale of Pickering, Yorkshire, for example, were dotted with Anglo-Saxon settlements (following Powlesland 1999, 64; in general, Hooke 1988a, 1998). Elsewhere in the British Isles, in general an age-old, largely pastoral way of life continued, though the area under arable at any one time was probably considerable in what was often likely

Plate II Upland landscape with fertile valley: enclosures and hut circles at Threlkeld Knotts, Cumbria, with Skiddaw in the background.

to have been in many localities more truly a mixed farming economy than exclusively stock-raising (Pl. II).

From the seventh century onwards to the eleventh, most people continued to gain their livelihood, directly or indirectly, from the activity of farming and its products. Society remained essentially agrarian. The evidence for this basis is, however, fragmentary as well as diverse, despite these centuries being increasingly 'historic'. We can build on a vivid description, comparable to that of Caesar (above), written by Bede *c*. AD 730:

> This island is rich in crops and in trees, and has good pasturage for cattle and beasts of burden. It also produces vines in certain districts, and has plenty of both land- and water-fowl of various kinds. It is remarkable too for its rivers, which abound in fish, particularly salmon and eels, and for copious springs. (*HE*)

From the seventh century, but even more so from the eighth and later, evidence comes partly and increasingly from documents and expands tantalisingly to include some manuscript illustrations (chapter 8); but, for farming itself, the bulk of it continues to derive from the present landscape, including its place-names, and from archaeological and related investigations.

The principal documentary sources are contemporary and later laws, biographies and land charters (chapter 2). Among the early laws, those of King Ine of Wessex (688–726), for example, set out to regulate numerous practical matters of the sort which arise when many individuals are seeking to wrest their living from the same area of land. His laws were consequently much concerned with cornland and fences, meadows and pasture, straying animals and the felling of trees. The general impression is of an agriculture effectively, even expansively, exploiting a range of resources in the Wessex landscape. Later Anglo-Saxon codes tend to follow Ine's pattern of attempted regulation, this common concern flowing from the basic importance of land to virtually everyone in an agrarian society. In somewhat different environmental and sociological circumstances in north Wales, the thirteenth-century Book of Iowerth, 'derived from ancient exemplars', 'reveals clearly that Welsh medieval lawyers . . . [also] recognized that land was the ultimate source of all wealth', as had indeed been the case there in earlier times too when it was crucial to integrate in a 'hierarchy of estates' the resources of lowlands and uplands in a mixed agrarian economy (Jones 1976, 15–17).

Biographies, such as Felix's *Life of St Guthlac* and Asser's *Life of King Alfred,* contain topographical descriptions. Charters contain much detail pertaining to specific areas of land, including headlands and woodland in working agrarian landscapes, mainly in Southumbria in the tenth and eleventh centuries. Manuscript illustrations include agrarian scenes, though few English examples, whatever their artistic origins, date before *c.* AD 1000 (chapter 9). A conversation piece, including a passage specifically about ploughing, also belongs to the end of our millennium (chapter 9).

If Roman farmers had found their landscape already 'littered with the cultural and environmental debris' (above) of their predecessors, how much more so must it have been as a distinctively Anglo-Saxon agriculture developed during the last centuries of the millennium (OS 1994). The land charters clearly show that the inhabitants of the time were aware of this: they referred to old tracks, burial mounds and lynchets of fields we know were prehistoric, to roads which we know as Roman (Pl. I), and to heathen burial places (Fowler and Blackwell 1998, 104–5, following Bonney 1976, Figs. 7.6, 7.7). Later, the impression is of a land extensively farmed in what had by then become England, with a lot of tree-cover which was probably regenerated woodland and managed rather than wild-wood. But the fact that we can read detail and see change does not mean that change happened everywhere; nor did it develop evenly, either across the land or in time.

It seems very likely that, as a result, the regional distinctiveness of farming in Britain developed during the first millennium. Previously, of course, regional differences existed, but perhaps more at coarser levels such as 'highland' and 'lowland' zones (Fox 1932; Fowler 1978b) than in the mosaic of locally differentiated areas which enabled Thirsk (1967, 1984b) to write of British farming in regional and sub-regional terms and each of a whole team of scholars to write about field systems alone in one particular region (Baker and Butlin 1973). To take an extreme example to make the point, the farming of south-east Wales and the Hebridean Isles was distinctively different by the fourth century. More subtly, the Anglo-Saxon and Danish transformation of the British landscape was less radical in the West Midlands than in the East Midlands (Gelling 1992, Foreword); and agrarian life in north-west Wales in the tenth century was, as now, somewhat different from that in Midland England as a whole. At a smaller scale, within a region, Wessex for example, dairy-farming of the clay vales was distinctively different by Domesday Book from the long-established traditional mixed farming of the chalkland valleys and downs (Aston and Lewis 1994). Whenever they began, such regional farming differences were clearly marked over much of Britain by the eleventh century and were presumably then, as during the second millennium AD, directly affecting life, thought, landscape and economies. Following Davies (1989, 3), we would do well always to remember in these matters 'the immense influence of land and landscape on society, religion and politics, as well as on economy'. It is certainly not now necessary to believe that Anglo-Saxon agriculture presents 'a general picture of uniformity' throughout England (Hallam 1988) or indeed that various agricultures, racially attributable or not, were uniform throughout Britain. Continuities through time there may well have been in some places, but diversity rather than uniformity is the key to any understanding of the process of farming in first-millennium Britain.

The archaeology of the period has tended to be formed by big, and sometimes spectacular, excavations of the obvious, now largely re-dundant, features of the first-millennium landscape such as Roman cities and villas, Anglo-Saxon cemeteries and Viking towns. *Verulamium*, Fishbourne, Sutton Hoo and *Yorvik* spring to mind (Frere 1972, 1983; Cunliffe 1971; Carver 1992; Hall 1984). There is much there of agrarian significance, most of it secondary but containing some crucial, direct evidence. The actual evidence in the field continues to remain intriguingly

Plate III Ancient woodland: 1946 vertical air photograph of the northern edge of West Woods, Overton, Wiltshire. The trees are recent but woodland has been here since prehistoric times, its mid-twentieth-century outline fairly accurately following that defined by the edge of 'Celtic' fields, *left centre*, in modern arable, and the bounds of two estates in the tenth century AD. The 'eyebrows-shaped' hedge, *bottom left*, is part of their common boundary *c*. AD 950. The woodland clearing, *centre bottom*, is late Anglo-Saxon *ers lege*, modern Hursley, then as now a nodal point in the local communications network in the first millennium. The partly deserted settlement, *Dean, top centre*, may have originated before AD 1000, and another, but unlocated, Saxon settlement, *Burham*, lay somewhere to its south-west, *left centre* or beyond, cf. Fig. 3.1.

pathetic, not least because much of the stage for British farming in the first
millennium was used for a continuous performance throughout the second. The consequential removal of evidence for earlier activity has tended
to reduce physical survivals in the landscape to such as, at one extreme,
slight undulations on the ground. The best-known archaeological examples of such, representing ridge and furrow of pre-1000 date at Gwithian,
Cornwall, and, perhaps slightly later, at Hen Domen near Montgomery
(Fig. 7.8; Pl. XIX; Fowler and Thomas 1962; Higham and Barker 2000),
continue to intrigue precisely because they remain rare rather than typical; but quantitatively, and almost certainly historically, their evidential
significance has been overwhelmed across a generation by the implications of widespread landscape survey elsewhere. Whether starting from
archaeological or from documentary approaches and methodologies, such
work has produced a kaleidoscope of local detail and, at the other extreme, has tended at one and the same time, as elsewhere in Europe
(e.g. Barker 1995), to illustrate both continual landscape change and established, long-term factors in the landscape. The latter emerge in the
form of such as 'permanent' boundaries, 'stable' economic units, and
preferred, long-lived uses of certain areas as, for example, traditional
arable or woodland (e.g. Andrews and Milne 1979; Hooke 1985a, 1989;
Fenland Survey Reports 1987–; Fulford and Nichols 1992; Hall and Coles
1994).

Archaeology itself has nevertheless been very successful in demonstrating the existence and nature of agrarian settlements, especially those
of the first to fourth and sixth to eighth centuries. Most such places,
almost by definition, are usually long abandoned; in the former period,
they are characterised by both timber and stone-footed, perhaps even
walled, buildings (Pl. IX; generally, Hingley 1989) while in the latter
they are characterised by many timber buildings (Pl. V). In many senses
the archaeology of so-called 'Roman' Britain has long been well known
(Salway 1981), whereas its counterpart between Honorius and Canute, at
least in agrarian terms, has tended until recently to have been unknown
and even simply disregarded (cf. the treatment of it in standard histories
up to such as Stenton (1971) with the recent 'step-change' exemplified
by Hinton (1998) and Sawyer (1998a).). Now, however, in places such as
Raunds, Northamptonshire, West Heslerton and Wharram Percy, North
and East Yorkshire respectively, and the Middle Thames valley, excavation
coupled with fieldwork has glimpsed the landscape context, and even social and tenurial links, within which agriculture may well have operated
in the middle centuries of the millennium (Fig. 1.1). More widely without settlement excavation, landscape study has successfully argued for

the existence of complex estate and tenurial arrangements providing the framework within which the routine of farming was carried out (e.g. Hooke *passim*; Wade-Martins 1975; Faull 1984; Welch 1985; Aston and Lewis 1994; Cleary 1995; Barker and Darvill 1997). Hints of pre-Anglo-Saxon origins for some elements of that framework have been noted throughout the country, for example in Kent, Wiltshire and Northumberland (Everitt 1986; Bonney 1972; Morris 1977).

Both 'Roman' and 'Anglo-Saxon' landscapes contained features specific to each, as indeed did 'British' landscapes in Wales and 'Pictish' landscapes in Scotland. The adjectives qualifying the various landscapes are in inverted commas here because, as should already be clear, no landscape existed at any moment as the exclusive demesne of, or was indeed created by, any particular group of people, whether it be defined by race, politics or belief system. We do not after all refer to a 'pagan landscape', even though in one sense it is an accurate descriptor of much of Britain in the first millennium AD. Curiously, if any landscape can be justifiably characterised as of a particular racial/political group, then it could be that of southern Britain in the first two centuries AD. Then, as forts, towns, villas, industry and roads impacted physically on the landscape, they also collectively represented a new way of operating, of working the land in different ways for different objectives within a European framework led by military considerations under the aegis of decidedly non-British gods. Corn-dryers, temples and shrines well illustrate this signal change. The workings of this 'Roman' landscape were rather different from the world of Cassivellaunus, though the politico-economic change probably made little practical difference to the daily life of the British farm-worker.

Similarly, characteristic structures appeared in the same landscape a few centuries later, arguing for a legitimacy in the use of the phrase 'Anglo-Saxon' landscape: a range of rectangular timber buildings from the sixth century onwards (Pls. XIII, XIV; Marshall and Marshall 1991); but to people from the early seventh century onwards the most obviously new, different and impressive buildings would have been churches, minsters and monasteries (Morris 1989). Such structures in one sense characterised, if not a 'Christian' landscape, then a 'Christianising' of an already old landscape, for some of their newly ecclesiastical lands were of much older components. Furthermore, an estate like that at Cerne Abbas in Dorset (chapter 4), and a monastery like Whitby, while being aloof in a religious sense, would have had to operate within the local economy (Cramp 1993), relating to a secular world of other lands and landlords and processes like commerce, food supply and agrarian practice.

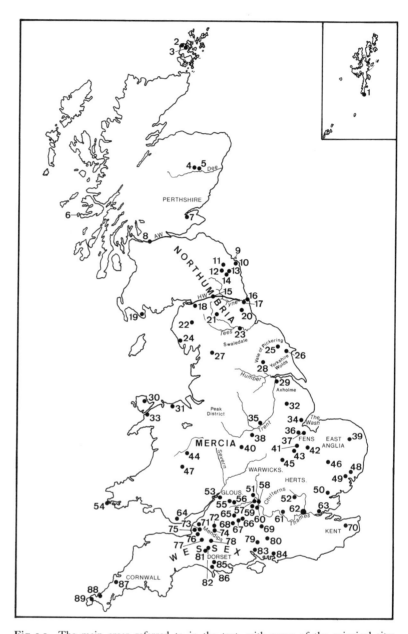

Fig. 1.1   The main areas referred to in the text, with many of the principal sites, numbered as follows:

1 Jarlshof, Shetland	8 Bearsden	16 *Arbeia*, South	23 Piercebridge
2 Brough of Birsay,	9 Lindisfarne	Shields	24 Ravenglass
Orkney	10 Bamburgh	17 Jarrow	25 West Heslerton
3 Gurness, Orkney	11 Yeavering	18 Carlisle	26 Thwing
4 Loch Davan	12 Breamish valley	19 Whithorn	27 Gauber High
5 Braerodolach Loch	13 Ingram	20 Hurbuck	Pasture
6 Iona	14 Chesters hillfort	21 Simy Folds	28 York
7 Black Loch	15 Housesteads	22 Threlkeld Knotts	29 Flixborough

Agricultural implements are well attested in contemporary sources for the first half and last century of the millennium; between the fifth and ninth centuries, evidence for them is slight. In the first four centuries AD, as we discuss in chapters 8 and 9, equipment, implements and tools appear in Roman literature and graphic art, mainly of the Mediterranean world, so nice judgements are to be made about relevance to practices and uses in Britain. Direct evidence of immediate relevance comes, mainly as iron tools, from the archaeology of Romano-British sites, especially in southern Britain (Manning 1985). Some of the few key pieces from post-Roman times come from less obviously Romanised contexts to west and north; very little has been produced by the archaeology of the south and east for this period. That agrarian equipment of course existed, largely in wood, is, however, not in doubt, though it is only from *c.* AD 900 that reliable evidence reassuringly reappears. This is notably in illuminated manuscripts (which again raise interesting questions of interpretation, see chapters 2 and 9), in written works, and in a rare, tenth-century hoard from Flixborough, Lincolnshire, mainly of carpentry and agricultural tools (chapter 9; Loveluck 1998, Fig. 8a).

Archaeologically, given the amount of relevant excavation now accomplished, the absence of unequivocal evidence of a plough from Anglo-Saxon contexts before *c.* 900 is almost certainly significant. No evidence exists that Anglo-Saxons brought with them proper ploughs or the 'open field' system, though the one certainly was, and the other may have been, physically present in Britain before their arrival (chapters 7 and 9). Since land cultivation was undoubtedly the basis of Anglo-Saxon agriculture,

Caption for Fig. 1.1 (*cont.*)

30 Din Lligwy	47 Whitton	61 Heathrow	74 Camerton
31 Dinorben	48 Sutton Hoo	62 London	75 Bleadon Hill
32 Goltho	49 Ipswich	63 Mucking	76 Cheddar
33 Caernarfon	50 Witham	64 Caer Dynaf	77 Shapwick
34 Boston	51 Shakenoak	65 Man's Head,	78 Oakley Down
35 Nottingham	52 *Verulamium/*	Marlborough	79 Winchester
36 Spalding	St Albans	Downs	80 Cowdery's Down
37 Holbeach	53 Great Witcombe	66 Fyfield Down	81 South Cadbury
38 Catholme	villa	67 West Overton	Castle
39 Norwich	54 Gateholm Island	68 Chisbury	82 North Cadbury
40 Tamworth	55 Barnsley Park	69 Silchester	83 *Hamwic*
41 Peterborough	56 Cirencester	70 Canterbury	84 Fishbourne
42 March	57 Farmoor	71 Cadbury	85 Cerne Abbas
43 Yaxley	58 Oxford	Congresbury	86 Maiden Castle
44 Hen Domen	59 Watkins Farms,	72 Bath	87 Mawgan Porth
45 Raunds	Northmoor	73 Lye Hole, Vale	88 Gwithian
46 West Stow	60 Barton Court Farm	of Wrington	89 Chysauster

however, the tilling implement commonly in use until at least the tenth century was therefore most probably a wooden ard without iron fittings (Pl. XXV). Such was almost certainly of bow and/or crook type, familiar in the arable fields of the first half of the first millennium AD and earlier, perhaps being replaced by a plough with mouldboard as our millennium ends (Pl. XXVIII). The existence of a fully fledged 'heavy' plough as illustrated in medieval sources such as the Luttrell Psalter (e.g. Passmore 1930, Pl. II, lower; here Pl. XXVI, lower) does not validate, contrary to common reference, technology or practice 300 and more years earlier.

Though specifically agrarian evidence remains sparse archaeologically for the earlier part of the period in particular, botanical studies of excavated plant remains, pioneered largely from urban deposits like Winchester, *Hamwic* and Gloucester, have now become significant in rural contexts. The main cultivars and aspects of cropping practices are emerging within an agriculture characterised by regional diversity. By the eighth century, a pattern had emerged which can perhaps be seen as a distinctively Anglo-Saxon crop husbandry compared to late Roman times (chapter 10). Nothing in the palaeobotanical evidence indicates, however, any major, long-term improvement in cereal-farming in the period.

Probably at no time was the situation static. The emergence of towns under Roman government and again from the eighth century (perhaps in the seventh in the south-east of England) would have significantly affected certain areas, particularly estates with urban centres; the growth of powerful estates, especially regal and ecclesiastical ones, and a probable rise in population in the later half of the period also imply agricultural change. The fundamental change in agrarian settlement pattern from the eighth century onwards, and possible technological improvements in such things as drainage, iron-smelting, milling, farming implements and harness, hint at a quiet rather than dramatic dynamism of an agriculture operating within a framework of non-synchronous regional diversity. It managed to maintain and develop an increasingly English countryside basically in good heart over a thousand critical years which saw the emergence of a number of distinctive insular societies.

Population

We do not know how many people were living in Britain in the first millennium AD, at its start, at its end or at any time in between; but we can make some informed estimates. The matter is not just a mathematical game, for it is vital to agriculture because numbers of people represent numbers of mouths to be fed and, when all is said and done, feeding people was first and foremost what agriculture was about. If there had been only ten people in Britain during the first millennium, there would have been no agrarian history.

By general agreement the inferred population of England was about 2 million people in the late eleventh century. An estimate of 3 million for the whole of Britain would probably be regarded as generous by demographers but we will adopt that and, erring even further on the side of generosity, take it as about right for AD 1000 (generous because what-ever the absolute numbers, the population increased during the eleventh century though we know not by how many or at what rate).

At the other end of the millennium, estimates are even shakier, for we have no written records to go on. Numbers have traditionally been extrapolated backwards from Domesday Book, on the assumption that they would be lower earlier. From the 1960s, however, the explosion of archaeological data, and the emergence of economic trends with their demographic implications during the millennium, have led archaeolog-ical thought to converge around a figure of about 2 million in the first century AD and 4–5 million at the peak of prosperity around AD 300. These numbers are very probably of the right order (though this author still tends to regard them as conservative) but, whatever the absolutes, all the indications are that the population of Britain, more specifically of what became England, went down, not up, between the fourth and eleventh centuries. Such matters are by no means resolved, though several lines of evidence, and the thoughts of influential researchers in the field, are converging around a few key ideas. These include that of a largely plague-induced population collapse in the remnants of Roman Britain about the middle of the fifth century, perhaps similar in effect to the 30–50 per cent decimation of the Black Death in the mid-fourteenth cen-tury; the arrival of a numerically small number of Continental Teutonic peoples thereafter, and perhaps consequently; and a long, slow rise in population over the half-millennium or so to 1086, with a quickening during the economic vitality of the century before Domesday Book was compiled.

Hazarding a guess at actual numbers, a cautious 4 million Britons and Romans could have become a more accurate 3 million Britons, Angles, Saxons and Danes by AD 1000. A 50 per cent fall in the maximum likely population of late Roman Britain (5 million) would allow a population of about 2.5 million to grow to 3 million, only approximately 15 per cent growth over 500 years. A sinuous population curve expressing this order of numbers was first published over twenty years ago and has since been much criticised, copied and yet not significantly altered (Fowler 1978b, Fig. 1; a topic otherwise fully referenced and interestingly discussed in Jones 1996, chapter 1, esp. p. 13). If, however, the archaeological estimates of population in the first four centuries of the millennium were 50 per cent exaggerations of the reality, then there would be no need to postulate a population collapse in the fifth/sixth centuries and a 'flat curve' for the millennium around the 3 million mark would suffice. That, however, has not been in the minds of recent writers on this topic; there seems general agreement that the population 400 years into the millennium was higher than it was at its end, with a dip of uncertain depth, width and profile asymmetrically in between.

Within those sorts of numbers, quite marked variations occurred, by and within types of settlement and across the regions. An instance of the former is provided by Holdsworth (1995, 36) with estimates of late eleventh-century urban populations, markedly of around 4000 and less, an order of numbers almost certainly comparable with that of Britain's Roman towns eight centuries earlier. Regional demographic variation is exemplified by the Upper and Middle Thames valley, which was probably always quite crowded from late prehistoric time onwards. In comparison Wessex, which was apparently teeming with people when Claudius' army fought its way through it, had possibly lost significant numbers by mid-millennium and seems to have stabilised by the eleventh century at a lower rural population level than was the case in the first. The quite small numbers of people in terms of population density over large areas of west and north Britain almost certainly hardly changed throughout the millennium; though locally, demographic events doubtless occurred across a range from abnormally high numbers of inhabitants to desertion.

Britain, peoples and languages

Genetically the peoples of Britain were already well mixed up by the first century AD. The first millennium added to the genetic brew. A few Romans from Rome and Italy, and small numbers of settlers from different parts of the Roman Empire, came and stayed. Thereafter, three 'invasions' of supposedly Angles, Saxons and Jutes followed, though it is extremely doubtful whether more than a few thousand people were involved in any of them. After a period of Viking raids in the late eighth/earlier ninth centuries, during the second half of the ninth century and on into the tenth, thousands of immigrants, variously 'Viking', 'Norse' or 'Danish', seem to have been involved in a widespread Scandinavian settlement of eastern and north-western England, northern and western Scotland and some islands, notably the Orkney Islands, and eastern Ireland.

Before any of those changes, Caesar (*BG* V.12) provides a clearly focussed view in the mid-first century BC, our first written description of the British population, its origins and its activities:

> The interior of Britain is inhabited by people who claim, on the strength of an oral tradition, to be aboriginal; the coast, by Belgic immigrants who came to plunder and make war – nearly all of them retaining the names of the tribes from which they originated – and later settled down to till the soil. The population is exceedingly large, the ground thickly studded with homesteads, closely resembling those of the Gauls, and the cattle very numerous. For money they use either bronze, or gold coins, or iron ingots of fixed weights. Tin is found inland, and small quantities of iron near the coast; the copper that they use is imported. There is timber of every kind, as in Gaul, except beech and fir. Hares, fowl, and geese they think it is unlawful to eat, but rear them for pleasure and amusement. The climate is more temperate than in Gaul, the cold being less severe.

Though Caesar was factually wrong on some details (notably about beech and fir trees), he otherwise reliably delineates for us – though that was not, of course, his objective – a numerous, divided but multi-ethnic population, living in a relatively temperate climate, occupying the land in a characteristically dispersed settlement pattern, and engaged in arable farming, stock-raising, silviculture, metalliferous industry and coin-based commerce while sharing some social taboos and pleasures.

Writing in the present tense nearly 800 years later, Bede (*HE* I) also describes a familiar place, Britain, 'once called Albion'. It is, he says, an island

> rich in crops and in trees [with] good pasturage for cattle and beasts of burden. It also produces vines in certain districts, and has plenty of both land- and water-fowl of various kinds. It is remarkable too for its rivers, which abound in fish, particularly salmon and eels, and for copious springs.

He goes on to describe the delights of Britain's sea-food, natural thermal baths, metalliferous resources, jet, amber, and the long summer days and long winter nights. Strangely, he interpolates into his catalogue of natural phenomena that 'The country was once famous for its twenty-eight noble cities as well as innumerable fortified places equally well-guarded by the strongest of walls and towers, gates and locks.'

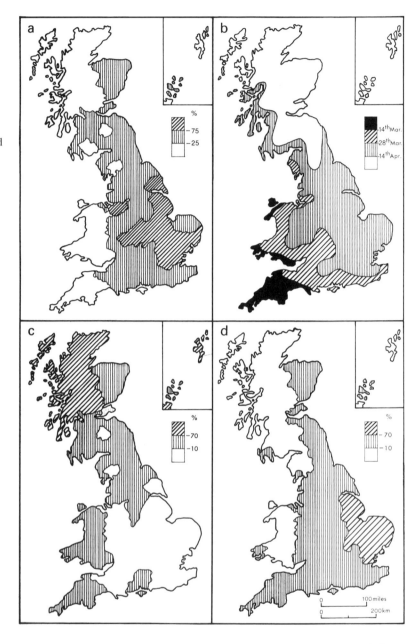

Bede (*HE* I.15) famously records the arrival of 'newcomers' from Europe about AD 450, 'from the three most formidable races of Germany, the Saxons, Angles and Jutes'. They became the 'English' of his contemporary description (*c.* 730): 'At the present time there are in Britain . . . five languages and four nations – English, British, Scots, and Picts. Each of these have their own language, but all are united . . . by the fifth – Latin' (*HE* I.1).

At the time of Julius Caesar, most if not all of the inhabitants of what is now Britain spoke a Celtic language, British. Four centuries later the vernacular was still British, but regionalism was leading to differentiation and then through dialects to 'daughter languages'. These were (Old) Welsh, Cornish and the long-vanished Cumbric of north Britain. The only Celtic additions were two. In Scotland north of the Antonine Wall a conglomeration of peoples known to the Romans, and Bede, as *Picti* used what may have been an archaic form of British. From the late fourth century, a scattering of Irish settlements from Cornwall to Argyll retained spoken (Primitive) Irish for a variable number of generations. That summarises modern scholarship's version of Bede's 'five languages and four nations', but says nothing about the language in which Bede wrote, Latin.

In Britain from the first century AD onwards, Latin, unlike British, was the primary vehicle for the written word (Jackson 1953). It was spoken, too, at least among some persons in the upper echelons of Romano-British society. In either medium, farm-workers' knowledge of Latin would have been, at best, rudimentary. Nevertheless, by the late fourth century, Britannia's citizens were familiar with Latin across a range from appreciating Virgilian verse to scratching rude words on potsherds; and in that context a regionally developing spoken British Vulgar Latin emerged, in a process similar to what was happening with British in Britain and with Latin in, for example, southern Gaulish provinces where Languedocian was evolving as a Romance language. Spoken Vulgar Latin, however, probably did not survive in Britain beyond the sixth century. In the two-thirds of Britain not affected by English settlement before *c.* AD 600, written Latin nevertheless continued to be used in the insular Church, from there coming to be used in the sixth-century courts of the new and nominally Christian native kingships. Within such a context developed in the seventh century an intellectual Christian–Latin culture of native character that seems to be largely of indigenous origin, though it seems to be of no agrarian significance (Thomas 1998). By the time Anglo-Saxon (or 'Old English') was well established, yet another two languages were added to the linguistic mixture in Britain: first Norse, and then Anglo-French in the years around the middle of the eleventh century. The effect of both was to add to, rather than basically change, a language which was by the end of our millennium widely spoken in England but which was to take much of the next millennium to infiltrate areas of Britain to west and north.

A significant factor in all this seems to be, not genetics or what subsequent people have argued about, but what various peoples felt about themselves in the first millennium. Some, for example, regarded themselves as having a group identity (e.g. 'West Saxons'), which was in some cases recognised by others (e.g. 'Picti'), though it is contentious whether such groups were races (e.g. 'Welsh'), tribes (e.g. 'Durotriges'), members of a political kingdom (e.g. 'Hwicce'), the followers of a prince or warrior (e.g. '–ingas'), or those who lived in a particular area/place at a particular time (e.g. 'Wilsaete').

Probably the most influential book in our field, Maitland's *Domesday Book and Beyond*, was published in 1897 and reprinted ten years later; it still lives in paperback (1960, the edition used here). During the twentieth century, the wave-making minds of post-Roman studies have tended, like Maitland, to study tenure and law, and then kingship, art and linguistics, and, archaeologically, brooches and cemeteries. The absence of similar concentrated effort in agrarian matters is indicated by the fact that, in the near half-century of its existence, even the specialist journal *Agricultural History Review* has carried only four papers on the topic in the later first millennium, one on the Roman period, and none on the millennium as a whole (see Appendix 1, esp. notes for chapters 6–11, for the bibliographical background).

Having introduced different types of evidence, and used them differently, in this slight introduction to some aspects of the first millennium, we can next turn to a survey of some of the evidence itself.

2 | Evidence

The land itself speaks Welsh.

RICHARD NEALE, WARDEN, LLEYN PENINSULA,
AT THE NATIONAL TRUST AGM, CARDIFF, 1998

Introduction

The idea that the land 'speaks', in any language, is one which resonates with many people – conservationists, town-dwellers, ramblers, poets, even some farmers. It is clearly not a very scientific idea, however, precisely because of one of its great virtues in practice, imprecision: answers to the question 'What do you hear?' will be varied, not repetitive. They will nevertheless tend to clump around abstract ideas such as tranquillity, antiquity and, in the uplands, space, freedom and wilderness. It is interesting to hear such qualities listed by present-day upland farmers as reasons why they chose their way of life and will continue to follow it, even though they labour and make a financial loss in the collapse of their stock market at the start of the third millennium AD. Whether such personal responses are an acculturated characteristic of post-Renaissance, European people or whether people in the first millennium AD thought similarly is a nice point. The evidence, such as it is, is that they did. We can look, for example, at Virgil's poetry and Giraldus Cambrensis' topographical descriptions just outside either end of our thousand years: emotions as well as visual images are recognisable to us in both writers' words. The point is central to our consideration of the evidence from within that millennium for, depending on whether our predecessors thought like us or not, our use of the evidence more than a millennium later could be producing interpretations either within or in parallel to their perception of 'reality'. However skilled our investigations, however logical our interpretation, our *rationale* may be their fantasy (cf. Cosgrove and Daniels 1988; Tilley 1994).

Another challenge in using evidence in our period is that historical generalisation is now both easy to be misguided by and difficult to identify. As we shall see, this is partly the result of a dynamism in the landscape,

and our recent recognition of it (chapters 3, 4). One response can of course
be not to recognise it. 'My book', wrote Everitt (1986, xvii),

> is not about the Romano-British period itself, or about the ultimate origins
> of Kentish settlement in the Iron Age or Bronze Age, since those are matters
> for the archaeologist. I have endeavoured to indicate places and neighbour-
> hoods where continuity of occupation with the Roman era seems likely;
> but I have not discussed pre-English settlement as such except where there
> seems reason to suspect that occupation was indeed continuous. However
> important the older strata of colonization may be to the archaeologist,
> however absorbing to the student of landscape, they are relevant to the
> historian of English society only where settlements actually survived, or
> where an older population or system of organization was incorporated in
> the new.

As a massively misconceived appreciation of past process and current
research that statement would be difficult to beat, particularly coming
from an important local historian but there seemingly writing in ignorance
or arrogance. Are we really supposed to believe that 'English society',
somehow uniquely different from all other agrarian societies, appeared
and developed in a cultural and environmental vacuum except where
some of its members occupied a few places used beforehand? Did not
'English society' farm? Did it choose the farmlands, create the seeds,
magic the stock and invent all the agricultural practices and implements
itself *de novo*? And did not the degree to which it did or did not do such
things affect the sort of society it was and became?

The benefit to those who eschew, or are unaware of, such archaism
is that we can now envisage a thousand years of great landscape variety
at any one moment and an agrarian history which is more involved with
change, quite sophisticated change at time, than with simplicity and stasis.
Landscapes were both home to and developing with numerous societies,
of which the English version was but one. It had nevertheless become in
economic and political terms the dominant one by the end of the millennium, in part because of its farming.

One of the nicer judgements to be made is the extent to which evidence,
of whatever sort, from before 1 BC/AD and after AD 1000, can be used
to illumine the millennium between those dates. Traditionally, the Roman
Conquest has been seen as marking a major break between the heretofore
and the Imperial future, with little of significance being carried forward
from prehistory; while much from the Norman Conquest onwards has
been transposed backwards into Anglo-Saxon England, e.g. about field
systems (see chapter 7). More useful, perhaps, is the thought that some

of the likely basics of first-millennium farming are probably illumined not so much by the specifics of medieval farming but by the realities of pre-industrial agrarian life and practices throughout most of the second millennium AD in western Europe.

Truism it may be, but basic to understanding how we come about any knowledge of the first millennium AD is to realise that most of the evidence is not only incomplete and patchy – but that is true of all periods and topics – but is seldom direct, especially about trends and developments. Yes, Tacitus recorded that Claudius invaded Britain in AD 43, and the scribes of the *Anglo-Saxon Chronicle* later meticulously wrote down dates of comets and droughts: some documents are good at recording events. On the other hand, however, nowhere does a document say anything as specific or helpful as 'Today, 1 April 900, the king decreed that henceforth English is the official language.' No contemporary document specifically records when the 'feudal system' started or indeed even discusses by name its growth. No one recorded how villages developed; no one, to judge from the silence, decided that an open field system would be better for some parts of England and not for most of the rest of Britain. To be fair, neither documents nor archaeology are good at recording such developments for any period, however important they may be in terms of longer-term significance, e.g. no government statement or official document recorded when the people of modern Britain became a 'post-modernist society'. The evidence is not, therefore, just being awkward for the first millennium AD.

Evidence

We are immediately confronted by a paradox. On the one hand, a very wide range of evidence is now available to be taken into account in considering farming in the first millennium AD in Britain. On the other hand, there is a widespread perception of paucity of evidence. Writing of what is admittedly rather a special part of Britain, for example, a distinguished authority began her study of the second half of the millennium by declaring 'It is not possible to write a history of early medieval Wales that will stand up to the requirements of modern scholarship' (Davies 1989, 1). One of the skills that modern scholarship in these matters has developed, however, is that, given an imperfect past world in the present, interdisciplinarity over a wide field can compensate for deficiences in one aspect. Davies of course knows that, as she proceeds to demonstrate in the rest of her book; but the fact is that our subject, agrarian history, is no longer only a diplomatic one.

It is not solely 'historical' in two senses: it no longer relies on, even stems mainly from, documentary evidence, nor is its objective only to arrange the evidence in such a way as to be able to tell a chronological narrative ('story'). It would, for example, now be perfectly possible to treat the first millennium AD as a prehistoric period and still generate a cogent perception of food production during it. The thought plays to the significant difference now, compared to Finberg (1972a) and colleagues writing a generation ago, of the availability of seas of non-documentary evidence, in particular the results of modern archaeological excavation (*passim*), air photographic study (this chapter) and environmental research (chapter 3).

One of the most significant shifts in the way that the period has been studied over the last generation has been to move from an approach at the general level of national history, illustrated by local examples which bear out the wider truths, to intense studies of localities from which local generalisations may emerge and from which, collectively, broad trends may appear. The first two volumes in the Penguin History of England series (Richmond 1955; Whitelock 1952) exemplify the former. Everitt (1986) and Blair (1991) are classics of the latter; they illuminate with much original research and scholarly percipience the counties of Kent and Surrey respectively, and the newly elucidated early histories of those counties illuminate southern England and a number of its key historical issues.

Archaeology, both fieldwork and excavation, has made a massive contribution, and continues to do so. Davies (1989) recognised the particular nature of this development in its early stages; not just the quantitative increase in the amount of data, but how quantity of investigation spread across the landscape was likely both to change the nature of the evidential base and consequently to alter interpretative perspectives. Hence our preference here for not wishing to be tied down in advance within a historical framework of periods and events which could well be irrelevant to, even obscure, agrarian significance through time. Particularly fruitful has been the combination, often under the label of 'landscape archaeology', of studies combining interdisciplinary research including scientific, documentary and fieldwork techniques. Almost by definition such work is best carried out at a regional or more local scale, and to a significant extent this essay is based on such studies. They have been particularly successful in identifying localised land arrangements, such as those of Anglo-Saxon estates, and in elucidating change through time in particular areas, notably in the work of Hooke (*passim*). Bell and Boardman (1992, 3) remarked that 'One of the great revelations of landscape archaeology ... has been the degree of continuity and time-depth in many landscapes' (but see Everitt below). That there have also been major episodes of discontinuity and disruption, locally if not nationally, should be added.

Why all this is crucial evidentially is because it is now so apparent that recognition of process is one of the keys to understanding: process not just of reinterpretation of essentially a static block of evidence, as with documents of this period, but process as the continuum whereby evidence is itself generated. This is particularly true not just of archaeological evidence but of field evidence as a whole. Bell and Boardman (1992, 3), for example, stress that

> much modern geomorphological research [implies] that the history of landscape is essentially that of episodically changing processes, at its simplest, the contrast between stability (soil development) and instability (erosion or deposition) . . . The difficulty of reconstructing erosional episodes, because by definition they involve loss of evidence, means that emphasis has to be placed on soils and sediments.

Much of the evidence of the history of the landscape that the farmers of the first millennium AD inherited had therefore been destroyed and removed before Claudius crossed the Channel; and it, together with the evidence from the millennium of our study, has been further smudged by another thousand years of climatic, geomorphological and human activity. Much of it, especially the palaeoenvironmental, where it exists at all is not in fact *in situ* but lies in deposits such as alluvium secondary to its place of generation (e.g. Evans *et al.* 1993; see also Bell 1992 and Appendix 1).

Theory

All evidence is recognised, collected, curated, assessed and interpreted, and then reinterpreted, within a framework of conscious or unconscious theory. 'Theory' here means the assumptions and premises underlying a piece of research or writing; we are not concerned with theory as popularly understood, as in theories about the mystery of the Ninth Legion's disappearance or whether or not the Bayeux Tapestry shows Harold about to pull an arrow from his eye (Stenton 1957, nos. 71–2, according to whom he was not). Theory in the intellectual sense profoundly informs such major studies as Frere (1967) and Stenton (1943), though neither said so. Stenton (1947, 695–9), for example, in the course of a scholarly assessment of his sources, unconsciously betrays his own version (or 'model') of where historical significance lies by listing fifth, and last, in his categories of primary sources 'Sources of incidental information'. They consist of coins, archaeology and architecture, place-names, literature and learning. Such a bias, unspecified by him but obvious now, clearly helps formulate the character of his book and therefore of the Anglo-Saxon England about which he writes so learnedly and which he creates in other people's minds.

Laboratory analyses are, despite their objective aura, based on theory too, and the myriad data they tend to generate can lead to general models – 'what we have to analyse is a system in which man himself is, and has been for a long time, an ecological factor as well as a member of the ecological community' (Dimbleby 1977, Preface). 'Science' is neither 'better' nor 'worse' than translating old documents as a way of elucidating the past and addressing some of the questions it asks; the important point is to use the appropriate approach and methodology. Ultimately, decisions on them may well come down to personal experience and judgement. 'Theory' in that sense clearly underlies this book, for in addition to trying to pursue particular emphases in it, that is to explore my selection of 'models', my particular mental constructs, experience and attitudes, not some abstract and achievable 'truth', make it what it is. That statement is itself 'theory'.

Apart from the co-authors in Finberg (1972a), no one seems to have previously attempted a British agrarian history of the first millennium AD as a whole; and even that great book, although conceptually a millennial unity, in practice did not escape the deeply rooted concept of the thousand years being divided into 'the Roman period' and 'the Anglo-Saxon period', perhaps with a somewhat murky-grey period in between and a marginal area (Wales) beyond. Its three main sections were written separately by three different authors (Applebaum 1972; Finberg 1972b; Jones 1972). Many others have, of course, written on the topic in terms of farming in Roman Britain or the Roman period and in Anglo-Saxon England, either in separate studies (e.g. Rivet 1958; Fowler 1976a), or as components of general histories of either period (e.g. Salway 1981; Loyn 1991). This division is itself significant in theoretical terms, since it clearly marks the way in which scholarship has approached the topic. Both approaches have been, and are, 'positivist', that is pursued in the belief that 'Roman Britain' or 'Anglo-Saxon England' existed and are recoverable, to a greater or lesser extent which it is the business of scholarship to explore. Clearly, theoretical stances are implied in all this, but are seldom stated; yet the sort of understanding we have, at the start of the third millennium, of farming in the first millennium is a direct result of the various theoretical positions previously adopted.

That understanding is largely based on the results of studying topics deemed to be worth studying; and, negatively, of other topics which have not been pursued. Largely unconscious assumptions rather than deliberate decisions underlie that fact. In the British Isles projected in Davies'

(1999) monumental history, for example, no 'farming' occurred at all and 'agriculture' was apparently, to judge by the index, confined to the Neolithic period and the late Bronze Age. What sort of history is it in which people did not eat after 700 BC? What did the bulk of the population do with its time after that? In a different context, but making the same point, the existence of Roman villas and Anglo-Saxon charters has significantly affected the nature of research into, and coloured the understanding of, the first millennium. That has come about, however, mainly because these two sorts of evidence are so obvious and accessible, not as a result of a cool appraisal of the relative merits of a range of primary sources. This is a truism but the consequent bias goes right back to the beginnings of a created history of the millennium. Hill (1981, maps 27–30, 41) makes this graphically clear in his maps of the differing cognitive geographies of Bede, viewing his world from Tyneside, and the *Anglo-Saxon Chronicle*, compiled by scribes based in southern England. Bede's is the only one of the five maps showing any significant appreciation of Britain north of York – *plus ça change*. A comparable, unconscious bias today is exemplified by the index (Wright 1991) to the first ten volumes of the much-esteemed journal *Anglo-Norman Studies*. It contains no entries under 'agriculture', 'cereals', 'crops', 'farming', 'pasture' or 'plough': a whole dimension of human activity and economy would not seem to exist in the minds of those now studying the ninth to twelfth centuries in western Europe. The 'history' of that place and period, as a *post facto* human construct distinct from what was actually going on then, does not contain the agrarian dimension. Historicity is a relative concept.

The historical/archaeological debate

One of the big debates in archaeology generally but very much in relation to the first millennium in particular is about the degree to which archaeological evidence should or should not be interpreted in its own right or within a documentary framework. To many historians, it is not an issue: archaeological evidence, if admissible at all, is ancillary to 'real' history, knowable only from documents. Even a historian generally sympathetic to and thoroughly knowledgeable about the archaeology of the second half of the first millennium can seem to be curiously harsh in his assessment of the subject while apparently blind to similar limitations of documentary evidence (Sawyer 1998a, 134–5). The debate continues, passionately but wastefully; for no one discipline can now alone satisfactorily address the range of critical issues in the first millennium, and the future lies in interdisciplinarity. Meanwhile, at least both history and archaeology are in

accord about one matter at the centre of our concerns here: the idea that
Anglo-Saxons brought open fields and heavy ploughs was abandoned by
historians in the 1960s for one set of reasons and archaeology, for different
reasons, agrees (though Kerridge (1992) disagrees with both).

Richards (1999, 44–9), an archaeologist, illustrates some of the sub-
tleties in the relationship not so much of the practitioners as between the
two main sorts of evidence, documentary and material. Writing of Anglo-
Saxon settlements in Northumbria, he remarks that 'one of the strengths
of archaeology is that it is able to complement history based on documentary sources and dominated by the deeds of kings and archbishops.
Archaeology, it is argued, is about the everyday lives of everyday folk.
Unfortunately, one searches hard for the everyday villages and farms to
place alongside the rich manuscript and sculptural evidence of seventh
and eighth century Northumbria.' He then proceeds to discuss the context for a particular piece of archaeological research which he interprets
entirely, and plausibly, within a documentary template. His particular conundrum was that a 'new' type of archaeological site, characterised by
large numbers of Middle and Late Anglo-Saxon coins and other artefacts
found by metal-detector users, had come significantly to outnumber settlements of the period known from more conventional archaeology. Were
they perhaps market places? The application of some precision excavation and landscape interpretation resolved the matter satisfactorily – or
at least generated a usable model – by suggesting that the new sites were
enclosed farmsteads of the eighth and ninth centuries 'with normal settlement debris' (for field-walking and excavation corrected the bias created
by metal-detecting), in the case study replaced by an adjacent ditched
Viking Age farm, with occupation 'relatively grand but short-lived, perhaps spanning some fifty years or a single generation only, from the late
9th to early 10th centuries'. The local inference is that the next move
was to nearby Cowlam, giving the present village a tenth-century origin.
Of wider significance was the regional model that 'the Scandinavian settlement disrupted existing settlement patterns and led to the nucleation
of villages'. And of potential national significance is the implication that
it can no longer be assumed that the many other ditched enclosures on
the Yorkshire Wolds, and perhaps elsewhere, date to the late prehistoric
and early first-millennium centuries (chapter 6; this matter has now been
significantly advanced by Ulmschneider 2000).

Sawyer (1998a, 270–1), incidentally, writing of the same material,
brings into the open another dimension not so much in the use of evidence as in its availability. In this case, because some of the evidence has
been produced by metal-detectorists, not necessarily pursuing scientific

understanding and more concerned with competitive advantage over rivals, locational information is kept secret or only communicated in confidence. This has for long been the case in the murky realms of art collectors and numismatists, and it is much to be regretted that secrecy should now have become the norm apparently in certain areas of archaeology. Evidentially, it runs completely counter to the ethic of scholarship, and is unacceptable.

Different scholars can handle the same or similar evidence in different ways (cf. Salway 1981, 766). This is particularly so where an artefact type, be it brooch or broch, is readily identifiable, or where one topographical area, especially an attractive one, contains a cluster of evidential material. South-west England in the first six centuries of the millennium, for example, provides attractive material like villas with mosaics and hillforts with Mediterranean pottery in a generally pleasant environment; it has attracted considerable attention (summarised with plentiful reference in Todd 1987; see on the specifics Branigan 1977b; Rahtz *et al.* 1992). In contrast is the archaeology of the same period between Hadrian's Wall and the River Tweed, an area dismissed as unimportant or only dimly perceived as a rather distant, dim and dreary no-man's land. Its archaeology, directly relevant to chapters 6 and 7 here, was effectively created by a small number of people consciously working in unfashionable territory in a cold climate in the second half of the twentieth century (Miket and Burgess 1984).

Härke (1997) addressed another sort of difference stemming from a single block of evidence. The problem, apparent in the 1990s, was about distinguishing social status in early Anglo-Saxon society, and was explained, so he argued, by a generational model:

> The disagreements have not been resolved, but the debate appears to have resulted among historians in a shift of opinion away from the assumption of an essentially free peasant society (as advocated in Stenton 1971). Among archaeologists, the intellectual shifts in the discipline have resulted in a split: many of the younger archaeologists who have studied Anglo-Saxon social structures have eschewed the use of written sources, while many of their older colleagues who are more comfortable with the use of historical concepts and sources appear to be more comfortable with the opinion of Stenton and his contemporaries than with more recent historical opinion.

Härke's observation of the particular is correct but rather misses the theoretical point. It is a matter not of being comfortable or otherwise 'with more recent historical opinion' but of being more familiar or otherwise with working in diplomatic or anthropological terms. That applies to theory and to practice. In this case, of course there is a perfectly valid theoretical point in eschewing 'written sources' and looking at Anglo–Saxon social structures on the basis of material culture alone (though that does rather beg the question of what is 'Anglo-Saxon'). The same would of course apply earlier too, prompting questions such as 'How Roman were the British?'

Historical models

History too has its ways of thinking; historical models are both uncon-scious, as in the Davies and Stenton examples above, and conscious. 'Most of the work of settlement was done, and the problems of the future were of a different shape from the struggles of the past' wrote Hallam (1988, 44) thinking at a national level of 'the land the Conqueror won from Harold [which] was one of the richest in western Europe'. He was writing of a land where good husbandry combined with rich natural resources to effect a considerable agrarian achievement by 1066. And he was trying to combine an anthropological with a historical model. It is in general credible, though it is extremely likely that further research, as is already happening, will tend to reinforce ideas of regional diversity in space and of non-synchronous changes in time rather than his model of continuous linear development.

One element of hard-won conclusion to a detailed study of Surrey (Blair 1991, 161) provides, in comparison, a 'local model'; but it also presents a clear model of settlement process which can be abstracted and tested, not just in Surrey but elsewhere. The moment in time is again in the eleventh century but such a date is not essential in the conversion of the conclusion into a general model: 'groups of farms which crossed geological strata tended to coalesce, and split into longitudinal townships, as lines of villages developed with pasture links to the north and south and incipient common fields. But settlement nucleation and common fields were largely confined to the fertile zones.' An immediate question is whether or not that proposal applies to other areas, to places others know as well as Blair knows Surrey, to places one knows oneself. It is certainly relevant to areas Hooke (1998, esp. 46–54) knows well, in Wessex as well as the West Midlands. It also provides an attractive, workable model 'explaining' what could well have been going on in the Wiltshire parish of West Overton. There, two medieval manors and tithings cross geological strata to form 'longitudinal townships', with 'pasture links to north and south', and two sets of common fields certainly present in the tenth century adjacent to two farm – 'tuns' which physically (not tenurially) coalesced into a medieval nucleated village and may well have done so as early as the tenth century (chapter 13; Fowler 2000c, chapters 10, 11).

First-millennium agriculture: history and historiography

We now summarise the growth of our topic bibliographically, more fully referenced in Appendix 1 for here it is rather a case study of how various evidence has been used.

The concept of a long, agrarian history preceding the Roman invasion of Britain in AD 43 should now be familiar, not only to prehistorians; yet echoes can still be heard of the basically wrong idea that Anglo-Saxons moved into a primeval, virgin landscape awaiting their pioneering, Teutonic axe. It is, after all, already more than forty years since the historian Lennard (1959, 1) began his study of the decades after Domesday with a first chapter entitled 'An Old Country'. All the same, it is slightly disappointing in that particular case to find that the 'distant past', in which were set the 'roots' of the England taken over by William the Conqueror, lay in a marginal 'Celtic Britain' older than a Roman civilisation which had 'evaporated without leaving any appreciable mark upon the new and vigorous communities which the Anglo–Saxon invaders established within the boundaries of the former province'.

Some landowners, and possibly their foremen, may have had some knowledge of 'best practice' during the early centuries AD when numerous books and treatises on various sorts of cropping were disseminated, though doubtless in small numbers (White 1970a). It is dubious, however, whether perhaps half-baked knowledge of principles and practice developed for Mediterranean conditions would have been particularly helpful in the British Isles. On the other hand, knowledge of vineyards and Roman gardens, including their plants both decorative and medicinal, travelled at least to southern Britain and, perhaps surprisingly, garden-lore persisted to north and west in post-Classical times (chapter 12). Whatever the impact of Classical agrarian understanding on British farming generally, however, it was a knowledge that faded and was forgotten, not to return until the Renaissance (Fussell 1972). About AD 1240 Petrus Crescentius collected together and synthesised into one volume much of the agrarian writing of the Roman world, though his volume was not published until 1471. European farming in the fifteenth to seventeenth centuries was nevertheless characterised by numerous agricultural volumes. All such knowledge was denied to British farmers in the second half of the first millennium, and it is only now and then, and late, that we catch glimpses in the occasional written word of sensible, tried practices on a monastic estate, for example, and of a doubtless strong vernacular tradition, pre-Anglo-Saxon, pre-scientific and pragmatic, about how things ought to be done. Thomas Tusser (1573) over 500 years later is not only in that tradition but is the articulator of it, writing about what to do when and how in a way which, some anachronisms apart, would have been recognised and often approved by the illiterate farmers of the first millennium AD had they been able to hear someone read his words.

Knowledge about the history of farming as distinct from the history of knowledge about how to farm is a very recent phenomenon. It did not loom large in first-millennium British history in particular until Finberg (1972a), nor has Britain been prominent in agricultural histories. Nevertheless, Dickson's *The Husbandry of the Ancients* (1798) began a topic which has received fitful attention for two centuries. Stukeley, characteristically, beat him to it, correctly identifying banks he saw on the Dorset Downs as those of abandoned fields. This line of recognition and argument led Sir Richard Colt Hoare in the early nineteenth century to recognise pre-Roman fields near Marlborough and strip lynchets as the product of ploughing (Bowen 1961, 67). Farming did not become historically focussed, however, as is illustrated by the fact that although the various editions of basic Anglo-Saxon documents edited from the early nineteenth century onwards (e.g. Kemble 1839–48; Birch 1885–93) contained, by definition, many references to agricultural matters, they were not taken up in agrarian or landscape terms until later. Only with the genesis of large, scholarly tomes dealing with the general – the history of Europe, the origins of feudalism and the like – from the mid-nineteenth century did agrarian history came into focus as a proper, and indeed significant, subject of study. It tended nevertheless to be a means to an end rather than a subject in its own right: *agraria* illustrated the growth of the manor or the state of villeinage at the grand scale, while parochial history dealt with descents and genealogies and never asked about the farm-workers. A remarkable academic output helped generate a growing public interest in such matters, in the case of our topic following a number of significant publications in late Victorian and Edwardian times, e.g. Seebohm (1890; 1914). These key studies not only laid the foundations for the modern subject but largely set the research agenda for the twentieth century, e.g. Maitland (1897). This 'grand' tradition has been continued through the twentieth century with magisterial *opera* from time to time, notably at the European scale, e.g. Randsborg (1991).

Three developments synchronously enabled the subject to flourish through the twentieth century: air photography, landscape archaeology and public service archaeology. The application of air photography by O.G.S. Crawford revolutionised approaches to the landscape and understanding of farming, both pre-Saxon and Anglo-Saxon (Crawford 1924; Crawford and Keiller 1928). Crawford and the Curwens in Sussex added 'Celtic fields' to the repertoire of *agraria* in the English landscape (Bowen 1961); the former's discovery, cartography and elucidation of 'Celtic' fields in the 1920s was masterly. Perceptions of older landscapes within the countryside further increased as the serious study of place-names began and, for example, Grundy pioneered the interpretation of Anglo-Saxon charters as descriptions of real landscape rather than just legal texts. His brave efforts were constrained by being desk-studies of Ordnance Survey maps rather than based on field-work but the compliment was returned as, in their turn, Ordnance Surveyors followed his identifications into the field and added, in Gothic writing, features of the Anglo-Saxon landscape to those of the twentieth century e.g. herepath. At the same time, a strong interest in 'open fields' and ridge and furrow in the Midlands reached a peak in the Orwins' *Common Fields* (1938; more significant was Thirsk's basic rebuttal of their thesis of origins and date in the 3rd edition, 1967). Hoskins (1955) single-handedly brought about a symbiosis of local history and the grand theme, rescuing the one from its minutiae and giving ascertainable fact in the field and document to illumine the other.

The third development involves government and public money: on the one hand the development of reliable record offices at national and local level, safe repositories relatively accessible; and on the other the massive expansion of archaeological investigation as a public service since *c.* 1970 as a response to the increasing demands on that most important of all historical documents, the landscape itself.

Overall, despite increasing efforts and intense academic interest over the last century in matters pertaining to or arising from our topic, there has been very little study specifically of farming in the first millennium until recently. Several books and numerous articles have examined the topic or some aspect of it in the Roman period (e.g. White 1967; see Appendix 1, esp. notes for this chapter and for chapters 6–11). Some authors, notably Loyn (1962; 1991), have squarely addressed the topic in their books on post-Roman Britain, or England. Finberg (1972a) apart, however, no book was devoted to farming in either the first or second half of the first millennium. Research papers were few and far between too. Some recent major studies are, however, central to the topic, e.g. Rackham (1994), and the number of significant agrarian papers is increasing. Fowler (1976) and (1981b), for example, are now completely overtaken. One of the most thoughtful studies is technically just beyond our millennium, but Hallam's (1988) is a brave and scholarly essay trying to relate post-Domesday agrarian history to antecedents in the eleventh century and earlier. Meanwhile, all over Britain scholars such as Crawford and a whole school of northern Scottish colleagues, and Williamson and colleagues in East Anglia, opened up new agrarian perspectives on landscapes both known and unresearched, at both ends of, and throughout, the first millennium. Maitland, had he been able to see the scholarly works being produced a century and more after his masterpiece, would immediately have felt at home with books such as Faith's (1999), but he would have surely been quick to appreciate too the works of others, e.g. Dark (2000), Hooke (1998) and Reynolds (1999), also expanding agrarian knowledge across the whole millennium but in ways unrealisable or even unconceptualised in his day.

Archaeological evidence

Archaeological evidence exists, in the first place, only in the landscape (including the sea). Contrary to common belief, it survives not merely in the ground but also on and above the ground surface. It is now recognised to be voluminous; as data, it is quite well ordered but spatially patchy and frustratingly incomplete. Here we only give examples of a few aspects particularly relevant to elucidating farming, and landscapes and their evolution, in the first millennium AD.

Most archaeological evidence from the first millennium is redundant for our purposes. Much of it is relevant as secondary or tertiary evidence in that the overwhelming majority of the objects and material were produced by or for agrarian societies. Sometimes individually but more often collectively, these items can say something about their contemporary society. Archaeology's main contribution, however, is in providing evidence for most of the settlement and other human sites of this millennium, that is the places where people lived, worked and worshipped. Without that dimension, particularly in the countryside, our understanding would still basically be stuck in the late Victorian cul-de-sac of history by documents alone. Archaeological fieldwork in the sense of minute examination of the detail of surviving earthworks has been an important part of that process, especially in woodlands and uplands, areas of low-intensity farming where artificial features tend to survive. Practically every piece of investigation in the landscape involves many periods of time and episodes of activity in the past. The level of detail recorded, in field, excavation trench, library and laboratory, can be excruciatingly exact, often indeed boring in itself but

the foundation nevertheless of many of the grand generalisations filling these chapters.

Excavation

Archaeological excavation alone has told us about, for example, early towns, otherwise at best known only from a name in Latin or Old English, and few matters are more significant for agriculture than urban settlements (see chapters 5 and 13). Archaeological excavation has provided practically all our knowledge about major aspects of agrarian technology in this period, for example mills (see chapter 8). Much more important than most of the individual sites, even the really important ones like the Tamworth mill (Rahtz and Meeson 1992), great Roman villas as at Gorhambury (Neal *et al.* 1990) and Fishbourne (Cunliffe 1971) or royal palaces such as Yeavering (Hope-Taylor 1977), are a few hard-won generalities that

Plate IV Crop-marks in the Upper Thames valley on valley gravel near Oxford, illustrating a typical landscape complex of settlements, enclosures, tracks and fields mainly of late prehistoric and first-millennium AD date.

Plate V Excavation on chalk at Thwing, East Yorkshire, showing work in progress on the foundation trenches and

have now emerged in particular from archaeological excavation, for example about settlement patterns, house types and social arrangements (see chapters 5 and 6).

Such have come despite one of the marked characteristics of archaeological evidence, that is the element of chance in its discovery. There is, for example, a rather grand tradition in which, for 200 years already, the insertion into the British landscape of major engineering works such as canals, railways and motorways has significantly affected the archaeological record (Ashbee 1972; Rahtz 1974; Fowler 1979). This continues strongly in the early twenty-first century, in the age of compulsory archaeological mitigation by developers and very deliberate, planned but reactive archaeological activity. Such has significantly affected the nature of this essay during its gestation. The following example is typical. On one part of the Channel Tunnel Rail Link through Kent were 'a 6th–7th century Anglo-Saxon cemetery . . . containing 36 burials [accompanied by] shield bosses, spear-heads, glass beads and dress items . . . A 1st–3rd century Roman cemetery . . . excavated close to Springhead Roman town . . . [was] aligned on a Roman road [and contained] some 600 cremation and inhumation burials.' As part of the same exercise, excavation uncovered a 'large area of the villa estate' of a previously discovered Roman villa at Thurnham, including 'numerous associated buildings such as a private estate, a massive aisled building and other agricultural structures such as corn-driers and wells' (see Appendix 1).

Particular subsets of archaeological evidence requiring particular expertises to 'read' lie in architectural remains and sculpture. Again, such evidence is not in general necessarily of direct agrarian relevance though some pieces are, e.g. agricultural tools sculpted to decorate a religious building or monument; but the fact of architectural remains, as for example of a villa or an early Christian monastery, is of considerable agrarian significance (see chapter 7).

Scientific evidence

The later twentieth century saw the development and impact of both the application of scientific methodology to archaeology and history, and their opening up whole fields of new types of evidence not available to earlier students. Broadly, that evidence has become available only in the last quarter of the twentieth century (e.g. Fowler 1981b), reaching an early point of generality and assessment in the all-important environmental dimension in Rackham (1994). Climate, for example, traditionally pieced together from annalistic and anecdotal texts, is now reconstructed from a range of evidence using various techniques: not just textual, but from, for example, carbon–14 and dendrochronological dating linked to environmental sampling in peat, ice-cores and glaciers (chapter 3; Lamb 1995); 'for first-millennium AD Britain textual sources shed little light on the nature of the environment overall. Reconstruction of the environment is, therefore, largely reliant on the same types of evidence used for prehistory – principally the remains of plant and animal communities, soils and sediments' (Dark 2000, vii). A palaeoecological approach to our topic is essential (Dimbleby 1977; 1985). Here it is simply necessary to note the huge amount of data now available from essentially the Natural Sciences, particularly with regard to past environment and climate, crops and fauna, evidence of a nature and range simply not available to earlier generations of agrarian historians.

Palaeobotany generally (synthesised in Dark 2000) is one of the fields most important for our purposes, in parallel with the enormous increase in the skills of studying animal bones (e.g. Grant 1989). Recently, the genetic potential of 'old bones', human as well as animal, has come to be recognised too (Jones *et al.* 1996; Muir 2001). All this is now central, not only to agrarian developments 5000 to 10,000 years BC but also to the first millennium AD and its farming in particular. Such evidence and scientific methodology, however, do not necessarily produce clarity or certainty, and in any case rigorous observance of traditional archaeological recording method remains – indeed, is even more important – on site, establishing the critical dimension of 'context' without which any evidence is severely diminished in value.

In a typical example we summarise part of an attempt to interpret animal bone evidence in its context on a site called Watkins Farm in the Middle Thames valley:

> Later Romano-British deposition is difficult to assess. Specific evidence for domestic activity is scant, with problems in the central area because of the redeposited Iron Age material. Most of the groups of sheep bone showed considerable degradation, though preservation is markedly better in the main enclosure. This degradation can affect the presence of skeletal elements, but in this case the percentage representation of species bones seemed to be unbiased. Due to the level of degradation the percentage levels of small skeletal elements of sheep are not as high as on other sites.
>
> In an explanatory model for the special distribution of bone debris, three interactive causes are postulated. The first two, scavenging and rubbish clearance from inside houses and from some external areas (e.g. external hearths), tend to disperse larger bones and fragments away from the central

area of intensive human activity. The third is the accumulation of coarse and fine debris from carcass butchery, near slaughtering and butchery areas. These are located at increasing distances from the houses and hearths relative to the size of the species carcass. Small carcasses can be butchered and cooked with a minimum of inconvenience in or near houses. The butchery of larger carcasses is more disruptive of household activity and is thus often carried out further afield. (Summarised from Allen 1990)

We shall be forced to use such evidence more definitely than in this example, for we cannot argue every case as here. It is especially important therefore for a student to realise the sorts of arguments and the uncertainties which actually lie behind the less ambivalent confidence of a synthesis.

Landscape

Maitland (1897) tried to break out of the documentary strait-jacket by recognising possibly significant historic patterns on maps; Seebohm (1890; 1914) was edging the same way. Their precognitions have subsequently flowered into a rich bundle of studies which, when conceptually and methodologically integrated, have proved extremely rewarding in understanding contemporary landscape in terms of its historic development. Britain has led the way in such studies. The first millennium AD is often key to such considerations; conversely, much of our understanding of landscape between Julius Caesar and William I comes from such studies. Approaches and methods are dealt with elsewhere (Crawford 1953; Aston and Rowley 1974; Tilley 1994), so here we need barely do more than touch on some of the main types of evidence used in 'landscape archaeology'. The main source of evidence is, it should be stressed, the landscape itself; it merely has to be read.

Two realisations have profoundly affected appreciation, rather than the nature, of archaeological settlement evidence in particular. Until the later twentieth century, archaeological sites were generally thought of as discrete entities; now they are appreciated less as sites in a setting than as a context containing numerous aspects of human behaviour. The move from the study of sites *per se* to that of context has been and is fundamental, moving archaeology on from glorified philately to a serious intellectual pursuit. This is one of the bases of 'landscape archaeology', with emphases on ecological context and environmental change and, in practice, the widespread application of field survey projects like that in the Fens (Fig. 4.1; Hall and Coles 1994). The second realisation, articulated by Taylor (1972), was that it was incorrect to perceive archaeological sites as 'normally' existing on higher land, especially hills and their slopes. Taylor made the crucial distinction between former existence and contemporary survival, demonstrating that the latter was the result of medieval and later land-use. Sites, in other words, survive (with their contexts) where subsequent land-use has been light, as on hillsides and uplands, but not where subsequent land-use has been continuous or temporarily intensive, as in valleys.

Medieval and later ploughing, for example, has erased the surface features of early medieval and earlier settlements. This demolished one of the crucial tenets of our period: that 'Ancient Britons', up to and including the Roman period, were hill peoples (with silent nuances, therefore, about their primitive and uncivilised nature); whereas, given the apparent absence of such settlements from the valleys and the presence there of extant villages often bearing Old English names, the new English settlers began by occupying the much better sites along those valleys, keeping their distance from the natives marooned up above. That became a demonstrable myth *c.* 1970. The existence of upland sites today is largely the result of selective land-use, their survival due to their lying not on hills as such but on post-Roman marginal land. The point came to be emphasised because the earthwork evidence of the traditional archaeological record was largely destroyed in the second half of the twentieth century. We now know from survey and air photography, however, that much more had been removed from the visible landscape long before that. Now, a completely different sort of hitherto unseen archaeological evidence has been revealed where, because the surface had long been flattened, virtually none was known to exist. One result is that we now know that thousands and thousands of people lived, not only on the hills but also along the valleys, in later prehistoric and Roman times. We examine some of this evidence in chapters 5 and 6.

'Context' in landscape study is, therefore, not only topographical and spatial but temporal and evolutionary, dependent on the study of documentary, palaeoenvironmental and other evidence as much as material culture. Documentary evidence is particularly important, and in that sense the 'landscape archaeologist' has to be a good documentary (and cartography) researcher too (the need is often met by a specialist within a landscape archaeology research group, cf., for example, all the specialist contributions referenced in Aston and Gerrard 1999). Elucidating place-names from Roman Britain, which after all come to us largely in the form of written evidence from antiquity, illustrates one sort of expertise (Rivet and Smith 1979); relating Classical descriptions to ards and ploughs in first-millennium Britain (and twentieth-century Languedoc) is another (chapter 9). Much of Kelly's *Early Irish Farming* (1998) adduces landscape and life-way from the superficially somewhat unpromising source of Early Irish law-texts; Hooke (1997) provides some excellent examples of readings of landscape enriched by readings of Early English documents. Sometimes, however, a correlation between field and documentary evidence is neither obvious nor immediately significant (see the 'rundale' example in chapter 11). Any such use of evidence is based on a judgement about relevance of one sort of evidence to another, and of both together to the topic under investigation. But with so much of that topic geographically in the west and north of Britain, and on the whole poorly documented, there is a strong temptation, justifiably succumbed to here, to use later sources and invoke analogy, especially 'ethnographic parallel' (e.g. chapter 9).

As students working in Britain we also tend in our insular work to fail to recognise the object of our particular study as an example of a phenomenon widespread in space and time. Transhumance, for example, has been and is a widely followed way of stock-farming in many parts of the world (e.g. Hole 1996, 271–8), but that may not be apparent in an insular local history which happens to notice its former existence without comment (see Appendix 1). 'The theoretical importance of settlement agriculture to early food production systems . . . has become clearer as scholars begin to examine the spatial significance and energetic contribution of near-residential and infield agriculture to . . . cultivation systems.' Without the quotation marks, that sentence could serve unremarked as conclusion to this section. It actually relates to prehistoric farming in Mesoamerica (Killion 1992, 1–2).

Place-names

Part of the acculturation of the landscape is its naming; we put our labels on the land and thereby claim and familiarise it. People like to be able to refer to where they are, where they have come from and where they are going to: they like to locate themselves, and to do so to others. So they give names to natural features and to places they have recognised and even made (Hooke 1998, 2–16, enlarges almost lyrically on the point). Often these names remain in use, or linger on in dialect or on a historical map; but they are always being replaced, for later people have their own names. Some early names have fallen out of use but have fortunately been recorded in medieval documents before they did so. It is often a matter of luck which old names survive, written, cartographically or orally, so the evidence we have available for study is fragmentary and eclectic. It nevertheless consists of thousands of place-names deemed to be of historical significance. Many, by definition almost, relate to farming.

A few place-names are over 2000 years old, just taking us back to a
pre-Roman British toponomy. 'Kennet' as in 'River Kennet' in Wiltshire
is one example, for it seems to have been Romanised into *Cunetio*, the
now-deserted Roman town on the bank of the River Kennet near present-
day Marlborough. Many place-names are known from Roman Britain,
most now forgotten except scholastically, but some persist in modern geography (Rivet and Smith 1979). Most of these Latin survivors are of
places rather than fragments of daily speech, so farming is not well represented. 'Villa', however, if not a genuine survivor in Britain (though it
is in Gaul), is at least a revived Latin name for a type of Roman farm;
and first-hand observation has led to the correlation between a Romano-
British settlement which may or may not be a villa and a place-name,
often just a field-name, incorporating the word 'chester' or derivatives
(from the Latin 'castrum', camp). At a basic level some names provide common nouns and adjectives describing the British countryside
(chapter 3).

Such are mere scraps. The signal importance of place-names, especially
with regard to the agricultural landscape, lies in the post-Roman period.
Two books by Gelling are pre-eminent (1978, 1984). The first relates
place-names to a historical framework, following a long and on the whole
unfortunate tendency by historians to fit place-names into a received narrative of English origins. More helpful on farming is the second book. The
very elements in the chapter heads reveal not only the range of landscapes
and activities deducible from place-names but the confidence of a mature scholar to discuss them. Gelling lists, and therefore has place-names
related to, rivers, springs, pools and lakes; marsh, moor and floodplain;
river-crossings and landing-places, roads and tracks; valleys and remote
places; hills, slopes and ridges; trees, forests, woods and clearing; and
ploughland and pasture. There the scope of the later first-millennium
landscape is laid before us, by late twentieth-century scholarship, agreed,
but by studying the very words, or their descendants, spoken by those
who farmed the land. The Gelling list of the range of landscape features
could almost be the agenda for this book, and to a large extent it is.

To illustrate the nature of this sort of evidence, an unusually long
quotation is adapted from Gelling (1992a, 124) rather than use a miscellany
of examples. She encapsulates so much about the nature and use of place-
name evidence here in the opening paragraph to her chapter 5 about some
of the commonest perceived features in the landscape:

> Hills, Slopes and Ridges: . . . OE **hlāw** . . . probably refers more frequently
> to burial mounds than to natural hills, and ON *haugr* . . . probably refers

to tumuli when it occurs in settlement-names in any of the areas of Norse colonization . . . Other 'hillock', 'rock' or 'ridge' terms . . . seldom occur in major settlement-names. There are a number of English and Welsh words beginning with *c-* in this category, such as OE *canc, clacc, clūd, cnæpp,* and the Welsh *cefn, cnwc, cnycyn* . . . some 'one-off' names like Cogges [Oxfordshire], Kilve [Somerset], Swell [Gloucestershire] . . . are descriptive of a hill near a settlement. A few anatomical terms are . . . OE **baec** and **hēafod** and Welsh **pen** . . . [others are] OE *bile* 'beak', *brægen* 'top of the head', *brū* 'brow', *ears* 'buttock', *hals* and *swēora* 'neck', *horn* 'horn', *tunge* 'tongue' and *wrōt* 'snout'.

Maps

Unfortunately we have no maps directly relevant to our purposes from the first millenium. On the other hand, maps from the sixteenth century onwards are a priceless source of evidence, for every map portrays a version not only of what is but, usually unconsciously, of what was. Maps are one case where experience has shown that post-1000 AD cartography can be used for backward projection. Historical maps, of open field systems and seventeenth-century estates for example, can be extremely helpful, showing features such as trackways and place-names now fallen out of use. In several respects, however, modern (though not the most recent) Ordnance Survey maps are the most important source of all. This has everything to do with the metrical accuracy of its survey and its military, then public service, brief. Furthermore, when it began its work around 1800 (Seymour 1980), large areas of the 'ancient landscape' of Britain still lay about the surveyors in its pre-industrialised maturity.

The importance of all these maps, however, is not their display of individual archaeological sites, but their amalgam in graphic form of features which have accumulated on the landscape over thousands of years. Many of these features are from the first millennium AD, probably more than we have yet recognised; but nevertheless, as with the landscapes it depicts, it is possible to read a map and make it sing, not only with the rigidity of the military mind engaged in 'map-reading' but like the musician reading a score.

Aerial photography (Pls. III, IV, VIII–X)

This single technique has arguably contributed quantitatively more to agrarian study in the twentieth century than any other source. Its interpretative contribution is significant too (Wilson 1975; 1982; Whimster 1989;

Riley 1980). Yet the technique is not specifically archaeological (St. Joseph 1977). Indeed, its use for the study of the past is a minor part of a multi-million pound international enterprise encompassing satellite imaging and global information systems. Its essence, for present purposes, is its power to facilitate both extensive and very detailed study of the present landscape and thereby elucidate landscape development through time. Aerial photography does indeed find new archaeological sites – tens of thousands of them, signally contributing to twenty-first-century views of a very busy British landscape in former times. In our context here, its contribution has been to provide us with a range of farmed landscapes, characterised by a variety of extensive land arrangements including – its unique contribution – a variety of field systems not otherwise documented. In particular, it has given us what we now recognise as several sorts of 'Celtic' field, and other agrarian arrangements of prehistoric and Roman date (see chapter 7). Neither fieldwork on the ground nor excavation necessarily confirms, however, what appears to be the case from above (Maxwell 1983); and conversely both can add enormously to what is visible on air photographs (Musson 1994 *passim*).

Documentary evidence

The documentary evidence is actually both considerable and complex, demanding high scholarship in several languages and disciplines to elucidate. Among it is, however, only a relatively small amount of writing specifically about farming, particularly about farming in the British Isles in the first millennium AD. An authoritative paper entitled 'Sources for Scottish agrarian history before the eighteenth century', for example, not only assumed that the only 'sources' were diplomatic, but began with thirteenth-century monastic records (Donaldson 1960–61).

Most use of documentary evidence is as gleanings from many scattered sources, for example Adomnan's *Life of Columba* for an incidental reference to a mill (see chapter 8), and as inferences from sources not written to provide answers to questions of agrarian history. These latter include such items as ancient geographies, political, legal and historical writings, and literary works such as biography, letters and poetry. Irish early medieval law tracts, for example, can be particularly revealing of practices changing little over time and probably relevant to later first-millennium society. They also refer to activities such as brewing, milling and beekeeping, the construction of fences and the value of trees. Sometimes they appear to be priceless; it becomes easy to understand why there is a documentary bias in the tradition of study of the first millennium when one document alone, *Críth Gablach*, 'describes a strict hierarchy of farmers, each listed with their possessions: agricultural tools and equipment owned personally or shared with others, crops, livestock and animal pens' (Edwards 1996, 48; see in general on Irish sources Kelly 1998).

Basically two languages, Latin and early English, are involved in the documentation, but so too in much less degree are languages spoken by the native British. Norse was also introduced from the ninth century onwards (chapter 1). Almost none of the indigenous material is contemporary, strictly speaking, in the sense that the written versions which have survived were generally written down after 1000 AD; whereas Tacitus, for example, was writing in the first century AD, Bede in the first decades of the eighth and the scribes of King Alfred's court in the later ninth, all contemporaneously with events they were describing at the ends of their histories (though characteristically we have to work with copies of their originals). Those three examples illustrate the bulk of the range of documentary sources – evidence in Latin from the Classical world and in a distinctly early medieval Latin from the emergent English world of church and state.

The main Classical sources are Caesar, Tacitus, Pliny the Elder, Virgil and Columella (Rivet 1958; White *passim* and esp. 1970a). They were of course writing for their domestic audiences, and their viewpoint, if they mention Britain at all, is external looking in. None of them, except Julius Caesar who summarises geographical research done on his behalf, was particularly concerned with Britain as such, nor were they trying to write authoritatively about farming in Britain. It is a moot point how much, if at all, Roman treatises on agriculture and gardening are relevant to Britain (chapter 1).

How valid is Classical literature for British farming and agrarian life? Indirect answers are implied in chapters 7, 8 and 9. The example of a Classical account of fishing in chapter 12 illustrates two answers to the question. In many technical ways, clearly it is not valid, especially when it is dealing with matters characteristically Mediterranean; but when it is dealing with things of a general nature, not specific to a particular environment or culture, then it can be useful even if not particularly revealing.

Written Latin is also the language of two of the main Anglo-Saxon documentary sources, laws and charters. The former are much concerned with the administration of an agrarian society by royal decree and refer in considerable detail to both social and landscape features. They require and depict a social hierarchy based on loyalty, property, gender, 'worth' and work, in which it is reasonably clear who were the primary workers in the field and what their functions were. Punishment for deviating from rigid performance indicators, as early twenty-first-century society would call them, is typically spelt out in excruciating detail (Robertson 1925; Whitelock 1955, Part IIA, *passim*).

Charters were almost exclusively concerned with grants of land. They survive in their hundreds, mainly for the West Midlands and Wessex. As a result of meticulous scholarly attention (Birch 1885–93; Whitelock 1955, Part IIB; Sawyer 1968), they have now been reasonably well sorted out into authentic and bogus (creating 'old' charters, and therefore 'establishing' traditional rights to property, was a favourite device after our period). Many have also been dated with some certainty and ascribed to a place; some have now been precisely placed upon the ground (see Hooke *passim*). Conversely, such fieldwork combined with documentary evidence can delineate and partly fill in an Anglo-Saxon landscape with vegetation, tenure and people (e.g. Fig. 3.1; Hooke 1997). It can even give glimpses at land-use so crucial to this study, for example by references to 'ploughlands' (cf. Fig. 13.1 and chapter 8).

Two other major written sources are different sorts of history. The primary documentary source for the history of the millennium is Bede's *Ecclesiastical History of the English People*, written in Latin and finished at the monastery of Jarrow in 731 (Sherley-Price 1955). It contains nothing substantial about farming. Its main contribution to our concern is anecdotal evidence of plagues, poor harvests and the like, though some of Bede's other works contain incidental agrarian information. His *œuvre* as a whole is deeply imbued with agrarian understanding and metaphor (chapter 4). The prime historical source for the later part of our period is *The Anglo-Saxon Chronicle*, written in Old English but containing very little about farming.

Some documents were illuminated, that is decorated, and although the prime motive was religious, a few of those which have survived contain agrarian evidence. We turn to this source in chapter 9 in particular, so it is germane to point out the particular interpretative challenge it presents.

> Are the busy and attractive figures which populate many Carolingian or Late Saxon illuminations reflections of their painters and patrons, or are they ghostly survivors of the Roman Empire, fossilized in a scribal convention? . . . The representation of a spade in a Late Saxon manuscript is . . . no guarantee that the illustrator knew what it was or that the Late Saxons had them. The Anglo-Saxons may have dug with Anglo-Saxon spades, but continued to draw Roman ones, imported, as 'image fossils', in the manuscripts that were copied; or they may still have been using spades of an essentially Roman type, so that a representation from life would escape notice. (Carver 1986, 117)

Finally, non-written word evidence, that is the oral tradition, and folklore beyond it, have their place. The potentials and pitfalls, as well as legitimate uses, are illustrated in the notable works of such as Estyn and Ewart Evans, Jenkins and Fenton (see Bibliography). Such evidence has a general relevance to some aspects of our concerns here, notably in agrarian processes from pre- or non-industrial, capitalistic and mechanistic societies but, as with documentary sources, just because something is 'old' or 'traditional' does not make it admissible as evidence of or for farming specifically in the first millennium AD. Fenton (1970), for example, advances the claims of a plough-song as a source of medieval aratral history.

3 | Environment

Cold the lake-bed from winter's blast . . .
Angry wind, woods stripped naked . . .
Snow is falling on the slope . . .
Storm on the mountain, rivers embroiled,
Floors of houses flooded . . .

CANU LLYWARCH HEN, QUOTED BY DAVIES 1989, 9

The agrarian environment consists basically of geology, air, climate, sunlight, hydrology, flora and fauna, soils and bacteria. This was true in the first millennium as now, though those farming would not have appreciated either all the content or the bio-relationships of that fact. They could have seen connections between the quality of their harvests on the one hand and, on the other, climate, amount of water on and in the ground and falling as rain, differences between 'good lands' and 'bad lands' depending on stoniness and the depth of earth, weeds and shade, and predators. They may not have had rabbits but they certainly had birds. But they can have had no informed knowledge of meteorology or the physics, chemistry or biology of the soil itself. That does not alter the fact, however, that what we now know of the interrelationships between those variables, especially in the soil, was happening in the first millennium as surely as it is in the third.

We need at the outset to remind ourselves of the basic influence of geology and physical geography (already outlined in chapter 1). They formed in many ways the basic component of the environment of farmers in the first millennium. It conditioned in the first place the sort of farming they were able to pursue. This element of determinism is there in British farming: even today, after the countryside has suffered an onslaught of heavy machinery and decades of dowsing in chemicals, the overall pattern of farming regimes is not fundamentally different from what we know was the case in late medieval times (Thirsk 1967) and, by and large, in the first millennium AD (cf. Coppock 1964; 1971).

Locally, the physical circumstances of an adjacent mountain or a river running through, to take but two factors, could significantly affect not only what farmers could do, but more particularly when they could do certain things. There is little point, for example, in planting autumn wheat if your

Plate VI Treeless landscape of stone-walled fields which, in pattern and type, were in existence here in the first millennium AD, Bosporthennis, near Zennor, Cornwall.

hill-fields are susceptible to a significant chill factor, as from easterly winds at 255 m AOD on Totterdown on the Marlborough Downs in southern England; or any crop in your bottom fields in very early spring if they frequently flood in March. Giraldus made the same point 800 years ago, contrasting the summits of the Black Mountains in Wales with the mild, damp cloudy conditions of 'the deep vale of Ewias, which is shut in on all sides by a circle of lofty mountains and which is no more than three arrow-shots in width' (as quoted by Davies 1989, 5–6). Such local variations can be critical, as all farmers and many agrarian historians have observed. Neither place nor period particularly matters to the importance of such factors of locality; my discussion elsewhere of the issue in its British prehistoric context is just as relevant here (Fowler 1983a, 22–24; cf. van Bath 1963, chapter 2).

Climate

Weather, then, is characteristically affected by physical geography, and so too is climate up to a point (see generally Lamb 1981; Harding 1982; Dark 2000). The phenomenon of 'rain-shadow', for example along the lands on the Pennines' eastern slopes, is very much part of the climate with a direct bearing on the farming parameters in those areas. We can be fairly certain that in general that was true in the first millennium too. But at a higher level – literally in some respects – climate is characterised by other major factors. Altitude itself can be a major factor at any time: it was in the second millennium BC and certainly was again in the first millennium AD. It can, for example, in combination with other factors, affect the length of the growing season in a particular area and the amount of rough grazing available to any particular land-use regime (Fig. 1.2; Coppock 1971, chapter 2). External factors, perhaps surprising ones like a high-level dust-cloud from a distant volcanic eruption, can be significant too. Such an event *c*. AD 540 may well account for what was noted at the time and later as a particularly dire moment in British agrarian history (Baillie 1994).

Such local factors and short-term events apart, in general the climate of Britain in the first millennium AD seems to have followed a pattern which we can now discern at least in outline from various evidence, not least that of soil cores and pollen analysis. In the early centuries AD it continued a slight but significant amelioration which had begun towards the end of the last millennium BC, resulting in something close to conditions *c*. AD 2000. A decline, in terms of temperature and wetness, occurred during the fourth and fifth centuries, with an improvement back to a kinder temperate climate beginning to take place during the sixth century, perhaps towards its close. The improvement may well have been maintained generally in western Europe resulting, as Stafford (1985, 9) remarks, in the early medieval period being 'part of a "Little Climatic Optimum" when the weather was on average 1°–2°F warmer than now, and drier. This should have been good for food output.'

Within Britain itself, however, regional differentiation seems to have been both present and agriculturally significant. In southern England, for example, the amelioration may well have continued for the rest of the millennium, with generally dry, warm summers from the eighth century onwards. Evidence from peat stratigraphy and tree-rings, by definition overwhelmingly from north and west Britain, indicates in contrast cool phases in respectively the seventh and eighth centuries. Simeon of Durham bears that out anecdotally in remarking on the hard northern winter of 764, when snow fell early, hardened into ice and lasted until the middle of spring, withering trees and killing marine animals (*EHD* I, 267). Hard frosts were indeed a characteristic of west European winters throughout the second half of the millennium; perhaps the skates from Viking levels in York illustrate a generality (Hall 1984). All sources, however, and indeed all commentators, seem in agreement that before AD 1000 the climate in general was improving as Europe, including Britain, began to enjoy a prolonged period of warm, dry but temperate conditions which lasted into the early fourteenth century. The establishment of this generally better climate is signalled by the vineyards catalogued in Domesday Book, as at Eaton Socon, Bedfordshire (chapter 10).

The relationship of climate and agriculture throughout the millennium is neatly exemplified by Wales:

> the climate of early medieval Wales probably experienced two major changes – a drop in the temperature and an increase in rainfall at the start, to levels below those of the present; and a gradual warming, intensifying at the very end, to levels above the modern [i.e. late 1970s when written] . . . It may well be, then, that productive capacity experienced a sharp downward jolt at the opening of our period but that gradually over several centuries conditions became more favourable until, by 1200, they were better than those of today. (Davies 1989, 7)

For an example of climate in relation to an individual site, we can turn, not for the last time, to West Stow, Suffolk (discussed as a settlement in chapter 5; occupied AD 400–650). It provides evidence that the climate was warmer and drier than in the late twentieth century between AD 250 and 400, and that the late sixth century brought with it colder summers and wetter overall conditions. Dark (2000, chapter 2) discusses this and other sites in much greater detail.

Soils

Soils are extremely complex. At the basic level, how they 'work' is not yet always understood fully. For example, there remains uncertainty about the desirability of creating a tilth for crop development (Russell 1961, 423). Experiment and observation have established that the 'most desirable size for the surface crumbs or clods to have from the point of view of plant growth lies in the range 1–5 mm.' (p. 423). It would be interesting to know whether the sorts of cultivating implements used during the first millennium AD, on various soils and subsoils, produced tilths within that range. We do not know, and it would have made a significant difference if, for example, tilling equipment in the eighth century was not on the whole producing suitable tilths for cereal cropping (cf. chapter 9).

Another reason for soils' complexity is 'that they have a population of micro-organisms living in them . . . [which is] continually oxidising the dead plant remains and leaving behind the nitrogenous and mineral plants needed by the plants for their growth' (Russell 1961, 135). Russell's chapters IX and X expound this dimension of the environment far more fully than can be attempted here. But the complexity is emphasised by the recognition that, important though bacteria are, other groups are also included in the soil micro-flora such as actinomycetes, fungi, algae and protozoa. Though the knowledge is modern, it presumably applies to the historic situation in the first millennium AD, and hence its relevance here. Micro-bacterial activity in the soils on which first-millennium farming occurred has not so far attracted much attention.

Modern research also brings out another environmental factor for those farmers. Soils can no longer 'satisfactorily be divided into a few simple groups' such as sands, clays and loams according to their particle sizes, 'nor can attention be confined to the surface layer' (Russell 1961, 22). As with the landscape as a whole, to understand them we have to know of their history. 'The properties of a soil depend not only on its parent material but also . . . on the climatic, vegetation and other factors to which it has been subjected' (p. 22). For much of the British Isles, one of the most important of such factors was people, not just farmers but others who had made myriad demands on the landscape already by the first millennium AD. People had left their mark in as well as on the soil. This was apparent in many situations: mineralised soils on the moors, impoverished soils on the downs, and in many a silt or colluvial deposit, 'natural' in a sense but as

Plate VII A quintessentially 'English' scene of church and manor house on a low knoll over-looking river, water-meadows and sheep; but everything visible here at East, now West, Overton, Wiltshire, far from being of 'time immemorial', is later than AD 1000 and the grouping itself is unlikely to be earlier than the tenth century. The grass on the valley floor in the foreground, however, covers a deposit several metres thick, an accumulation largely from prehistoric times, with extra layers added in the first millennium AD.

often as not influenced, even triggered, by anthropogenic actions (Pl. VII; e.g. Bell 1981).

On Overton Down, near Marlborough, Wiltshire, for instance, a crumbly, demineralised topsoil, the washed out remains of a cultivated humus in the second millennium BC, was already supporting in the later centuries BC the 'old grassland' which later fed one of the largest monastic flocks in the Middle Ages. That short-lived attempts were made to recultivate it in the first and thirteenth centuries AD adds weight to the proposition rather than weakening it (Fowler 2000c, chapter 5; here Pl. XVIII). Farming in the first millennium was not therefore, in any sense, starting with a 'clean slate'. Some 'good lands' had already been impoverished; others were relatively newly created, by erosion products for example, and almost wherever soil was being cropped, so was its 'goodness' being maintained by manure. Even woodland was likely to have been at least managed, so that species composition and distribution, for example, might not be entirely natural; and the chances are that the much-loved if largely mythical 'pioneer Anglo-Saxon woodsman', felling his way through the trees, was chopping down secondary growth. Just how complex was the relationship between soils, pedological change and the changing human occupancy of the soil in the first millennium is well illustrated in the Fens (Hall and Coles 1994) and a particularly sensitive area of sands and clays in Suffolk (Warner 1987; 1988). In both cases, put simply, soil contributes signally to the peculiar character of each. Clay, as drift geology and more recent deposits, traditionally creates 'cold' soils to which has therefore been attributed a 'secondary' or even 'marginal' status in land-use terms by students of farming and settlement. Facts suggest this view not to be well founded: as Warner showed, claylands do not appear to have been settled 'late' simply because of their base. For example, Romano-British settlements occur either side of the A1 through the claylands of middle Northumberland, and elsewhere were hit one after another as another road, the M5 motorway, sliced its way through the Keuper Marl of Gloucestershire (Jobey 1982b; Fowler 1979).

A particularly sensitive zone of soil change in the first millennium was Britain's coastline. It was changing throughout the first millennium, both in the vertical dimension in relation to changing sea-level and horizontally in relation to deposition and scouring. Climate change was part of the reason, but other factors were at play including anthropogenic ones. Agrarian significances of this dynamism along the interface of land and sea are not widely studied but certain zones are both sensitive to such changes and the scene of considerable research. General relationships are illustrated through time in the Somerset Levels, and are particularly well illustrated in terms of settlement patterns in the first millennium AD in and around the Wash on England's east coast (Fig. 4.1). There, however, not all the changes were natural; some were artificial, involving dykes as sea-walls, canals for transport, and extensive drainage works to create and maintain good farmland, especially in the early centuries of the millennium. Similarly, on the western mud of the Severn estuary, works there may well have sought to increase the land-take, for occupation and pasture (Dark 2000; Appendix 1 here).

Woodland

Just after the end of the first millennium 'England . . . would not have looked like modern Borneo, but rather like modern France.' Rackham (1990, 53) goes on to elaborate – perhaps advisedly, given the variety in both Borneo and France – explaining that the 'Norman Weald, like the modern Vosges, was well over half tree-covered' while in areas open to the skies, then as now, like the Yorkshire Wolds and Wiltshire Downs, 'as around Chartres today . . . one could go many miles without seeing a wood' (p. 54; Pls. XI, XVII).

Much of the landscape would have been between those extremes, a mixture of arable and pasture with woods in between (Fig. 3.1; as in Pls. II and III). Caesar, for example, describing his campaigns in Kent and Hertfordshire, very much gives an impression of that sort of landscape, even though his concern was with tactics, not environment; his opponents' tactics were to hide in and fight close to more heavily wooded areas, more like that illustrated in Pl. III. In Kent, in one incident, a small number of Britons were working in the fields as a ruse while far greater numbers were laid up in the woods, waiting to attack the Roman legionary corn detail 'when the soldiers were scattered and busy cutting corn, with their arms laid down' (*BG* IV.32). Elsewhere, he notes rather wryly how Cassivellaunus 'would retire a short way from the route [of Caesar's army] and hide in dense thickets, driving the inhabitants and cattle from the open country into the woods' (*BG* V.19).

Kent remained significantly wooded – or became well wooded again – in the early medieval period (Everitt 1986, 2–3). South-east England as a whole remains relatively well wooded but it would be easy to carry away from there and certainly from the rest of Britain in the last centuries BC and throughout the first millennium an impression of too many forests, woods and trees. Boyd (1985), for example, concludes of the evidence from four Roman sites (Bar Hill, Croy Hill, Wilderness West, Bearsden) in southern Scotland that it 'provides a moderately uniform picture of an

Fig. 3.1 Late
Anglo-Saxon landscape
with names, land-uses
and vegetation adduced
from two tenth-century
charters for East and
West Overton estates,
now the parishes of West
Overton and Fyfield,
Wiltshire (from Fowler
2000c).

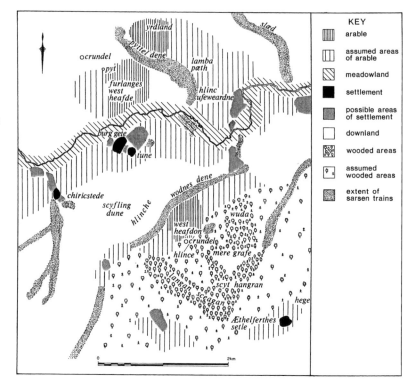

open, largely pastoral landscape in which the Antonine Wall was built'.
He notes that 'a similar picture is recorded for the area of Hadrian's Wall,
with extensive woodland clearance occurring during the three centuries
prior to the Roman presence in the area, and with the emphasis on the
formation of pasture land'. In Caesar's time, in reality, much of Britain was
already treeless (Pls. IV, VI, VIII, XVIII), and the countryside of Britain
in general, certainly of England if not of Kent, was not well wooded.

It is not therefore surprising for Rackham (1990, 55) to have concluded
that by the time of Domesday, 'It is unlikely that any wildwood still remained in England.' If we project backwards from William's time the
15 per cent of land that was wooded in the countryside assessed in the
Domesday survey, then the state of the woodland as a part of the environment is unlikely to have been significantly different during the first
millennium. Indeed, given the enormous demands placed on woodland
resources to maintain the Roman economy and life-style (chapter 13), it
seems probable that extensive felled woodland would have existed along
with intensively managed woods. Buildings, the army, kilns, furnaces,
central-heating, quays, boats, bridges – they all needed timber. It is likely
that management of such a vital resource – for building and fuel even when

Roman industry collapsed – was the key to one of the more remarkable statistics to emerge from analysis of Domesday, that is that one in four of Anglo-Saxon woods is still there (Rackham 1990, 44). Perhaps the same is true of five centuries earlier when both arable and woodland from the first century AD seem to continue in use, and management (cf. Pl. I).

Woods and wastes: three distinctive landscapes

Woodland could be 'waste' and a 'waste' could include woods; and both could be used for the same purpose, extensive pasture (chapter 11). Here we select them, woodland and two sorts of waste, marsh and moor, from a variety of environments which had developed throughout Britain by and during the first millennium AD. We could have followed other examples in visits to riversides and wolds, coasts and islands, downland and peat bog, and elsewhere. But our choice is partly because woods and wastes were important economically as well as visually, partly because impressions of them are visually so different, and partly because their rather unkempt, even 'natural', appearance belies their managed nature and the human impact upon them. They would have belonged to someone; they too were elements in the organisation of the land. Indeed, precisely because of their particular assets, apparently 'marginal' lands such as woods, moorland and marsh were often prized resources of an estate, lying perhaps distant and detached from the centre but quite as much owned, farmed and managed as other demesne land. They after all could provide facilities such as building timber, rough grazing and peat, not available perhaps in the more intensively farmed core of an estate (Sawyer 1998a, 138–40, 146–7, summarises some good examples).

Despite an emphasis here on the extent to which the land had been and remained cleared during the millennium, woodland was nevertheless an important feature of both the landscape and the economy. Further, it provides an indicator of process. Gelling (1992, 6), as so often, provides a vivid example from the 200 years between the mid-eighth and the mid-tenth centuries, relating place-names first to land, then to process, finally to history:

> the place-name element *lēah* is a reliable indicator of the presence of ancient woodland at the date when English speech was gaining the ascendancy in the greater part of southern Britain. . . . The sense of 'clearing' is very much the commonest. Names in which this sense is appropriate frequently occur in clusters . . . In the West Midland counties [the distribution of] this element provides convincing evidence for the extent of woodland in the middle Anglo-Saxon period. The reference will sometimes be to ancient,

> pre-English settlements in a forest environment . . . sometimes to areas on
> the outer fringes of ancient forests which were being progressively cleared
> by the Anglo-Saxons when the names arose.

She ends that detailed study by distinguishing between primeval forest
and areas which had reverted to woodland after being cleared in the
Roman period. In Warwickshire (Gelling 1992, 11, here and throughout this paragraph), some of the *lēah* settlements in a forest environment
were probably already flourishing when Anglo-Saxon colonists arrived,
the implication being that they were avoided by newcomers more intent on
acquiring farmland to work than military conquest. So other settlements
were founded as pioneer efforts in newly cleared woodland. And in the
West Midlands, as doubtless over large areas of Britain, woodland to be
cleared did exist in extents uncharacteristic of the Thames valley. Some of
it was indeed cleared, perhaps not so much during the immigration phase
of the fifth/sixth centuries but rather from the eighth century onwards
when, after a century or so of stabilisation, colonisation developed into
economic expansion. 'There was probably a good deal of relatively undis-
turbed woodland until the middle of the Saxon period' in Warwickshire,
from which time onwards it was partly cleared – the impression, indeed,
that southern parts of the county's countryside continue to give. There
are both similarities and contrasts with the rather different landscapes of
the Middle and Upper Thames valley, only 100 km or so to the south. We
can sense the inhabitants' sense of proximity, of people bumping into one
another as farmers and families adjusted to neighbours new and old as
well as to an ancient landscape of traditionally open areas, long-established
clearings, former clearings with regenerated scrub and young woods, and
new clearings edged by vertical cliffs of bruised but standing trees where
the woodsman stayed his axe.

The Fens surrounding the Wash are a flooded alluvial plain (Stafford
1985, 5–6, is the basis for this paragraph). Post-Roman flooding produced
the extended fenlands around the Wash rivers, altering the coastline and
estuaries. To the east, sedimentation produced a silt fen bordering the
Wash, with a peat fen behind it dotted with islands capped with boulder
clay. The peat fen was unstable and liable to flood, and no Domesday
villages are recorded on it. Settlement here was confined to the islands.
Large inland lakes existed, the largest being Whittlesey Mere in Hunt-
ingdonshire. The silt fen of the seaward edge was settled, a line of villages recorded in Domesday Book marking the eleventh-century coastline
(cf. Stafford's Fig. 2 from Hill 1981). Wisbech, Spalding and Boston were
coastal villages. Marsh and fen stretched up the Witham almost as far

as Lincoln; they were also a feature of the lower reaches of the Humber, and fen-wastes lay around the Trent estuary. The valleys of Ancholme and Axholme were marshy and waterlogged. Erosion of off-shore shoals in Roman and later times increased the danger of flooding: the *Hafdic*, a sea-dyke, was built before 1066, perhaps in the tenth century by newly settled Danes, to protect the Lindsey coast; a similar dyke closed the estuary between Holbeach and Fleet. 'Nothing is known of the construction of these banks, but they join other impressive earthworks of the Dark Ages as testimony not only to the engineering but also to the organizational skills of our ancestors' (Stafford 1985, 6). She also reminds us (p. 16) that, despite this humanising of the landscape, still in the tenth century Abbo of Fleury saw the Fens as 'Desirable havens of lonely life where solitude could not fail the hermits.'

Overall, marshes and fens were much more extensive in the second half of the millennium than now, not only in our example in eastern England. As in North Lindsey, 'they inhibit settlement, agriculture and movement' (Stafford 1985, 6). Similarly bleak-looking areas, the moors of upland Britain were, in contrast, for the most part extremely useful. These 'wastes' were in part thinly settled at times in the first millennium, for example in the third/fourth centuries, but they were nearly always used for extensive grazing. This could have been from outlying farms at some times; but they were characteristically supporting summer human migrants coming with their flocks from settled places as part of the agrarian system known as transhumance (chapter 11). They supplied raw resources too: peat, for example, as fuel, and heather for honey-bees. 'Wastes' were not wasted in modern parlance, but active components in a much-used environment.

Flora and fauna

The flora and fauna of first-millennium Britain are to an extent well documented. Welsh Laws, perhaps surprisingly, abound in references to the natural and man-made environment. They refer to eleven different species of tree: alder, apple, ash, beech, crab (apple), elm, hazel, oak, thorn, willow and yew. They do not refer, however, to pine, common in prehistory, or sycamore, yet to be introduced (Davies 1989, 13). Since species of plants and animals appear frequently throughout this book in one form or another, here, rather than generalise, we exemplify with three case studies, one from a site in the Thames valley, Oxfordshire (see also chapters 2 and 6), a second of a rather different nature from Scotland, and a third from north-east England.

Watkins Farm, Oxfordshire

Insect remains indicated a relatively open, although not entirely treeless, landscape in which pasture was important at about the time of Caesar's invasion and on into the early first millennium. Waterlogged seeds suggested various sorts of disturbed ground and scrub. Seeds of the aquatic plants water crowfoot and duckweed, alongside others, suggested that the ditches contained stagnant water, while the occurrence of *Planorbis planorbis* suggested that they did not dry up seasonally. Dung beetles suggested a significant presence of domestic animals grazing on grassland. Seeds of plants associated with arable agriculture were, however, poorly represented; insect remains did not indicate arable farming either, and indeed a prevalence of pasture continued from late prehistory into the first centuries AD. The appearance of *Valvata cristata* suggested that at least one gully may have been drained then, when there continued to be an absence of evidence for flooding in an open landscape with even less woodland than was available in the last centuries BC. The range of annual and plough-tolerant seeds was similar either side of the Roman Conquest, with charred grain perhaps indicating locally grown cereal after it. Wherever the cereal was kept, it contained *Stegobium paniceum*, a minor pest of stored grain. On an adjacent site, the predominant seeds were of stinking mayweed, a species now associated with arable agriculture, but one which formerly grew in abundance around settlements. Overall, the environment of the early centuries AD here was comparable to contemporary sites in this region, with a strong presence of pastureland and an uncertain arable presence (after Allen 1990).

Scottish environment and the Roman invasion

Our second case study is related to a general environmental issue far to the north of Watkins Farm but also in the early first millennium – though there are many subsequent occasions in which it might be tempting to look for palaeoenvironmental evidence bearing on the nature of a recorded, military event. In Scotland a controversy continues not so much about man's impact on the environment in general but in particular whether or not drastic environmental change was occasioned by the Roman invasion in the later first century and thereafter. To answer, we need to know how much environmental change had happened and was in train at the end of the first century AD. Van der Veen's (1992) assertion that landscape clearance did not occur prior to the Roman period is rebutted by Whittington and Edwards (1994, whose account we largely follow).

Three well-dated eastern Scottish lake-sites show remarkable resolution levels in their pollen analysis and so are adduced as bearing detail pertinent to the general issue. At Black Loch, the sporadic appearance of barley-type pollen and microscopic charcoal indicated some agricultural activity. Between AD 40 and 640, however, there was apparently a severe decline in clearance and agricultural activity. Oak, hazel and birch increased whereas open-land taxa decreased. Cereal pollen disappeared from the analysis, and loch sediments and charcoal deposits decreased, suggesting a slackening of arable activity. This collapse of a well-developed agricultural regime does not appear to be associated with either soil exhaustion or degradation or with climatic change. At Loch Davan, between 1560 BC and AD 35 an initial pastoral land-use was followed by mixed arable and pastoral activity beginning about 400 BC. From AD 35 through to 1125, there were a dramatic regeneration of birch and hazel woodland and a decline of open-land taxa, again indicating an abandonment of agricultural land. Braerodolach Loch, the third site, produced comparable results. In particular, early mixed arable and pastoral activity was followed by increases in birch and hazel alongside a depression in herbaceous and open-land taxa during the first millennium AD. The implied drop in the scale of agricultural activity was reversed in medieval times when woodland was reopened and mixed agriculture revived.

Overall there is clear evidence for a marked regression and change in agricultural activity early in the first millennium AD; but that is still a long way from being able to attribute it to any one cause, let alone Roman military action. In Continental Europe a similar decline in agricultural activity has been noted from pollen evidence immediately after conquest, supposedly 'simple agricultural systems' implausibly collapsing under increased demands of Roman authority. In eastern Scotland, however, where permanent annexation was impossible, there may well have been good military reason for driving the inhabitants out or at least severely disrupting the area's farming economy and standard of living. Certainly, here in this evidence in the far north, unlike that along the Antonine Wall and in southern England, there is no heightening of agricultural activity as a result of invasion; rather the marked change early in the millennium in the agricultural landscape suggests a destructive Roman army.

The relevance of this case to the rest of Britain, precisely because it occurred in highly marginal land, politically as well as militarily and economically, is that it demonstrates what might have happened elsewhere, but assuredly did not. Virtually everywhere else, where there is relevant evidence, we see the environment being changed, being put under inferred strain perhaps as cropping demands were increased, as Roman urbanisation intensified perhaps, but not reverting to extensive, low-energy-input types of farming. Unlike what may have happened in eastern Scotland under Roman impact early in the first millennium, in general farming survived the English national, military collapse of 1066 well. Domesday Book hints, however, at what may have been locally similar episodes to this Scottish case in the 1060s and 1070s, and the 'ravaging of the North' was no idle story.

North-east England

'If we are interested in looking at the agricultural economy . . . over the long term we cannot get very far by using the archaeological record alone.' Thus a recent researcher writing of the north-east of England; here we follow his assessment (Fenton-Thomas 1992). The area examined was between the rivers Tees and Tyne from south to north and from the east coast to the high Pennines in the west, over the period *c*. 300 BC to *c*. AD 900. As elsewhere, natural processes and land-use since AD 1000 have destroyed and masked land surfaces and their features of the first millennium, so the evidence available for environmental investigation is both partial and, because of the biases in archaeologists' sampling (chapter 2), unbalanced. Nevertheless, the thirteen pollen analyses available range from the high moors above the North Tyne at Fellend Moss to Neasham Fen on the Tees; though, as usual, the pollen evidence can best be related to long-term trends and patterns, not events.

Our period interests are clearly shown in Fenton-Thomas' Figs. 2–5 where, broadly speaking, we see the impact of farming on the region. Overall, from relatively high proportions of trees and shrubs in the first half of the first millennium BC, we see progressive reductions and relative increases of agricultural species (implying arable land in this exercise) about 100 BC and AD 400, with a slight reversion in the ninth century AD. The author argues for a movement of environmental activity within such a regional generality, seeing clearance spreading from the lower Tees area in late prehistory northwards and westwards until about the mid-first millennium AD. Sites in Roman military areas evidence intensification of activity in the early centuries AD, with decline 'not apparent until well into the sixth century AD' (Fenton-Thomas 1992, 54). This begs questions about mono-causal explanations for land-use events: neither food requirements for the army alone, nor supposed climatic deterioration which would have affected these high places relatively harshly, explain the increase or the decline in agricultural activity. By the seventh century, however, while agricultural activity around the southern Magnesian Limestone escarpment decreased, agricultural activity and more tree cover is apparent at some other sites elsewhere in the region. In contrast, evidence of 'a sudden and short-lived phase of agriculture' appears up-country early in the sixth century. The 'presence of arable cultivation at [high altitude] has implications for the prevailing climatic conditions of the period as well as providing a possible context for archaeological sites . . . nearby . . . (Coggins 1986)' (p. 54).

The study goes on to discuss pasture, woodland, the possible impacts of Scandinavians (cf. chapters 6 and 14). In terms of the environment, one of the more important conclusions is the demonstration within quite a small region of two sub-regions, distinctive in their land-use histories as well as in their physical characteristics. Essentially south and east of the River Wear the area was cleared early and maintained that status throughout the first millennium irrespective of climatic variations and possible peoples' coming and goings; whereas west and north of the Wear, environmental change in the landscape pursued its own course, clearance pre-dating and post-dating Romans but possibly reflecting the arrival of new Anglian landlords. This sub-regional distinction, as the author says, 'could be seen throughout the Middle Ages'; rather could it be expressed as the significant but subtle distinctions in the rural cultural landscape of north-east England of the second millennium AD were established during the preceding thousand years.

Between the Roman and Norman conquests the environment of course continued to be modified, but not by military violence so much as gradually by increased agrarian exploitation. As Dark (2000, 156–68) remarks in her own conclusions, overall

> many of the regions that had undergone the greatest change in vegetation and agriculture in the Roman period seem to have experienced a relaxation in the intensity of land use in the post-Roman period . . . some sites in the north of England show an increased impetus to clearance and agricultural activity in the Viking Age, while others experienced abandonment of land and woodland regeneration.

She articulates a widely held view that the phenomenon of valley sedimentation in the uplands reflects an expanding agriculture between *c.* AD 900 and 1250, a final facet, as it were, of the many natural and man-induced environmental changes which by the eleventh century had produced a Britain of considerable variety, complexity and diversity, notably in its landscapes.

As more was asked of those landscapes, so did relationships between people and land become more intense.

4 | Land

Throughout the whole of the first millennium, the land, its appearance
and its uses were affected by the ways in which it had been formed and
arranged in nature. The land was, however, generally organised into management units, often proprietorial in nature, and its uses were determined
by people, not nature. The combination of these two symbiotic, occasionally opposed, factors, natural and cultural, was the result of, and also
produced, distinct landscapes which were collectively characteristic of the
land of Britain between the first and eleventh centuries AD. There is a
very clear connection between that land as it had matured by AD 1000 and
the somewhat more bedraggled land we occupy in the early twenty-first
century.

In this chapter we follow those three themes in that order: the natural
arrangement of the land; human arrangement of the land; and distinct
landscapes which affected and were influenced by farming in the first
millennium.

The natural arrangement

Despite the widespread evidence of human impact on it during the first
millennium (chapter 3), the environment still contained many a natural
landscape, or at least ones where human influence was not immediately
apparent. An anonymous monk's description of the Fens provides an
example about a thousand years ago: 'The great fen begins on the banks
of the river Granta . . . swamps and bogs, an occasional black pool, exuding
dark mists, sprinkled with islands of marshy heaths and crisscrossed by
winding waterways' (Stafford 1985, 16).

Recognising 'nature' in that sense, we would like to reinvigorate the academically old-fashioned idea that there is actually a direct connection, and countless indirect ones, between literally the lie of the land and gaining a livelihood from it by farming (cf. Pls. II, VI). Evans (1967, 276) put it precisely: 'In cultivating the land man has always been compelled to adapt his methods to the type of soil, the prevailing climate and the tools he has at hand.' And, he continued: 'A change in any one of these, forces him eventually to change his methods, and by changing his method to change . . . the organisation of his farming, and finally the community associated with it.' He could have added another facet of the relationship: that man the farmer can very much affect nature. The important point is that Evans was in effect recognising that far more is involved than merely writing of 'natural' and 'human' arrangements as if dealing with two matters either side of a division. As we are painfully rediscovering in the early twenty-first century, a dynamic relationship is at work, one which has sociological and agricultural consequences in general and therefore, by implication, in the first millennium.

Archaeologically, one of the effective ways of descrying former land and its uses is by compiling and interpreting distribution maps (Hill 1981). East Anglia provides a good example (Scull 1992, Figs. 2 and 3). The map of 'Romano-British sites and finds' shows what at first seems a fairly dense distribution of symbols right across the map, but at a second glance two facets catch the eye: clumpings of symbols at particular places, as in the vicinity of what later became Norwich, on the coast of north-west Norfolk, and along the river valleys draining into the Wash. These preferred locations reappear in the quantitatively sparser distribution of comparable Anglo-Saxon data from the fifth to mid-seventh centuries. The significant point is the likelihood that the same land was being selected and used in similar fashion, if not continuously over six centuries then in two archaeologically differentiated periods. In contrast, the Fens at two different points in time show different distributions (Fig. 4.1), using data from field survey probably as intense as we are likely to mount in England. Settlement and other activity extended from the areas used in the early centuries AD on to previously flooded land, indicating factors were in play such as dyke-building, drainage, coastal deposition and marine regression (or land lift). Such need not, of course, be exactly synchronous. In this case, the 'Saxon' settlement expansion is likely to be dependent partly on a seventh-century phase of 'natural' depositional activity further affecting the land–sea relationship, and partly on decaying engineering works undertaken under Roman aegis.

Fig. 4.1 Distribution
of settlement sites in and
around the Fens, AD
200 (squares) and 600
(circles) (after Hall and
Coles 1994).
P = Peterborough;
C = Cambridge.

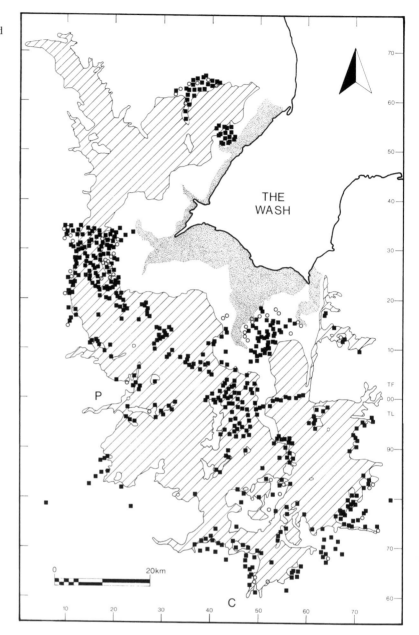

The human arrangement

For most of the first millennium AD people organised the land into territorial, often proprietorial, units (Hooke 1998, chapter 3). They decided
and regulated its uses too. The land was certainly not a wilderness; it
was managed, exploited and looked after. And it had been like that for
at least 2000 if not 4000 years previously. As we have seen (chapter 1),

Lennard's (1959) 'Old Country', even if it referred only to England, not Britain, meant not just a land which had achieved political and constitutional 'solidity' (his word) but the Anglo-Saxon country in which 'the peaceful energies of men have extended their beneficent sway over all parts of it, turning the wilderness into ploughed fields and utilizing the resources of the land, according to the measure of knowledge and skill then obtaining, for the fulfilment of human purposes and the maintenance and betterment of human life . . . The framework of rural England as we know it was already laid out' – that is by AD 1000 in his perspective, but in several other respects long before that.

As a result, concepts such as 'pioneer farming' are simply irrelevant in most of Britain in the first millennium, for example in much of eastern Scotland (RCAHMS 1994; Whittington 1974–75), the English East Midlands (Brown and Foard 1998) and in the Cerne valley, Dorset (Barker 1988), and in thousands of similarly farmed places during the period AD 500–1000. The dimension of time is vital to our appreciation of what farmers in the whole of the first millennium found, however, and how they too in their turn changed the landscape. Just how much the landscape had already been 'set' in appearance, if not quite literally in stone, e.g. with long-lived cairns and walls, before and during the early years of the millennium must be taken into account. Two recent, similar but independent accounts exemplify the point of 'time-depth'. Each sums up what happened at one spot on the landscape, one on the chalk of Fyfield Down, Wiltshire (quoted in chapter 7, p. 141; Pl. XVIII), the other in the Pennine limestone landscape of Swaledale (Fig. 7.6); and each ends by taking off into imaginative interpretation. Fleming's flight (1998, 160) is:

> Frameworks for systems of planned land division were probably set up in the Middle Iron Age, around 300 BC, if not earlier. In the Roman period the landscape must have looked as 'settled' as that of today, if not more so, with broad walls running up and down the dalesides, perhaps topped with elm hedges, and interrupted at frequent intervals by walled enclosures containing groups of ovoid huts, with others close by, each on its own terrace.

Lennard's somewhat Arcadian view of the farming life of Anglo-Saxon England can be extended to the first half of the millennium, for affairs of the land were remarkably similar then too. In particular, the only difference in terms of the land was essentially cosmetic in that the labels for the land-units were different; the agrarian process, and the system of the majority working for the few, were effectively the same. Swaledale also exemplifies land-clearance, i.e. hard work, early in the millennium, this time through pollen analysis. After a phase of major land clearance in the later centuries BC, a short-lived period of increased tree-cover – birch, hazel, oak and alder – 'seems to relate to the period around the Roman conquest' (Fleming 1998, 140). 'Then there is a major rise in evidence for clearance and open country', probably right through the second to fourth centuries. Interestingly but not unexpectedly in this particular place, the result of the human effort which lies behind the palaeobotanical data was that heathland 'became firmly established, probably spreading as a consequence of more intensive use of this relatively fragile environment'. Again, that is the sort of ecological reality which underlies the formal land arrangements variously discernible throughout the millennium.

Another source of information about land is names, especially revealing at local level, occasionally giving us a glimpse of how a place was seen by people nearly 2000 years ago. Post-Roman place-names are noted in chapter 2; field-names are collected by Field (1972). Romano-British place-names were adopted, perhaps even invented, to meet Roman needs. Some common nouns and adjectives, for example, describe features of the countryside, as in *Glannoventa* (Ravenglass), from **glanno-* = shore or river-bank and *-venta*, probably 'site of customary market'; or *Litomagus*, Scotland, **litano-*, 'broad', 'extensive', and *magos*, 'plain' or 'large area' becoming 'place' (see Rivet and Smith 1979 for many examples).

Large land units

A number of different mechanisms for arranging land into large units was created in Britain during or soon after the first millennium. Many were not primarily agrarian in intent, their purpose generally being to administer law to and collect taxes from a predominantly agrarian society; but their effect on farming was direct and sometimes significant. The fact of Britain's provincial status within a foreign, centralist government's imperial domains for three and a half centuries is of signal import; those who manned its provincial governmental infrastructure knew what they were there to do (Black 1995). Hints of Roman 'imperial estates', in Wales, the Peak District and on Mendip to control metalliferous extraction, in the Fens and just possibly on Salisbury Plain to manage food production, may indicate areas involving either or both state-led capital investment and state concern to secure vital supplies. Either way, the significant factor is state control, perhaps even state ownership, of large estates of political as well as economic significance at the 'national' (strictly imperial) level. In the Fens, for example, state initiative first under Hadrian in the early second century can be envisaged as the driving force behind extensive land development involving canals, roads and the 'planting' of large numbers of farms and villages to farm sheep and manufacture salt (Hall and Coles 1994). Presumably such 'imperial' estates were at the top of the pyramid of Roman Britain's land arrangements, and if so then, although names and place of control were different, they were the equivalent of the royal estates of Anglo-Saxon England. Stafford (1985, 143) writes of those later centuries but her eloquent words stand also for the whole millennium:

> The larger units … were not irrelevant to the peasantry. [They] determined where dues were paid, services performed, tribute taken, cases heard. But it was the boundary of the local landscape, known … in its intimate detail, which always figured most prominently in peasant life.

Peasant life nevertheless usually existed within the outlines of large-scale organisational arrangements. Fiscal dues and labour duties were characteristically attached to that framework.

For practical purposes, the largest units of the millennium's early centuries do not exist any longer, though their extents can be placed more or less with confidence and their names occasionally still resonate faintly. Thus the broad divisions of Upper and Lower Britain, and regional administrative units, the *civitates*, of Roman Britain are well known (Salway 1981, chapter 17; Dark 1994, Fig. 23). Modern Dorset is an example of the name of one of their number, the *Durotriges*, persisting from late prehistoric times. We know of the provinces into which later Roman Britain was divided (Dark 1994, Fig. 1). We catch glimpses of tribal areas, in some cases perhaps revivals, in other cases new, in the middle of the millennium when the order of Roman governance fragments rapidly into warrior allegiances, both indigenous and introduced. King Arthur on the one hand and Hengist on the other can serve as metaphor for each respectively, without the need here to argue their historicity or otherwise. Thereafter the large units are best known to us today as counties, often 'shires'. Most of the older ones among their number acquired their present names, size and shape towards the end of the millennium but many have origins in earlier arrangements. Some incorporate older land units, rationalised into the English county system not only in Wales and Scotland but also in England itself, e.g. Cornwall, Northumberland. But territorial units larger than counties existed in the first millennium, notably the large early kingdoms such as Northumbria, Mercia and Wessex, and the result of a political settlement in the tenth century, the Danelaw. Parts of some of their boundaries physically existed, for example Watling Street and Offa's Dyke, even though each of those kingdoms enjoyed both fluctuating boundaries and subdivisions still larger than most counties. Northumbria, for example, even in its reduced form north of the

River Tees rather than north of the River Humber, largely consisted of a kingdom by another name, Bernicia, close in size and shape to present-day Northumberland and Co. Durham combined. Within it were subdivisions, for example Bamburghshire, Bedlingtonshire and perhaps the medieval 'Islandshire' (Morris 1977; Brown *et al.* 1998, Fig. 19.1), each with its own history and identity then though neither exists today except as conscious antiquarianism.

This may all seem rather remote from farming, but when, in what has become a famous story, Bede tells us that in Edwin's early seventh-century Northumbria the king had established a peace such that a man could walk safely through the countryside and drink from bronze bowls hanging at the wayside, any farmer can recognise the essential precondition he craves to carry out his work and gain his livelihood. Security and safety were as important for viable farming as were herds, flocks, fields, woods and land itself. Beneficial influence from above – the state or a king – and mechanisms to deliver security as well as collect services were significant factors which affected the nature and practice of farming in the first millennium.

Gelling (1992, 139–40) uses the word 'province' to describe the early administrative units that she perceives in the West Midlands. She stresses, however, that *provinciae*, or *regiones*, were 'probably in origin associations of people rather than arbitrarily demarcated areas', so that when she speculates about the *Beormingas she is relating not so much to the equivalent of the estate of Birmingham City Council as to Birmingham Rugby Football Club as an association of people. A province nevertheless inevitably came to have a locational meaning, as in *Pecsæte*, the people of the Peak District. This sort of arrangement seems to have existed in this area up to the time of the major disruption caused by the Danish wars in the decades around AD 900. Perhaps soon afterwards and certainly before the late tenth century, the West Saxon shire system was developing, probably being imposed, a quite different system in which specific areas were administered from royal estates. In Wessex itself, it is possible again that some of these new shires, and in some cases their names, reflect earlier arrangements. Wiltshire, for example, derives from *Wiltunscir*, itself peopled by *Wilsætan* – 'the dwellers on the Wylye' (itself a British river name like Kennet) – in a grouping which 'falls into line with early divisions of the Mercian kingdom mentioned in the Tribal Hidage, compiled in the 8th century or possibly even in the 7th' (Darlington 1955, 2). Nevertheless, a glance at a map showing the counties of the former kingdom of Wessex (Hampshire, Wiltshire, Dorset, Somerset) rouses the suspicion that their comparable sizes represent an imposed, bureaucratic rationalisation. If so,

it was presumably intended to bring order, peace and the better collection of dues to a hard-pressed royalty leading an embryonic kingdom of
England through the Danish aftermath. This was early in a century which
was to become one of the most formative in terms of agrarian history of
the first millennium. A key factor was undoubtedly the establishment, by
and large, of peace; and that, in part at least, was the result of a strong
administrative system from above, implemented fairly efficiently at local
level through *ealdormen* or elders.

Hundreds and equivalents

The counties were too large for many local matters, so they were subdivided, in much of England into *hundreds*; in much of the Danelaw their
equivalent was the *wapentake*. There were five hundreds, for example,
in Staffordshire, twenty smaller ones in Herefordshire (Gelling 1992,
Fig. 55, and p. 144). Most such land units became much altered, and
the hundred today is an administratively irrelevant and largely forgotten
mechanism for local government. We do not know what its equivalent was
before the tenth century, when it became the norm over much of England;
though hundreds and their equivalents probably developed from earlier
arrangements in some parts of the country. Some of their boundaries
survive, particularly where they follow earlier earthworks. Comb's Ditch
in Dorset is a good example. A boundary of a 'Celtic' field system was followed when a bank and ditch were built and later enlarged in post-Roman
centuries, creating a large earthwork which was, or became, the hundredal
boundary. The earthwork physically survives and still marks the parish
boundary (RCHME 1970, 313–14).

One reason for thinking of earlier origins is that hundredal meeting-
places often seem to be at focal points in landscapes much older than
late Saxon. Typical situations are on important routes, at river crossings,
on estate boundaries and – rather making the point a near-certainty –
at places distant from late Saxon settlements. These have not avoided
such places, nor has the meeting-place been deliberately sited far from
where people in the tenth century were living. It was simply that new
units of administration played to strength by putting their meeting-place
where people had for long met as a matter of convenience for different
settlement patterns. A classic example which could quite plausibly go back
to late prehistoric times is on the Marlborough Downs at Man's Head,
Wiltshire – 'a long and low but well-defined hill' to redeploy Gelling's
(1992a, 161) description of the meeting-place of Manshead Hundred in
Bedfordshire. The spot is now about as remote as it is possible to be in
central southern England, 4 km from even the nearest riverside village

and 6 km from its parochial village, but it would have been remarkably convenient for an earlier population living along the downland slopes and shepherding on the downs.

Estates

How the land was arranged locally in Roman Britain and beyond is uncertain. The most plausible model suggests a myriad of small largely self-sufficient 'estates' in some sense belonging to local 'head-men', with such local arrangements in some places being grouped into larger 'territories' under a sub-regional chief or 'lord'. Much, on the whole later, evidence suggests such arrangements need not always have involved single blocks of land making up the entire 'estate' or 'maenor' but could consist of a 'caput' – a place of the sort known to us archaeologically as a hillfort, dun or round – central to a viable economic operation involving the exploitation of lands and resources dispersed over a considerable area. This concept of the 'multiple estate' as a basic form of land organisation and management, not only in the west and north where it is evidenced but perhaps also in lowland Britain where it has subsequently been replaced, has been much studied, notably in Wales (Jones 1972), and its documented existence is now displayed both explicitly and implicitly with variations and in detail in Ireland (Kelly 1998). The complexity of extant landscapes there is illustrated by Norman and St. Joseph (1969).

Villa estates in southern England have often been discussed (see Appendix 1). There are, however, few Roman villas on the river gravels, certainly in the Thames valley where so much of the recent archaeological work on rural land-use and settlement has been conducted. Here we concentrate on land organisation and settlement patterns, following Fulford (1992) and Hamerow (1992). The land witnessed a radical change between Caesar and Claudius: its use intensified, and continued on that trajectory into the second century (Fulford 1992). If this was so, then clearly such a change has profound implications for the first millennium AD, perhaps as a whole. It is, however, important first to establish norms of later prehistoric landscape before being able to judge the extent to which 'the Roman occupation interrupted or altered existing settlement and subsistence systems' (Fulford 1992, 23). In fact, it seemed to do both, for there is both continuity and disruption in time – though not immediately – and a socio-chronological distinction apparent in the archaeological evidence which not only tells of new information but allows an unexpected sort of interpretation.

In the south-east of Britain proto-urban settlements had developed before the Conquest, phenomena edging into central southern areas at

sites like *Calleva* (Silchester), Mildenhall, beside Marlborough, and, possibly, Bagendon near Cirencester, Gloucestershire. Some such places, like
Verulamium, continued their urban development, to become Roman towns
and cities. In such cases, the Conquest brought no hiatus, so an agrarian
implication is that a new urban demand for food both was sustained and
grew over the first two centuries AD. There immediately is a reason for
countryside intensification of the sort that archaeological evidence seems
to be indicating. But, as Fulford observes (1992, 24), a distinction is to be
drawn between intensification as 'no more than a redirection of existing
resources with the existing framework' and 'radical changes in the way
the countryside was farmed and, consequentially, in the organization of
rural society'.

On the gravels of the Upper and Middle Thames, settlement density
between the two Roman invasions and on beyond the Conquest was as
great as in medieval times (one example each of a larger settlement and
a farm are detailed in chapters 8 and 9 respectively). Practically all the
known settlements are multi-period and characteristically shuffle around
their locality. The site where people lived in one period, for example,
becomes the stockyards of the next when the inhabitants move on to a
'green field' site, quite literally in some cases like Farmoor, Oxfordshire
(Lambrick and Robinson 1979). Mixed farming was the valley's general
basis, with an orientation towards stock-raising, itself perhaps a hint of
urban demand; yet, at the older Iron Age settlements, in general the material culture of the inhabitants was low while often being the only evidence
indicating Romanisation into the late first or early second century. Using
later analogy, perhaps life on the Thames valley gravels was not apparently
very attractive because the settlers there were landless labourers, leftovers
from earlier times or newcomers who had moved out on to low-lying
marginal land, 'free peasants' who paid for their freedom in insecurity
and an impecunious standard of living; or, as seems more likely, they were
tenants at the lower end of the social hierarchy rendering unto a local lord
and then a possibly distant Roman estate-owner a significant part of their
output. We cannot know, as we do seven centuries later when we have
documents, whether the rent included free labour.

The contrast between their material culture and that of some 'native'
sites only about 50–100 km to the west in Gloucestershire and Somerset
is striking; even more striking in its way is the similarity to the material
culture of comparable sites far to the west and north where Roman objects
are few and Romanisation taken to be weak. For farming settlements in
the centre of southern Britain, they stand out because, at what is generally
considered to be a time of economic and in particular agrarian expansion,

they had been deserted by around AD 100. Perhaps there is some selective economic or tenurial factor operating from the Conquest which,
consciously or otherwise, was weeding out certain settlements from the
landscape. Assuming a Roman imperative to increase productivity, a re-
duction in settlement numbers is plausible in the interests of efficiency;
but did the older farms stink, lie in the wrong place or simply house
more recalcitrant peasants? Why these particular sites were chosen or
self-selected is indeed puzzling. 'In some of these settlements we are as
near as we are ever likely to be to the peasantry of Late Iron Age and early
Roman Britain' is Fulford's assessment (1992, 26). Perhaps too near for
Roman sensibilities; and perhaps not only on the gravels.

Other settlements flourished, some becoming decidedly Romanised
and lasting until at least the end of the fourth century; but we cannot
go into comparable detail here, though two individual sites are discussed
in chapters 8 and 9. Overall, for the Middle and Upper Thames valley
and following Fulford (1992, 37–8), many Early and Middle Iron Age
settlements did not survive more than a couple of generations into Roman
Britain; and before their desertion, they were little Romanised. The settlement pattern on the gravels, and perhaps of lowland Britain, which
becomes that of Roman times was established in the period between the
mid-first century BC and the mid-first century AD, coincidentally or otherwise in parallel with the development of urbanism and the imposition
of imperial taxes and administration. These new, late prehistoric settlements continued into the fourth or fifth century, in part at least probably
because they were better managed (by being part of a Roman estate?)
and developed a more diverse cropping regime. They also became more
'Romanised', notably in some of their timber buildings of which a few
may be 'villas' by any other name, in their farming arrangements and in
their material culture. A parallel development in a type of site which may
show Romanised traits but definitely did not become villas was among the
'rounds' and 'raths' – circular enclosed settlements – of south-western
England and Wales. Many of them originated in late prehistoric times
and some at least were flourishing in the mid-first millennium AD (see
Appendix 1).

In none of these matters, however, is there much apparent continuity
with settlement and land-use after the fifth century. With very little doubt
good farmlands of course largely remained in use, in Cornwall, eastern
Scotland and southern Wales for instance. That is likely too of the Thames
valley, though land-use may have changed locally, for example from arable
to pasture (Hamerow 1992). Settlement was already pulling back from
the first river terrace in at least the Upper Thames valley by the late

Roman period, as shown by excavation at Claydon Pyke, Gloucestershire (Miles and Palmer 1982). In the fifth century the elaborate drainage system which had enabled the floodplain to be grazed and the first terrace to be cultivated was silting up. New settlement foci were developing along the second terrace, between and close to the sites of Roman farmsteads on higher, drier and possibly safer land if newcomers really were pressing up-river. At the Barton Court settlement, Oxfordshire (Miles 1984), at least one of the buildings, perhaps a timber villa, was in use well into the fifth century and may even have been still standing when the first Anglo-Saxon buildings were constructed (chapter 9). The important implication here is that, whoever was doing the farming, new Saxons or suborned Britons, the land itself almost certainly saw no break.

Many new settlements, here and elsewhere, both occupied former farmland and presumably maintained the rest in working order (Hamerow 1992, 43). Such settlements as Barton Court Farm, and Mucking, Essex (Fig. 5.1c), Shakenoak, Oxfordshire, and Orton Hall, immediately south-west of Peterborough, provide one sort of answer about whether and how we should distinguish between 'continuity and contiguity' (Fowler 1976a, 36). 'Continuity', at least archaeologically, is conventionally taken to mean continuous occupation of one site, though Finberg (1957) was writing of landscape continuity in his pioneer study. Continuity in function, as in farming the same area of land, can be expressed by contiguous settle-ments, as the sites just mentioned would appear to suggest; so clearly at least one sort of continuity does not require habitations to be super-imposed physically on the same spot. Continuities of proprietorial and tenurial succession of a given piece of land could also be present without an archaeological sequence of continuous occupation of one settlement. The farming itself in the Thames valley examples continued to be mixed in the fifth to seventh centuries (chapters 11 and 12), so some sort of land-use continuity is implied, with the further possible implication that some of the existing major boundaries survived. This could be so even if there was, as seems likely in as crowded a landscape as the Middle and Upper Thames valley, considerable fragmentation, enlargement and rebuilding of territorial units ('estates'?) during the fifth to sixth centuries.

Elsewhere, in what became England after the sixth century, some of the land issues illustrated in the Thames valley west of Reading are also now becoming familiar. Overall in England the traditionally good land for both living and farming along the river valleys was where early Anglo-Saxon settlement concentrated. Whatever the nature of that settlement in general, and whatever the bellicosity or otherwise of the inhabitants, they were primarily farmers not just looking for good land but seeking to occupy the best land they could acquire. 'Best' involved not just the quality of the soil but drainage, access to land-routes, river crossings and natural resources such as building materials and stock-feeds. Sometimes, for whatever reason (but one suspects it was because the land was crowded in some areas), the very best land was not available close to a river. A shift slightly up-slope, or even further upwards from Romano-British settlement areas, can be glimpsed, for example, on the side of the Nene valley at Orton Hall (Mackreth 1978) and on greensand ridge and downland slopes in Sussex and Hampshire (Hamerow 1992, 40–1). Two well-known sites are also up-slope: Mucking locally in relation to the Thames estuary (Clark 1993; Hamerow 1993) and Shakenoak regionally relative to the Cotswolds (Brodribb *et al.* 1968–78). So probably many more Early Anglo-Saxon settlements existed away from the gravels but not beneath the present villages which generally take root at a later stage of settlement evolution towards the end of the first millennium.

In the reality of farming there was not of course as sharp a distinction between the desirability of light, gravel soils and the rest of the land as previous paragraphs may have implied. There was also, and always during this millennium, almost certainly the matters of ownership and tenure, often emanating from the highest level. Yeavering, for example, and nearby Milfield in north Northumberland, are documented royal sites of the seventh century (Hope-Taylor 1977); they lie on gravel in the Milfield basin on the banks of respectively the rivers Glen and Till, near their confluence. Either or both, but probably Yeavering, is likely to have been successor to the internally crowded hillfort of Yeavering Bell, high above the valley and certainly occupied in the early centuries AD (Fowler and Sharp 1990, pl. on pp. 64–5; Frodsham 1999). Yeavering royal site of the early seventh century was successor physically to an earlier fortified site on the same gravel ridge, so there may well be a three- or four-phase succession of great power here, of which the last was 'regal'. Whatever the extent of that power – and it certainly varied in time as we know from Bede's account of the early Northumbrian kings – locally an estate could be expected to support the regal life-style and its predecessors, wherever the 'court' happened to be in any one week.

Air photography and fieldwork have recently been revealing details of other sites which may well have been on that estate and which could help define it (Gates and O'Brien 1988; O'Brien and Miket 1991); other major places, in the same east-draining river basin but a little further afield as at Sprouston (Smith 1991), are now also seen as potential estate centres. There must surely have been a range of settlements and farms in the vicinity of the Glen/Till confluence, up above as well as along the valleys, situated on a range of subsoils and not just the gravels. Morris (1977) has attempted to define the Anglian land-holding structure in Northumbria and the Viking impact upon it, including a documented royal estate a little down the coast from Yeavering at Bamburgh, and others are doing likewise elsewhere (e.g. Blair 1996b). We know royal and other major estates existed. They represent an important type of land arrangement, and they can help bridge the period in the middle of the millennium between hypothetical imperial and villa estates and known, properly documented institutional ones from the early eighth century onwards.

A good example is at Cerne Abbas, Dorset, ostensibly a 'late' estate but in some form or other perhaps spanning our millennium (following Barker 1988). In 1086, there were two *Cernels*, both held by the Bishop of Salisbury. One, to the south, is now called Charminster, the Cerne with a *minster*, a church or college of secular priests serving a large area which emerges later sub-divided into eleven parishes. The abbey at Up Cerne or Cerne Abbas owned more than 14,000 acres and was locally influential in government and over the fortunes of many small rural communities. In the Cerne valley itself there was a degree of impressive precision in the land arrangements.

> Of the twelve Cerne's that merited separate entry, two were important local centres, Charminster and Cerne Abbas ... Liability for tax or *geld* was calculated in *hides*; in some cases we find the hides to be related to an actual, well-defined area of land . . . we find these hides to be almost equally divided between north and south part of the valley, the dividing line marked by the southern boundary of the later parish of . . . Lower Cerne . . . The adjustment of a single hide would give us an exact pair of estates, and a local centre with each. (Barker 1988, 29)

Hide numbers are often grouped in fives, perhaps relating to military purposes, but here, if a multiple exists, it is nine, 'shared almost equally between Cerne north and south'. But a perhaps more profound question is the time at which such arrangements came into being. They are certainly not Norman, though they could reflect one aspect of the monastic reorganisation in the tenth century; but they could have originated much earlier because, bearing out Lennard's words, long before AD 987, the first documented date for the monastery, the Cerne valley was cleared and cultivated, owned and parcelled out. During Anglo-Saxon times there were many more settlements than now,

> strung out along the valley floor making a descent of nearly six hundred feet from the slopes of High Stoy to the banks of the Frome . . . Within [a] very neat topographic framework the bounds of individual communities

ran from the stream up-slope to the flanking ridge giving an axial, cross-
valley arrangement very characteristic of Dorset chalk [and elsewhere in
Wessex], and probably of considerable antiquity.

Good local archaeological evidence exists of earlier settlement, including
Dogbury Camp 'at the head of the valley which we may endow with a
territorial significance' (Barker 1988, 28–9).

There is much in that which is representative. It has a hint of prehistoric
territoriality, large early estates, metrical elements in land organisation,
and the Church as land manager as well as owner. If the rural framework
was already present in 1086 and had been developed during the second
half of the millennium, what of the earlier centuries? In general, and
throughout, the bulk of the land belonged to the few in the upper levels
of a social hierarchy; land tenure was never democratic. To say as much
about the last century of prehistoric Britain and then of the centuries of
Roman domination is, however, an interpretation, a guess, for we lack the
documents such as we have for Anglo-Saxon England telling us of territorial units and the names of landowners. Nevertheless, detailed fieldwork
and excavation can suggest plausibilities. Two cases in Somerset come to
mind.

In one, a small farmstead is tucked into its local landscape of fields and
tracks overlooking the Vale of Wrington (Fig. 7.3) and a Roman villa, amid
its own, quite different fields, at Lye Hole down below (Fig. 7.4a). The
former may well have lain within a putative villa estate which stretched
across the contours from high ground to valley floor, the existence of this
former possible entity being reflected in the medieval ecclesiastical parish,
itself an almost unchanged version of an Anglo-Saxon estate (Fowler 1968;
1975b). Much more intensive investigation characterises the second example at Shapwick (Aston and Gerrard 1999). This basis induces the
confidence to envisage a similar occurrence but on a wider canvas: 'by
the end of the fourth century, villagers in small, nucleated agricultural
settlements . . . provided customary service to the owners of "villas" on a
series of estates along the northern flank of the Poldens' (p. 20). Another
locally significant landscape reorganisation occurred in the tenth century
'when the dispersed population was apparently suddenly re-housed in a
compact, nucleated village with open field systems to east and west under
the orders of Glastonbury Abbey' (p. 45). As we have noted, such estate
management at that time fits in well with similar changes elsewhere. At
times, interpretative confidence can be so great that it can also overturn
vegetational preconception too. Taylor (1983, Fig. 38), for example, cap-
tioning an air photograph, states that at Lidgate, Suffolk, 'In an area

alleged to have been forested until medieval times [was] a great Roman villa. It was undoubtedly the centre of a prosperous farming estate.'

Ecclesiastical estates

The Church became a great landowner, especially in England though it also held important estates in south Wales for instance. Its estates shared many characteristics with other estates in terms of land and farming; but of course they fitted into a different organisational framework. This was demonstrated above all in the second half of the tenth century when it was possible to impose reform centrally from above on a diversity of religious organisations holding land. The process of land-acquisition had begun when Augustine arrived from Rome in 597 and, as a base for his mission, was given property in Canterbury by the king, a gift setting a very significant precedent. Thereafter, at Monkwearmouth/Jarrow, for example, in the later seventh century the king of Northumbria gave lands, probably a working estate, not only on which to build first one, and then a second, monastery, but as the agrarian resource on the basis of which the monasteries could pursue their mission. Such grants were really endowments, intended to provide food and other supplies from the land and rents from tenants – and a number of resident souls to be saved. The motivation was of course selfish: to provide for the donor a sort of insurance policy, or at least a lottery ticket, for the Life hereafter. Status came into the act too, for what the king did today his nobles and dependants tried to do tomorrow. Whatever the motivation, as a result the Church prospered as landlord, and its holdings influenced both its way of working and its status. Sawyer (1998a, 272) summarises succinctly:

> Before the Norman Conquest, pastoral care was provided by bishops operating from their cathedral churches and by episcopal minsters, many of which had been founded on royal estates in the seventh and eighth centuries. These minsters each had what is now conventionally called its *parochia* . . . originally the royal estate (or the district that contributed to a king's *tun*) in which the minster was established. Monasteries, which are often difficult to distinguish from minsters, also had pastoral responsibilities.

He notes that this situation was complicated by the secularisation of many minsters and monasteries, and in the ninth century by Vikings. Parishes as units for ecclesiastical administration and the saving of souls did not certainly exist before AD 1000 and were not called such until the twelfth century; but local units of administration, many of them with a church, were operating in a contiguous and continuous network across much of

England before then. Variants of this system, or at least local units and their central place with different names like 'Townland' and 'Church-town', occurred to west and north in England and further afield. The essence of these land units was that, unlike other ones, the areas defined were not the property of an institution or an individual, though almost certainly the land involved would be part of someone's estate or, later, manor. Nevertheless, parishes and their predecessors as such did not belong to any one body or individual; they were a communal resource, later colonised by the Church.

Those land units which later came to be called ecclesiastical parishes enjoyed two relationships with Roman roads. In various parts of the country, notably East Anglia and Somerset, they appear to be earlier than Roman roads. Improbable though it may seem, it is very difficult to set aside the visible evidence of hectare after hectare of 'parochially' allotted land crossed uncomfortably by kilometre after kilometre of Roman road. The clear implication is that at least parts of the early first-millennium landscape contained as a new item, or inherited from prehistory, systems of land allotment of the same order in terms of size as large areas of Bronze Age Britain; in terms of territorial organisation and social function, what eventually emerged as the medieval parochial system could be viewed in similar terms, that is an effective parcelling up of land for management purposes at a level hierarchically one up from that of individual holdings.

Land units, some later to become ecclesiastical parishes, were also laid out in relationship to Roman roads after their construction (or did some of the major roads run along existing boundaries?). This was a relationship which was surely known to those living on the land at the time; it is also clearly discernible to us on our maps and air photographs. It is probable though unproven that Roman roads were used as local territorial boundaries in the first four centuries of the millennium; they certainly were later, though we do not know from what date. Some 'ancient' boundaries related to Roman roads probably continued in use where it was useful so to do; others probably used roads where they were obvious features in the landscape to help define local units of property and farmlands in that continuing process of local parcellation that went on throughout the first millennium.

Some of the results, still there in our landscape, are startling. About thirty parishes, for example, are laid out in a remarkably symmetrical pattern at right angles to some 48 km of Ermine Street immediately north from Lincoln (Owen 1976; Stafford 1985, Fig. 4). We do not know when this extensive piece of wholesale landscape organisation occurred, but it

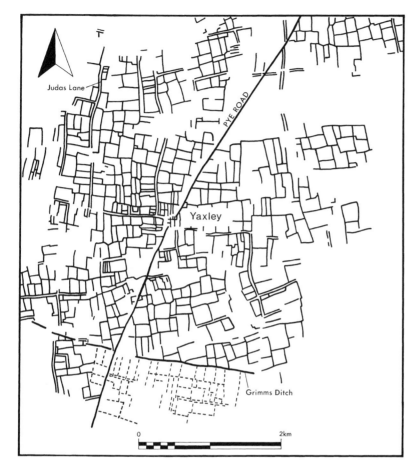

Fig. 4.2 Roman road and Grimm's Ditch overlying enclosed landscape, Yaxley, Suffolk (after Williamson).

is tempting to regard it as a deliberate act of planning and Roman in date. Even if it is not as early as that, and instead perhaps the handiwork of Anglian farmers or Danish settlers partitioning out their new lands, the arrangement bespeaks a significant element of landscape continuity, with the pattern likely to pre-date by at least several centuries the documented definition of parishes after the end of our period. In no way, however, does it imply that the road itself remained open to through traffic.

Yet noting all sorts of territorial units, some with new names if not actually new themselves, will tend to convey an impression of creativity and hierarchy; whereas in fact the most significant process going on in relation to land in the later first millennium may well have been fragmentation. Proprietorial units, if not administrative ones, were being broken up, perhaps with a loss of productivity. Expressed the other way round, the holder, owner or otherwise, of a small land unit would have had to look to greater efficiency to maintain, never mind increase, the land's productivity, so providing a context in which changes in the distribution of resources and working practices could occur. Sawyer (1998a, 155–6) sees it as a context for

> a fundamental change in the concept of land ownership in the course of the eighth and ninth centuries. Before that the land held by individuals was thought to belong either to their families or to their lords . . . These early attitudes to land ownership were already changing in the seventh century, largely as a result of the need to endow churches with permanent rights over land, a need met by the granting of royal charters . . . In time similar grants were made to laymen and when, thanks to such a grant, an individual was seen to own land it might well be remembered as his, especially if he chose to make it his permanent home . . . The new attitude to land ownership was accompanied by, and indeed contributed to, the fragmentation of many large estates.

Our discussion here has skimmed lightly over a very complex and voluminous topic, for our need is simply to emphasise that the agriculture of the first millennium occurred within a series of frameworks of land organisation. We have tried to indicate some of the units and something of the hierarchies within which they were arranged; we hope we have implied that at no time were there free or free-ranging pioneers, farmers or cowboys able to do whatever they wanted on land beyond any jurisdiction. Nevertheless, we cannot discuss, even exemplify, the range of organisational mechanisms operating in the whole of Britain over a millennium. We have used mainly English and late material simply because it is so readily available and relatively well evidenced, but some of the general principles underlying its divisions of the landscape should apply elsewhere. The various ways in which the landscape was organised are wonderfully diverse and often locally well studied, but the important point for a general agrarian history is not their detail, except to exemplify, but the facts that they represent. For the second half of the first millennium certainly, and very probably for the first half too, farming in Britain was carried out within an organised landscape of territories, estates and proprietorships with tenure to the fore. It was a landscape not only in which just about every acre was owned but also in which every resource needed by an agrarian way of life was managed.

5 | Settlements

When Cadog went away from Llancarfan, his first buildings fell down.
And the poet ... looked sadly at the deserted and overgrown settlement
of Urien: nettles; grass, brown stalks, brambles, thorns and dock leaves
thrive; a pig roots in it; a chicken scratches around it.

DAVIES 1989, 14

Settlements, places where people lived, were created at a remarkable rate
over much of Britain throughout the first millennium. They form a basic
component of any consideration of agrarian history in this period, for they
were the work-places and homes where the members of an essentially
agrarian society spent their daily lives (Fig. 5.1). Some of these places
survived as habitation sites a long time, some even into the twenty-first
century; most were abandoned and fell down; and a few, like Cadog's, fell
down but were inhabited anew. The buildings in them were, in general,
of organic materials; few buildings were intended to be permanent –
Roman public and military buildings (Pl. VIII) are an obvious exception –
and most were conceived of as temporary or at least replaceable. It was
Bede who commented on the church at Whithorn (Galloway), 'the white
building' ('*Ad Candidam Casam*'), as being of stone 'in a manner unusual
among the Britons' (*HE*, chapter 4).

Other stone buildings appeared from time to time, notably villas, temples and other Roman-style structures, in town as well as country, in the
early centuries AD, though many were timber-framed on stone foundations or walls (Pl. IX). The majority were in fact of wood until the
'Norman rebuilding', and some ecclesiastical buildings, like Whithorn
church and the Monkwearmouth/Jarrow monastic churches, were outstanding, as was the intention, in being of stone from the seventh century
onwards. Stone churches and other ecclesiastical buildings had become
more common by the end of the millennium (Taylor and Taylor 1965).
Otherwise Bede was right, and not only for his own time. Throughout
the millennium, across the whole range of settlements, buildings were in
general not of stone but constructed in organic or impermanent materials
such as wood, vegetable matter like straw, and earth, mud and clay, often in
combination. Not one single such building survives, though sub-surface

85

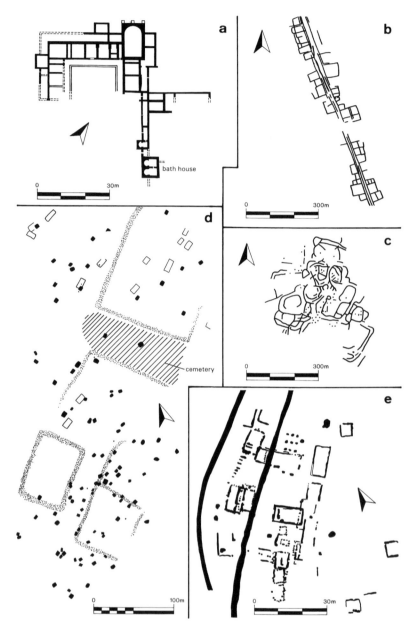

Fig. 5.1 Plans of five examples of settlements to indicate the range in the sorts of places people lived in during the first millennium: (a) Box villa, Wiltshire, from which came a large iron ploughshare, probably of the third/fourth century (after Smith 1997); (b) a settlement in Warter parish, one of the many 'ladder' settlements on the Yorkshire Wolds, similar to some in the Fens (Fig. 4.1), with long, linear arrangements of rectilinear enclosures along a ditched 'street' leading from and into the surrounding countryside (after Stoertz 1997); (c) overlying the junction of two great Neolithic cursuses, this settlement of curvilinear enclosures lies close to Rudston village, on the floor of the Great Wold

excavated evidence of their former existence is now an archaeological common-place (Pl. V) and several have recently been built as intended replicas (Pls. XIII, XIV). The original evidence is obviously grossly in-adequate, nevertheless, particularly in structural, functional and three-dimensional visual senses (cf. the critique in Morris 1979, 71–3); but we know quite a lot about settlements themselves, where many were, their times of habitation, their morphological differences, their range of func-tions and, less confidently, of social status, and their remarkable diversity across the land.

This chapter is about larger types of settlement in the settlement hier-archy, generally of village size and upwards (Fig. 5.1). We shall generalise a little at its end but our main intention is to look at a number of indi-vidual settlements and their details, including some buildings. Smaller settlements, generally of farm size and smaller, are discussed in chapter 6 (Pl. X). Such a division crudely by size is fraught with a potential to mislead but, given the thousands of known examples of settlements from this millennium, any way of handling the evidence has some drawback. A morphological approach, for example, can run into the difficulty that similar shapes do not necessarily mean similar dates or functions, and a functional approach can disguise one of the principal dynamics of settle-ments, that is that they can change their function as well as their form. At Flixborough (below), for example, Loveluck (1998) remarks that it is tempting to 'view the settlement as a high-status vill centre (*caput*) which became a monastery, prior to a further transformation back to a secular estate centre or nascent "manor"'. Form too can be the result of process: as we find them now, conglomerations of structural remains may appear to form large settlements, but of course the individual buildings may well be of widely differing dates, reflecting successive use of the same place. Mucking, for example, is now interpreted in this light (Fig. 5.1d; Hamerow 1993).

Nevertheless, the material could have been tackled here by date, ge-ographical area, nationality, function, status or quality of evidence (for

Caption for Fig. 5.1 (*cont.*) Valley, North Yorkshire, with pits (black dots), perhaps *Grubenhäuser* (after Stoertz 1997); (d) part of the excavated approximately 800 m length of settlement remains at Mucking, Essex, illustrating not one huge settlement but suc-cessive small ones, here of the earlier phases including rectangular timber buildings and *Grubenhäuser* (black squares) plotted against features of prehistoric times and the early centuries AD which are presumed to have been still visible *c*. AD 500 (after Hamerow 1993); (e) Middle Anglo-Saxon settlements at Wicken Bonhunt, Essex, with rectangu-lar timber buildings and the major ditches characteristic of the period and later (after Reynolds 1999, following Wade). NB The scales vary.

Plate VIII   Hadrian's Wall and fort at Housesteads, Northumberland, in a 'busy' agrarian landscape of fields of several phases between late prehistoric and post-medieval. *Bottom left*, by the stream are fragments of early fields showing as white lines, and a similar field system outside the nearest, east fort gate, and on the slopes north of the wall and fort, appears to be overlaid by the fort. The rectangular enclosures outside the west gate, *top right*, are part of the extensive extra-mural civil settlement, also indicated by the exposed buildings outside the south gate. The excavated Roman terrace lies between the museum and farm buildings, *top centre*, with the more obvious terrace system, downhill and *top left*, both overlaid by the block of fields, *left centre*, and extending out of the picture along the south-facing slope to the west.

Plate IX   Typical valley-side siting and preserved remains of a Roman villa, at Great Witcombe, Birdlip, Gloucestershire, showing wings and central corridor arranged around a court, with a plunge bath in the foreground. A large, probably late Roman, iron ploughshare, now in the British Museum, came from here.

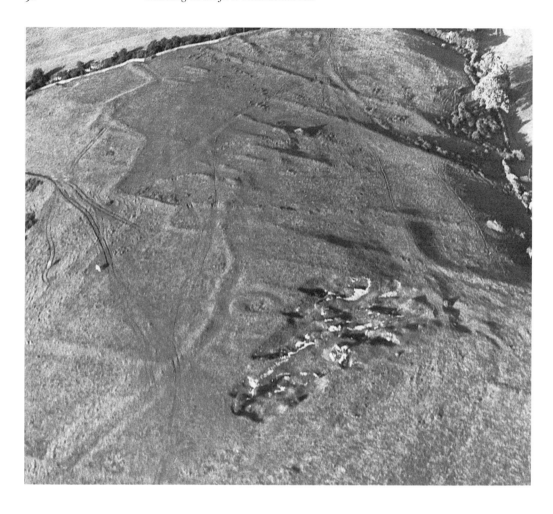

Plate X Settlement and fields arranged either side of a contemporary trackway along Bleadon Hill, Somerset, in the first half of the first millennium AD. Discounting the modern quarrying, *lower centre*, the complex is an earthwork equivalent of the crop-marks in Pl. IV above.

example, excavated or not). Wales provides a good example of a chrono-logical treatment in a discussion of material from the second half of the millennium and after (Edwards 1997). Alcock (1988, 11–24) returns to the primary evidence in mid-millennium Northumbria, isolating the ac-tual terms for settlements in contemporary use – *civitas, urbs, castellum, villa, vicus* – and correlating them with archaeological evidence. He argues (p. 11) that the five terms represent a threefold hierarchy in which, taking as example an element of settlement pattern with clear agrarian impli-cations, 'the *villa regis* may have been the centre of a royal estate with subordinate *viculi*'. In contrast, the evidence of settlements in Scotland, also recently discussed, has been categorised morphologically under six heads, using late twentieth-century archaeological jargon: forts, cellular buildings, crannogs, timber halls, *Grubenhäuser* and Pitcarmick houses (Armit and Ralston 1997). This pragmatic approach, descriptive of visible differences not particularly related to any criteria except the current state of research, 'works' with the material available. It is further elaborated for the far north (Cowley 1999), which emphasises that the material is more relevant to chapter 6 than here. That bears on one of the two main points to emerge from this material in a British perspective: from both west and north, it is clear that, outside and beyond Roman implants – a few places like Caernarfon – truly large settlements are absolutely rare west of the Wye and Severn valleys and north of Hadrian's Wall for the whole of the millennium. The material nevertheless serves as a useful corrective for the settlement range in first-millennium Britain to that of an English mind-set dominated by Classical and Teutonic concepts such as 'villa' and 'villages'. Not only are such concepts irrelevant for much of non-English Britain, but even in England beyond the lowlands they can mislead rather than help.

'Large' settlements were always relatively few in Britain throughout the millennium. The key words here are 'large' and 'relatively': the former is used here in the sense of the latter, not as an absolute as in the sense that 'large' means settlements with over a hundred inhabitants. Settlements large in size and population relative to other settlements in their contemporary regional settlement pattern were nevertheless present in Britain throughout the millennium, always with major implications for feeding their inhabitants and therefore for farming. The most obvious examples were *oppida* in the century and a half before the Claudian conquest (Cunliffe 1976), various types of fort (but excluding Roman military ones) notably in the first, fifth–sixth and ninth–tenth centuries, and towns (in several different manifestations) in every century except between the mid-fifth and mid-seventh.

Generalisations about any such types of settlement always disguise complexity and ambivalence. Unlike most other types of British prehistoric settlement, what we call *oppida* were actually seen and described by a contemporary writer, Caesar: 'Cassivellaunus' stronghold . . . was protected by forests and marshes and had been filled with a large number of men and cattle. (The Britons apply the term "stronghold" to densely wooded spots fortified with a rampart and a trench, to which they retire in order to escape the attacks of invaders.)' (*BG* V.21).

Though that description is almost certainly correct as far as it goes, it leaves open questions about the functions of such places at times other than during military threat, for example in relation to the agricultural economy in general and cattle in particular. Similarly ambivalent are hillforts, fortified sites containing hundreds if not thousands of Britons at the moment of conquest, as at South Cadbury, Somerset (Pl. XI) and

Plate XI   In striking contrast to the agrarian landscape in Pl. X is South Cadbury Castle in south Somerset, a place of power in prehistory, and at the beginning, in the middle and at the end of the first millennium AD. The Roman army attacked it in the mid-first century, its role was sufficiently grand for imported Mediterranean pottery to arrive there in the sixth century when it was refortified, and it was refortified again when it was minting coins in the tenth century. At no time, however, do we know the nature of its relationship with the rich farming lands round about.

Maiden Castle and Hod Hill, Dorset. Apparently they presented a brave front but may well already have been anachronistic, at least in much of southern Britain by the forties AD; and their reuse in the fifth century, while superficially similar in some respects, was of a different kind in a different social context (see Cadbury Congresbury below).

Towns included public buildings, mints, market places very much involved with the exchange of agrarian produce, ports and defended places, notably Roman foundations in the first and second centuries and Saxon and Danish burghs in the ninth and tenth centuries. They ranged in their origins from military accretions to state creations through riverside trading settlements as illustrated respectively by Carlisle, Oxford and Northumbria's *Eoforwic* across the Ouse from Roman York. Some Roman towns, for example Caerwent and probably Caernarfon, continued to be occupied after AD 400 and others were occupied (still or anew?) in the fifth (*Verulamium*: opposite St Albans), sixth (*Virocornovium*: Wroxeter) and seventh (*Durovernum*: Canterbury) centuries; but we remain uncertain in general whether such occupation retained the status of urban settlements like those as 'large'. The impression from Bede of Canterbury about AD 600 is of political stability and religious renewal among standing buildings (*HE* I.25–6), a view of the urban physical fabric which, in general, is not sustained by archaeological revelations of ruins, 'dark-earth' and traces of wooden structures by that date (see Appendix 1). Towns subsequently developed from the eighth century onwards, sometimes on the site of earlier towns with or without a break in occupation but characteristically as trading places on new sites. Their significance in agrarian terms is that at various points in time they became one or both of two factors: places generating new points of consumption and increased demand for agrarian products; and centres facilitating trade in agrarian products as commodities rather than as food being grown for direct, local consumption.

Villages

There were also several different sorts of non-urban but relatively large living-places such as unwalled rural settlements along roads or at communication nodes in the 'Roman' countryside. Whether they should be classified as 'small towns' or large villages remains unclear, and may well be a matter of function, status and tenure rather than merely size. Settlements which are more clearly villages have been proposed, for example, on Salisbury Plain and along the Fen edges in the early centuries AD (Bowen and Fowler 1966; Hallam 1964), and throughout lowland England by the tenth century AD. The origin of villages is a vexed question but, as was clearly established in the 1980s, not only is there no simple answer, there is no single answer (Faull 1984; Hooke 1985b).

One of the earliest so-called villages in our millennium is Chysauster in West Penwith, Cornwall (Pl. XII, Fig. 7.2; Hencken 1933; Smith 1996). This is open to the public as an archaeological 'village' of 'courtyard houses'. In fact, the structures are but a local variation of a multi-purpose homestead, adapted to the local environmental circumstances and now explained in their farming and land-use contexts (chapter 7). A good example of a large British settlement, Caer Dynnaf, in Romanised Wales is illustrated by Musson (1994, 29, bottom right). Taken by itself it presents a typical spread of building sites and small enclosures, presumably houses, farm buildings and yards, along irregular streets (or perhaps the more appropriate word is 'lanes'). Similar-looking settlements, existing as grass-covered earthworks remnant from either collapsed stone or timber

Plate XII House 3 photographed from House 4, looking west-south-west across the village of the early centuries AD at Chysauster Cornwall, and down towards the valley.

walls or constructed banks and ditches, are quite rare now in relation to what must have been their number in, say, AD 400, but they are nevertheless a known type, occurring for example on Bleadon Hill, Somerset (Pl. X), on Salisbury Plain (McOmish 1998) and on the Yorkshire Wolds (Fig. 5.1c; Stoertz 1997). The particular interest of the one at Caer Dynnaf, near Cowbridge in the Glamorgan lowlands, is that it lies within the abandoned defences of a late prehistoric hillfort, though such a placement is common far to the north too. Chesters, overlooking the Breamish valley in Northumberland, is a particularly well-preserved example of a phenomenon meticulously recorded in the region by Jobey (Mitcheson 1984).

In non-hillfort country, large 'native' settlements of the early centuries AD and in varying degrees justifying the status of 'village' have been a familiar feature of settlement studies since the mid-twentieth century. A range of examples is illustrated in Frere and St. Joseph (1983), notably street villages at Chisenbury Warren, Wiltshire (Pl. 122) and March, Cambridge (Pls. 130, 131), settlements whose symmetry contrasts geometrically with the characteristic sprawling extents of sites such as those at Lamming's Bridge, Holbeach, and Rookery Farm, Spalding Common, both Lincolnshire (Pls. 132, 133). Both the last fall within a wider extent of settlement pattern in and around the Fens, systematically explored in the 1960s in a way which revolutionised understanding of 'villages' and indeed other types of settlement of the early centuries AD (Phillips 1970). Such work has more recently been followed up with widespread and intensive field-walking as well as air photography and some excavation, the whole now providing a vivid illustration of the settlement pattern and, to an extent, the rural history of one of the areas which was undoubtedly among those most intensively farmed for crop production during the early centuries AD (Fig. 4.1; Hall and Coles 1994).

Morphologically, villages come in various shapes, two of the best-known forms being the 'street village', of properties and buildings arranged either side of a road, and the 'green village' with its properties arranged around an open space, often as a rectangle or triangle (Roberts 1987). While the village continues to entrance the English as a form of living representative of their history, we now know, however, that village shapes are characteristically the product of long-term process and recent change as well as acts of planning. Furthermore, large settlements of village type were present in the late prehistoric countryside and were created in the early centuries AD too. The 'English village' was neither reintroduced nor introduced by Anglo-Saxon immigrants in the middle of the millennium but developed as a late arrival in the English countryside of the ninth century onwards. On the other hand, most existing villages in England were in place by 1086, though in general villages in Wales and Scotland formed later than that under English influence.

Some extensive Anglo-Saxon settlements prove on examination to be much smaller at any one time than the area of settlement remains. At Mucking, Essex, for example, the 'village' proves to be a small settlement which moved around the landscape in the same area in three different phases over some 200 years (Fig. 5.1d; Clark 1993; Hamerow 1993). We have to think of an area of settlement of which only a part was occupied at one time while the rest was probably used as yards, paddocks and fields, some of them markedly fertile as they used up the nitrogen in the soil from former occupancy. West Stow 'village', on the other hand, may well have consisted of only one or two farm homesteads at any one time.

Other large settlements tended to accrete around some feature, natural or man-made. Residential sprawls, for example, came to be associated with forts (Pl. VIII) and industrial workings such as metalliferous extraction or artefact manufacture, e.g. lead-mining on Mendip and pottery production along the Nene valley near present-day Peterborough, and settlements also agglomerated around fixed and significant features such as monasteries and churches (Holdsworth 1995). Following its extensive excavation, Whithorn (Hill 1997) now provides a vivid example of the last, while the air photograph of Gateholm Island (Musson 1994, 60, lower left; Davies *et al.* 1971) gives an excellent visual impression of what could be involved spatially. Bede himself probably bears out the idea of such places being relatively large settlement nodes in his mention of 600 people at Jarrow, surely a reference to those living around the monastery and on its estate, not to the number of brethren.

Other fixed points in the landscape might well be centres of secular power as represented by the temporary residences of travelling kings and great lords or the principal residence of the local chief or landlord. The archaeologically well-attested Roman villa was probably often a central place for hundreds of dwellers and workers, rather like the Victorian country house at the centre of both an agricultural estate and a social round. Royal courts may well have been at times a collection of houses and tents but they could also be on the grand scale and with 'permanent' installations even if not inhabited all the time. Yeavering in Northumbria (Hope-Taylor 1977; Alcock 1988, 7–9) and Cheddar in Wessex (Rahtz 1979) provide the excavated examples. Less exalted in social terms, maybe, but locally significant power-centres could also grow to become relatively large. Though they look completely different and are indeed archaeologically distinct, there is in this last context probably a similarity between, for example,

Jarlshof in Shetland and Goltho in Lincolnshire (Hamilton 1956; Beresford 1987).

Several of these types of larger settlements show clear evidence that they were planned, that is they developed to fit in with a preconceived shape rather than just accreting. This characteristic is most evident, of course, in the Roman towns of the first half of the millennium, applying Mediterranean concepts of urbanism, but they also appear in the later Anglo-Saxon town, though probably in pursuit of objectives more pragmatic than the aesthetics of Classical conformity. A degree of spatial organisation has been observed within the quasi-urban settlement at *Hamwic* (below), for example, and, using Flixborough again as examplar, one of the common features of sites contemporary with it is the 'widespread use of major enclosure boundaries to structure settlement layout'. Loveluck (1998) then speculates that 'many Anglo-Saxon rural settlements had at least a loosely planned layout within or associated with enclosures or linear boundaries, in their Middle Saxon phase'. The point is graphically exemplified by Fig. 5.1e.

Structurally planned or otherwise, other types of large site are also indicated archaeologically by crop-marks (Pl. IV; Fig. 5.1b) and spreads of artefacts in plough-soil, and doubtless the landscape still contains much to change our present picture of first-millennium larger settlements; but such archaeological evidence need not always indicate a place where people actually lived. The Yorkshire Wolds, for example, have now produced artefact-rich sites which may well be later first-millennium market places (below), while in the chalk-country of Wiltshire a category of artefact-rich site has emerged which seems to be primarily a 'disposal area' set aside to deposit over centuries from later prehistory into the first millennium AD anything from corpses (cemeteries) through metal hoards to debris (rubbish dumps) (Lawson 2000).

Six exemplary settlements

This choice of the few examples that space allows is influenced by the wish to obtain a spread of settlements through the first millennium, through Britain and across the range of the upper end of the settlement hierarchy from 'village' to 'town'. The selection also requires examples of short-lived and long-occupied settlements, and, as far as possible, sites where you can go and see something. The agony of choosing, and the inadequacy of the choice in representing former reality, emphasises in the writer's mind the quite extraordinary range of larger settlements in Britain in the first millennium AD.

The six large rural settlements (Fig. 1.1) summarised are:
    Castle Copse villa, Wiltshire
    Cadbury Congresbury, Somerset
    West Heslerton, North Yorkshire
    West Stow, Suffolk
    Flixborough, North Lincolnshire
    Brough of Birsay, Orkney

Castle Copse villa, Great Bedwyn, Wiltshire

Examination of this Roman villa, one of hundreds of excavations at rather than of the near-thousand such sites, demonstrated a familiar sequence showing that villas were often not simply built as 'Roman' houses in a conquered countryside (Hostetter and Howe 1997). The impression instead is of a gradually Romanised 'native' site, an idea more familiar in more obviously 'peripheral' areas like the South-West than in central southern England (Branigan and Fowler 1976). The earliest features, ditches and beamslot structures, were of the second half of the first century AD and seem to have foreshadowed the plan of later structures arranged as a rectangle around an open space. Mixed farming and animal husbandry were tentatively indicated in the vicinity.

Either side of AD 200 a gravel terrace was built right across the site and a series of post-hole structures in the now-buried rectangular plan were constructed upon it, some of them perhaps with plastered walls and terracotta roof tiles. A masonry 'villa' followed, with an aisled building – a flint structure with chalk floors – on the north and a long rectangular building on the west; both were given tessellated floors in the fourth century when the courtyard effect was probably completed with buildings on the south and a wall on the east. The development seems to have been from a winged corridor villa to a courtyard villa. 'This shift from timber structures to a masonry villa and the elaboration of the villa in the fourth century appear to reflect a process of gradual change and evolution within a single cultural group' (Hostetter and Howe 1997, 371). In this case excavation did not find, however, the range or ranges of ancillary buildings, for farm-workers and for various specialist tasks like bread-making, that should have existed in the vicinity. 'The villa reaches its *floruit* in the mid-fourth century when [its] west and north wings were luxurious quarters with hypocaust heating, imported Bath stone capitols, glass windows and . . . a possible plunge bath. Mosaics were laid in styles and patterns familiar from other central southwestern villas . . . and wall painting was executed in a variety of colours using local and imported pigments' (p. 372). The villa's 'decline and impoverishment' (p. 374) is, however, clearly marked archaeologically: at least one 'crude building' unsymmetrical with the courtyard was built on its west, probably in the early fifth century when patching of mosaic floors and use of residential areas for industrial activity had already occurred. The site was then abandoned.

The farming economy, judging from animal bones, was the familiar one of predominantly cattle, followed by sheep and pig, most probably butchered on site. A hint of sheep-raising for wool in the late phase is also familiar. Spelt wheat was grown in the early period; cereals including bread wheat and the glume wheats remained prominent throughout, with olives and figs providing hints of luxury in the diet.

Cadbury Congresbury, Somerset

Cadbury Congresbury is a small hillfort overlooking the River Yeo and the North Somerset Levels to the south-west of Bristol, an area now largely drained but still mostly only just above sea-level. In the fourth to seventh centuries it was an area of alluvial marsh from which protruded small, low islands like that on which a documented St Congar founded a monastery at the foot of the hill beside a crossing of the Yeo (Rahtz *et al.* 1992).

Excavations on the hill itself showed that, like others in the region, it was frequented in the fourth to second millennia BC, and both defended and occupied in the last centuries BC when it harboured some sort of cult centre involving the human skull. It was marginal to local activity in the early centuries of the first millennium AD, when local people were farming from small homesteads set among surrounding fields along the sides of the Vale of Wrington (Fig. 7.3) Some local villas along the lower ground in the Vale may have headed local estates, foreshadowing the later arrangement of parishes here, but the local power-centre was a substantial establishment at nearby Gatcombe, a valley-side settlement with a range of agricultural buildings within a massively stone-walled enclosure (Branigan 1977a). At Henley Wood beside Cadbury Hill, a Roman-style temple stood just outside the derelict late prehistoric ramparts; a cemetery began to develop there (Watts and Leach 1996).

Yet in the late fifth century people with a Romanised material culture, perhaps refugees from Gatcombe (though whether owners, estate-workers or slaves cannot be determined), reoccupied the hilltop which, soon afterwards, was refortified. A new rock-cut ditch with stone rampart was constructed across the narrowest part of the hill; through it was an entrance with double doors hung on iron hinges. Inside were at least eight timber structures of *c.* AD 500 and later through the sixth century. One seemed to be a circular, timber temple with a screened entrance; another was a rectangular timber building containing numerous objects

including fragments of pottery of both table ware and amphorae from
the eastern Mediterranean. Indeed, in the sixth century the people living
here had clearly achieved high status, having access to ceramics and glass
not only from the civilised Mediterranean world but also from eastern
'Anglo-Saxon' England, north Africa and possibly France or Spain. They
were also patronising craftworkers and using objects in iron, copper alloy,
gold, lead and enamel. Reinforcement about the nature of the society on
the hilltop in the sixth century is provided quite independently by one
of the key conclusions from study of the animal bone: 'The high percentage of immature animals . . . indicates that stock were slaughtered for
the sake of their meat and hides, rather than the meat being a bi-product
from worn-out plough oxen, wool-producing sheep etc. This suggests an
affluent society' (Noddle in Rahtz *et al.* 1992, 186). By AD 600, however, the *floruit* of this colourful and enigmatic community was over. The
settlement was abandoned, its people disappeared from the archaeological record, perhaps to a new village around St Congar's church, and the
hilltop was never again permanently occupied.

West Heslerton, North Yorkshire

West Heslerton, North Yorkshire, is the name of an existing village. It
may well have been first established in the mid-ninth century or a little
later as a response to Viking raids which had arguably brought to an end
life on its probable predecessor, a now totally deserted site nearby which
has been extensively excavated, 1986–95 (Powlesland 1999, 64–5). This
Anglo-Saxon settlement, known archaeologically by the same name, will
become a major site of reference as the information and ideas resulting
from its excavation, currently in preparation, become available. Three
main interim reports are in print; this account is based on the latest one
(Powlesland *et al.* 1986; Powlesland 1997; 1999).

The settlement lies on the southern side of the Vale of Pickering. Its
occupation began in the late fourth century and had ended, according
to coin evidence, by the middle of the ninth. Early Anglo-Saxon features
extended over more than 13 ha; they were preceded by some form of ritual
activity in the late Roman period which may well have continued, providing a focus for settlement there. North of the settlement was a cemetery,
used only during the 'Anglian', or 'Early to Middle Saxon periods ending
at *c.* 850' (Powlesland 1999, 62). Morphologically and functionally, the
settlement was well organised, with indications of 'deliberate separation
between secular and ritual space. Much of the northern half of the settlement was without any internal divisions or property boundaries. The

occupation and associated activity in the southern half of the settlement [shows] an extensive network of ditched and fenced enclosures' with the 'ritual space' marked by substantial timber structures around an active spring to the south (pp. 57–8). This last area included 'a complex of bread ovens' and 'extensive spreads of oyster and mussel shells', perhaps equivalent to 'the sort of food bars we find at pilgrimage sites today'.

The first establishment of an Anglian settlement saw the settlement at its most extensive. During the Middle Saxon phase (*c.* 650–850), it contracted 'to cover little more than the Roman core of the site' though it was then, 'during or soon after 724', that a well was constructed. The settlement's four zones consisted of housing to the north-east, with rectangular timber buildings and a few *Grubenhäuser*; industrial and craft activity to the north-west, with many *Grubenhäuser*, metal-working furnaces, 'a malt-kiln and very extensive butchery deposits' (p. 59); an area perhaps for crop processing and stock management to the west, marked by a triple-ditched enclosure beside a stream; and a 'multi-function zone' with extensive enclosure complexes around the spring and to the south.

This large, well-organised initial settlement exhibited 'a very high degree of architectural uniformity' evidenced by the approximately 220 excavated structures which included 130 *Grubenhäuser* and at least ninety post-hole structures, all envisaged as having raised floors. The very considerable amount of artefactual material includes significant quantities of Niedermendig lava quern-stone fragments and hone-stones but, in general, little out of the ordinary.

The excavator (p. 58) judged that the picture to emerge is 'not one of a cluster of small farmsteads gradually being replaced in such a way as to move the settlement across the landscape' (cf. Mucking below, and Hamerow 1993). He saw two of the most significant aspects of the site to be 'the emergence of a large and clearly zoned settlement during the Early Anglo-Saxon period [which] indicates a well-organized society. The uniformity of the structural remains might indicate an egalitarian society rather than one dominated by a small social elite; this view is also given some support from the examination of the grave assemblages which do not appear to indicate massive differences in the availability of disposable wealth' (p. 64).

West Stow, Suffolk (Pls. XIII, XXXVII)

This early Anglo-Saxon village within the Breckland was occupied *c.* AD 400–650. From it has come one of the largest faunal assemblages to be

Plate XIII
Reconstructed
Anglo-Saxon buildings,
West Stow, Suffolk. The
two in the centre, 'The
Living House' and 'The
Farmer's House', built
on their original sites,
were twelve years and
two years old when
photographed, 1999;
'The Sunken House', to
the right, was
twenty-three years old.

recovered and analysed from a British archaeological site (chapter 11). It lay on the bank of the River Lark, specifically along the river terrace where fluviate gravels are overlain by blown sand deposits. These deposits, and the absence of later occupation, have increased the level of preservation at the site. Local resources would have included the river itself (providing fish and waterfowl), river valley (meadow and pasture), and slopes and uplands beyond (rougher grazing land).

Modern vegetation in the uncultivated areas of the river terraces here often comprises heath, bracken and sand-sedge; at West Stow grass-heath and *Calluna*-heath are predominant alongside *Carex arenaria* (sand-sedge). The present-day environment here has been anthropogenically affected, however, and, taking climatic variation into account, conditions on the dry, poor Breckland soils in the mid-first millennium AD could have been different. Lamb (1985), as we have already noted, suggests that the climate was warmer and drier than today between AD 250 and 400, and that the late sixth century brought with it colder summers and wetter overall conditions. Here there appears overall to be a local 'fit' with such a broad correlation between climatic change and land-use, habitation having enjoyed generally warm and dry conditions, modified by a certain riverside dampness.

Excavation provided what seems to be a relatively complete plan of a significant part of an early Anglo–Saxon village (the word consistently used by the excavator and here followed, though it is clearly questionable). The buildings date to three phases: the fifth century; the sixth century; the late sixth to seventh century. Seventy sunken-featured buildings (SFBs) appear to be clustered around seven small post-built structures (possibly halls). The sunken features were probably covered by a raised plank floor resting on sill-beams, immediately improving the air circulation around the planks and therefore their longevity, a major improvement in design irrespective of whether or not the hole beneath was used for anything. Some indeed seem to have been lined with vertical planking and used as cellars or storage areas. As reconstructed on site (Pl. XIII), this interpretation of the contentious 'SFBs' carries conviction. The planking floor too immediately strikes the visitor as providing a major improvement in the quality of domestic daily life compared with living on bare earth, an improvement which would have been particularly helpful in a village planted immediately above the generally damp circumstances of a valley floor (above, chapter 3).

The preferred interpretation is of a settlement consisting at any one time of only one or two halls surrounded by about seven other buildings for specialist functions such as animal shelters, crafts and sleeping. Each such unit is envisaged as belonging to an 'extended family unit' which would meet for meals, decision-making, entertaining visitors and evenings of story-telling in the hall.

Flixborough, North Lincolnshire

Flixborough is the name of both the parish and present village. The site of archaeological excavations 1989–91, and on a slighter scale thereafter, should be called North Conesby, not Flixborough (Loveluck 1998, here followed closely and updated by Loveluck 2001). The main focus of Anglo–Saxon occupation and settlement-related activity, between the early seventh and early eleventh centuries, was on the summit of a windblown sand spur overlooking the floodplain of the River Trent 8 km south of the Humber estuary. There, some forty buildings, boundaries and other structural features were excavated, together with an extremely rich collection of artefacts and over 250,000 animal bones. The whole occurred in a vertical stratigraphic sequence of nine main phases. The settlement area overall, including a cemetery, was larger than that excavated and seems to have acted as a continuous focus of settlement from the early centuries AD for a thousand years and more.

Within the settlement, long-lived building plots were superimposed, and habitation was periodically interspersed with major phases of dumping associated with refuse accumulation. The main phases of occupation within the excavated area were from the late seventh to the mid-eighth century; from *c.* 850 to 950; mid/late ninth century to early tenth century; and early tenth to early eleventh century. Between the mid and late ninth century the organised layout of the previous period was abandoned, and smaller buildings were erected, most less than 10 m long and less than 6 m wide. Nearby were domed, fired-clay ovens. 'At some point between the early and mid tenth century, the small buildings, possible granaries and ovens were completely demolished, to be replaced by the largest buildings . . . within the occupation sequence . . . None of the new buildings was positioned to respect earlier building plots' (Loveluck 2001, 89). The largest building (7) was demolished during the mid-tenth century, and covered by a large rubbish dump including a great number of animal bones. Between the mid-tenth and early eleventh century, occupation of the excavated area ceased as the whole of it was used for dumping rubbish. Settlement may at this time have shifted slightly eastwards around the site of All Saints' church, documented from the thirteenth century and possibly overlying a late Saxon predecessor. Twelfth- to thirteenth-century pottery in a ditch across the excavated site suggested that it was then peripheral to a settlement focussed around the now-destroyed church to the east. The site was buried in windblown sand after the fourteenth century.

The buildings were all rectangular, aligned NW–SE, and with dimensions ranging from 9 m × 5.30 m to 19.70 m × 6.50 m. The largest, and among the latest, Building 7, was 19.70 m × 6.50 m. Hearths were usually in the eastern half of the interiors; construction involved post-hole, continuous trench and sill-beam structures. Details within the settlement included an east–west boundary ditch, metalled pathways linking different building plots, and activity areas associated with craftworking and ovens.

Artefacts indicated the site's context in inland, coastal and overseas exchange networks. On-site, a range of craft and industrial activities were pursued, including grain treatment, carpentry, textile manufacture, bone-working, leather-working, iron, lead, non-ferrous and fine metal-working, and possibly glass-making. Particularly important was the exceptional collection of wood-working tools (chapter 8). Someone was literate too: twenty-seven styli and two inscribed objects give a lustre of literacy to the site normally reserved for monasteries.

Arable cultivation and grain processing were evidenced by an iron hoe-sheath, charred seed grains of cereals and pulses, and a large collection of rotary quern fragments, many from the Eiffel region of Germany. What was at first thought to be an iron plough coulter is more likely to be a bill-hook. Cattle, sheep/goats, pigs, geese and chickens predominated among the domestic animals, with horses and cats also represented; but their relative presence varied through time, with important interpretative implications for the site's functions and status. Wild fauna and flora came from a variety of environmental habitats: cranes and various ducks indicated wildfowling, perhaps in the Trent floodplain; deer, hare, woodcock, and shells of snails, birds' eggs and hazel nuts indicated hunting and foraging over open ground and woodland edge; oyster shells, marine and riverine fish bones and net-sinkers indicated fishing along adjacent river and open sea. Unusual were the number of cetacean skeletal remains (porpoise, dolphin and pilot whale). Overall, the inhabitants were 'sustained by the products of a mixed agricultural regime, supplemented by wild fowling, fishing and the hunting of other wild fauna' (Loveluck 1998).

Even making allowance for the exceptional state of preservation on the site, and for the probability that its functions changed over 300 years *c.* AD 700–1000, the evidence suggests some sort of place with high status, at least for some of the time. Between the late seventh and late eighth centuries, it seems to have been an aristocratic estate centre, perhaps with a household or family church and leaving behind a collection of rubbish suggesting 'conspicuous consumption', e.g. of goods like exotic glass vessels and lava querns, and of consumables like dolphins. During the first half of the ninth century the number of cattle slaughtered markedly decreased, while the exploitation of domestic fowl, particularly chickens and geese, reached a peak. Styli and window glass were in use; craft production increased; the dominance of sheep may have related to wool and textile manufacture, perhaps for export. The overall impression is of 'a minster, and of an estate involved in the supply of finished commodities to nascent urban centres' (Loveluck 2001, 116), perhaps based on a monastic community. Thereafter, from the mid-ninth until the early tenth century, the settlement was much involved in textile production, with smaller buildings and less conspicuous consumption; but by the early decades of the tenth century, consumption returned, though this time in the form of the 'ostentatious use of timber in the largest buildings within the occupation sequence, and also massive consumption of animal resources', namely 'luxury feasting . . . traits consistent with the emergence of an Anglo-Scandinavian "manor", probably associated with the name Conesby – "King's settlement"'. Thereafter, in the tenth century, 'the more limited patterns of craft and industry . . . probably reflect the level of specialist services required to furnish the needs of a secular estate or "manorial" centre, set against the background of change in the roles of urban settlements' (all quotes in this paragraph from Loveluck 2001, 117). What the site meanwhile emphasises is the economic importance of the Humber as an interface between inland England and North Sea coastal exchange, periodically over the second half of the first millennium AD.

The Brough of Birsay, Orkney (Pl. XVII)

Far to the north are numerous settlements of Viking people who colonised the coasts and islands of what is now Scotland. One of the best-known, most impressive and relatively easily visitable is on the Brough of Birsay, a tidal island off the north-west corner of Orkney Mainland (Hunter 1986; Morris 1996; Graham-Campbell and Batey 1998, chapters 9, 10). There a late Norse (early twelfth-century) small stone church and stone-walled enclosure are the most obvious remains, but they represent only the last phase of a long sequence of religious and secular activity in the vicinity over several centuries during the first millennium AD. The two major phases earlier than the church were when the site appears to have served an important religious function during its Pictish phase, and then a period of extensive Viking settlement from the ninth century onwards leading up to its 'becoming a major focus of the earls of Orkney in the mid-eleventh century' (Graham-Campbell and Batey 1998, 188).

The grassed area around the church contains the remains of numerous other buildings, some sub-rectangular and laid out up and down the slope with a degree of symmetry to the west and a complex of superimposed structures to the east. The latter are of the Viking period overlying Pictish buildings; the former seem to be Viking longhouses and halls forming part of an extensive settlement stretching beyond the laid-out remains, being indeed perhaps part of a settlement complex continuing back towards the extant village on the Mainland. Excavation has shown settlement remains from immediately preceding centuries to underlie many of the 'Viking' buildings. The latter were also modified in their turn when they were in use as part of the complex we can now see. 'The Later Norse settlement was characterised by little more than substantial alterations to existing structures, usually with the retention of part of the original floor area and wall footings' (Graham-Campbell and Batey 1998, 190, quoting Hunter). Excavation also demonstrated the existence of pits and minor structures in the areas between the structures now laid out for visitors.

Conclusions

Two points stand out in this necessarily brief summary of the topic. One is the extraordinary range of large settlement types that existed during the first millennium AD. Though the size of the largest is nothing like that of the twenty-first century, between 1000 and 2000 years ago in effect much the same variation among the larger settlement types existed as is the case now. From cities to small villages, from open to enclosed settlements, from ribbon development to nucleated complexes, from stone to timber, from port to ecclesiastical settlement, from coastal to inland and from lowland to hilltop – they are all there, and much more is known about them, both in general and in considerable detail, than we have been able to indicate here.

The second generalisation concerns the patterns in which these types have variously arranged themselves at different times, and the dynamics of change in those settlement patterns. Ideas such as seeing deserted settlements as 'caused' by Anglo-Saxons driving Britons out westwards at a particular moment in time are quite inadequate and simply wrong. The overall pattern is of spatial movement, with major exceptions like some extant cities and towns being on or close beside the sites of Roman and medieval urban settlements. Even there, however, detailed examination shows significant local movement, at *Verulamium*/St Albans for example. In general, sites were abandoned as economics affected their livelihood, as environmental factors made them untenable, as communities moved for a host of reasons – and as new sites, nearby or distant, were chosen, occupied and developed. All this would have had agrarian consequences, if only at the practical level of where farmers took their 'surplus' products to market; more significantly, such changes could have been altering not just the location but also the nature of supply and demand.

Particular settlement trends can be seen in particular areas at particular times. In Co. Durham, for example, firmly in the area of early Anglian settlement,

> some nucleations [of settlements] . . . are likely to be of pre-Conquest origin, but . . . it is not possible to say whether they are early or late Saxon developments . . . most of the pre-1200 holdings associated with these villages display tenurial features which can definitely be linked with a pre-Conquest estate structure . . . [in some] a clear distinction can be drawn between the desmesne and bond parts of the settlement. This distinction is consistent with their former status as central settlements within an earlier Saxon estate. (Campey 1989, 85)

Campey's conclusion is very similar to that reached for the other end of the country, in the land of the South or Middle Saxons or Jutes (Blair 1991, 160–1). From such independent pieces of research a generalisation begins to emerge, in this case making us realise that significant settlement change can be as much about tenure as it is about physical occupancy of the land. That is undoubtedly true of farms too.

6 | Farms

[T]hey content themselves with wattled huts on the edges of the forest, put up with little labour or expense, but strong enough to last a year or so.
GIRALDUS CAMBRENSIS, CHAPTER 17 (THORPE 1978, 252)

Tens of thousands of farms came and went during the first millennium AD. Some were as temporary as Giraldus observed (above); the sites of others are still in use and occupied. Only a very small percentage, inhabited or dead archaeological sites, have been scientifically investigated, despite the centuries of antiquarian delving into local records and fossicking into Roman sites in particular. Most of our usable information comes from the later twentieth century and some of that is not properly available. Here, we begin by defining a farm, examine a few examples and then embark on a selective, regional survey.

A farm is both a place to live and a work-place. There must be a house; characteristically it will be home to a family, perhaps an extended family as argued for the units making up the Anglo-Saxon 'village' at West Stow (chapter 5). There may be two houses, for two brothers, for example, or for working family and aged parents and relatives. Until recently, most farms also contained accommodation for temporary workers, for example specialists to shear sheep or labourers to help with harvest. There will also be non-habitative buildings, though minimally a farm could consist of one house with its only indoor working space attached as a byre – making a longhouse – or barn. Depending on the type of farming being pursued, and the status of the farm, the other buildings will be from a range of byre, barn, stables, pig-sties, granary, tool and equipment sheds, poultry-coops, and smithy or other specialist work-place (the range of functions is well illustrated by the old photographs in Fowler 1983b). 'Mixed' farms will tend to have all or most of those; on the one hand a farm might only have buildings for storing grain and keeping its cattle, harness and implements, while on the other, buildings will be to shelter animals, store their feed and keep the few implements needed to obtain it. In addition, there will always be a water supply on-site or nearby, and an outdoor working area to do the

Plate XIV
Reconstructed
Anglo-Saxon buildings,
Bede's World, Jarrow,
South Tyneside. That to
the rear is based on
Building A excavated at
Thirlings,
Northumberland, and
the nearer one on a
'monastic cell' excavated
at Hartlepool, Co.
Durham.

farm's on-site work – such as a handling yard or pens for doing various things with and to animals, sorting sheep for example, and a rickyard for storing and threshing grain. And there could be all sorts of specialities involving structures, though not necessarily buildings: outdoor ovens for various purposes for example, a pond, even a mill.

Examples of all of these, and more, will arise in the following descriptions and discussion. A frustration in all this is that we know what a farm should consist of generically but it is actually quite difficult to assemble a working *ensemble* on or about any one site from either or both archaeological and documentary evidence. Numerous examples of what can reasonably be interpreted as farms exist, however, in the archaeological record (Fig. 6.1).

A fairly standard type of farm in the centuries of Roman rule is the small rectangular or rectilinear ditched enclosure, usually showing a single, clear entrance and, sometimes, the outlines of one or more buildings inside (Fig. 6.2). A typical example is illustrated by Musson (1994, 29, bottom left) from Cae Summerhouse, near Ogmore. This is actually double-ditched and, like others in the Vale of Glamorgan, may well have

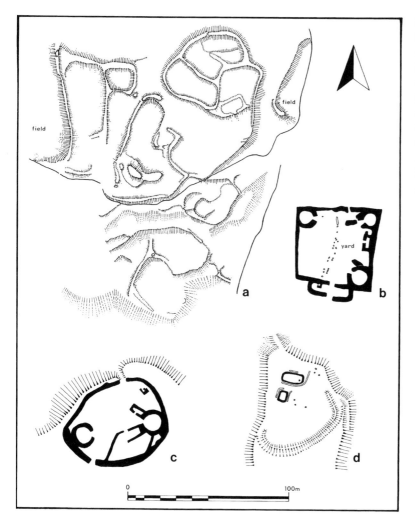

Fig. 6.1   Plans of four first-millennium enclosed farms: (a) Westmead, Row of Ashes, Butcombe, Somerset, before excavation; (b) Cefn Graeanog, Gwynedd; (c) Pant-y-saer, Anglesey; (d) Dinas Powis, Glamorgan, after excavation.

originated in pre-Roman times, acquiring a range of stone-footed buildings and some material prosperity during the next one or two centuries.
Such enclosed farms were not necessarily surrounded by a ditch or ditches,
nor in a rectilinear form. Their surround could be an earth bank alone or
a walled bank, perhaps even a palisade, and the shape could be of curved
rather than straight sides. A particular type of settlement enclosure in
north Wales is called an 'enclosed hut group'; a polygonal example is
illustrated by Musson (1994, 82, bottom left, at Hafoty Wern-las, near
Caernarfon). Such types of site often produce evidence of metal-working,
showing the difficulty of ascribing farming functions to such sites with
confidence. But perhaps the problem is the other way round: it is of

Fig. 6.2 Plans and reconstructions of a Romano-British farmstead at two points in time: (a) the third quarter of the first century AD; and (b) the first half of the fourth century. Whitton, Glamorgan (after Mitchell in Jarrett and Wrathmell 1981).

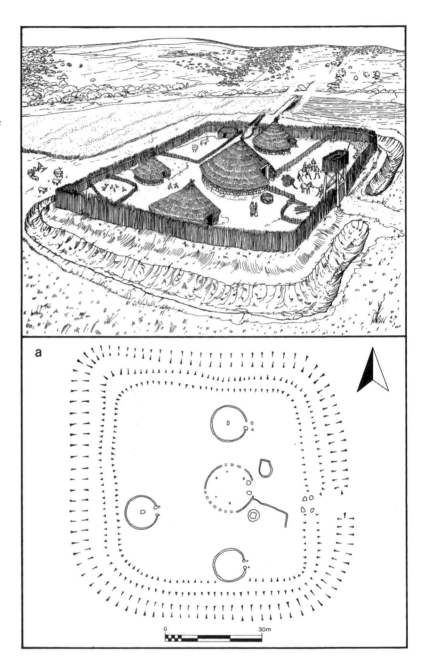

identifying how many of a possible range of activities were carried out on any one farm. Musson claims (p. 86) the native communities continued farming the surrounding countryside (despite being beaten by Agricola), though the rarity of early Roman finds suggests they were perhaps excluded from Roman life. He continues, with respect to north Wales: 'The latter part of the Roman period, however, sees the full flowering of the

Fig. 6.2 (*cont.*)

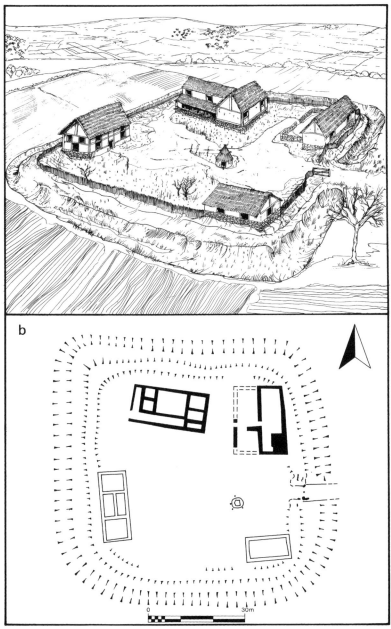

settlement types known as the "enclosed hut group", its variations perhaps reflecting differences of social status and life-style amongst the families who made their homes in these distinctive stone-walled homesteads of North West Wales.' One of them, Din Lligwy, on Anglesey (Pl. XV) is five-sided and perhaps the home of a local chieftain wealthy enough to employ an iron-worker. Its buildings were both circular, probably domestic,

Plate XV
First-millennium
settlement, Din Lligwy,
Anglesey, showing the
remains of some of the
round and rectangular
buildings within an
enclosure of which one
side is by the fence in the
mid-distance.

and rectangular, for farm purposes and workshops. It was occupied during the later Roman period and perhaps later. Not far away on the island is a different homestead enclosure, Caer Lêb (Musson 1994, 89, lower), of Roman date and also with stone-footed buildings round and rectangular, but enclosed by earthen bank and ditches.

The farm at Westmead, Butcombe, Somerset, is a good example of such characteristics: a late prehistoric circular building succeeded eventually by a rectangular stone-based, flagstone-floored building beside which was a small round stone structure, perhaps a stack-stand, the whole within a small stone-walled embankment surrounded by similarly enclosed pounds or yards within a landscape of enclosed fields laced with trackways (Figs. 6.1a, 7.3; Fowler 1970; 1975a; fields, see chapter 7). Such a picture, in that case spanning the years from mid-first to late fourth centuries, is typical of many sites throughout Britain, even though the variety of structural materials may make different sites look very different. Coles and Hall (1998, 53), for example, use different descriptive words of a site, namely Hilgay on the eastern edge of the Fens in Norfolk, which is neverthe-less essentially similar to Butcombe on the other side of England: 'the earthworks of a small farming settlement . . . consist of two raised (house) platforms set in rectangular and square enclosures marked by shallow gullies. Two small ringworks lie near the farmstead . . . with narrow annular ditches [and] were probably stack-stands.'

One of the several attempts to interpret this mass of evidence in terms of historical process in the early centuries AD proposes four models in considering the change from 'Celtic farm to Roman villa', a proposal which has wider and useful implications (Branigan 1982, 83–92, with site references). Model 1 was of 'an existing, pre-conquest farmstead, with a moderately wealthy occupation such as might suggest its owner belongs to the tribal nobility, shows increasing signs of Romanisation after the conquest and within no more than two generations sees the construction of a villa house'. Examples are widespread in southern Britain, e.g. at Gorhambury, Hertfordshire, and Holcombe, Devon. In Model 2, a pre-Conquest farm adopted new farming strategies or methods after the Conquest but only progressed slowly towards the replacement of existing farm architecture by villa-style buildings, e.g. Barton Court, Oxfordshire, and Odell, Bedfordshire, where a fourth-century villa overlay a first-century farmstead.

With Models 3 and 4 we move to sites originating after the Conquest but, after that later start, essentially reflecting the rapid and slower changes of the type envisaged in Models 1 and 2. In 3, a native farm founded shortly after the Conquest, perhaps in a government-directed expansion of rural settlement, might be simply of native style or show signs of Romanisation from the start but, in both cases, moved rapidly to the appearance of a villa house by the late first century or first half of the second century, e.g. Gadebridge and Boxmoor, Hertfordshire, Brixworth, Northamptonshire, Shakenoak, Oxfordshire, Winterton, Yorkshire, and 'Gargrave in the heart of the Pennines'. In Model 4, the villa was built much later, e.g. Langton, East Yorkshire, where a new five-roomed villa was built on a 'native' farmstead early in the fourth century, with a new bathhouse and new farm layout and buildings. All four models are, of course, based on assumptions of continuity from pre-Roman to 'Roman' farm (Models 1 and 2) and within the Roman period (Models 3 and 4). Other models are needed to cover cases of disruption and abandonment which are likely to have occurred not only during obvious periods of transition, as in the mid-first century and our Phase 5 (see chapter 14), but also within blocks of historical time such as 'Roman Britain', here ignored and treated as four phases of agrarian history (chapter 14, Phases 1–4).

Change on the farm through time, therefore, to a significant extent belies the generalisation above that many farms in the first millennium appear broadly similar as archaeological evidence. Considerable variety and regional distinctiveness in fact exist within the forms of thousands of first-millennium farms. This is so, even though their function was basically the same and not particularly sophisticated. A small library of modern surveys of farms extant in the late twentieth century stresses this point about both the steadings and their houses (see Appendix 1). There is no reason to suppose that the first millennium was different; the whole of Britain shows that it was not. In the west, for example, small enclosed settlements with various local names like 'round' and 'rath' were probably mostly farms, some beginning before the first century AD and characteristically occupied over several hundred years during the early and middle centuries of the millennium. Din Lligwy, Anglesey, possibly a pale reflection of the idea of a villa transmuted through the British tradition of a farm, has unusual features but is essentially a good example; it is also publicly accessible (Pl. XV). Many other examples are discussed elsewhere in their western regional contexts (Appendix 1). On the Yorkshire Wolds, to take another region, such is the wealth of settlement evidence now available that, quantitatively at least, excavation can make but little impact on the whole. Nevertheless, while morphologically many of the late prehistoric/earlier first-millennium settlements seem entitled to be called 'villages' rather than just 'farms', hundreds if not several thousands of farms of the first millennium probably lie within the detail displayed across a whole landscape – and in the implications of the thought that we cannot know what was not air photographically visible at the time of the survey (Stoertz 1997). That study identifies villas and subdivided enclosures, large regular enclosures and some of the linear settlements with ditched trackways as certainly or likely to fall within the first part of the millennium, with *Grubenhäuser* (as in Fig. 5.1c) and, cautiously, the eleven curvilinear complexes in the second part. The last indeed look complex, and are perhaps small groups of farms, with successive components, rather than single farms (Stoertz 1997, 55–9, 62, 67, Fig. 30; cf. 'market' sites in chapter 13).

North Britain north of Yorkshire contains dozens of investigated farms of the first millennium AD, particularly in the north-west of England (Bewley 1994), Northumberland and southern Scotland (Clack and Haselgrove 1982; Wilson *et al.* 1984). Jobey's well-known work in particular (bibliography in Mitcheson 1984) illuminated distribution patterns and types of small settlements between Tees and Firth of Forth in the earlier centuries AD. One morphologically distinct type stands out as a characteristic farm of the Roman phase in the region: a small, sub-rectangular enclosure, two-thirds of it an open space or yard with a track through it leading from the entrance in one end to one or, more usually, two round buildings on a slightly raised level at the other (three examples are visible on Pl. XX). Two excavated farms from the region are also often quoted because they belong to the last centuries of the millennium, when dating settlements, indeed finding them, is difficult. Gauber High Pasture, Ribblehead, North Yorkshire, and Simy Folds in Upper Teesdale, Co. Durham, suggest their nature in their names as upland and fairly remote places, probably primarily with pastoral concerns on the margin of settlement whatever their date. They were occupied respectively in the eighth and ninth centuries and, unlike so many earlier farms, were not enclosed, consisting essentially of a loose grouping of two or three buildings at any one time, informally related to a yard (both are well summarised and illustrated in Reynolds 1999, 147–51).

Further north still, the sheer numbers and the sub-regional diversity of farm-sites continue in the forms of hut-circles, brochs, wags and other building forms. The round-house had already been a highly successful building form for at least two millennia BC and it continued as the basis of farms well into the early centuries AD. Large-diameter, substantially built, circular houses with a stone wall of the final centuries BC and early centuries AD, for example, characteristically accompanied souterrains – stone-built, underground passages with or without chambers. A round-house stood on Buston crannog as late as *c.* AD 600.

The locally named 'wags' represent a distinctive local variant of small farming settlement in north-east Scotland. They are 'circular or oblong structures with stone pillars supporting a slab-built roof, very much associated with the availability of Caithness flag, a local sandstone which splits into the massive slabs' (Cowley 1997, on which this paragraph is based and from which come the quotations). Characteristically about 4–5 m wide with proportionately wide walls of up to 2 m thick, the building type may well have been in use for much of the first millennium AD, clumped in mid-millennium, and possibly representing infilling of a farmed landscape by colonisers. Perhaps in the later first millennium AD, rectangular buildings became more common and 'the overall extent of settlement may have contracted . . . and developed into the pattern of farmsteads and townships that survived until the clearances of the early 19th century'. One case of rectangular buildings, apparently associated with expansion on to marginal land in the later centuries of the millennium, occurs down the east coast in Perthshire. There 'round-ended sub-rectangular buildings of Pitcarmick type', a name 'derived from a group of structures at Pitcarmick in Strathardle', measured from 12 m × 5.8 m to 33.8 m × 7.1 m overall. Some, if not all, of these buildings may have been

Plate XVI   The internal divisions with hearth and entrance viewed across the interior of the broch at Gurness, Orkney Mainland, a site in use in the early centuries AD.

byre-dwellings and have formed steadings at the centre of mixed farms ('P' on Fig. 7.7).

Another local type of small settlement, the broch (Pl. XVI), has a wide distribution and disputed status, but is always likely to have been a farm in some sense. Locally, its distribution can be variable and suggestive: in Sutherland, for example, the small number of brochs cannot have housed the totality of the population, whereas in Caithness 'it is easier to envisage a larger proportion of the population living in and around brochs' (Cowley 1999, 73). In both counties, however, as on the Yorkshire Wolds and over much of Britain, there must have been many other unenclosed, archaeologically less visible farm-sites. Some may even have been hamlets.

Hamlets

Just as earlier we saw that it is in practice difficult to draw a line between 'villages' and larger settlements, so it is difficult to draw a line between villages and 'hamlets' and indeed between hamlets and 'farms'. The farm is often the basic unit within such larger forms of settlement: a large village could actually consist of, say, eight individual, single farms without there being a large, communal, non-farm building, and two farms could minimally make up a hamlet.

The hamlet is one of the most characteristic settlement forms over the west and north of Britain. Discussed by numerous writers, it is pertinently assessed by one of its more recent students who makes the emphatic point that its small size is not the result of failure to become a village

Plate XVII On the same island as the broch in Pl. XVI, another settlement complex but of the later centuries of the first millennium AD lies on the Brough of Birsay, now a tidal island at the north-west corner of Orkney Mainland. In this general view looking towards the Mainland, a Viking-age hall house is in the foreground, with the later ruined church in its stone-walled enclosure in the middle distance.

(McDonnell 1990, 20). More positively, it is characterised as a viable social and economic unit, usually not dependent on other settlements and free of functions as an administrative centre, lay or ecclesiastical. Many of the small first-millennium settlements, especially those known only from archaeology as abandoned, and therefore in some sense failed occupation sites, meet and can probably be interpreted by such criteria. On the other hand, such a definition does not embrace all small existing settlements, some of which are demonstrably shrunken remnants of larger, sometimes much larger settlements.

Certainly, the classic definition of the hamlet would insist that it be larger than a single farm. McDonnell (1990, 39) argued that it could consist of up to fifteen households, even up to twenty in the Pennine Dales. If that be accepted, then many of the abandoned settlements of the first

millennium identified and sometimes excavated by archaeological methods were hamlets; and the hamlet was a much more ubiquitous form
of settlement than appreciated. Some of the excavated Anglo-Saxon 'villages' too, like West Stow, and Chalton and Cowdery's Down, Hampshire,
would become 'hamlets'. The terminology is important here, not merely
to describe individual sites correctly but to interpret settlement patterns
and even hope to see tenurial relationships. We ought to know what we are
dealing with in trying to understand the frameworks and units of the first-
millennium landscape and, if so minded, to explore possible correlations
with what the documentary evidence is talking about. Archaeologically,
'hamlet' seems reasonable as descriptor for a settlement of four to ten
households; larger, and 'village' seems more appropriate. But such definitions cannot be absolute, for although size is important it is also a function
relative to social organisation, population density and land-use. And it also
varies with time and place. A fifteen-household 'hamlet' of lowland Britain
in AD 300 could be the size equivalent of a relatively large settlement by
the local standards of, say, contemporary northern Ireland or western
Scotland. Size is also important to perception: the Domesday surveyors
did not 'see' hamlets.

The classic view of hamlets as independent seems untenable. They are
always in tenurial matrices when documented, and that status is argued for
in pre-documentary times too. The hamlets of north Wales were arguably
dependants of *maenors*, for example, and the farms and farm hamlets of
Surrey forming within the disintegrating fabric of large estates nevertheless took with them obligations as well as rights (Jones 1979, 11–12,
18; Blair 1991, 160). Nor are they independent geographically, for they
are always part of a settlement pattern, characteristically of a dispersed
nature but certainly not exclusively so. Roberts and Wrathmell (1998)
provide a new assessment of the complexity based upon a national survey
in England.

The small size of a settlement now can be seen sometimes to be the
result of fragmentation rather than an inability to grow large enough to
become a village. This has been not so much failure to grow as failure to
sustain the fabric – physical, economic, tenurial – of a larger settlement.
Many other processes were also at work locally creating small settlements
in the medieval landscape (e.g. Aston *et al.* 1989). Doubtless such was also
the case a thousand and more years ago. The fact is that the countryside is a
dynamic organism, and hamlets, though often individually old settlement
sites, are to an unknown degree a symptom of that dynamism just as
much as the better-known deserted medieval villages of England and the
'wandering settlements' of the 'Migration Period' in Continental Europe.

Another characteristic of the 'ancient' hamlet is that it concentrated on pastoral farming. Today this is a truism as we note the familiar pattern of hamlets across the uplands, but the association is of some, and probably of great, antiquity. Upper Swaledale, for example, was settled from Cumbria by 'Irish Norse', presumably late in the first millennium and certainly before the thirteenth century when the first documentary evidence occurs (McDonnell 1990; cf. Fleming 1998). It speaks of 'vaccaries' and 'bercaries', that is cattle and sheep farms, some them perhaps hamlets rather than single households. These new words, surely, reflect traditional land-usage originating well before the documented settlement, especially as Swaledale contains impressive extents of pre-medieval land arrangements which have survived as earthworks precisely because of low-intensity non-arable land-use (Fleming 1998, Fig. 1.5). In other words, even here, in a relatively remote upland area, there was already a long history of farming and the formation of a cultural landscape well before pastoral farms appear in documentary evidence. Swaledale could well serve as metaphor for virtually the whole of Britain in that respect.

Even in the uplands, however, the 'simple' form of settlement called 'hamlet' is not necessarily the only outcome of newly arrived farmers; and variations can be sub-regional. Not far from Swaledale, for example, is Malham Moor, where the 'Norse-founded *hus* farms' showed little or no development into hamlets (King 1978). At Bordley, two tenant farms side by side fronted on to a single large farmyard. Uphill, a boundary dyke separated Bordley land from Madtiles Moor, the arrangement being of 'an Anglian rather than a Norse origin'. If such land-use arrangements high in the Pennines originated well before the tenth century, then they speak volumes about the relatively early filling up of the farmable landscape in lower, agriculturally more attractive topographies.

A former wider distribution of hamlets in lowland areas may be both conjectured and also associated with that characteristic of hamlets, pastoral farming. We may, for example, identify them in early medieval and medieval times on the claylands of the Essex/Suffolk border, pasturing their sheep and cattle on the heaths while participating in the evolutions of settlement patterns today characterised by single farms and small, green-side settlements (Warner 1987).

Three excavated farms

To complement the generalities, we now look in more detail at three examples of first-millennium farms which have been excavated. The sample is obviously not statistically representative but it is hoped that the choice represents an appropriate range of evidence and of farm types. The first offers something about farming settlements in the earlier centuries AD in the Middle Thames area and probably further afield too; the second is a hilltop site, probably not only a farm though of a farming nature, in Scotland in the middle years of the millennium; and the third is at Lindisfarne off the east coast of Northumberland in the eighth century.

Watkins Farm (Allen 1990)

The name is of both an existing and an archaeological farm. The latter is one of a group of archaeological sites in the Stanton Harcourt area, Oxfordshire, situated on the low-lying First Gravel Terrace, which shelves very gradually on to the floodplains of the rivers Thames and Windrush. The limits of the floodplain and First Terrace are difficult to define, although the whole terrace around the settlement may have been an oval island which included two settlements. One was centred around a large ditched enclosure of the Middle Iron Age with two phases of occupation in the early centuries AD, and, 200 m north, a settlement area also in use early in the first millennium AD was represented by a scatter of pits and ditches. At the former, occupation soon after the Roman Conquest reused the main Iron Age enclosure ditch. Further ditches defined a small enclosure on the south-east; other features included scattered pits, wells and post-holes. Ditches externally flanked the eastern entrance, with small rectangular pens attached to the northernmost of these. West of the main enclosure was a large rectangular enclosure whose west side was formed by a group of intercommunicating, sub-circular enclosures. The whole suggests an establishment involved in stock management, a function which probably continued, for the occupation during the Roman period was characterised by a succession of sub-rectangular enclosures containing a few deep pits or unlined wells. Indeed, the settlement area to the north, occupied from the later second century AD, was perhaps the homestead using the former site as stock pens. It too was ditched, with two phases of occupation. The absence of third- and fourth-century occupation on each site suggests that by this time the area might have been managed from elsewhere. Wetter conditions indicated by the environmental data may have reduced settlement possibilities. It is also possible that some degree of settlement nucleation was occurring at this time, e.g. to Northmoor.

On the Roman site, all the wells consisted of circular pits with vertical/near-vertical sides and flat bottoms, with a less steep slope on the east but one still too steep for safe access for stock. Droitwich salt containers from the first centuries BC–AD were found on both sites. Loomweights and spindle-whorls indicated wool-working, and typical bone artefacts included a narrow needle made from a pig fibula, a sheep tibia, a decorated weaving comb made out of a long bone of cow or horse, and a cylindrical polished handle made of antler. All of this is utterly unremarkable, though the pair of Roman shoes from a waterlogged context indicates what can be assumed to be missing on drier sites. Like other contemporary settlements in the area, overall this was a low-status site, involved for the most part in local trade.

The animal husbandry at Watkins Farm, as at other sites, was probably part of a relatively self-contained subsistence pattern, which concentrated on animal rearing and dairying, with sheep playing a secondary role for meat and wool. Possibly, specialised breeding and training of horses oc-curred too. Cattle, followed by horse, were the most common species in the early centuries AD; overall there was a significant presence of domestic animals grazing on grassland. Sheep/goat and pig were present but not apparently significant; but dog was well represented. Cereal was processed on a small or domestic scale, and flax may have been processed too, but seeds associated with arable agriculture were poorly represented and the insect fauna gave no indication of arable farming. *Stegobium paniceum*, a minor pest of stored grain, probably indicates acquired rather than grown cereal. Trees, stagnant water and various sorts of disturbed ground and scrub were present but the environs were a relatively open landscape with pasture an important element.

While much of such generalisation is based on later prehistoric contexts in this case, the evidence from the early centuries AD also suggested an open landscape, with even less woodland than was available in the preceding period. Similar pastureland conditions appear to have prevailed, arguably providing us with a marked case of 'landscape continuity' into the first millennium AD. Certainly the character of the landscape and its use seem to have been formed well before the Roman period, and to have continued irrespective of political change in the first century AD. The earliest documentary evidence for the area is in 1059 when it was a 'moor', not a settlement. 'Northmoor' does not appear in Domesday Book.

Clatchard Craig, Tayside (Close-Brooks 1986)

Morphologically, Clatchard Craig is a small hillfort and therefore a sur-prising, perhaps even unjustified, example of a 'farm' to use here; yet many of the places in which people lived in the west and north of Britain were ba-sically small enclosures, so in at least two major features it is representative. In any case, here we are primarily concerned with a site's function, not its social status; and even if the site was of a 'princely' or similar nature, it would still necessarily be linked into a local agrarian economy at this time. Nevertheless, it was (the site has been destroyed) apparently much too large for a mere farm, for its D-shaped plan of five lines of ramparts, each curving south above an east–west cliff face, occupied 2.27 ha. It is used as an example, nevertheless, because the innermost enclosure was only some 1850 m² in area, less than 10 per cent of the size of the site overall, and it was from there alone that excavation produced evidence of habitation. This included a late, well-built hearth in a possibly rectangular structure. Furthermore, the inhabitants were of 'a farming community' and, unlike the great majority of enclosed upland settlements, Clatchard Craig is well dated. Its five radiocarbon dates clearly indicate the mid-first millennium AD for its construction (rampart 1 itself very probably between the mid-fifth and the mid-seventh century).

All the dates came from oak used in the construction of the ram-parts, but we cannot know whether such wood was acquired locally or imported. Apart from a fragment of an artefact of hazel – to which the same caveat applies – that is virtually the only direct environmental evidence available for this site. The location and appearance of the site itself suggests relatively high-status occupants. Some of the material evidence indeed reinforces such an impression for it included a few objects of glass, shale, silver and bronze, and one rare tin (or tin-bronze) decorated disc. There was also clear evidence of metal-working, specifically in this case the manufacture of iron using low-level technology, and the making of penannular brooches. Spindle-whorls indicated that the humdrum task of weaving was also carried out – a common sort of evidence through-out Britain in the first millennium. Indeed, while the metal-working is of considerable interest in its own right, overall the material evidence, in its very ordinariness and small quantity, is probably representative of many a less prominent homestead.

The evidence for farming and food preparation and consumption was unremarkable. Stone artefacts included rotary quern-stones, though we cannot know whether the grain they ground was grown in the fort's own fields or brought from elsewhere. Querns of themselves do not prove local cultivation. Iron artefacts included a possible 'spud', a tool used for cleaning spades or weeding. The evidence of animal bones indicated the presence of pigs, cattle and sheep; animals were probably being killed and butchered on the site as well as being consumed there; at least some bones were gnawed, probably by dogs. Animal husbandry may well have been based on extensive grazing of cattle and sheep under cowherds and shepherds for as much of the year as possible, perhaps bringing herds and flocks back in winter to feed between the ramparts on carefully cultivated hay.

Green Shiel, Lindisfarne (Brown et al. 1998)

On the same tidal island of Lindisfarne famed for its early medieval monastery, excavations since 1988 have sought to examine a near-contemporary secular farm complex. A summary by those involved in the investigation meets our requirements exactly so is quoted almost in full:

> The site consists of a group of five buildings and associated yards, now located in an area dominated by sand dunes. The occupation is dated by nineteen coin finds to the middle decades of the ninth century (*circa* AD 835–871). At least two of the structures were probably dwelling houses, divided laterally into areas for animal and human shelter. The buildings are usually over 20 m long but crudely made with wide, irregularly coursed walls . . . there are few artefacts, suggesting either poverty of material culture, or a short period of occupation, or both . . . Cattle dominated the animal bone assemblage . . . and an analysis of material from [one building] indicates that some 45 per cent of the total number of animals recorded were calves under two years of age at death. More cows than bulls are present . . . The age distribution and the preponderance of female animals over males suggest a cattle economy based on dairying. To the south is an area of broad rig and furrow ploughing which may be contemporary with the site and which was certainly not covered by sand until the sixteenth century. (Brown *et al.* 1998, 139)

Other reasons for the sparsity of artefacts could include the possibility that most of the material culture was in wood and other organic materials, or that the inhabitants left only after carefully gathering up their goods and cleaning up the site – perhaps they liked to leave it in good order because they intended to come back? The paper cited, however, seeks to demonstrate that 'the site was abandoned for socio-political reasons almost certainly well before the environment became marginal due to sand dune migration'. Elsewhere, the excavators draw attention to the fact of the site's survival and discovery as a result of the inhabitants' use of stone for building, a break with the Northumbrian tradition of vernacular building in timber; and to the existence of other, broadly contemporary farmsteads in northern England with stone-based structures 'in what would now be considered marginal areas' (O'Sullivan and Young 1995, 88).

An overview

Farms in the first millennium AD in truth deserve a book of their own. The above short treatment of such a large amount of evidence and ideas is admittedly partial and unsatisfactory; but from it and the other 99.9 per cent of the material perhaps six general points emerge.

1. Farms in the first millennium, as in the second and doubtless third, existed in considerable variety, in terms of regional diversity of form, size and function.

2. Nevertheless, they demonstrate a functional consistency and a basic homogeneity of form despite the variety – 'a farm is a farm for a' that'.

3. A constant difference, economic and functional expressed in form and location, was that between arable and pastoral farms; though an absolute difference was at the edges of the range only, for most farms were engaged in mixed farming, varying primarily in their emphases, and not absolutely distinct.

4. Farms span archaeological and historical periods quite happily; changes regarded by students as significant for political and chrono-logical reasons do not automatically, perhaps not even characteristi-cally, lead to the abandonment or creation of farms.

5. Farms changed through time in details of building forms and mor-phology, nationally, regionally and locally though not necessarily synchronously; but their biggest change was distributionally, where their location appears – as now – extremely sensitive to external and medium-term factors such as economics, demographics, tenure and climate, expressed in particular along marginal interfaces.

6. Given such changes, and yet also the basic diversity, no particular merit seems to exist in considering farms in historico-racial terms. Explanations of changes in farms in Britain do not lie primarily in the ethno-cultural domain, nor are differences between farms in, say, England in AD 300 and AD 800 necessarily explained or clarified by labelling such as 'Romano-British farms' and 'Anglo-Saxon farms' respectively.

7 | Fields

[W]ith what fresh eyes I could see a field, this field. It was no longer just a bit of earth.

COLLIS 1975, 39

Definitions

We do not actually know the British word for 'field'. Our sense of ignorance can only be inflated by the thought that there were probably several. How indeed did first-millennium people talk about fields? Following the introduction of Latin, some at least must surely have used a word or words derived from *acer*, 'a field', a word underlying not only the English 'acre' but also the loan-word *erw* in both Welsh and Old Cornish. The only non-Latin field-word common to the other three languages is *park/parc*, an enclosed piece of land, introduced in an Anglo-Norman context. Otherwise, many of the Celtic words seem to have begun as simply terms for small utilised or physically defined units of land, some perhaps with reference to actual boundaries. The Welsh *cae*, Cornish *ke*, for example, meaning a hedge or field-wall, also came to mean, in Wales, 'a field'.

The modern English 'field' is of course from OE *feld*, of Teutonic derivation, though *feld* did not carry the modern meaning of 'field' until late Anglo-Saxon contexts. Indeed, its meaning varied regionally and changed through time. Before the tenth century it often meant the opposite of what we normally mean now: *feld* = 'open country', as distinguished from, for example, woodland. A place-name like Felton, Northumberland, is then describing a 'settlement in open land' – as indeed it still is today, on the edge of largely treeless moorland. *Feld* meaning specifically arable land seems to be a development very late in our period, perhaps only in the second half of the tenth century; it never meant *enclosed* field, arable or pasture in the first millennium (Gelling 1992a, 235–45). We can nevertheless be assured that at least some people in Britain were using the word, spoken as well as written, in communicating about rural matters in the centuries leading up to 1000 AD.

Plate XVIII   Fields and tracks of the early centuries AD on Fyfield Down, Wiltshire. Ignored by modern tracks, two clearly defined but long-abandoned double-banked tracks – from *top right* and across the *bottom* of the plate – meet at a T-junction, *centre bottom*, which has attracted a probable small settlement. All form part of a 'Romanised countryside' with villages and farms connected by a network of local communications winding through a landscape of small, enclosed arable fields. Here, those with west-facing lynchets reflecting the bright, low sunlight on the *left* were enclosed in the later first century AD by dry-stone walls, soon covered by plough-soil. Later reverting to pasture, the fields were briefly recultivated in the thirteenth century as is indicated by the overlying ridge and furrow.

As *feld* implies, much of Britain remained unenclosed throughout the first millennium but a lot of such land was nevertheless within the food-production system, albeit at a relatively extensive level of use and a low-intensity productivity. It is a moot point whether such areas should be regarded as unenclosed field systems or even a series of very large unenclosed fields, but we would not wish to debar them here simply because they were in most cases extensive pastures, not arable. Clearly two issues of definition arise: are fields defined by being enclosed and/or by their land-use? The answer seems to be 'no' in both cases. 'Enclosure' and 'field' are not synonymous, nor are 'field' and 'arable' or 'cultivation'.

Fields, whether or not arranged in field 'systems', are fairly basic in our perspective here for they covered much of first-millennium Britain and much of the agrarian activity of that millennium occurred within them.

They were present extensively and in some variety in the Britain invaded by the Romans (Fowler 1981a; 1983a). We have no contemporary, distinctive name or names for them, however, so a name had to be invented for them when they were discovered, largely through air photography, in the 1920s. ' "Celtic" fields' was a name chosen to draw the distinction between these generally small, rectangular fields stretched in a skein across the landscape and long, thin strips of land arranged in furlongs in 'open' fields characteristic, as was then believed, of 'Saxons' or 'Anglo-Saxons'. 'Celtic' fields is a deeply unsatisfactory phrase now, for several reasons which need not detain us, but no agreement exists about an alternative as an umbrella term, so we continue to use it here. We now know, however, that, within the generality of 'Celtic' fields, a variety of field types, and of types of field system, existed in Britain throughout the second and first millennia BC and through at least the first half of the first millennium AD (and we suspect somewhat later too). We also know of later prehistoric and later fields which are not in any sense 'Celtic'. Furthermore, 'Celtic' fields were conceptualised monopolistically as a type of arable field, distracting attention from the equally important pastoral side of the landscape and economy. Where possible, therefore, we shall describe salient characteristics of fields and field systems, rather than pretend that to use the phrase ' "Celtic" fields' is sufficient explanation in itself (Pl. XVIII).

The extent and variety of arable field systems increased during the early centuries AD, largely within the British or 'Celtic' tradition but with Roman influences adding villa field systems, and expansions on to coastal wetlands as around the Severn estuary (Rippon 1999). We have very little specific or precise information about fields for the next three to four centuries but overall it seems best to assume that British tradition, whether continuing to be refined by Roman influence or not, remained as the basis for the field systems over the whole country. By AD 800, if not in the eighth century, changes in the organisation of field systems were beginning to occur, and during the ninth and tenth centuries much diversity in field morphology and field system organisation appeared in numerous local arrangements seemingly breaking away from British and 'Roman' predecessors. Nevertheless, in parts of lowland England, the principal field boundaries evolved directly from Romano-British or prehistoric systems of land division (Williamson 1999, whose summary we henceforth largely follow in this passage). By 1086, open fields existed across the Midlands from Dorset to Yorkshire with the 'arable land divided into strips or *lands*, grouped into bundles or *furlongs*. These in turn were grouped into two, three or four large fields one of which lay fallow each year, and open to the grazing of the village livestock' (p. 183). 'Open field' was by no means a standard system of land allotment or working, however, and a

Plate XIX   The pre-Norman ridge and furrow at Gwithian, Cornwall, survives as the slightest of earthworks on a south-facing slope beside the now-silted-up inlet represented by the hummocky area in the centre of the photograph. The ridges lie up and down the slope at right angles to the modern tracks across the lower half of the photograph. The mound, *upper left centre*, was the site of the contemporary settlement.

considerable amount of difference was exhibited within the regions using it. Further, much of lowland England, East Anglia for example, as well as the greater part of Britain to west and north, was not using that system. So given a range from prehistoric-type 'Celtic' fields to open field systems with strip fields, variety rather than homogeneity was the characteristic of the fieldscape at the end of the millennium and during the eleventh century.

One useful definition of 'field systems' is 'the layout of agricultural holdings and the organisation of cropping within them' (Williamson 1999, 183). The essence of the concept 'field' seems to be similarly twofold: the definition of an area of land to create a terrestial space where agrarian functions can be pursued in reasonably controlled environmental circumstances. An advantage of such an abstract definition is that discussion about enclosure is then clearly seen as a second-tier issue, that is about a particular form of defining an area of land and of controlling its use.

Modes of enclosure (with a wall, hedge or fence, for example), to create particular field shapes and sizes (square or rectilinear, for example), for particular uses (growing cereals or grazing sheep, for example), then become third-level matters. Such issues as the height of the enclosing wall, the size of the square field and the species of cereal to be grown in it all then become fourth-level matters, of historic interest and local importance, no doubt, but nevertheless of relatively less significant detail.

A fair deal of academic debate about such matters has failed to make such or similar distinctions and has consequently, in concentrating on fourth- and lower-level matters, not always attended to the 'big picture'. Conversely, many a work, particularly secondary books, has come up with generalisations not firmly grounded in the sort of evidential detail characteristic of those lower levels of the hierarchical model. Yet it is at those levels of detail that the student has to make interpretative decisions about the detail, and that the farmer at the time had to make pragmatic decisions. It was more important, for example, for the latter to make the right decision about the height of his fence around the area in which he wished to shear his sheep than to ponder too long about whether such a temporarily fenced area constituted an 'enclosed field' or not. Similarly, he would be well aware of which fields were his, whether or not they lay in a compact block, forming a field system, or whether they were scattered in different places around his locality. The important point was the ability of his holding to provide a livelihood for him and his family. That it may or may not have contained a field 'system' was not the way farmers thought of their land in the first millennium. A 'field system' is a modern concept useful to academics, spilling out across time and the landscape from the phrases 'open field system' and its derivatives 'common field system' and 'three field system'. The word 'system' does not appear in contemporary documents.

Arable/pastoral

One problem in academic use of the 'field system' concept is the tendency to try to characterise such a system as being 'arable' or 'pastoral'. In practice, land, whether or not parcelled up into enclosed fields, could be used for *both* rather than exclusively for one or the other. Even within one year – and we can be certain this was happening in the first millennium – the same field or field system could produce a crop from arable and then provide good autumn pasture on the stubble. Over several years, the use of a field could be changed in the normal course of local management practice, resting an arable field in fallow for a year, for example, or rotating its use on a, say, five-year cycle, through a series of crops, including grass for hay or pasture. Furthermore, on a longer-term cycle, perhaps more to do with climatic or economic trends than local practice, a field system could broadly change its function from arable to pasture and *vice versa*. In such circumstances, as we can see over large areas of the British landscape today, a change from arable to pasture, for example, means that a former system of cultivated fields ceases to operate as a system – its field boundaries become irrelevant – but the land itself does not likewise fall out of use. Its use merely changes: cattle or sheep graze where cereal waved. Not only can we assume all three such changes occurred in the first millennium; in places we can actually see or infer the first two types in documentary sources and detect examples of the last archaeologically.

Ownership

That general caution is necessary now that Britain has produced more examples of first-millennium fields and field systems than it is possible even to mention in one brief chapter. Such was not the case, particularly for the second half of the millennium, even a quarter century ago (cf. Fowler 1976). The topic is even more extensive if we take account of Ireland, where some of the best field systems in the British Isles occur in a generally well-recorded context (Edwards 1996, Figs. 20 and 21; Kelly 1998). We see there, as elsewhere, that ownership tends to be very closely associated with ideas of both definition and control, though 'ownership' may be as much and as often of rights as it is of pieces of land. A distinction between a land-area and land-tenure is often critical in agrarian societies, not just in Britain and Ireland, and was apparently well known to people in the documented parts of our topic (and therefore presumably likewise in the undocumented parts).

   Kelly (1998) is able to grasp that particular nettle in seventh- to eighth-century Ireland in his book (esp. chapters 11, 'Farm lay-out', and 12, 'Land-tenure'). His chapter 11 includes 'Fields and greens' where it is possible to identify, and distinguish between, infield and outfield, the latter in one case containing tilled fields. Nevertheless, 'The written sources tell us about field boundaries [p. 370] but rather little about the fields themselves' although they mention 'cornfield', 'woad-garden' and 'orchard'. It also seems possible to correlate archaeologically detectable, small, roughly rectangular fields radiating outwards around some raths, with a written form of land-holding called *airlise* (Norman and St. Joseph 1969, 64–5; Kelly 1998, 368). Such detail about physicality and function contrasts with the tenor of Kelly's chapter 12, which contains much of relevance to Britain. We can but exemplify by quoting: 'A distinction is made [in seventh- to eighth-century law-texts] between a person's inherited share of kin-land . . . and land which he has acquired personally . . . [and they also] provide information on the entitlement of wives or sons to veto or defer contracts which might affect their economic well-being' (pp. 399–400).

This Irish evidence primarily stresses the normality in first-millennium society of a basic legal distinction literally in the field, here as in contemporary Anglo-Saxon England (from which we could have used analogous evidence). It is that distinction between, on the one hand, the 'hard' reality of structures and functions in the landscape like fields and cultivation and, on the other, 'soft' realities of kinship and tenure which actually held the whole together. In other words, there is far more to the consideration of fields than their shape, size or archaeological context; and without documents it is virtually impossible to perceive that tenurial dimension.

Categorisation of fields (Fig. 7.1)

Nevertheless, at least for academic purposes, it is necessary to impose some sort of framework on the evidence that archaeology has produced, not least because most of it occurs without specific documentation. Bowen (1978, 117) tentatively reached for a morphological distinction embedded in technique and function: 'considerable later prehistoric and Romano-British development [of "Celtic" fields] . . . in these later periods [compared to the second and early first millennia BC] there are indications of fields being enlarged, of new long types, called by the author "Celtic" long fields which . . . suggest the introduction of new techniques and, very likely, new crops . . . In the Roman period the existence of asymmetric winged shares, and thus by certain inference fixed mould-board ploughs allows the possibility of ridge and furrow'. (See below for ridge and furrow; and chapters 8–10 for ploughs, shares and crops.) Another reaction is to reach for a typology. Riley (1980), for example, faced with the task of making initial sense of a large amount of hitherto unknown evidence of early fields in the north Midlands, devised a typology of field system plans labelled 'brickwork', 'nuclear' and 'irregular' (also summarised graphically in Muir and Muir 1989, 28). Such morphological distinctions embrace most of the material touched on here but one suspects that, except at the grossest level, there is not much correlation between field-shape and time, process or product. Nor do we propose a strictly chronological approach because it is so difficult to date so much of the material. In any case, what is the date of a field – its original creation, its use, its reuse, its alternative use, its abandonment, its absorption into a different type of field system or land-use?

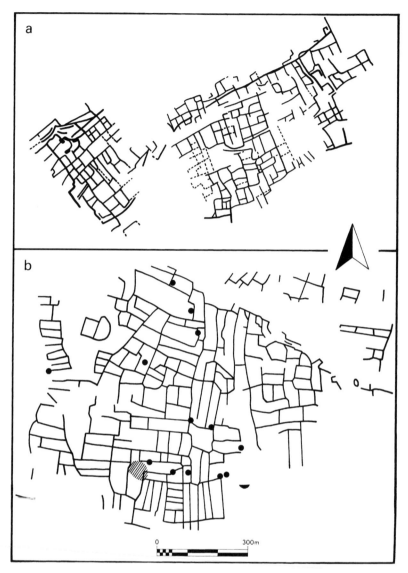

Fig. 7.1 Plans: (a) first-millennium field systems in Europe: a. the general type, b. Skörbaek Heath, Denmark; (b) opposite, schematic representation of some first-millennium field systems in Britain, following the categorisation and criteria in the text; *top two panels*: both category 1a: two widely different examples of category 1 ('continuing prehistoric system') fields coming under criterion (a) ('abandoned in the first-millennium'): *left*: 'Celtic' fields, southern England, with enclosed settlement; *right*: unenclosed settlement with cord rig in large enclosed fields, north Britain; *middle two panels*: two different examples of reuse of earlier fields: *left*: 2a ('adaptation of a prehistoric system', the whole 'abandoned in the first millennium'): as commonly happened in the early centuries AD, 'Celtic' fields converted into larger fields by taking out or overploughing some boundaries and superimposing a new enclosed farm within earlier arrangements; *right*: 3a ('new field system created on top of a relict field field system', the whole 'abandoned in the first millennium'): ignoring earlier

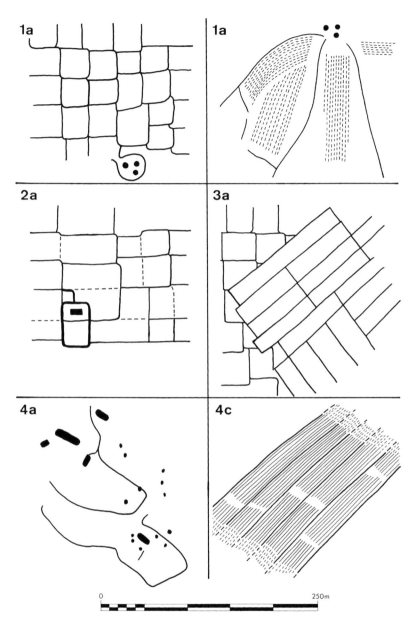

Caption for Fig. 7.1 (*cont.*)   arrangements and superimposing a new system of typically
'Roman long fields'; *bottom two panels*: two morphologically very different models, both of
the later first millennium: *left*: 4a ('new field system . . . abandoned in the first millennium')
large irregular enclosures, not necessarily for arable, with 'Pitcarmick' houses and cairns;
right: 4c ('new field system [which] continued in use into the second millennium when it was
abandoned'): large regular, linear enclosures as swathes across the landscape, subdivided
into long, narrow fields as inferred in late Saxon eastern England (an alternative model
could be of long fields radiating out from a nucleated village).

Edwards (1996), in contrast, echoing Irish law-texts (Kelly 1998, 389), uses a three-part division based on the potential and state of the land in considering Irish material, broadly clumping it into cultivable and uncultivable land (not cultivated and uncultivated). She categorises cultivable land into three grades:

1. level, clear of undergrowth and persistent weeds, and sufficiently fertile for a range of crops to flourish without manure;
2. on uplands;
3. land yet to be cleared of woodland with an axe.

Her perspective, however, is very much that of the arable farmer. A danger of any one template is indeed that it is likely to colour the resulting perspective.

There are in truth, with this material as with other sets of data, numerous ways in which to organise it. A chronologically led categorisation is tempting for, despite the above remarks, at least an outline temporal framework is discernible in the first millennium AD. It suggests that arable fields of the first millennium present themselves in three categories:

1. 'dead' archaeological field systems of undoubted pre-first-millennium AD date, found by modern archaeologists and not necessarily perceived as part of their landscape by first-millennium persons;
2. actual, archaeologically attested, physically surviving fragments of 'dead' fields used in the first millennium;
3. fields which survive, not as archaeological remains, but as patterns extant in the living landscape (this class perhaps being actually the main evidence if we could but see it).

We propose to adapt that model here into a more formal framework based on a more contextual approach. We can immediately then see tracts of countryside in the first millennium covered with abandoned prehistoric field systems, i.e. relict landscapes in the eyes of first-millennium people (if they noticed them at all). Into this category would fall many field systems of the second millennium BC, long abandoned as working units even if the land they occupied was now being used for extensive grazing. We will not include them, however, in our first-millennium categorisation for, except where they were reused or adapted (categories 1 and 2 below), they were 'dead' as field systems. By definition, the following categorisation can only deal with evidence which is known and therefore available for study. But that is an important caveat: it is distinctly possible that extensive areas of first-millennium field system survive in the existing landscape, but as yet unrecognised and therefore incapable of being studied. We have in mind not so much now-redundant archaeological remains – relict field systems – as more particularly 1000- to 2000-year-old physically surviving field arrangements embedded within the living fabric of the extant countryside, e.g. field boundaries now in use as parish boundaries (Pl. VII).

We can identify five main categories of first-millennium fields and field systems: those which were

1. a continuing prehistoric field system;
2. an adaptation of a prehistoric field system;
3. a new field system created on top of a relict field system;
4. a new field system created on land without remains of earlier fields;
5. a new field system imposed, as an act of reorganisation, on a working landscape.

The distinctions may be fine and in reality the categories tend to merge into a continuum; but they are nevertheless suggested by actual examples as much as a review of theoretical possibilities. We can then filter those categories through an additional rather than an alternative criterion relating to historicity and current status: thus fields/field systems which

(a) were abandoned in the first millennium;
(b) were abandoned in the first millennium and reused in the second;
(c) continued in use into the second millennium when they were abandoned;
(d) have continued in use into the third millennium.

The examples below illustrate – again somewhat briefly - some combinations of criteria 1–5 and a–d in a selection across Britain and through the first millennium.

1a. A continuing prehistoric field system abandoned in the first millennium AD (Fig. 7.3)

Until the 1990s, it would have been easy to provide examples of this type, for it was assumed that many of the 'Celtic' field systems of southern Britain fitted this description exactly. Now, a few exceptions like Chalton, Hampshire, where prehistoric 'Celtic' fields were in use in the early centuries AD, seem to be the odd ones out. There, however, it is not absolutely certain that that use had been continuous, so the case might well fall into what now seems to be the norm. A number of investigated cases have shown 'Celtic' fields to be either abandoned in prehistoric times or remodelled, even created, in the first millennium AD, so it can no longer be assumed that such fields normally fall into this category (1a). On the Berkshire Downs, for example, as thorough an investigation using excavation as has yet been carried out pointed fairly unambiguously to the extents of 'Celtic' fields there originating in the early centuries AD (Bowden *et al.* 1993; see also Overton and Fyfield Downs, (2a) and (3a) below).

Some of the late prehistoric but otherwise characteristically imprecisely dated field systems of west Cornwall and north Wales are much better candidates, for there is in general little doubt of their pre-Roman origins, nor of their continuing use in the early centuries AD. The real doubt is how long they continued to be used, but arguments tend to centre around the middle centuries of, rather than after, the first millennium (Herring 1993; Kelly 1991). Otherwise, we have to turn to the 'invisible' field systems of river gravels and other soils where no surface remains survive. There we can work from a few cases where excavation has shown ditched late prehistoric fields to continue in use into the early centuries AD and infer that in general field systems of this category (1a) exist among the extensive evidence (cf. Pl. IV). Some systems survived, however, only into the middle decades of the very first century: all over the country, pre-Roman fields and perhaps even field systems were taken out by Roman structures, forts and other constructions, along Hadrian's Wall for example (Pl. VIII), and by roads in Wessex (Pl. I) and parts of East Anglia (Fig. 4.2).

2a.   *An adaptation of a prehistoric field system abandoned in the first millennium (Pl. XVIII)*

The note on category (1a) has already indicated that refugees from there would be found here. The Berkshire case has been mentioned; we look in a little more detail at another example where excavation has been applied to well-known 'Celtic' fields on Wessex chalk.

On Fyfield Down, at the south-west corner of the Marlborough Downs, Wiltshire, excavation tested three lynchets forming three sides of a 'Celtic' field where no ridge and furrow intruded (some lay immediately east; Fowler 2000c, chapter 7). Excavation was planned to illuminate both chronology and questions of why and how such large lynchets had accumulated on a natural slope of only 3 degrees. The main excavation, tantamount to sectioning a hillfort rampart, was through a lynchet nearly 3 m high (Fowler and Blackwell 1998, Fig. 26 and colour pl. 14). At the base of the topsoil was a scattering of potsherds mainly of the first to second centuries AD (and not later), presumably the accidental byproduct of manuring. The bulk of the cultivation may well, then, have taken place by soon after, if not before, AD 100, by which time the top of the lynchet, essentially the present ground surface, had reached its existing height above the old ground surface. Well down the slope of the scarp forming the front of the lynchet was a small drystone wall. It stood on a ledge only

15–25 cm wide and consisted entirely of smallish, broken sarsen stones packed around with large flints. It had never been a large structure, two or three courses at most probably constituting its original form. It would not therefore have kept animals in or out, so its most likely function, if not just decorative, was perhaps tenurial, marking the edge of a property as well as a field. For present purposes, its significance is its date: it had been inserted in the later first century AD into a prehistoric lynchet. This 'drystone-wall' phase of field remodelling on Fyfield Down is taken as fitting in with the locally widely attested period of rapid and substantial landscape reorganisation towards the end of the first century AD.

These famous Fyfield Down 'Celtic' field lynchets, undoubtedly pre-historic in origin, were nevertheless bounding fields being cultivated in their existing form *c.* AD 100 and were, at least in part, built. At an early stage of their last use, with drystone walling just showing among arable fields, the landscape would have looked somewhat different from the downland grass sheep-runs and horse-gallops of today, an aspect it finally began to acquire from the second century AD onwards. In southern Britain, this example probably represents a generality.

2b. *An adaptation of a prehistoric field system abandoned in the first millennium and reused in the second*

With the emphasis on 'adaptation', this category too is widespread (whether or not use was chronologically continuous). Two examples must suffice. Above the Breamish valley, Northumberland, extensive archae-ological landscapes survive, particularly 2 km south-west of the village of Ingram. There current research is establishing complex sub-surface sequences, mainly prehistoric, as well as analysing the surface evidence. Ridge and furrow of at least six varieties and of several periods from probably later prehistoric to post-medieval exists in what is now sheep-cropped pasture. It can be examined with no more trouble than visiting the area and walking out on to the valley sides in what is now the Northum-berland National Park.

Though much of the area included in the vertical air photograph (Pl. XX) is strikingly overlaid by medieval rig, at least some of this same ground is highly likely to have been cultivated in the first millennium AD and remains of that may well exist east (left) of the narrow valley of Middledean Burn. 'Romano-British rig' has been both claimed and denied in the central area where a settlement complex contains three sub-circular, enclosed farmsteads of the early centuries AD and a probably medieval rectilinear farm enclosure. A fourth early farmstead has been damaged by later ploughing (*right centre*). The D-shaped, bivallate enclosure (*top left*)

Plate XX Ridge and
furrow of at least six
varieties and of several
periods from probably
later prehistoric to
post-medieval on the
south side of the
Breamish valley, 2 km
south-west of Ingram,
Northumberland.

is a late prehistoric fort. The long, linear dykes overlying the ridge and
furrow may include elements of early enclosure but generally represent
a post-medieval land-use change from arable to pasture. It is difficult to
identify with certainty elements of first-millennium arable farming among
the plethora of detail but it seems highly likely that the spread of 'open
field' ridge and furrow is blanketing arable land cultivated in late prehistoric times and through at least some if not all of the first millennium.
The caveat is entered because the village name, Ingram, seems to derive
from the Old Norse element *-eng* betokening that 'pasture' or 'grassland'

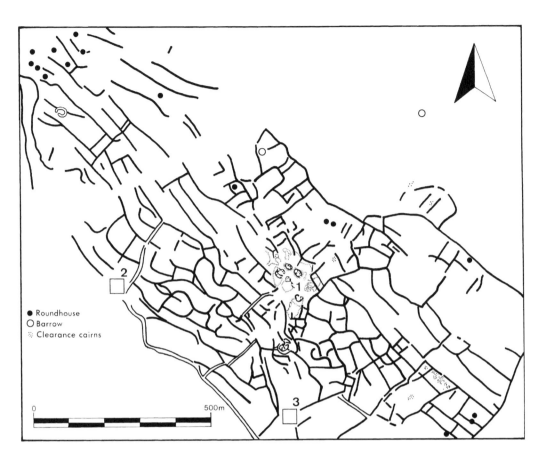

● Roundhouse
○ Barrow
⁖ Clearance cairns

0   500m

was a characteristic of the place. Perhaps, then, despite all the evidence on the ground for long-lived and various patterns of cultivation, by the end of the first millennium at latest the treeless sheep pasture of Pl. XX was already well established.

At the diametrically opposite corner of England, Chysauster and its surroundings in west Cornwall provide an example of a recently published modern, interdisciplinary study of a field system and associated features (Fig. 7.2; Smith 1996, here followed very closely, including verbatim in places). This provides much data and several insights into how at least one stretch of landscape may have developed and been used before and during the early centuries of the first millennium, and perhaps right through it and into medieval and modern times. The place is centred on a well-known and publicly accessible archaeological 'village' of curious structures rather ponderously called 'courtyard houses' by archaeologists (see chapter 5; Pl. XII). They have now been put into their farming and land-use contexts. Indeed, this work suggests that the settlement was inserted into an enclosed landscape of *existing* fields.

Fig. 7.2 Plan of late prehistoric/first-millennium AD field systems, Chysauster, west Cornwall (after Smith). 1. Courtyard-house village, 2. Carnaquidden Farm, 3. Chysauster Farm.

The overall study proposes that the earliest field system, of the second millennium BC, was largely modified by a more irregular and strongly lynchetted field pattern, probably associated with more intensive agriculture both in later prehistoric centuries and early in the first millennium AD. In general, the layout of all the fields on a generally south-facing slope of 4–7 degrees was rectilinear and followed the topography, with boundaries either contour-following or cross-contour. The contour-following boundaries are lynchetted, normally with a stone wall revetting the lynchet and rising above it. Typically the stone wall might be 2.2 m wide, 0.5 m high on the uphill side, 1.6 high on the downhill, indicating that the lynchet itself was 1.1 m high. The boundaries visible on the surface included, in addition to stone-faced lynchets on steeper slopes, unsupported stony lynchets on shallower slopes, stone banks incorporating orthostats, stone-faced earthen banks, and simple earth banks. Simple stony banks with some orthostatic embellishment relate to fields of the early centuries AD and earlier, and stone-faced earth banks relate to probably medieval reuse of the area. Lanes passed through the field systems, but tracks are later.

The present-day pattern of small, apparently irregular, strongly lynchetted, stone-walled fields which perpetuate ancient field patterns are likely to be no later than the courtyard house settlements which are themselves of the first centuries AD. 'The medieval field pattern developed within the confines of the pre-existing layout.' It seems that 'in the typical West Penwith hamlet the farmers' holdings were scattered through the small rectangular fields, which acted as the equivalent to strips in a system of subdivided arable (Herring 1987, 33)' (Smith 1996). The pattern of maintained field walls at Chysauster Farm is largely unchanged from the 1843 Tithe map.

Excavation of field boundaries showed evidence of long periods of modification and lynchet accumulation, including evidence of podzolisation and erosion. Above the Chysauster settlement, soil loss may have been as much as 50–70 cm from the negative lynchets. The typical brown podzolic soils of the slopes below the settlement may consequently be in part colluvial in origin. It is possible therefore that field boundaries were constructed to help control this later prehistoric or early historic soil erosion. Certainly arable agriculture was contemporary with podsolisation in later prehistory and the early centuries AD. The cultivation techniques in use then led to deterioration in soil status and to soil erosion. The changes, through deforestation, cultivation and erosion, influenced the plant communities in the nearby valley. Here is direct evidence of what has often been suspected in general: that exploitation in the

'Roman' centuries led to degradation and field abandonment in the mid–
first millennium.

Further interpretation, as in using other types of evidence, has to rely
on hints and judgement rather than merely follow hard scientific fact.
The landscape above the courtyard house settlement may have been divided into arable fields up to around 200 m in altitude, with grazing of
the moorland above. The substantially terraced fields immediately adjacent to the courtyard houses were probably subject to more intense
or prolonged ploughing than the more lightly terraced rectilinear fields
which, in the early centuries AD, were perhaps pastoral 'outfield' of the
main settlement. All phases of the settlement were basically exploiting the
same fairly narrow topographic zone, on the favourable south-west-facing
slope between approximately 130 m and 180 m OD with better-drained
soils than both the moorland plateau above and the valley floor below
(Pl. XII).

3a.   A new field system created on top of a relict field system and abandoned in the first millennium

Several good examples of this category are now recorded, for example on
Totterdown, Fyfield Down, Wiltshire, where markedly rectangular fields
are imposed on prehistoric fields (Bowen and Fowler 1966; republished
with excavation data in Fowler 2000a; 2000 c). The type of field, consisting
of long, relatively narrow enclosures, often occurring in this category was
recognised at the start of the modern phase of field research by Bowen
(1961, Fig. 4C) and nominated as likely to be 'Roman'. One of his notable
examples on the chalk of Chisenbury Warren has recently been dated by
excavation to the early centuries AD, and a similar date has been confirmed
for the Totterdown fields.

Judging again that very probably we are dealing with a generality, that
is with the recultivation in the early centuries AD of an area in new fields
of distinct, contemporary systems, we take but one example, deploying a
little detail. It lies on Overton Hill, Wiltshire, immediately north of the
A4 road where the modern Ridgeway strikes north across the Marlborough
Downs (Fowler 2000c, Fig. 2.5). The field system is in two parts, both
on the north side of the Roman road from *Cunetio* to *Aquae Sulis*. Its
southern part is aligned north–south, at right angles to the Roman road, a
fact regarded as highly suggestive dating evidence. This distinctive block
of fields consists largely of long, rectilinear fields characteristically about
70 m long but only about 15 m wide, a length to width ratio of around 1:5.
This morphology separates them visually from the typically 50 m square
fields of the surrounding field systems of the second millennium BC which

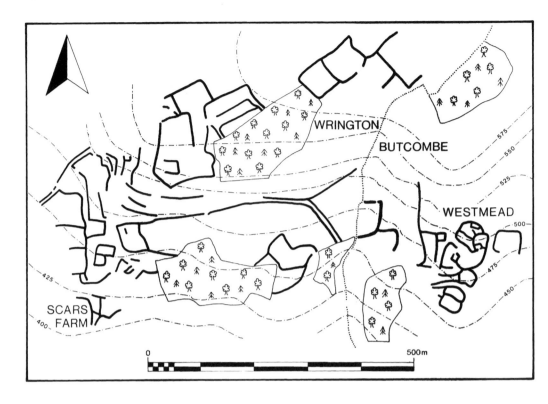

Fig. 7.3 Plan of early first-millennium fields with trackways and settlements (Scars Farm and Westmead; cf. Fig. 6.1a), overlooking the Vale of Wrington and Lye Hole villa (Fig. 7.4a) to the south, Somerset (from Fowler).

they both overlie and have obliterated. Further north is a contiguous block of fields characterised by an orientation 7° west of True North with distinctive rectilinear fields about 100 m long or longer and 40–50 m wide. These are not just larger than conventional 'Celtic' fields but of a different shape and proportions, i.e. roughly 2:1 or more, up to 5:1. Overall, the Overton Hill system covers some 3.6 km north–south by 0.6 km, an area of almost 200 ha.

Strip-like fields are also characteristic of a second example in this category, chosen for their rarity at the moment in dating between the second and fourth centuries. The site is that of the former sewage settlement tanks between the western ends of the two main runways at Heathrow airport; the archaeology is a typical complex of features on a gravel plateau in the Thames valley (Fig. 7.5). The fields form a group just as firmly overlying several earlier phases of field system as on Overton Hill, but their present ambience suffers in comparison and their archaeological context is invisible. The system overlay and cut through ditches and other features of mid to late Bronze Age date, but in part respected some features of mid-Iron Age date. The fields themselves were defined by parallel ditches aligned in a north-east to south-west direction, with shorter lengths at

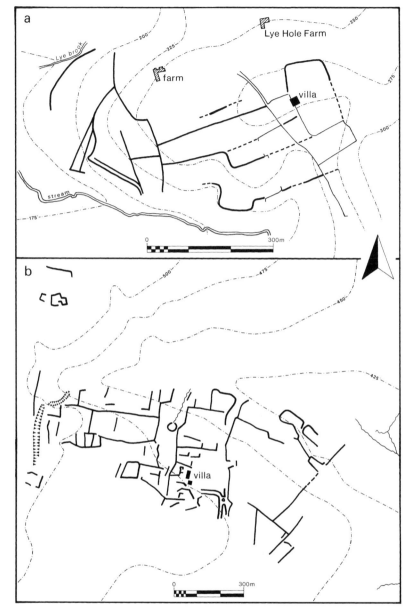

Fig. 7.4 Plans of
Roman villa fields:
(a) Lye Hole, Somerset;
(b) Barnsley Park,
Gloucestershire (from
Fowler).

right angles forming rectangular enclosures, presumably the actual fields.
The whole area so enclosed was of some 5 ha; the main alignments were
about 32 m apart, widening to about 45 m, with individual fields roughly
32 m × 15 m. Overall, the pattern is similar to other Roman examples of
field systems, for example that on Overton Hill, but the dating to a period
within the second to fourth centuries is of particular interest. Unfortunately, there is no later cultivation here for some considerable time so it is

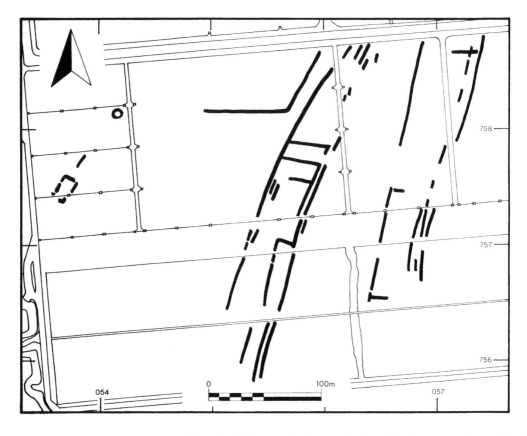

Fig. 7.5 Plan of
second/third-century
AD field system, defined
by ditches, excavated in
advance of the proposed
Terminal Five,
Heathrow Airport,
Middlesex, 1999.

not possible to link the morphology or the local land-use to early medieval
arrangements.

4a. *A new field system created on land without earlier field remains and abandoned in the first millennium (Pl. XIX; Fig. 7.8)*

Our sample of this category has to be relatively poor for there are many
instances. It is perhaps the commonest in Britain if only because the very
abandonment of new, first-millennium field systems has frequently created archaeological remains which archaeologists can find and study. That
is not, however, absolutely true: there must be many cases of abandoned
field systems having been subsequently buried by such as erosion products like alluvium in the Thames valley (Lambrick 1992) and windblown
deposits such as the sand which covered plough-marks at Gwithian and
ridge and furrow at West Stow. The paradox that we can quote such examples which have been found does not invalidate the general point. We
can nevertheless discern five main types of field and field system within
this category:

(i)   new Roman villa field systems of the first four centuries AD;
(ii)   new non-villa field systems of the early centuries AD, in the British
       tradition but apparently under Roman influence;
(iii) new field systems in the British tradition, with variants, at various
       times throughout the millennium;
(iv)   new field systems of non-traditional British form in Anglo-Saxon
       contexts in the second half of the millennium;
(v)   new field systems in Scandinavian contexts in the second half of the
       millennium.

We cannot deal with examples of all such instances, but we will briefly
look at examples of all types except (v), well-summarised by Muir and
Muir (1989, chapter 2) and picked up in discussion below.

   (i) *Villa fields:* 'Villas would almost certainly have been surrounded by
extensive field systems, as illustrated by recent excavations at Roughground Farm, Gloucestershire. Here a villa built in the early second
century was surrounded by a series of rectangular enclosures (perhaps
paddocks), and larger open fields covering at least 15ha (Allen *et al* 1993)'
(Dark 2000, 81–2). Bowen (1961) first seriously explored the topic, providing examples; Applebaum (1972) discussed the topic learnedly and
speculatively. Rudston, N. Yorkshire, is another example with actual field
remains (Stead 1980); the surrounds of the villa at Castle Copse, Wiltshire,
suggest where the villa field system should have been, but the investigation
could not actually produce a plan of its lineaments (Hostetter and Howe
1997, Fig. 156, and pp. 138, 348 and 353 fn 16). We therefore revert to
one of the best examples where a system of actual fields surviving on the
ground could be physically associated with a villa, supported by excavated
evidence of structure and date.

   In Barnsley Park, Gloucestershire (Fig. 7.4; Fowler 1985), the system
covers at least 32 ha (80 acres) and is made up of mainly rectangular fields
characteristically some 27 m × 82 m, a ratio of breadth to length of 1:3.
The width (about 35 m) is a repeating measurement. The fields themselves
are now demarcated by very low banks, becoming small lynchets on the
gentle slope to the small stream on the north. Excavation showed these to
have no built structure within them, certainly not stone walls (*contra* the
caption in Taylor 1975, Fig. 7b), but interestingly pointed to a distinction
between them and stone-walled yards or paddocks immediately around
the farm buildings. In the fourth century, when the field system was in
use, its individual fields may well have been marked out – and how permanently? – only by unploughed baulks, variously distinguished by different
vegetation at different times of the year. Of course, it presumably did

not suffer from demarcation disputes since ownership lay with the villa estate, but in general it may well have looked remarkably like an open field of several centuries later. But how much later? Potsherds suggested arable cultivation (and manuring) continued through the fifth and sixth centuries at least, cultivated from somewhere other than the villa; and the medieval fields pushed up towards what is now the remnant Roman field system from the present village 0.5 km to the south. Medieval cultivation undoubtedly occupied land belonging to the villa and destroyed its field arrangements on that side (Fowler 1975b, Fig. 8.6).

(ii) This type is well exemplified by the Overton Hill fields (3a above), placed there because the fields are overlying British fields but otherwise a good example of the type of 'Celtic long field' in mind and typical of other field groups on Wessex chalk in particular, e.g. McOmish 1998. Our main example, however, chosen largely because in a part of England not often associated with 'ancient fields', comes from north Nottinghamshire and south Yorkshire, entirely the result of assiduous air photography in the 1970s by Riley (1980, chapter 3). He categorises 'field plans of the brick-work type, which resemble [in plan] the pattern formed by the joints in a brick wall'. Such systems often cover large blocks of land, up to 200 ha. The divisions are ditches, as much as 2 m wide and 1 m deep, defining long strips of land from about 50 to 100 m wide. These strips are divided by cross-ditches making up the fields and giving the impression of 'bricks' laid out across the landscape, albeit visible only as crop-marks. Despite an overall impression of cohesiveness and regularity in numerous field systems, in fact the systems show considerable variety, in size if not in shape. A 'normal' size is about 1.5 ha, with 83 per cent of the total number of measurable fields falling in the range 0.5–2.8 ha. Most fields are roughly twice as long as they are wide, but in the detail of Fig. 3, for example, lengths at Edenthorpe average about 160 m while ranging between about 100 and 200 m. At Barnby Moor an average is about 290 m but there seems a significant clustering of lengths around 275 m. Some fields are crossed by a Roman road but in general these systems seem to have been in use during the early centuries AD. Morphologically, they could readily be of the second millennium BC but, if they are indeed of the first half of the first millennium AD, then they provide another example of widespread landscape organisation, perhaps for both arable and pasture fields, about the time of, though not necessarily entirely after, the Roman Conquest. Whatever their date, caution would expect a process of development rather than an event for their creation, despite their arresting appearance. Nevertheless, as Riley (1980, 11, 15) observes, 'This was a planned system of land division, perhaps partly controlled by the physical geography, because the long boundaries tend to run at right angles to the general direction of the courses of the river, but it was not standardised, and there are differences in the field plans from north to south of the region.' The temptation to go further and think of them as largely a consequence of Conquest is apparent when he adds: 'The remarkable thing about these fields is their orderly planning, which may well have been set out in largely unoccupied territory.' Collectively, however, as a series of organised landscapes, Riley's discoveries did not come through into the medieval landscape in the sense of influencing its pattern in the way that early field remains did elsewhere, cf. group 4d below. They apparently fell into disuse – we know not why – and became lost and forgotten sometime in the middle years of the millennium.

(iii) New field systems in the 'British' tradition, with variants including 'Celtic' fields, continued to appear at various times throughout the millennium. At Roystone, Derbyshire, for example,

> fossilized field banks and terraces survive on a steep slope about 400 m south of the grange. Six low banks running up the steep slope dividing the natural shelves between can be seen on the ground . . . Excavations indicate that the hillside was terraced for allotments in late Roman times. Odd stones were probably placed against a thicket hedge to define a strip owned by each family. In some lights the narrow lines of lazy bed, spade cultivation, can be seen. Cultivating this slope was probably the last resort when pressure on other sources of food was becoming desperate. (Hodges undated; see also Hodges 1991, 79–91; cf. also Swaledale, Fig. 7.6).

The Vale of Wrington in north Somerset is another limestone area with several examples of early fields, very much in a Romanised context in the third to fourth centuries. One group is spread along a south-facing slope overlooking a villa with its own field system, with a marked morphological difference between them (Figs. 7.3 and 7.4b). Together, they both contrast and exemplify (Fowler 1975a; 1976). The fields associated with an excavated farmstead, perhaps on the villa estate, are similar to those in systems of small fields, squarish and irregular in shape, in use in the early Christian period in Ireland. Perhaps there they were often used for 'minor crops such as the woad mentioned in both legal and literary sources' (Kelly 1998, 371) but, given their characteristic contexts in Ireland (as well illustrated in Edwards 1996, Figs. 20, 21) and the widespread existence of such fields over much of Britain, they must have been cultivated for main crops too.

Fig. 7.6 Plan of
first-millennium fields
and settlements,
embedded in the existing
landscape of enclosure
(thin lines) in Swaledale,
West Yorkshire (after
Fleming 1998). The area
shown is about 800 m
wide west–east.

Field systems in this tradition have now been identified in eastern
Scotland, dating between the seventh and eleventh centuries AD. Some
such seem to find their contexts with buildings of Pitcarmick type
(chapter 6). In Glen Cochill one well-defined and distinct field system
covers some 4 ha (Fig. 7.7); along the Ballinloan Burn are 'six Pitcarmick-
type buildings and their associated field systems'. In addition, several
examples of strip fields 'may be linked to rig cultivation and perhaps date
to the first millennium AD or possibly later'. A further field system is
almost certainly associated with another settlement of Pitcarmick-type
buildings. It comprises a series of small, irregular fields about 0.5 ha in
area as well as a larger field (in excess of 3 ha). The large field contains
traces of three patches of rig, aligned on three different axes, and numerous clearance heaps, some of which are aligned with the rig and are
presumably associated with it (Cowley 1997, 162–70).

(iv) New field systems of non-traditional British form in Anglo–Saxon
contexts in the second half of the millennium are beginning to appear
archaeologically only very slowly. The Gwithian, Cornwall, example actually consists of two pieces of evidence, different in nature and date
(Fowler and Thomas 1962). The field, rather than a field system (Pl. XIX;
Fig. 7.8a), is a rectangular area of ridge and furrow which analogy would

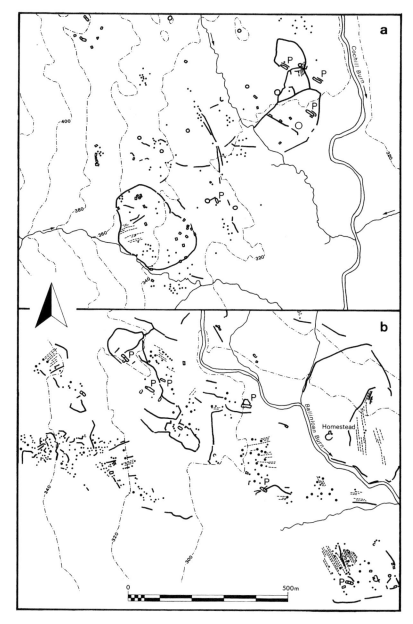

Fig. 7.7 Plans of first-millennium field systems, Perthshire: (a) west of the Cochill Burn, showing large, stone-walled enclosures, scattered cairns (black dots), hut-circles (open rings), sub-rectangular buildings ('Pitcarmick' houses), patches of rig (broken lines) and apparently unattached lengths of wall/dyke; (b) similar arrangements (expressed using the same symbols) on both sides of the Ballinloan Burn (after RCAHMS).

now suggest to be more likely to be a lazy-bed, or at least a patch of hand-dug ground, than a ploughed area. Not closely dated in itself, its context was nevertheless with one or more phases of the adjacent settlement in the eighth to ninth centuries. Quite separate from that 'field' were parallel plough-marks and clear traces in sand of turned furrows, of a field probably under cultivation in the ninth to tenth centuries. That a proper plough, with coulter and mouldboard, was in use is clearly indicated (chapter 9).

Fig. 7.8 Plans of
pre-Norman ridge and
furrow: (a) Gwithian,
Cornwall; (b) Hen
Domen, Montgomery-
shire (after Fowler, and
Barker and Lawson).

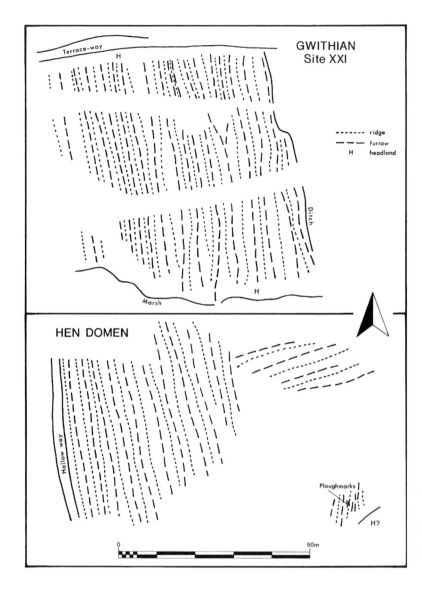

Such is also the case at the other long-known example of this sort of evidence late in the millennium, Hen Domen, Montgomery (Barker and
Lawson 1971; Fig. 7.8a). There field survey recorded narrow, slightly
curving ridge and furrow outside a Norman motte and bailey castle of
1071–86, the line of whose defences seems to have acknowledged the
field's existence (Musson 1994, 149). Excavation detected the same ridging, and parallel plough-marks, beneath its outer rampart (Higham and
Barker 2000). The possibility of aratral remains has subsequently been
entertained both beneath East Wansdyke, Wiltshire – that is, earlier than

c. AD 500 – and beneath the eighth-century Offa's Dyke in Shropshire
(Everson 1991).

4b. **A new field system created on land without earlier field
remains abandoned in the first millennium and reused in
the second**

Rightly famed for its Roman fort and much-visited adjacent stretches of
Hadrian's Wall (Pl. VIII), Housesteads, Northumberland, and the immediately surrounding area provide a 'window' into a northern, upland
agrarian landscape of rare complexity and detail. Stukeley hinted at its
presence even to the untrained eye (Crow 1995, Fig. 1); it is clearly visible
to us, and delineated in expert detail by RCHME in an unpublished plan
(of which Crow 1995, Fig. 69 is an inadequate version for present purposes; cf. Hedley 1931). The palimpsest of remains is, however, atypical in
that much of the earlier farming activity that it represents was to do with
its location in a military zone and close to a major fort; but, on the other
hand, the area was being farmed long after AD 400 and has remained a
favoured settlement location until the present (Crow 1995, 98–106). Indeed, placing the Housesteads evidence in this category is contentious.
In the first place, farming of this land before the Roman installations is
probable; in the second, it is uncertain whether farming actually ceased
here in any one of the several field systems in the second half of the millennium. Certainly, new arable arrangements were laid out at least three
times in the second millennium, with cultivation in the medieval period,
in the seventeenth and eighteenth centuries, and again in the nineteenth.

For long it was wondered whether any of the remains were of Roman
construction or even earlier date; answers have come from both fieldwork
and excavation. A distinct block of narrow fields lying up and down the
slope just up from the 'Roman well' could be of pre-fort date. On the north-
east of the fort, between it and Knag Burn, the Military Way cuts through a
group of small irregular fields which on its west is also apparently overlain
by the fort's wall (see Crow 1995, Fig. 69 for location). Immediately
south-west of the museum, excavation glimpsed a detail possibly of such
early fields: 'Traces of gullies and temporary enclosures of Roman date
were found, followed by a pit filled with domestic rubbish dateable to the
second century AD. The line of a fence had crossed the filled pit before the
radical creation of terraces running east to west across the hillside' (Crow
1995, 74–5). The fort's extra-mural settlement(s) also passed through a
timber phase, so 'the construction of the settlement in stone was a major
redevelopment and probably forms part of the wider reorganisation of
the landscape when the terraces were built in AD 200'. The terraces were

built up and fronted with stone revetments, carving the south-facing slope dropping from the fort into parallel 'steps' stretching 0.5 km to the west (Crow 1995, Figs. 48, 49). This event was clearly of great importance for the fort's garrisons and adjacent population, presumably responding to an urgent need for more cereal. It is also of considerable academic significance in that it has provided us, and the English landscape, with the only proven example of a flight of terraced fields of early first-millennium AD date in Britain. Despite their location in an apparently remote northern upland, at the time the place was at the cutting edge of Roman affairs, and with a direct line to Rome. We should probably therefore accept them for what they look like: not medieval strip lynchets, though clearly later strip cultivation has affected them, but Roman-style terraces in Mediterranean mode. Any enthusiasm for the idea should not, however, garnish it with grapes or olives.

4d. A new field system created on land without earlier field remains which continues in use into the third millennium

This category is growing significantly and has the highest potential as we refine our skills at detecting the old in the living landscape. Long-known individual examples include, from early in the millennium, Lye Hole villa in the Vale of Wrington, north Somerset, where some elements of the villa field system are perpetuated in existing field boundaries (Fig. 7.4a). From later come whole field systems such as that suggested at Povingdon, Dorset (Taylor 1975, Pl. II) and, showing 'traces of nucleal land and quillets of former hereditary land', the long-lived one at Llanynys, Denbighshire (Jones 1972, Fig. 45 and Pl. III). Now, the recognition has extended to whole landscapes, outstandingly in the two great wetland surveys of the Fens in the east and the Severn estuary in the west (Hall and Coles 1994; Rippon 1997).

5d. A new field system imposed, as an act of reorganisation, on a working landscape

This category may be the most significant of all. It emerges from category 4d but without the emphasis on the existence or otherwise of earlier field remains or continuity to the present (though, paradoxically, the permanence of these new systems may well be obscuring our perception of them where they have not been destroyed by, for example, modern Enclosure). The important, positive aspect of this category is to allow for large, new, planned field systems replacing, not relics, but whatever arrangements for land parcellation existed in a particular place at the time of the change. This possibility may have occurred locally before *c.* 900, e.g. when land newly granted to an ecclesiastical estate was being reviewed by its new owners. It was, however, first glimpsed as perhaps a general develop-ment in a specifically Scandinavian context in easten England (Finberg 1972a, 491–3) and has since been given credibility in Northamptonshire (Hall 1988) and in Yorkshire (Harvey 1983). In the former, a date around AD 900 and later is envisaged when reorganisation of field systems across the landscape could have taken place. In the latter, two periods were iden-tified as possibilities: in the late ninth century onwards, i.e. as part of the settlement of the land by incomers under new landlords in the Danelaw, and in the late eleventh century. On both occasions, favourable circum-stances may well have existed 'for the creation of planned field systems in the Wolds and Holderness' (Harvey 1983, 103).

Field boundaries

We have already touched on boundaries in considering varieties of field. Walls, hedges, fences, ditches and banks of various sorts are all evidenced, archaeologically, documentarily and both. Boyd (1985), for example, re-ports at Bar Hill, southern Scotland, on 'Fragments of some 45 well-preserved hawthorn branches 2–6 years old from an infilled ditch over-lain by the fort of *c* 142 AD. Their natural growth had been disturbed, suggesting that they may have been from a hedge.' Edwards (1996, 53) discusses four types of documented Irish boundary: a ditch dug with a spade where the spoil was piled up to make a bank, and a stone-built wall, both around arable fields; a stout oak fence cut with an axe to partition woodland; and, most commonly, a fence constructed with a bill-hook and made of posts and wattles with a blackthorn crest along the top to prevent animals from jumping over (see Kelly 1998, 372–8 for Irish field bound-aries generally). One wonders whether that sort of detail for such specific purposes applied to, for example, the suggested thorn hedges around fields of the early centuries AD in an open landscape at Farmoor, Oxfordshire (Lambrick and Robinson 1979, 121–2). And the nature of the bound-ary itself can even depend on translation: was the 'hedge' erected by Ida of Northumberland around his new settlement at Bamburgh in AD 547, for example, a hedge of the sort just mentioned or a 'hedge' as in Cornwall still, that is a large, solid earth bank with stone faces?

Field contents

The most important material in a field is its soil. What the field can do, and how it is worked, largely follow from that. The soil is helped to do its job by various devices, of which crop rotation and adding chemically or nutritionally rich material to the soil, as in liming and manuring, were certainly practised in the first millennium. Rotation can be detected sometimes in the palaeobotanical record, sometimes in the soil itself, e.g. at Denton, Newcastle on Tyne (below), 'the soils buried by [Hadrian's] Wall were cultivated in rotation with grassland probably used for livestock rearing' (Payton in Bidwell and Watson 1996, 43). Archaeologically, fields characteristically contain durable bits of rubbish, notably potsherds and stones including worked or non-local ones. Such material is, in a circular argument, assumed to be the non-organic elements of manure from domestic middens and therefore adduced as evidence of manuring. The dating of many of the examples quoted in this chapter depends on the deposition, survival and recovery of bits of pottery from plough-soils. Conversely, various field systems such as those at Fyfield Down, Barnsley Park and Gwithian, respectively towards the beginning, middle and end of the millennium, would be interpreted as having been manured.

Fields can also contain various features, not just the crops and animals they are designed to hold but evidence and structures of their working. Boundaries, for example, can exist within a field – baulks, fences, perhaps temporary, lines of stones, invisible lines between marker, or mere, stones – to subdivide it into parcels or strips. Such may be a tenurial mechanism, or for proprietorial or practical purposes, dividing one crop from another for example. The Latin word *scamnum*, a specific term in Pliny and Columella for a baulk or earth ridge produced by a plough, somehow gave rise to Welsh *ysgafn* (with a slightly different meaning), providing a hint of the farming reality behind the generalisation.

Fields can also contain the evidence of their cultivation. This comes mainly in two forms, ridges and furrows, discussed here, and so-called ard-marks and plough-marks, discussed in chapter 10. Ridge and furrow varies enormously in width and extent in the first millennium. At one extreme are quite large extents of narrow (1–1.5 m wide) 'cord rig' in north Britain (Topping 1989), broadly late prehistoric, certainly continuing into the first millennium AD and persisting in places, at least in the north and west, into the second millennium. At the other, theoretically rather than yet proven before AD 1000, is 'broad rig', the more familiar 'medieval' ridge and furrow trending towards 6–7 m and wider in breadth (Pl. XX). Theoretically, in technological terms there is no reason why 'broad rig' should not have been produced in late Roman contexts, and the share from Dinorben, Clwyd (Gardner and Savory 1964) and plough-mark evidence from Gwithian show that it could indeed have been produced in pre-Saxon western Britain. Nevertheless, the fact is that no broad ridge and furrow is yet proven to be of a date before *c.* AD 800. It is indeed somewhat ironic that, on archaeological grounds, considerable extents of narrow ridge and furrow – cord rig – which blanketed much of northern Britain up to and just into the first millennium AD seem to disappear at precisely the time when one might have looked for the technique to develop, that is in the later first and second centuries when greater demand and better tools might have been expected. 'Seem' may well prove, however, to be the operative word. While the intrinsic validity of the archaeological evidence is not in doubt, much of that used for dating purposes can be so used because it is related to Hadrian's Wall and associated structures, i.e. it comes from contexts pre-AD 122 and, as in the case of the unequivocal example beneath a Roman camp at Greenlee Lough, Northumberland, occasionally closely dated pre-Hadrianic episodes (Topping 1989).

Radiocarbon dating is indicating, nevertheless, that we may be glimpsing local cessations – perhaps for military purposes? – rather than the disappearance in the first to second centuries of a north British method of cultivation. Narrow ridges beneath 0.4 m of peat at Machrie North on the Isle of Arran date (albeit on the basis of but two dates so far) to the seventh century AD. Of two examples of such ridges near Lairg, that at Allt na Fearna Mór seems to have fallen out of use not earlier than the fourth century AD in an area where blanket peat was forming into the fourteenth century; while that at Gruids seems to have continued in use until about the same time, that is in the medieval period (Carter 1993–94; but this last dating is based on a single radiocarbon determination). Interesting links are argued, on the one hand, with the technique of narrow ridge cultivation of *c.* 1000 AD at Lindholm Høje, Denmark, and, on the other, with potato cultivation in lazy-beds in nineteenth-century Ireland (Carter 1993–94, 88); and such are now distinctly possible if 'cord rig' is conceived as representative of a technique of seed-bed preparation rather than a purely cultural or technological trait. Theoretically, as a technique it could easily have spanned not just the first millennium BC but also the first millennium AD and indeed on into the full medieval period; and although we anticipate new evidence will substantiate the 'first millennium AD' part of such a thesis, the use of 'cord rig' thereafter is likely to have been as a continuing, traditional adaptation to particular circumstances, as in the wetter and colder west and north, rather than in the technologically increasingly advanced south and east with, as we argue in chapter 9, a fully developed plough by the end of our period. No one using such a plough will have wanted to waste time, literally, with narrow ridges.

Such ridging may in fact have been practised for any one or more of several reasons – technological, tenurial, hydrological, climatic. The critical advantage provided by the technique, as with lazy-bedding, is not so much to drain land as to lift the root system of the growing plant above wetter, lower levels of a probably only shallowly disturbed seed-bed. But the most compelling factor is its merit of holding the warmth of the sun for just a little bit longer than unridged soil. Local temperature variation is therefore less, and temperature is maintained at a slightly higher level than would otherwise be the case (Smith 1992). It is distinctly possible that 'cord rig' was the product of both the spade and a plough or, more likely, an ard, rather than one or the other (Carter 1993–94, 88; see below, chapter 10).

One other major type of feature can occur in fields and be directly related to their use, though it is seldom discussed in first-millennium contexts. It consists of cairns, mounds of stone, large or small, and notoriously of any date or many dates. They are a well-known agrarian feature in fourth- to second-millennium BC contexts; but, given that many of them represent clearance, some could be of the first millennium AD – or indeed even later. New land was being taken in episodically throughout Britain during the first millennium, and so stone clearance must have been carried out, either creating new cairns or adding to existing ones. New cairns seem to be associated with new fields and rig in Glen Cochill (Fig. 7.7). And another report, also from Scotland, provokes serious thought about cairns as a largely unexplored aspect of first-millennium farming: at Kildonan, Sutherland, ard-marks sealed by peat were earlier than about the tenth century AD and a cairn was on peat dated to *c.* AD 600 (Russell-White 1995, 33).

Summary

There were always several types of field system operating in Britain in the first millennium AD. Some were for pastoral purposes, some for arable. They related variously to previous types of field system and to newly broken-in land. From the first century onwards to the seventh or eighth, various types of field system in the British tradition were in operation throughout Britain, the only exceptions being some villa field systems (though known examples tend not to be very Romanised). Quite large areas were enclosed in systems of long, rectangular fields in the early centuries AD, on marginal lands like chalk downs, limestone slopes and newly drained wetlands. In such treeless landscapes, the visual aspects of such systems may well have been 'open', even if their working was neither co-operative nor 'common'. Larger, and possibly 'open' fields appeared in the Romanised parts of England in the third and fourth centuries and it seems likely that such fields, along with the typically stone-walled fields of west and north Britain, continued through the middle years of the millennium. Some, indeed, still continue in use.

From *c.* 800, changes were occurring, differently in many areas, with new enclosure and extensive arable spreading across waste, along wood-edge and through rough grazing in England. New enclosed fields were also being cleared in eastern Scotland and it is unlikely that they were alone. Areas of open field may have begun to operate in the west, and certainly were doing so in Ireland. Possibly of great relevance to the rest of Britain is Kelly's (1998, 371) observation that 'farming procedures described in the law-texts suggest that the open-field system may also have been in operation at this period' (second half of the first millennium). Farmers were contributing oxen to make up common teams and 'One might expect that this practice would lead to co-ownership of a large open-field in which each farmer had separate strips', while expecting an independent single farmer 'to sow . . . in one or two large fields rather than in many small fields' (p. 371). Whether or not open fields were present before the twelfth century, 'It is likely that fields were generally larger in the Anglo-Norman system, with open-field cultivation in strips of winter-corn (wheat and rye), spring corn (oats), and fallow in rotation' (p. 20).

In England at about the same time and probably for two or three centuries earlier, originating in part from very long strips of land, strip fields intermixed and probably increasingly farmed in common, progressively developed as permanent features of the countryside from Lincolnshire to Dorset, perhaps under strong direction from monastic and growingly assertive local landlords. Planned field systems, some arranged radially from the now commonly nucleated villages of the North and the Midlands, appeared in the tenth century in an increasingly regulated English landscape. All the ingredients for a more mature common field system were already present by 1000; perhaps all that was needed was more systematic and centralised authority to regularise it as the norm for the 'champion' countryside, thereby unconsciously emphasising differences, not necessarily less sophisticated, from the rest of Britain. The Muirs (1989, 41–2) summed up the process as 'until the eighth century the land [in England] was mainly farmed from scattered hamlets and farmsteads set in fields of Roman or earlier date [and thereafter] there is good reason to believe that many open-field systems were originally composed of long strips lying in long furlongs'. Their conclusion (pp. 47–8) on the specific point of 'how' open fields began was that 'landowners were establishing churches in the new centres or at focal points which were destined to become permanent villages. The introduction of open fields was apparently the result of deliberate planning by the landlords and their agents.' Even so, it was probably only the peculiar hierarchical nature of Anglo-Saxon society that enabled this to happen so early relative to western Europe.

In Britain beyond England, the 'open field' question as a historical conundrum was a non-issue, for throughout the first millennium visually open fields, as distinct from small enclosed plots, physically existed in some places, in others not; where they did, their use tended to involve more co-operation. By the end of the first millennium a varied British landscape of fields encapsulated a long history of agrarian, social and tenurial change quite as much as technological developments.

8 | Technology

He asked for implements to work the land with.

BEDE, *LIFE OF CUTHBERT*, CHAPTER 19 (CROSSLEY-HOLLAND 1999, 68)

The Venerable Bede was not a farmer but those of whom he wrote were sometimes using farming technology. Eosterwine, for example, second Abbot of Jarrow-Monkwearmouth monastery, put 'his hand to the plough along the furrow, hammering iron into shape or wielding the winnowing fan' (Crossley-Holland 1999, 193). He thereby incidentally told us of the existence of one of his world's most important implements, a plough – though unfortunately not what sort (see chapter 9); of the method, cold-forging, used in making iron objects; and of a simple, very ancient 'machine' applied to one of the most important tasks of the farming year, sorting the grain from the waste after threshing. Such agrarian technology was crucial to the practice of farming in the first millennium AD and is important, but not dominant, in our perspective of it.

That technology, despite Bede's words, was not primitive: for the most part unsophisticated perhaps, but certainly not primitive. Indeed it might be deemed adequate to the needs of society at the time, though to think so is to beg the question of whether society was conditioned by its technology or whether the absence of technological sophistication belies a social consciousness of pressing social need. Nevertheless, certainly as far as handtools were concerned, the range available to farm-workers was virtually the same as that of the medieval peasant and indeed of the British agricultural labourer up to the earlier twentieth century. All the basic inventions had been made by Bede's day, most of them a long time previously.

Such an assertion is borne out by radiocarbon dating of a range of agricultural implements, including cultivating implements discussed in chapter 9 (Lerche 1995). Mainly from Danish contexts of the first millennium BC but stretching back much earlier come digging sticks, spades and a yoke. The range of undoubtedly prehistoric implements, even if often not individually closely dated, in use in Britain is well illustrated by Rees

161

Plate XXI Wooden hand-tools, Hyelzas, Lozère, Languedoc, France, 1999: a spade, a flail and a fork, all in use into the mid-twentieth century, leaning against a wooden gutter, still operational.

(1979a). Table 8.1 here lists the dozen implements from Europe with radiocarbon dates in the first millennium AD (abstracted from Lerche 1995). It shows a range of near-complete, and parts of, cultivating implements, two types of spade and a harrow. Given the somewhat haphazard nature of the items dated in this way, the table hints that wooden equipment of a greater range was probably widely available in western Europe throughout the first millennium AD. It is likely, for example, that forks, flails and yokes were also available but simply have not been preserved,

Table 8.1   Radiocarbon dated agricultural implements of the first millennium AD (after Lerche 1995)

---

1   30–10 BC (170 BC – 80 AD cal +/− 1 st. d.): beam of bow ard; alder; Lochmaben, Dumfries, Scotland
2   10 AD: yoke; alder; Knudmose
3   220: beam of bow ard; Mammen
4   440: paddle-shaped spade; alder; Blegind
5   630: spade; Dannevirke
6   670: arrow-shaped ard share; Bramminge
7   770: arrow-shaped ard share (no. 8); yew; Samsüø
8   780: arrow-shaped ard share; Grindsted
9   800–850: crook ard with detachable arrow-shaped share; Dabergotz
10 890: harrow; Viborg
11 960: arrow-shaped ard share (no. 2); yew; Samsüø
12 985: spade; Jelling

For item 1, the date range at one standard deviation is given to emphasise that the piece could just as well be in the early first millennium AD as the late first millennium BC. Otherwise, in the interests of simplicity, a date of just one calendar year is provided, though all of the pieces have 'dates' of equal validity within a similar range at one standard deviation. Lerche's (1995, 172–5) own caveats about the uses of radiocarbon dating in general, and as applied to agricultural items in particular, should always be borne in mind in using these simplified data. That said, here the items are listed chronologically. All except the first are dated AD, and all are from Denmark and of oak unless otherwise stated.

rediscovered, conserved and dated (Pls. XXI–XXIII). Such a thesis is strengthened by the discovery and recognition in Britain, notably in the later twentieth century, of wooden parts of cultivating implements (chapter 9) and a range of other wooden equipment (Earwood 1993).

Against that background of a well-developed range of wooden equipment for many agricultural tasks, it is not difficult to understand that the major development in the early centuries AD, at least in southern Britain, was not so much in agricultural technological innovation as in an increased availability of iron for tools and implements. More specialist implements developed as a result, for example heavy iron ploughshares (chapter 9) and large scythes. Some items may well have been recycled for a time after AD 400 but the technological advance was then lost over much of Britain between the fifth and eleventh centuries because, although iron tools continued to be made by blacksmiths and were available locally on demand, the industrial production of iron ceased. Over much of Britain, however, the loss would scarcely have been noticed because many of those working

Plate XXII   An ox yoke, Hyelzas, Lozère, Languedoc, France, 1999: an oak neck-yoke about 1.60 m long viewed from the front, for a pair of oxen as used locally into the mid-twentieth century.

the land outside the Roman Civil Zone had probably not shared in the first place to any appreciable degree in the 'iron-tool farming economy' of the second to fourth centuries AD.

To farm in this millennium, basically everything had to be picked up by human hand, activated by human muscle, and done using the same means. Compared to medieval and later times, the big difference was the almost complete absence of machines and alternative power-sources. Neither wind nor gravity nor other natural element, and water not widely, was tapped as a source of power. People and cattle provided traction. Exceptions were one or two specialist items, possibly including a wheeled reaper, which may have been available on more advanced Roman estate farms; and the horizontal mill for grinding grain which was certainly in mid-millennium Ireland and somewhat later in Midland England (below). Water was also controlled in drainage works and fish-weirs, and may have been used in irrigation. Otherwise the only alternative power-source was the domestic animal, overwhelmingly the ox to pull carts, wagons, tree trunks and cultivation implements.

A specialist technology to mitigate the effects of nature was barely available at the 'sharp end' of agriculture. There was no glass-house, for example, or other means of propagating or protecting crops, and no very large sheds for over-wintering herds of cattle. Back one step from the field, however, some matters began to be better managed than before. Cereal and food storage, for example, improved at least for a time in southern Britain and Ireland, for underground storage pits disappear from the archaeological record and, on the positive side, large pottery jars, corn-drying ovens and granaries appear (Pl. XXIX). The matrix of agrarian life contained other technologies too. Bede, for example, was apparently intrigued by building work, glass-making, cement-mixing and wood-working, particularly lathe-turning (Blair 1976, 205–7). Kilns, properly built structures, came into use for various industrial processes, like pottery manufacture,

but they appeared on the farm too, to dry cereal and perhaps other produce. Specialist buildings in stone, like granaries, byres and barns, also
appeared, at least in the south in the early centuries AD. Among other
specialist structures were weirs, as described, for example, albeit in the
early twelfth century, at Durham (Crossley-Holland 1999, 204):

> . . . buildings backed
> by rocky slopes peer over a precipice.
> Weirs hem and madden a headstrong river,
> diverse fish dance in the foam.

Farming technology in the early centuries AD was, then, in some respects
more advanced than in late prehistoric times as a result of direct introductions from the Roman Empire. We could therefore expect among Latin
loan-words into British certain nouns for two types of thing: things where
a Roman version of a superior kind generally replaced a British one, and
things previously not present in Britain. The Latin word *pons*, 'a constructed, engineered bridge', is an example of the first, replacing British
briua and adding *pont* and *pons* respectively to Welsh and Cornish and perhaps even adding the place-name *Tripontium* to the British countryside at,
literally, a three-span Roman river-bridge (though Rivet and Smith 1979,
476 disagree). Real ashlar masonry with mortar was another technological
addition to that countryside, and remains of it are probably the origin of
the post-Classical Latin *maceria* underlying place-names like *Magwyr* and
Magor, Monmouth, and *Maker* and *Magor*, Cornwall. A curious masonry
building, Romanised rather than Roman, lay at the last (O'Neill 1933).

Agricultural implements are barely well attested in contemporary, first-
millennium sources, but their likely range and functions are discernible,
to a greater or lesser degree of accuracy, by records of and objects from
pre- or non-industrial societies in western Europe.

The basic tools (Fig. 8.1)

A brief look at the tool-kit of 'peasant' land-workers throughout western
Europe since prehistoric times points strongly to a similarity over an
extensive area and implies that, given the same basic level of technology
and range of tasks to be achieved, a similar range has existed for a long
time. The pre-machine tradition of farming and craftsmanship goes back
thousands of years. We can reasonably infer that many of the types of
actual implement not only were old in the first millennium AD but also
were in many cases basically the same in design and use then as they were

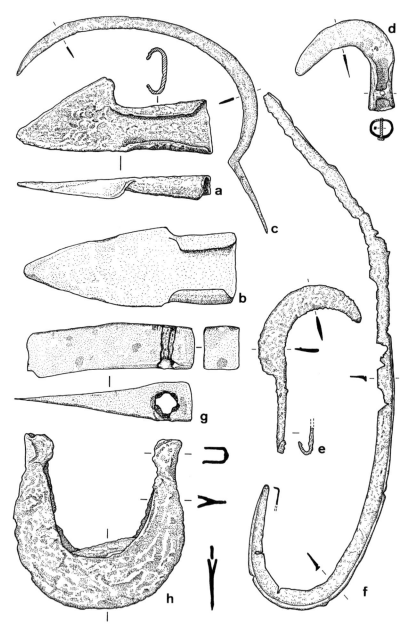

Fig. 8.1 Farm tools of the first millennium AD (various sources): (a) asymmetrical ploughshare, third–fifth century, Dinorben (after Manning 1964, 59); (b) symmetrical ploughshare, ?early centuries AD, Bucklersbury House, London (Manning 1964, 59); (c) sickle (Manning 1985, F22); (d) socketed sickle, first century AD, Camerton, Somerset (Jackson 1990, Pl. 27, 265) (e) tanged sickle, first century AD, Camerton, Somerset (Jackson 1990, Pl. 32, 309); (f) scythe, fourth century, Farmoor, Oxfordshire (Manning 1985, F19); (g) axe-head, 23 cm long, Fenchurch Street, London (Manning 1985, B1); (h) edging for the bottom of a wooden spade (Manning 1985, F9). All the objects are illustrated at approx. $\frac{1}{5}$ actual size except for f, c 140 cm long, at approx. $\frac{1}{10}$.

when illuminated in medieval pictures and indeed as recorded, not merely as archaic survivals but in use, in the nineteenth and twentieth centuries (Jenkins 1965).

Agricultural technology, the tools and implements used directly in farming tasks, were themselves part of a broader range of hand-tools used by other specialists, or at least used for specialist tasks needed to keep agrarian society operating. In various parts of Britain, then, would be found, for example, leather craftspeople, tanning and currying leather and making harness, saddles, perhaps boots and shoes, and, in the second half of the first millennium in particular, vellum for making large bibles and other great works. They would be using a variety of knives, punches, mallets, hammers, decorative tools, needles and awls. Different in design and function, but of the same order of technology, would be the tools of, as another example, the blacksmith. Such a craftsman in the first millennium AD would not have such a range and complexity of tools and equipment as became the norm on the big nineteenth-century farm (as presented today at various farm museums, notably Beamish, Co. Durham); but nevertheless, to do his job at all, his first-millennium predecessor – a person characteristically of high status in a horse-riding society (see chapter 13) – would have had a forge, bellows, anvil, tongs, chisels, punches, hammers and pliers. Similarly, another crucial specialist, the thatcher, would have had to have his range of tools, including straw- or reed-holders and, again, special knives. Other specialists, not present in every community but still necessary, would have included a farrier, mason, net- and rope-maker, charcoal-burner, cooper, carpenter and wheelwright (cf. Bourne 1923).

One of the main needs in farming is means to keep animals apart from each other and off growing crops; so hedgers, fencers and wattle-hurdle makers were key workers. They too required their own tools, principally various types of knife and hook for splitting wood, on the bush with hedgers, as lengths of chopped wood for fencers and hurdle-makers. In some districts, the fields were enclosed by walls, so drystone-wallers were the local requirement. Some idea of the variety in their walling work and other ways of dividing land is afforded in Evans (1958, 41–2). He also described (especially chapters 10–14) traditional tools and practices that might be relevant to first-millennium farming, though it is difficult to be sure even when the function is the same. In the case of Ireland, it would be easy to underestimate the effect of seventeenth-century and later English influence and of potato cultivation, both anachronistic for our purposes. Nevertheless, the recent tool-kit of an island which above all illustrates the remarkable variety of detailed differences likely in a small area – over 150 different types of spade blade, for example – included ards and the technique of cross-ploughing, ploughs, mauls for breaking up clods, weighted thorn bushes for harrowing, a linen sheet tied around the neck to hold seed while broadcasting (cf. chapter 12), a digging fork and a long-handled shovel. For harvesting grass to make hay, the scythe and iron hook Evans saw in use originated in pre-Christian times, leading him to opine that 'some of the methods of securing the crop can have changed little in two thousand years' (1958, 95). Possibly much the same could apply to the sickle and reaping-hook used for reaping oats, the choice of cereal in a wet climate.

The range of agricultural tools and implements was considerable, especially during the early centuries AD when, in a state-controlled market economy, commercial iron production for the first time ensured a ready supply of them. At least in southern Britain, many a farm would then have possessed adzes, a pickaxe, perhaps a couple of scythes, a field anvil for straightening out and resharpening tools damaged at work, a chain, various types of knives, and several sizes of axe, sickle, hoe, pruning-hook and bill-hook. Wooden rather than iron, though probably nailed together, were specialist agricultural items such as harrows, rakes and two-tined forks. Spades too were mainly wood, with iron sheathing around the edges of the blade: a unique, virtually complete one of ashwood with a T-shaped upper end to its handle was excavated at Stonea Grange, Cambridgeshire, and is on display at the British Museum.

The sort of farming life in general which we can envisage, and the tools in particular, sound familiar when we encounter them elsewhere in modern ethnographic studies. In Denmark, for example, 'farming proceeded entirely along lines drawn by ancient traditions' until the agricultural reforms there in the latter half of the eighteenth century (Michelsen and Rasmussen 1955). The same authors refer to the plough as the farmer's principal implement, then describe the whole process of producing food from crops as involving in technological terms a wooden harrow, a shallow wood-bottomed basket with sides of straw for carrying the seed-corn during broadcasting, for harvesting the sickle, and short-handled and long-handled scythe, for threshing and after, the flail, the threshing bat, a sieve or trough for separating the chaff from the grain, the rotating quern and vertical (in English technically horizontal) water-mills. Their mid-twentieth-century description could have been about the basic technology of peasant farming in most of western Europe before the time when local reform occurred. Even in a different climatic zone, the functions and therefore the range and types of equipment for pre-mechanical farming remain remarkably similar. Behind the detail, the agricultural tool-kit illustrated,

Plate XXIII Flailing, Causse Méjean, Lozère, Languedoc, France, probably in the first half of the twentieth century.

for example, from twentieth-century Languedoc (Pl. XXI) and Provence *d'autrefois* (Marchandiau 1984) is hardly alien at all. We see a range of ards and ploughs and other specialist equipment like a wooden-frame harrow (cf. Pl. XXIV) and several types of hoe; they vary considerably in detail among themselves, just as in Ireland, and no one could argue that any one item was the same as one used in first-millennium Britain. On the other hand, in their range, and in their types, and most importantly in the processes they represent, overall they are probably very close indeed to the equipment that would have been in use in first-millennium Britain at one time or another and variously across the regions.

The main reason for such a belief is not a theory of cultural homogeneity but simply an observation of function. Farming at the technological level prevalent throughout Britain in the first millennium AD basically consisted of a series of tasks that had to be carried out if several different processes were to be activated and successfully concluded. The ground, for example, had to be prepared as a seed-bed and, several months later, the cereal harvest had to be secured and prepared as food; oxen, cattle and sheep had to be maintained in certain ways to produce energy, meat, hides, milk, wool and their progeny; wood had to be grown and prepared for different uses; other resources had to be husbanded, collected, used. The range and emphases of functions varied somewhat from area to area but the basic functions had to be repeated endlessly. Similar tools were required to carry them out; so similar tools were everywhere needed throughout Europe until the invention and differential implementation

Plate XXIV Man with wooden harrow, Galicia, Spain, 1974. The harrow consists of a frame braced by struts through which teeth are wedged. The curve of the handle is mirrored in the background in the stilt of the bow ard tucked in under the eaves of a wooden four-post granary resting on granite piers.

of various technological changes came about in post-medieval times. 'In general it was with the flail that the grain was threshed right up to the beginning of Queen Victoria's reign' (Fussell 1981, 152) sums up the situation – and that was in England, not on some small, remote Atlantic island. The quotation also expresses the nub of the thesis which has led discussion of first-millennium farming into ethnographical evidence. Such evidence is in itself almost a thousand years too late but, at least functionally, could well have been contemporary.

Field implements

The plough and its predecessors are dealt with in chapter 9, and there is no need to discuss in detail the full suite of largely wooden implements which we can fairly safely assume were in use commonly throughout Britain in the first millennium (Pl. XXI). Although relatively little actual material, particularly its organic component, has survived, the evidence has been well studied and well published (see Appendix 1). We illustrate a range of the material from England (Fig. 8.1), and a harrow from Galicia of a sort which could well have been used in first-millennium Britain (Pl. XXIV).

Spades were much more important in farming then than they are now: a principal implement for cultivating the ground, in lazy-beds for example, as well as for cutting peat (Gailey and Fenton 1970). Like so many such implements, they varied enormously in detail of design, notably by region but also through time. In the tenth century and certainly on to the late eleventh, for example, on either side of the English Channel the blade was asymmetrical, flanged to provide a foot rest on only one side of the handle. Other hand-tools for ground preparation included forks, mattocks and hoes, all with at best only minimal ironwork. Hoes, of the mattock type with rectangular or triangular blades, not Dutch hoes, were, like spades, much more important than now in Britain, for they were used to break up small, awkward, perhaps rocky patches of land where even a light ard and two-ox team could not operate. In any case, not everyone had access to such equipment, and the hoe and spade were the poor man's cultivating implements. A mattock-shaped tool, but with two prongs instead of a blade, also existed. Sculptural reliefs on the one hand and, at the end of the millennium, decorative scenes provide visual illustrations of such material.

Harvesting implements included short-handled sickles of various sizes and double-handled, long-bladed scythes, the latter perhaps introduced by the Roman army which had a constant need for fodder, notably grass, for its horses. A small sickle was probably a common method of cutting cereal ears, leaving the stalks to be cut separately with a larger implement. The method was in use until recently in various places in Europe. Similarly the flail survived into the twentieth century in parts of Europe as the normal method of separating the grains from the ear and there really can be little doubt that its use was the common method of threshing throughout the first millennium (Pl. XXIII), though the organised trampling of cattle is a complement or alternative. Both flailing and trampling require a hard surface on which to beat or crush the ears of cereal, and such can easily be seen outside in the fields and in threshing-yards still in current or recent use in southern Europe. They have not, however, been recognised archaeologically in first-millennium Britain, a curious lacuna; though it is possible that the generally moist climate drove the activity indoors, as was the case in the second millennium when it traditionally took place in the space between opposing barn doors. Threshing is shown on one particular manuscript which also illustrates a cart, a plough with a share, a T-handled spade, a bill-hook, a straight-bladed scythe, a pitchfork and a whetstone (Carver 1986, table 9; Temple 1976, no. 87) – a typical range, and a good example of how important a source of information such manuscripts can be.

Pastoralism never required so much equipment as arable husbandry but, as could be expected, wooden hay-forks, sheep clippers and cow or sheep bells are all known to have existed. Long-handled scythes, essential for cutting grass for hay, are known in both the earlier and later parts of the millennium, for example at Farmoor, Oxfordshire (Fig. 8.1f), at other places in southern Britain (Rees 1979a; 1979b) and at Hurbruck, Co. Durham (Wilson 1960, Fig. 11). Loomweights and spindle-whorls, found archaeologically by the thousand, indicated wool-working, and typical bone artefacts include needles and carding combs. An exceptionally important tenth-century collection of tools and implements from Flixborough, Humberside (Loveluck 1998), included an iron hoe-sheath, a bill-hook and a possible plough coulter or heavy knife/chopper. All the stages of textile manufacture were represented – fibre preparation, spinning and weaving, and embellishment of cloth. Other crafts indicated by specialist tools included leather-working and carpentry. Wood-working tools in the hoard included axes, adzes (including T-shaped ones), shaves, spoon bits for drills, rasps, wedges and chisels. In general, axes, saws and pruning-hooks were elements of the tool-kit for woodland work. The Roman tools and descriptions seem particularly appropriate to southern Britain in the earlier centuries AD (White 1967; 1975), while the illuminated manuscripts, and indeed the Bayeux tapestry, contain numerous arboricultural scenes showing such tools in use.

The main pieces of equipment used in food processing were a knife and a rotary hand-mill (querns or quern-stones in the archaeological literature where they appear frequently, especially on settlement sites of the first half of the millennium). Grinding stones and pestles and mortars were also used.

So much for generality and theory. Now we examine what was actually found at two representative sites and in later cultural contexts, then summarise the material as a whole by function.

A farm and a villa

We descriptively compare here the agrarian technology as indicated by iron objects excavated at two contemporary settlements in southern England in the third to fourth centuries AD. One is a farm, Site XII, on Overton Down, Wiltshire, the other a villa, Gorhambury, near *Verulamium*, Hertfordshire.

Site XII, Overton Down, Wiltshire (Fowler 2000b; 2000c; Fowler and Blackwell 1998)

This was a discrete small farm, or a small farm component of a larger settlement, occupied for about a century from *c*. AD 340. An impressive assemblage of ironwork included a number of items of direct or secondary agricultural application, several noticeably grouped in or around the robbed remains of a building (Building 3) which seems to have served as a multi-purpose barn. In general the objects can be regarded as of later fourth-century date, though some may well have continued in use into the fifth century. Only one was of direct agricultural use: one of two pairs of shears, medium-sized and probably for sheep shearing or coarse cloth cutting; the other pair was for domestic uses. An iron pitchfork was too small as a field implement and may have been used as a hand-tool in much the same way as a gardening fork today.

There was, however, a good range of tools and equipment needed on any farm and in its household. For using animals, two snaffle bits were both from the two-link snaffle type which was the most common bit used in Roman Britain. Two ox-shoes join a few other dated examples from Roman Britain to prove that such shoes were used throughout the period. A common type of cleaver and three knives are what you would expect. Six chisels and a gouge indicate the carpentry normal on any farm, though other work, as with leather, is likely too. A spike, for example, may have been a leather punch. Gouges were also mainly used in wood-working, although this one is a particularly substantial example.

Structural and architectural fittings included nearly 2000 nails, fifty cleats, eight reinforcing strips or ties, and six staples. Two swivel loops were possibly parts of cauldron chains or simple levering systems. Five other loops, and a loop-headed object thought to be driven into masonry, or more likely wood, could have been all-purpose attachments. A fragment of a drop-hinge had punched perforation.

Household and domestic items were an unusual tripod iron vessel, a bucket and a wooden box. The one needle is likely to have been used for sewing coarse fabric, or a tough material, perhaps leather. Two latch-lifters were also present, plus an unusual T-shaped lift-key and a barb-spring padlock: security or personal privacy seems to have been an issue. Personal effects included, rather unusually in iron, brooches (others were in copper alloy), and two styli plausibly suggesting that at least one of the inhabitants of the farm was literate.

Neither agricultural nor domestic was a rather surprising group of iron objects – weapons. How typical were these of first-millennium farms? This one possessed four military-style spears. The two smaller spearheads were of a type which was probably intended either for throwing javelins or as cavalry lances; the larger two were probably intended for hand-to-hand fighting. In the context of a rural settlement, these items may represent nothing more than hunting equipment; but in the context of a rural settlement in the later fourth century AD, we can wonder whether these weapons could represent the need for such a place to be able to defend itself.

Gorhambury villa, Hertfordshire (Neal et al. 1990)

The collection of ironwork here was much larger (555 published items), from a much larger excavation; and its emphases are different from those at Overton Down XII in terms of agrarian equipment. In general there is, nevertheless, a similar range of metalwork. Just as a cluster of objects was noted around Building 3 at OD XII, much of the Gorhambury material came from in and around three buildings: an aisled hall, Building 53 and Structure 43 (Wardle 1990, 113–15, an account which the next paragraph follows).

As is to be expected, the metalwork included many items of personal and domestic use and function, e.g. brooches, keys and bolts. The range of iron tools included an axe, adze, saw and file and possible plane-blades, all for wood-working; with carpentry represented by a drill bit and chisels – in general, similar to that at OD XII. More specifically farming needs were covered, however, on the animal side, by ox goads, a farrier's butteris, and a large collection of hippo-sandal fragments, used as temporary horse-shoes. No such objects were found at OD XII. Arable farming was represented by ploughshare tips, a spade sheath and a rake tooth, sickles and scythes, none of which was found at OD XII either. The types of farming tool and implement in use on this villa may reflect different economic activities as much as its being a socially and economically distinct type of settlement compared to OD XII. Given the undoubtedly arable basis of Gorhambury's farming, the absence of specifically arable objects from OD XII highlighted by the villa's equipment may well indicate a pastoral basis for the downland farm.

Harnessing power

Two of the major technological developments of the millennium concerned the harnessing of water power and the harnessing of the ubiquitous beast of burden, the ox.

Water-mills

Water-mills were introduced into Britain in the early centuries AD from the Roman world as part of a general development of control and exploitation of water, for example in drainage and irrigation systems (Moritz 1958). The Romans, as Salway (1981, 632) remarks, 'were capable of constructing extremely elaborate systems to exploit the power of water'. Water-mills have been assumed to be of vertical type but this is not necessarily so. Examples, none anything like complete, have been identified in military contexts at Chesters and Birdoswald on Hadrian's Wall, and in the River Tyne immediately below the fort(s) at Corbridge (Snape 1997); in towns at Great Chesterford and Silchester; and in the country at Stanwick, Northamptonshire, Orton Hall Farm, Cambridgeshire, and Fullerton, Hampshire. Such advanced machines were certainly present in the fourth-century countryside of southern Britain but, like some other technologies, seem to disappear thereafter.

They appeared for the first time in Ireland some 200–300 years later, without exception with horizontal wheels, introduced, or reintroduced, from the Roman world. The earliest examples in Ireland, the earliest of all a tidal mill, have been dated dendrochronologcally to *c.* AD 630 and 782; the 'only Old Irish word for "mill", *muilenn*, is a borrowing from Latin *molina*, of the same meaning', and several mill-parts also enjoy Latin-derived names (Kelly 1998, 485). The connection between the Mediterranean and Atlantic worlds is, then, at least in this case, close; though possibly the idea of such a machine, like other aspects of British culture in the middle of the first millennium, crossed from *Britannia* rather than the Continent (cf. also Rynne 1989; Edwards 1996, 63–4).

Possibly religious, even Christian and monastic, connections played a role here. On Iona, for example, Columba '*horreum egreditur, et ad monasterium revertens media resedet via. In quo loco postea crux molari infixa lapidi hodieque*' ('[Columba] left the barn, and returning towards the monastery sat down midway. In that place [stands] a cross that was later fixed in a mill-stone'). The editors (Anderson and Anderson 1961, 522–3) of Adomnan's *Vita*, written *c.* 690, are adamant about the stone: 'This was the stone of a hand-mill' (fn 5). But their reason for saying so appears to be simply that 'it is unlikely that there was a water-mill of any kind as early as the sixth century' (p. 115). Now that the molinological scene has been quite transformed by discovery and research over the forty years since the Andersons wrote, one is bound to wonder whether Adomnan is not actually providing us from first-hand observation with prime evidence of the use and disuse of a proper mill-stone during the seventh century; and of its reuse as a cross-base before that century's end (cf. the reuse of a later mill-stone as a cross-base on Tor Abb within Columba's monastery: Fowler and Fowler 1988).

Such a reinterpretation of Adomnan's words about Iona during Columba's lifetime may not be too far-fetched. After it was written, a report (*British Archaeology* 53, June 2000, 5) recorded a mill at Nendrum Early Christian monastery, Mahee Island, on Strangford Lough, Northern Ireland, only some 200 km south of Iona across the North Channel. The mill was first built in AD 619–21, that is during Columba's lifetime. Though driven like other early mills in the British Isles by water (below), the Nendrum example is unique at this date in being a tidal mill. A millpond in the intertidal zone was 'filled with seawater at high tide, which was released through a sluice and fed along a channel to the mill's horizontal wheel as the tide receded . . . The earliest embankment [of the millpond dam] was a massive structure, some 9m across at the base, with timber-revetted sides enclosing clay layers and a central core of wattling.' Surviving mill-parts included wheel-paddles, three morticed oak hubs of mill-wheels and parts of early timber flumes, plus some grain, probably barley. By any standards, this was a significant installation, involving technological skill as well as capital investment, and it may well have been intended to cope with much more grain than that either grown or needed by the monastic community alone. Perhaps its functions as well as its technology were imported as part of the 'Roman' Early Christian migration of ideas into Ireland, either direct from the Mediterranean, from late Roman Gaul or Spain, or from western Britain. But whether that was so or whether the technology developed indigenously, archaeology and documentary evidence combine to demonstrate that the mill idea caught on in Early Christian Ireland during the seventh and eighth centuries, well before there is comparable evidence from Britain (Edwards 1996, 64; Kelly 1998, 245, 482–5; Rynne 1989).

Quite when mills reappeared in mainland Britain is uncertain; possibly one or two in the west really did continue to operate or at least the idea was not completely lost. English documentary sources do not equal the Irish in this respect and archaeology has not so far produced examples until two centuries after the Nendrum mill. Examples from the ninth century onwards include ones at Old Windsor, Berkshire and the Earl's Bu, Orphir, Orkney. The latter, with chamber, leat and lade (head race), illustrated the type in stone at the end of the millennium (Graham-Campbell and Batey 1998, 192–4). The best example so far in England is that at Tamworth (Fig. 8.2), constructed as

> a horizontal-wheeled watermill in the mid 9th century or earlier, [and] powered by a leat which drew water from the River Anker . . . [A] second mill was built on the residues of the first . . . [in] the mid 9th century or possibly a little later. It was also of the horizontal-wheeled type, with a millpool at a higher level, fed by a reconstructed new leat . . . Among the finds were the sole-tree of the mill, with its steel bearing; one of the wheel-paddles; many fragments of millstones, of local stone and imported lava; fragments of the clay bed in which the lower millstone was set; and the residues of lead window-cames. Grain . . . included oats and possibly barley. (Rahtz and Meeson 1992, xi; see *also* 'Conclusion', pp. 156–8)

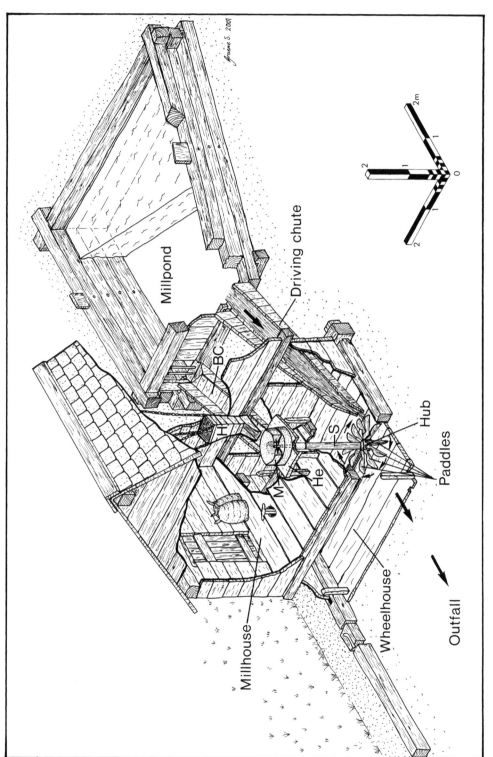

Fig. 8.2 Diagram of Anglo-Saxon water-mill, Tamworth, Staffordshire (after Rahtz and Meeson 1992).

Mills became a feature of Anglo-Saxon land charters from the ninth century onwards and were a common, taxable asset recorded in Domesday Book (some 5000 of them, with about 400 on the coast). They represent 'a mixture of skills and technologies, involving carpentry, millstones, metals and siting' (Hill 1981, 115 and map p. 197). Above all, though, they represent a significant conceptual advance in Britain, the harnessing of a non-human, non-animal source of power, implemented by an increasing social ability to concentrate the resources required to achieve such installations. Such concentration, in various societies through the British Isles, came through the increasing authority of 'lordship' or local chieftainship – the actual name differed from place to place but the idea was the same. Local dominance came to be associated with particular territories, particular places and particular families. The distribution of mills in England was neither general nor random, but densest in a west country band NNW–SSE from the Severn valley to the Solent, with outlying groups in Kent and East Anglia.

Wine was being produced in England in both Roman and Anglo-Saxon milieux, so some form of wine-press must have existed unless the grape was entirely trodden. An illuminated manuscript in the British Library (BL Cotton Claudius B.IV: f.17) shows a wine-press which could well be a version of such a piece of equipment in England at the end of the millennium.

Vehicles, harness and yokes

Wagons and carts, of both two- and four-wheeled types, were in use in Britain throughout the first millennium. All are likely to have been made almost entirely of wood, though iron wheel rims existed in the early centuries AD. Their use was primarily on and for the farm, using unmetalled and unpaved tracks; but of course proper roads were built and maintained in the first to fourth centuries, mainly for through traffic, and in places continued in use throughout the millennium. Bridges, fords and ferries also existed, the first mainly in the early centuries AD, the others throughout the millennium. Periods of improved transport, as during the Roman administration and in the last two centuries of the millennium, were critical in permitting and indeed encouraging the more efficient distribution of agricultural produce to market – and therefore in stimulating agricultural production. The urban market networks and their intercommunications were very significant in this respect.

Such activity depended on many factors, not least the minutiae of harness to enable animal draught power to be efficiently applied to farm implements and road vehicles (discussed *in extenso* by White 1962 and

Langdon 1986). Horses, oxen, donkeys and mules, collars, yokes and other harness equipment like bits, together with whips/goads, shoes, cues and hippo-sandals, are all involved here, though their detail need not detain us. Those animals may have been used sometimes in pre-medieval Europe, for carrying and haulage perhaps rather than ploughing; but, as Langdon (1986, 8) says, 'oxen carried all the burden for ploughing and hauling in ancient times'. So much was this the case that their role became enshrined in an Anglo-Saxon proverb (Swanton 1993, 255): 'Plough with your oxen and sacrifice with your incense: those men are foolish who imagine that they please God when they slaughter their oxen.' The oxen's load, literally, depended critically on the yoke, and since the ox was undoubtedly the principal, non-human power-source in farming throughout the millennium, we shall examine it, briefly, but strongly influenced by Langdon (1986).

The yoke is but one method of harnessing the object pulled to the animal pulling. No evidence suggests that anything other than oxen yoked together was used to pull cultivating implements in the first millennium in Britain, so we are not concerned any further here with other animals or other means of harnessing an ox-team to a cultivating implement (the matter is further developed in chapter 9). In the first half of the millennium, from north Africa to Co. Durham, we can literally see in different circumstances two oxen pulling various types of ard depicted in mosaics and sculpture (White 1970a, Pls.19–23), though in none of the reproductions is the detail of the yokes as clear as one would like. On the Piercebridge ard-team model, for example, the ambiguously bisexual team (Manning 1971) wears a neck yoke, perhaps even more correctly a shoulder yoke, the ends of which are carefully etched into the bronze above the top of the animals' 'outside' shoulders; but details of the yoke's attachment to the halter around the animals' necks are ambivalent (Pl. XXVa; Fig. 9.2a). Similarly, ambiguity continues with two votive model yokes from Sussex which for long were not recognised as yokes at all. Even now exactly what their detail represents is not certain, though each clearly represents a yoke for a pair of oxen (Manning 1966).

So confident are Whitelock (1955, 371) and Langdon (1986, 22 fn 1) about the exclusivity of oxen in cultivation in the second half of the first millennium that they infer oxen from the mere mention of a yoke in Ine's *Laws*. And that situation persisted to the end of our millennium and beyond: oxen dominate Domesday. The yoke is crucial because consideration of implements which actually cultivate the soil, other than hand-tools, is impossible to pursue without taking into prior account how they were pulled through the ground. Without oxen fitted with yokes, first-millennium cultivating implements would not have moved. Without movement, ploughs do nothing.

Various types of yoke are illustrated and discussed by Haudricourt and Delamarre (1955, 165) and Langdon (1986). No yokes of the first millennium AD have yet been found archaeologically, and yokes are either omitted or not shown in much detail in the relevant illuminated manuscripts. We very much have to look, therefore, to later sources and analogy on the reasonable assumption that the design of the ox yoke has not changed fundamentally since its early development (Pl. XXII).

For our purposes two basic yoke-types exist which enable a pair, or pairs, of oxen to work together. One is the 'neck' or 'shoulder' yoke which pulls together and keeps separate two animals across their shoulders at the base of the neck. This type has the advantage of making the animals pull at their zone of greatest strength, that is they lean into the traction, taking the pull across their shoulders. The other type seems less plausible and perhaps even cruel (as Columella claimed) but it works just as well. The 'head' or 'horn' yoke fits across the top of the two necks, lashed to the front of the horns (Pl. XXX; Marchandiau 1984, pl. on p.19 illustrates the method clearly on live oxen). It has the advantage, perhaps because it is somewhat less comfortable for the oxen, of making the animals keep their heads up and then pull through the full length of their bodies including their neck muscles.

The early Irish tale *The wooing of Étaín* indirectly indicates that both shoulder yokes and head yokes were known, the head yoke being the more primitive (Kelly 1998, 472), in at least the second half of the millennium. This author's conversation in 1999 with the last man to lead the ox-team at Hures la Parade, Causse Méjean, Languedoc, some fifty years previously, confirmed that there both methods were used indiscriminately and indeed that the same yoke was used for both methods. In both serious experiment and pragmatic day-to-day use, head yokes have found favour at both Butser 'Ancient Farm' and Bede's World's 'Anglo-Saxon farm'. In contrast, however, is an eighteenth/nineteenth-century claim that head yokes were introduced to Ireland then: is this an example of continuity or revival or reintroduction? Bell's (1983) conclusion that the horse from England largely replaced oxen *c.* 1500 may be generally correct but oxen were still in use in Ireland in the nineteenth century. This was so in Britain too, for example in Northumberland, especially by gentleman farmers. Fortunately for scholarly purposes, the authentic practice continued in outlying parts of Europe long enough to be recorded (Pl. XXII; *l'araire* and yoke in Passmore 1930, Pl. IX, top; cf. Barker 1995; Fowler 1981c; Reynolds 1981).

Conclusion

Essentially, with the technology at their disposal, the many and varied communities of Britain throughout the millennium exploited a plethora of natural resources to produce their food supply fairly successfully from a wide range of habitats. They did not, however, control Nature to any significant degree, and were therefore very much at the mercy of climate and weather, soils and topography, in a seasonally based cycle within which their technology enabled them to cope, but little more. We have remarked already how even the *Anglo-Saxon Chronicle* notes exceptionally bad weather and famines (chapter 4); vernacular sources are full of that awareness of the thin edge between survival and hard times in a basically hostile natural world. Knowledge of local conditions and practicalities, accruing from practice over a thousand years and more, was almost certainly quite as important in enabling farmers to cope from season to season and year to year as any technological knowledge. Husbandry was surely as much traditional – in the proper sense of that word – as technological.

9 | Ard and plough

Remarquez la différence entre les araires et les charrues.

CAPTION TO PHOTOGRAPHS OF EARLY
TWENTIETH-CENTURY PLOUGHING SCENES,
MUSÉE DE LA FERME D'AUTREFOIS,
HYELZAS, LANGUEDOC, FRANCE

The ard and the plough were crucial to farming in the first millennium AD; but the ard was by far the more common of the two. The plough, however, especially in the third, fourth and tenth centuries, proved the more significant in the light of what happened in the second millennium. Coming between technology as a whole (chapter 8) and the processes which it served (chapter 10), this chapter acknowledges that these principal cultivating implements have become a somewhat arcane minor field of study in its own right with its own literature.

'Ard' is a modern name invented and much used by archaeologists in particular to distinguish a cultivating implement without coulter or mouldboard (see Fig. 9.1 and Glossary). An ard is the earliest of the draught cultivating implements, with a history going back to the fifth millennium in Europe; the type survives not only as the common cultivating implement in today's Third World but was in use in western Europe until recent times (Lerche 1994, 23). In Mediterranean Europe it persisted into the 1950s in, for example, Languedoc (Fowler 1998), and in southern Italy until the 1970s (Barker 1995). In Atlantic Europe it was the normal implement in use in montane Galicia into the mid-1970s (Fowler 1981c; Reynolds 1981), and in the north it was recorded, for example, in 'use here and there in Zealand [Denmark] in the nineteenth century' (Michelsen and Rasmussen 1955, 13). It was certainly widely in use in north-western Europe in the last two millennia BC and, as radiocarbon dated examples show, throughout the first millennium AD (chapter 8, Table 8.1). Principally illustrated through the accident of survival and discovery by Danish material, but with examples from places as far apart as Britain and the Ukraine, we can note two principal types of ard in use in the first millennium AD, the crook ard, exemplified by that from Dabergotz, Germany, in the ninth century, and the bow or composite

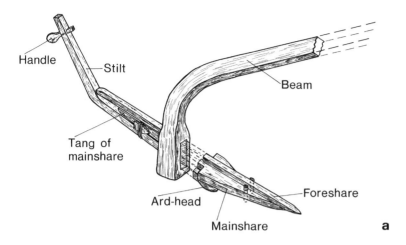

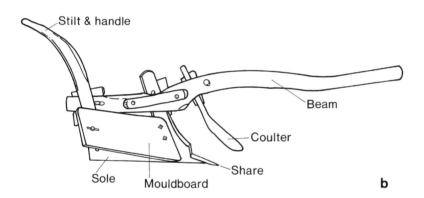

Fig. 9.1 Diagrams to illustrate the components and their names of: (a) an ard; (b) a plough (based on Bowen 1961 and Lerche 1994).

ard, exemplified by the beam of one from Mammen, Denmark, in the third century and by several examples of wooden shares of various dates throughout the millennium. The implications for Britain are difficult to avoid.

Obviously, arable farming in Britain could not have been carried out in the first millennium without reasonably efficient versions of a cultivating implement. The problem is what sort or sorts of cultivating implement, and when the different types were introduced. In particular, what cultivating implement or implements, if any, did the Romans introduce and the Anglo-Saxons bring with them to Britain? And when did the plough (*la charrue*) replace the ard (*l'araire*)? Was this in the first millennium AD and, if so, did it happen once or several times, and was the displacement general or partial, sudden or gradual? The mere asking of such questions immediately places us a long way from the traditional, and academically long-abandoned, view that the Anglo-Saxons introduced a 'heavy plough' into Britain. One of the few things we can be certain of in this matter is that they did not.

Merely by homing in on that particular topic, however, we fall into the old Anglo–centric, historical trap. Looking at Britain as a whole, and at the whole of the first millennium, gives a different perspective. An equally weighty question, for example, is whether a plough, heavy or otherwise, existed in Roman Britain; and the answer is 'yes', though the fact must not distract from the rather more important fact that it co-existed with the indigenous ard, which was the much more common, widespread type of cultivating implement. The latter is well documented in Classical literature and modern ethnography; the former is documented only outside Britain but archaeologically attested within. Later in the millennium, on the one hand documents tell us how land was marked out into estates and how people should behave to their agricultural neighbours; but, on the other, not a single document unambiguously describes either the common cultivating implement or a specific example of one, so we do not know how the land was actually being cultivated. An Anglo-Saxon riddle about a plough late in our period illustrates the problem (below).

Archaeologically, there is quite a marked contrast between the first and second halves of the millennium in respect of cultivating implements. From the first, we have several parts of ards and ploughs, and models and depictions in various art forms; from the second we have almost nothing, at least in Britain, until the tenth century and later. Given the large amount of relevant excavation now accomplished, the absence in particular of unequivocal evidence of a plough from Anglo-Saxon contexts before the tenth century is almost certainly significant, particularly in comparison with the existence of equivalent evidence from earlier in the millennium. So here we first summarise the present situation, and then expand on terms, details and sites in subsequent discussion.

The ard was in common use throughout Britain for most if not all of the millennium; it was complemented by the introduction of a 'Roman' or 'Mediterranean' type of plough with heavy share and coulter, and possibly a mouldboard (see Glossary for all such technical terms), used perhaps only on the more advanced estates in the agriculturally richer parts of the province, like the Somerset/Gloucestershire area. The great bar-shares from Box, for example, and the large iron coulter from Great Witcombe, both Gloucestershire, all bespeak heavy, wooden-framed ploughs of a general type which would not have been out of place on an eighteenth-century farm in the same area. The idea of, and therefore the practice with, both types continued, though differentially on a regional basis. On the rare occasions when cultivating implements have been archaeologically suggested

(a)

Found at Pierce Bridge Co Durham.

Plate XXV Bow ards in use at the beginning and end of the first millennium AD: (a) bronze model of *c*. AD 100 from Piercebridge, Co. Durham (British Museum); (b) illustration of ploughing in a cycle of seasonal activities (similar to that shown on the frontispiece), *c*. AD 1000, Harley MS 603, fol. 66r (British Library).

(b)

in contexts of the second half of the millennium, they are invariably ards, not ploughs, until the context is tenth century or later (see Appendix 1). No evidence exists that Anglo-Saxons brought with them proper ploughs.

Since land cultivation was undoubtedly the basis of Anglo-Saxon agriculture, however, farmers in the second half of the millennium must have had some form or forms of tilling implement. That most commonly in use in England until at least the tenth century was therefore most probably a wooden ard without iron fittings. Such was almost certainly of bow and/or crook type, familiar in the arable fields of the first half of the first millennium AD and earlier, probably being replaced by a plough with mouldboard in England as our millennium ends. If so, no firm evidence links it with specifically Viking introduction or development, though much about the socio-economic context of tenth- to eleventh-century England suggests that the insular emergence of a real plough would have been appropriate, not least to cultivate large, long fields (above, chapter 7).

A few ostensibly late Saxon iron shares could have fitted on to ards and are not in themselves proof of a framed, wheeled or mouldboard plough (Fowler 1981b). The Gwithian evidence of plough-marks and a turned furrow belonged to a pre-West Saxon context (Fowler and Thomas 1962) and is most likely to have occurred so far to the west precisely because it emanated from a different cultural context altogether, reminding us that the cultural reservoir in the post-Roman Celtic West may have included *agraria* as well as religious, linguistic and scholarly traditions (cf. Thomas 1998). Nor is Gwithian an isolated instance in this respect: the mouldboard plough existed, after all, in early medieval Ireland (Kelly 1998), a phenomenon more likely to have continued from a Roman introduction in the first half of the millennium than anew from Anglo-Saxon England. The appearance of the water-mill in Ireland and western Britain in the seventh century and later is similarly as likely to be an insular survival from Roman technology before the fifth century as a reintroduction from Mediterranean or Continental sources after AD 600. The Bayeux Tapestry itself illustrates such a plough, *une charrue*, whether it was sewn from life in Normandy or England (Stenton 1957, pl. 12; below).

Types of cultivating implement (Figs. 9.1 and 9.2)

Ards

Ards are characteristically quite small, 1.25–3.5 m in length. The smallest and simplest are light enough to be picked up in one hand; one can easily be carried over the shoulder. Modern ards can be made of iron, e.g. as displayed in the Eretz Israel Museum, Tel Aviv, but in the first millennium

SAXON PLOUGHS

Above. 10th century, from Cædmon's MS.   *Below.* 11th century, from the
Cottonian MS.

AN EARLY ENGLISH PLOUGH

An illustration from the Louterell Psalter, 14th century

Plate XXVI   Copy of Pl. II in Passmore's *The English Plough* (1930), illustrating key parts
of the evidence as perceived in the first half of the twentieth century for the 'introduction' of
a proper plough into England by Anglo-Saxon settlers. All three illustrations are genuinely
from authentic medieval manuscripts of the dates indicated, but to imagine they tell us
anything of aratral technology 500 and more years earlier is an insupportable assumption.
The top two, nevertheless, very probably do reflect types of plough not brought from
Europe in the fifth and sixth centuries but as developed in fields in England from the later
part of the first millennium onwards.

they were made entirely of wood. An exception, to do with their function, not construction, was that some were fitted with a metal cap over the tip of the share or foreshare and others were fitted with proper shares (below). The ard can, however, become heavier and more complex without its basic character being changed. Their main types are:

Crook ard: essentially made from one piece of wood, the beam being a branch angling off a block of tree-trunk cut down and shaped so that it will slice through the soil. Easy to find on standing timber and to make, the type was nevertheless apparently always rare in prehistory (Glob 1951) and, with the exception of the 'Odell ard' (below), is unknown in the first millennium AD in Britain. It is not the type illustrated as 'The Crooked Plough' by Passmore (1930, 66) (see sole ard below).

Bow ard (PL. XXVIIa): essentially consists of a main piece of wood in the shape of a bow forming the ard-head and stilt, with a beam projecting forward. The type is illustrated in all its effective simplicity around the end of the first millennium AD in Harley MS 603 (Pl. XXVb, as shown in Passmore 1930, Pl. I, upper). The beam could join the main part of the ard in a variety of ways in several places. The junction could be used to fit in also a foreshare and share, as in the Donnerupland ard (Plog 1951; Manning 1964, Figs. 2, 3), the quite complex carpentry involved resulting in a rigid structure as the parts became jammed together as the ard moved forwards through the soil. It could also be fitted with an iron cap on the foreshare or even a complete iron share: that this may well have become the norm by the first century AD is suggested by the four from Camerton, and one from nearby Stantonbury Hill, both Somerset (Jackson 1990). For lighter soils, in order to push earth to one side if not actually turn it over, it could be fitted with 'wings' behind the share, as described by Virgil ('*binae aures*', two ears; Manning 1964, 55–6, Pl. VIII, (1)) and illustrated here from Galicia in 1974 (Pl. XXVIIb). It could also be fitted with a coulter as illustrated in Eadwine's twelfth-century Psalter (Pl. XXVI, same as Passmore 1930, Pl. II, middle), though to do so makes it a plough, a *charrue*.

The bow ard type was the commonest throughout prehistoric Europe and later. An arrow-shaped share from a bow ard in Esjberg Museum, Denmark, is, for example, radiocarbon dated to *c.* AD 700 (Lerche 1994, 36). It was in use in Britain too throughout the first millennium AD. It is not therefore surprising that there is a strong argument, advanced below, that it was from this type that the 'Saxon' or 'English plough' developed; and indeed that is what Eadwine's Psalter shows precisely.

Sole ard (Pl. XXVIIb): this is distinguished because instead of being basically of one piece of wood, like the two previous types, it is by design of three. A heavy block of wood forms the basis, the sole; into its top were fitted separately a handle at the back and a beam at the front. Passmore's (1930, 66) 'Crooked Plough' is exactly of this type, otherwise known in prehistoric Europe but apparently not in first-millennium Britain, with one well-known, apparent exception. An unprovenanced miniature votive bronze ard from Sussex in the British Museum is of the early centuries AD though not absolutely certainly of British origin; it can be interpreted as a sole ard, with a stilt and beam attached to a central piece and share (Fig. 9.2b; Manning 1966). It is unusual as an illustration of an ard because of its 'keel', apparently fitted to the base of the sole, and its two 'ears' splaying back from the share or ard-head. Though we cannot rely too much on the detail of an object only some 8 cm long overall, and intended for worship rather than agrarian scrutiny, such a winged share design was useful in pushing dry soil especially to one side or the other in preparing a seed-bed, a technique described by Virgil and witnessed by this author in Greece and Spain in the 1960s–1970s.

A sole ard with 'wings' may well be what was in the mind of the bronzesmith who cast the best and best-known representation of ploughing from Britain during the Roman occupation. The piece, a model from Piercebridge, Co. Durham (Manning 1971), is of a whole ploughing scene, showing a ploughman at work, holding a plough (or ard!) being pulled by two cattle, one male and the other, on negative evidence, female (Pl. XXVa; Fig. 9.2a). This is a combination of ceremonial significance, so perhaps the detail of the model should not be pressed too hard in agrarian terms; yet some details are encouragingly clear while others are, characteristically, ambiguous. The ploughman's clothes, for example, are an interesting combination of tunic, leggings and hooded cape (chapter 13); the fine detail enveloped by the cape shows a 'Classical' and not a 'Celtic' face. The yoke is well defined up to its ends (chapter 8).

The most ambiguous element is the plough itself, or more correctly the cultivating implement, which is in general depicted as an ard. It clearly consists of a stilt, sole and beam, with a projection outwards on both sides from the junction between stilt and beam; but it is the relationship between these parts which is unclear, probably because the whole is cast rather than through artistic obfuscation. Manning (1971, 130) opted for the reasonable conclusion that the implement is a modified bow ard. He picked out as significant two details: a hole in the top of the beam, arguing that this could have held a coulter on occasion, and the two side projections which could have held 'ground-wrests'. The implement could equally well be, however, a sole ard, with the stilt fixed into a separate sole or plough-head, rather than curving down into the plough-head as a single piece of wood.

(a)

(b)

Plate XXVII   (a) Bow ard, Hyelzas, Lozère, Languedoc, France. The bow, with its carved stilt, passes through the end of the beam where it is wedged into position; and the tang of an iron foreshare, in the form of a bar-share, is wedged between the front end of the bow and the sole (the iron brace holding beam and sole together is unlikely in a British first-millennial context). The sole splays and its rear end is flanged on both sides, enabling the implement to push soil to one side or the other, i.e. it is a two-way ard. The beam is truncated by the photograph because it is so long, as if for at least two pairs of oxen. (b) Sole ard, 1974, Galicia, Spain.

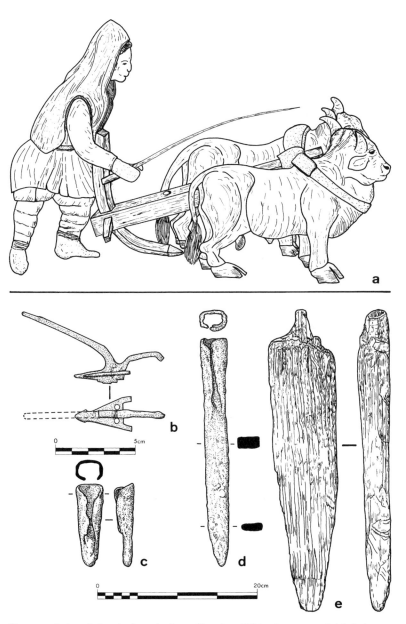

Fig. 9.2 Ards and ploughs from the first millennium AD (various sources); (a) the bronze model from Piercebridge, Co. Durham, interpreted after detailed examination in a drawing to project what the bronzesmith might have achieved if he had been able accurately to represent life; (b) bronze model of an ard from Sussex (Manning 1964, 59); (c) socketed iron ard-tip, Camerton, Somerset (Jackson 1990, Pl. 25, 256); (d) socketed iron bar share, Stantonbury, Somerset (Jackson 1990, Pl. 32, 305); (e) front end of wooden mainshare from a bow ard, the part fitting in the middle of the composite bow and as illustrated in Fig. 9.1a, with a notch and other markings on the pointed front for or of an iron share-tip as illustrated in (c) to the left, second/third century AD, from Abingdon, Oxfordshire (Fowler 1978a).

The beam could then have been fixed into the stilt. The junction of the latter two parts is not good on detail though, since no beam-end seems to jut out backwards behind the stilt, presumably the beam was morticed into the stilt – if this model was meant to be an accurate representation. Doubts on that score mount in considering the two curious projections to either side. They seem unlikely to have been the 'supports for earth-boards' (mouldboards) of Manning's suggestion (1971, 132) since the plane of such a fixture would have sloped the boards upwards from the ard-head to the projections, instead of being in the same plane as the sole as on recent, actual examples of such ards. Though the projections are not in exactly the same place as modern examples, they could themselves be the 'aures' which, by contact with the plough-soil when the ard was tilted to either right or left, helped mound up the soil to one side or the other. The fact is, however, that we cannot be certain of the exact type of ard in use in this model, but the important points are that the cultivating implement in this very Roman model is not a plough but an ard, with no apparent share or mouldboard even if it could be fitted with a coulter; and that the group as a whole is witness to one of the perpetual verities of agrarian life in Europe, not just Britain, in the first millennium AD.

Ploughs and prose

The two pieces of English (as distinct from Classical) documentary evidence bearing directly on the details of the cultivating implement and its use come, as could be anticipated, from right at the end of our millennium. One, Aelfric's *Colloquy* (Swanton 1993, 169–77), is a 'conversation piece', a favourite teaching device in which an imaginary conversation was written down in Latin and then read out, in this case perhaps in the monastic school at Cerne Abbas, Dorset. Here, a Master asks his pupils to role-play various characters in contemporary (probably late tenth-century) society: 'What do you say, ploughman? How do you carry out your work?', he asks, pointing to a pupil. And the 'ploughman' replies, in words mundane at the time but priceless to us.

> PLOUGHMAN Oh, I work very hard, dear lord. I go out at daybreak driving the oxen to the field, and yoke them to the plough; for fear of my lord, there is no winter so severe that I dare hide at home; but the oxen, having been yoked and the share and coulter fastened to the plough, I must plough a full acre or more every day.
>
> MASTER Have you any companions?
>
> PLOUGHMAN I have a lad driving the oxen with a goad, who is now also hoarse because of the cold and shouting.
>
> MASTER What else do you do in the day?

PLOUGHMAN I do more than that, certainly. I have to fill the oxen's bins
    with hay, and water them, and carry their muck outside.
MASTER Oh, oh! It's hard work.
PLOUGHMAN It's hard work, sir, because I am not free.

That little exercise gives us in its prosaically vivid description details of
the plough, clearly not an ard, and other aratral objects, of the processes of
cultivation, manure collection and animal care, of the ploughman's status,
and of the human perspective on the work – long hours, miserable working
conditions, fear of 'the boss' and an absence of any choice in the matter.

We can now turn happily to appreciate an anomalous piece of evidence,
always quoted but still significant. Anglo-Saxons were fond of riddles and
one that has come down to us in written form, perhaps originating in
the eighth century, is 'Riddle XXI' from the Exeter Book. A modern
translation runs like this:

> I keep my snout to the ground; I burrow
> deep into the earth, and churn it as I go,
> guided by the grey foe of the forest
> and by my lord, my stooping owner
> who steps behind me; he drives me
> over the field, supports and pushes me,
> broadcasts in my wake. Brought from the wood,
> borne on a wagon, then skilfully bound,
> I travel onward; I have many scars.
> There's green on one flank wherever I go,
> on the other my tracks – black, unmistakable.
> A sharp weapon, rammed through my spine,
> hangs beneath me; another, on my head,
> firm and pointing forward, falls on one side
> so I can tear the earth with my teeth
> if my lord, behind me, serves me rightly.
>   (Crossley-Holland 1999, 240)

Allowing for the metaphors, the description is fairly clearly of a proper
plough, with a share ('snout'), coulter ('sharp weapon rammed through
my spine') and mouldboard (another 'sharp weapon', 'firm and pointing
forward, falls to one side'), the whole being led by a man ('grey foe of the
forest', an oblique reference for us but clear to the contemporary mind
impressed by images of rough and wooded land being cleared for arable
farming). Very telling is the image of the equipage moving forward with
'green on one flank' – the unploughed land, more particularly perhaps the
previously uncultivated land – and 'my tracks', clearly the furrows already

ploughed, on the other. Here is apparently clear evidence of the fully developed medieval plough at work in late Saxon England. The whole, however, may well reflect what the translator rather than the original scribe had in mind.

An earlier, overtly literal translation (by E.J. Morley for Passmore 1930, 3–5) reads:

> My beak is downwards, I go deep and dig along the ground, I go as the enemy of the hoar-wood guides me; And my lord goes not straight, my guide at the tail pushes me over the field, drives and urges me, sows in my track. I go nose forwards, brought forth from the grove, bound by skill, driven on the wagon; I have many wonders. As I go, it is green on my (one) side and my track is clear, black on the other (side). Driven through my back, hanging under me, is a well-forged pointed weapon, another in my head firm and pointing forward; what I tear with my teeth falls to the side. If any serves me well at the back, he is my lord. What am I?

We can easily answer: 'A cultivating implement – but whether an ard or plough we cannot be certain.' Passmore (1930, 4) was, however, in no doubt: 'This plough certainly had a beam, a coulter, a share, a mouldboard, and either a handle or a pair of handles; there are also perhaps references to a share-beam, wheels, and the practice of curving at the headlands. The writer was Saxon and almost certainly had in mind a plough which at the very least was a primitive form of those shown in Caedmon's MS' (here Pl. XXVI, upper). We remain unconvinced; there seems nothing in that literal translation that could not apply to an ard, though the modern translation convincingly describes a plough. The Caedmon manuscript, of the same late millennial time as the written version of the riddle, shows a plough, not an ard, though goodness knows what a 'primitive form' of it was meant to look like – other than an ard. The fact is that this evidence is ambiguous, but it certainly does not suggest, let alone prove, the presence of a plough in early Anglo-Saxon England. Passmore's 'evidence' to that end is worthless (Pl. XXVI). In particular, the wheeled carriage between plough and team helped give rise to the myth of the 'Anglo-Saxon heavy plough', though there is no evidence that such wheels were common even in medieval times, cf. the plough in the Luttrell Psalter (Pl. XXVI, bottom). His illustrations are nevertheless, if ironically, helpful for the end of the first millennium: each implement is fitted with a coulter, a share and a mouldboard; and both teams are harnessed with neck yokes. Our argument here is that such scenes could have occurred around AD 1000, but that they were new in the tenth century and not part of a technology introduced 500 years earlier.

Cultivation and its implements naturally feature in the various agrarian treatises by Roman writers (Gow 1914; see in particular White 1967, chapter 7, here used for examples but not otherwise repeated). Varro, for example, described in the late first century BC 'all the processes of cultivation from sowing-time to harvest' in Book One of his *De Re Rustica*; while Columella, writing in the first half of the first century AD, described 'field-crop husbandry' in Book Two of his *De Re Rustica* (White 1970a, 23, 27). Virgil gave an excellent, detailed description of one type of ard (cf. Payne 1948; Fowler 1981c; Reynolds 1981). Classical background material like this was well known to Classically educated writers on the subject in the modern period, but they were completely unaware of the archaeological evidence for agriculture and ploughs, in particular in northern and western Europe. Such evidence was changing in status in the early decades of the twentieth century from that of disparate curiosities to a body of coherent information (Leser 1931; Glob 1951). Nevertheless, most of the earlier historians' misjudgements understandably arise from the absence of that information. The most expansive academic treatment of what he described as 'a small section of the history of the plough in Europe' was, at the time, Passmore's *The English Plough* (1930). It was a signal publication for our purposes, its influence still not dissipated.

Remarking that 'The early records of ploughs covering the centuries prior to the Norman Conquest...are scanty', Passmore nevertheless plunged straight into '1. Pre-Saxon Ploughs'. Essentially he saw the development in ancient times of the digging stick which then became a spade and then a more sophisticated hand-plough. In the absence at the time of prehistoric archaeological artefacts, he then jumped to two medieval manuscript illustrations to make his point about the difference between a spade and hand-plough on the one hand and a 'primitive plough drawn by oxen' (p. 2). He discoursed aptly on the 'araire' of Provence and Languedoc, and was clearly aware of plough types not only from the ancient world but also as distributed in space and time; yet he makes no connection with 'the English plough'.

His problem is conceptual. Even if the Roman plough was introduced into Britain during the first four centuries AD, he argues, 'it is certain that it is in no way a foreunner of the English plough. It is also improbable that any plough which existed in Britain before the coming of the Romans affected the development of the English plough. The various indications show that the Saxon brought his own plough . . . or that [the Saxon plough type] was developed by him after he settled in these islands' (p. 3). Passmore was wrong on all three counts. This was unfortunate for the understanding

Plate XXVIII
One-way plough with
bar-share and mould-
board suspended from
the beam, but no coulter,
Hyelzas, Lozère,
Languedoc, France.

of first-millennium farming, for his views held the field in effect for a generation, and still linger. A result is that aratral scenes at the end of the first millennium are seen as showing 'Saxon' ploughs, when in fact they show types of prehistoric ard, and medieval illustrations are used to suggest the back-projection of 'heavy' plough types into pre-Conquest days (Pl. XXVI).

Our concern with this detail seems to be justified when, in complete contrast to Passmore's enthusiasm for the idea of the Saxon plough as a mid-millennium import, a modern study comes to a very cautious judgement after a cogent assessment of the case (Langdon 1986, 245): 'It would seem, on balance, that the English peasantry of the last three centuries of the middle ages [1200–1500] used mould-board ploughs rather than ards.' Many, their thoughts dominated by heavy ploughs behind eight-ox teams churning their way along curving strips at any date from 1066 if not earlier (cf. Richardson 1942), may not have realised there is even a case to consider.

Cultivating implements and field types

Bowen (1961) laid out the principal types of ard and plough and of field evidence of cultivation, namely several types of field systems and of ridge and furrow. His focus was very much in southern England but he boldly made the correlation between types of cultivating implement and types of field evidence. For example, ard = cross-ploughing = squarish 'Celtic' fields; mouldboard plough = ploughing in long runs = long rectilinear plots = (sometimes but not necessarily) broad ridges defined by a furrow either side = (sometimes but not necessarily) open fields. Fenton (1962–63) pulled all the relevant archaeological evidence together from Scotland and brought into focus the fact that ards were not merely a foreign, Danish phenomenon but had also existed in early Britain. He put into context wooden parts of wooden ards from later prehistory found in Scotland. His approach, itself influenced by Glob's, was consciously influential in the academic treatment of wooden – not iron – ard-shares which have subsequently been excavated in contexts of the early centuries AD in southern and western Britain.

Two from the west were excavated in Wales, at Usk and at Walesland Rath, Pembrokeshire (the following paragraph summarises Fowler 1978a, 87). That from the latter was understandably first published as a 'spear-tip' (Wainwright 1971, 94–9). When Manning subsequently appreciated its significance, it provided a new perspective on the existence, use and survival of wooden ards and their parts in western Britain where previously stone (Rees 1979a) and iron shares, as at Dinorben (Manning 1964, Fig. 5C), had been the archaeological expectation. Two other wooden shares came from lowland Britain. One was on the floor of a probable gravel quarry at Odell, Bedfordshire (Dix 1981), infilled during the first half of the first century AD. The profile of the worn and shaped piece of oak suggests that the piece is the complete sole and share, plus the stump of the beam, of a crook ard of Glob's Type II, a crook ard with a long beam and broad sole (cf. Glob 1951, 14–29). The ard from Papouro, Poland (*ibid.*) is an almost complete example of what the Odell piece may have come from – if indeed it was an ard. The doubt about its identification rests almost entirely with the thinness of the stump of what would have been the end of the beam: no wonder it snapped at what was the point of most tension in a crook ard. Perhaps the piece was intended to be part of a crook ard but was either unfinished or broke in a trial run which provided the convincing aratral scratch-marks on its sides and the wear on its leading edge or 'share'. Though this type of ard was rare in prehistory, it was known in the first millennium, as illustrated by the ard from Dabergotz, Germany, radiocarbon dated to the eighth century AD (Lerche and Steensberg 1980, 82).

Much more convincing was the oak share of a bow ard deposited around AD 250 in a stone-lined well of a farm at Abingdon, Oxfordshire (Fig. 9.2e; Fowler 1978a). Although it has subsequently disintegrated, at the time of examination it showed clear evidence of having been fitted with a presumably iron 'cap' or share-tip, and also of differential wear on its surfaces which enabled numerous suggestions to be made about how it had actually been used. Nevertheless, as many as three interpretations were offered as to exactly how it had fitted on to exactly which sort of bow ard. For present purposes, however, the significant point is that 'it represents the continued use in the heavily romanized Abingdon area of a prehistoric type of wooden ard' (Fowler 1978a, 87). Though not such a surprising conclusion now, it was a point that needed emphasising in the 1970s when outdated thoughts about 'Belgic', Roman and Saxon 'heavy ploughs' lingered still.

These examples of wooden ards represent exactly the sort of evidence which should, and one day will in this writer's view, be found in Anglo-Saxon contexts of the seventh to tenth centuries. Meanwhile Postan (1966, 149 ff), pondering on the origin of the mouldboard, correctly addressed one of the two outstanding problems in European terms but misjudged significance by focussing on the origin of the wheeled plough when the presence or otherwise of wheels is not basic to the plough in terms of technological development; though characteristically a feature of west European ploughs from the eleventh century onwards, rather is a wheel-carriage a mechanism for improving steering and adjusting share-depth to field circumstances (Lerche 1994, esp. chapters 2, 9).

One archaeological object characterises cultivation in practice in Britain in the first millennium. It is the miniature, bronze model of an aratral scene from Piercebridge, Co. Durham (Fig. 9.2a). We have already commented on the yoke and the cultivating implement, a bow ard (see pp. 179, 189–92). The ard itself shows a projection on both sides of the lower stilt, perhaps for shoving it down into the earth with either foot, perhaps simply the peg to hold the stilt in the beam. The ploughman, clad in hooded cloak, clasps the stilt in his left hand and holds the end of a stick, perhaps a goad or whip, in his right. Overall, it presents a pan-European image of the ploughman engaged in his arduous task. The image must have been familiar throughout the millennium; it becomes familiar to us at the end.

Illuminated manuscripts

We now turn to a completely different evidential source, graphic art and illuminated manuscripts in particular. A few works are of great importance in this matter, for they depict agrarian, and specifically aratral, scenes (frontispiece; Pl. XXVb). These make sense to an agrarian historian but crucial in their agrarian use as evidence of technology is the date, not just of the actual manuscript but of the components of the picture. Lerche (1994, Fig. 2.5), for example, draws attention to the square-framed wheel plough on the Bayeux Tapestry, a contrast to the wheel-less plough of a later English manuscript noted by Leser (1931, 159) to which might be added the famous wheel-less plough of the Luttrell Psalter, dated *c.* 1340 (BL Add. MS 42130 fol. 170; Pl. XXVI, bottom). Though such sources provide a *terminus ante quem* if, as in these cases, the artwork itself can be dated, its components may well not be contemporary and can have origins essentially of earlier date and in distant sources. We are dependent on art historians for their assessment of these matters. Here we follow Backhouse *et al.* (1984), aided by Temple (1976). We first follow, however, the exception to the generalisation, an archaeologist. Carver (1986) set out to answer his own question, 'How far do the pictures in early medieval manuscripts reflect contemporary life?'

By way of illustration, we take two manuscripts of *c.* 1000 AD. They are not a random choice: both are particularly significant in terms of ard, plough and yoke; and both contain scenes of people ploughing (here frontispiece, Harley MS 603, fol. 21r, and Pl. XXVb, Harley MS 603, fol. 66r). It does seem extraordinary that while the great debate, sometimes assumption, continues about the existence, even ubiquity, of the 'Anglo-Saxon heavy plough', here are two well-known scenes right at the end of the first millennium on manuscripts which clearly show people using ards. Langdon (1986, 244–5), like Lerche (1994, Appendix IV), considers that such scenes may well have continued; she meant in Europe, he meant in England. In the latter, such would have become increasingly less common after the eleventh century, but of course they probably remained the norm for various lengths of time in other parts of Britain and Ireland as well as north–west Europe.

The Harley Psalter (BL, Harley MS 603, fol. 66r; Backhouse *et al.* 1984, no. 59), shows an agrarian sequence containing a ploughing scene with a bow ard (Pl. XXVb). It is one of over a hundred eleventh-century multi-coloured drawings by several hands. They, and the Latin manuscript as a whole, seem fairly certainly to have been created during the second and third decades of the eleventh century, copying at Christ Church, Canterbury, a monochrome original of the Utrecht Psalter made at Rheims *c.* AD 820 and brought to England about the end of the tenth century. Thinking of the illustrations in terms of the material culture they depict, everything shown must be earlier than AD 1040 at the very latest. Some details may be of *c.* 1020 if insertions into or contemporary versions of original items; some would be earlier than 1000 if properly copied from the imported Psalter; and some could be early ninth century and Rhenish if originally drawn from life. It could well be argued, therefore, that any connection between agrarian life as depicted in the Harley Psalter and late

Anglo-Saxon farming is remote. There are strong reasons for thinking that such is not the case.

We have already used Carver (1986) in an exemplary role (chapter 2) and for his information about various tools and implements (chapter 8). Fortunately, the thrust of his research was precisely to try to answer the question of the extent to which late Anglo-Saxon illuminated manuscripts could be used as evidence of contemporary artefacts. He concentrated on Harley 603, 'a copy of the Utrecht Psalter begun at Canterbury in the early eleventh century', while also considering other contemporary manuscripts; he did not, however, discuss processes. His 'preliminary conclusions are that the illustrator is most likely to be recording contemporary life' and he also judged that 'many of the *Harley 603* innovations . . . proved to be inventions of tenth century England in general, rather than the Harleian hands in particular'. Given that different artists worked on the illumination over perhaps a period of 30–40 years, 'Hands IA and IF prove to be accurate observers of their surroundings' (pp. 120–1). In that context, we look at the depiction of a plough in Harley 603, an illustration which Carver places in Hand IF's second phase when 'he displays a far greater originality and fondness for naturalism, which extends even to the testicles on a ploughman (f.66)' (p. 132).

The ard is fairly certainly of a single piece of wood, shaped to give a not very thick and slightly sinuous stilt, a thick heel and a tapering sole which is not tipped with anything. A beam, unconvincingly attached to the base of the stilt, passes at a slight angle between two oxen, but no yoke is shown. The ploughman feathers a notably straight stick in his right hand, holding it rather like a fishing rod, its far end hovering above the oxen's noses. He holds the base of the stilt with his left hand, just above the junction with the beam, clearly lifting the heel of the ard off the ground so that the ard-tip is at an angle into the soil. The artist equally clearly attempts to show that the ard makes a furrow (see below). The ploughman's right shoulder leans into the top end of the stilt. He is barefoot (and apparently bare-bottomed too), his left leg advanced, his right pushing from the back. This whole posture, together with the depiction of the implement itself, indicates that the ard is quite small and very light: the ploughman has to 'work' it rather than just expect it to follow the oxen through the soil under its own weight. Typologically, the ard could come out of a Danish prehistoric peat-bog and, medieval clothes apart, the whole scene off a Swedish Bronze Age rock carving (cf. Glob 1951, 48–51). It is certainly pan-European in agrarian terms, and may not even be English.

One interesting further detail is that the surface of the ground being cultivated is quite deliberately shown as undulating. It bears five depressions (grooves or furrows) and four small, rounded ridges between them. The ploughman's right foot is in the deepest furrow to the rear, the oxen's forelegs in the furthest to the front. Ahead of them is flat ground, so clearly the artist was attempting to distinguish between ploughed and unploughed land. He may well have run into the familiar problem of perspective, not knowing quite how to show in the same plane two things, ploughing and the effect of ploughing. His drawing, in other words, may be his best attempt to show what had been done backwards and forwards along the same axis while at the same time showing what the ard was doing at the moment of his depiction. On the other hand, to offer a functional rather than art historical interpretation, his depiction may show precisely what would have had to happen with an implement of this sort: cross-ploughing.

The Harley Psalter (BL MS 603, fol. 21r) shows seven stages in the crop production process (see frontispiece and chapter 10). Here we are concerned with the first, another ploughing scene. All the remarks above about the making of the manuscript and its use here apply. The implement is an ard, technically a bow ard, but its representation is schematic, not detailed. It may be of one piece of wood but its shape suggests it is composite. A possible share-tip and an outward-turned stilt-end to act as a handle are nevertheless apparent. The implement is being pulled by two shafts, whether wood or rope/leather is not clear, attached to the lower part of the stilt and converging immediately behind the rear legs of the two-ox team. They are teamed by a neck yoke. The ploughman is correctly standing to the left of the equipage, holding the stilt handle in his right hand and a light stick in his left, its end just flicking the inner horns of the animals. He is balanced somewhat agitatedly on his right leg with his left off the ground, exactly the sort of snap-shot effect that could be obtained as the ploughman endeavours to keep the implement in trim while trying to keep the team moving smoothly. The scene has all the verisimilitude of what actually happens: whoever drew it, drew from direct observation or at least knowledge of what happens, or of course was copying an original drawn in such circumstances.

The explanation of both drawings must be either that they are a correct contemporary witness early in the eleventh century; or that the monk artist(s) of that date was out of touch, delineating archaisms; or, most probably, that the scenes are basically copies of earlier illuminations in which such ards would have been accurately portrayed because they were then in use and no other sort of cultivating implement was known. So, at the very least, such pictures indicate what we can infer was the normal cultivating implement in the Rhineland in the earlier ninth century and, perhaps, contemporaneously in England. In themselves, these two scenes at face value tell us nothing about what was happening in England in, say, the period AD 600–1000, though in the early eleventh-century world of the English illustrator, ards were apparently the norm.

Such was probably not, however, the reality in the fields outside the monastic windows in much of southern England by that date. The 'Caedmon manuscript' (Caedmon MS 154; here Pl. XXVI, top), also *c.* AD 1000, shows drawn correctly in perspective a plough-scene depicting a two-ox team harnessed by a neck yoke, and a proper plough with coulter, share-tip, two mouldboards and, between plough and team, great big wheels carrying the beam – almost certainly an accurate contemporary depiction, even though it is meant to be Noah ploughing. Perhaps the monk actually looked out of the window and drew what he saw there (Gollancz 1927; Temple 1976, no. 58; Backhouse *et al.* 1984, no. 154). There may indeed be a generality behind the remark about a slightly later illumination: 'The scenes of the Israelites' everyday life . . . depict usages and customs of 11th century England' (Temple 1976, 103).

Later still in the eleventh century is, as we have already noted, the Bayeux Tapestry, a work of art not exactly famed for its agrarian interest but with some relevant detail nevertheless (Stenton 1957, Pl. 12). We merely mention the single mule with harness but no yoke pulling a marvellously detailed, wooden-wheeled plough-carriage and full-blooded, adjustable plough with coulter, share and mouldboards, attended by a ploughman with his (invisible) feet presumably in the furrow and a 'traceman' with a long stick in his right hand, apparently shouting at the ploughman to get a move on! Of course, the whole equipage may have been seen in the fields of Normandy, not Sussex, though Stenton and colleagues favoured an English location for the creation of the Tapestry.

Such improvements in a basic technology that we see in Caedmon 154 and on the Tapestry had in practice been accumulating, perhaps in spurts, throughout the first millennium. This is strongly expressed for Ireland in one illustration (Edwards 1996, Fig. 22), making the point that plough improvements in share and coulter went with comparable changes in hand-tools. Langdon (1986 generally, here pp. 15–17) saw 'changes in plough design' as one of several major technological innovations developing from about the middle of the millennium. He follows others, for example, in seeing the breast-strap harness arriving in Europe (from the East) about the sixth century. His perspective, however, is concentrated on identifying the rise in the value of the horse, not the ox, as a beast of work early in the second millennium AD, so his perception of 'the spread of the heavy plough in northern Europe as a replacement for the earlier scratch plough or ard' is 'as a change to which the available traction had to adjust' rather than one of significant detail in changes to cultivating implements. For him, all innovations, in harnessing and horse-shoeing for example, 'gradually coalesced into a new system or systems of traction' which enabled horses to do more, but 'Ox traction was less affected [and] arrangements for harnessing or yoking oxen in the middle ages were still essentially the same as in ancient times.' We need not, therefore, look too closely for major improvements in the traction arrangements for ploughing the land in the last two centuries of the millennium; nor do we need to look at alternative traction power itself because, despite the Bayeux mule, 'oxen were the sole plough animals in use at the time of the Domesday survey' (Langdon 1986, 33).

Summary

The source of traction-power, oxen, remained the same in medieval England as in prehistoric Europe, but there clearly is a case for considering that significant changes in the design of the principal cultivating instrument in England – essentially the change from ard to plough - occurred decisively in the tenth to eleventh centuries. We use the word 'decisively' to indicate that the change was made for good and all in England and, over the next centuries, in Britain. Unlike parts of the European mainland where it survived, the ard became anachronistic, and arable farming has not subsequently reverted to its use.

An equipage of two oxen yoked at the neck pulling a bow ard was the only one available to most farmers throughout most of the first millennium AD in England and, probably, in Britain as a whole. Cultivating implements with coulters and large shares, but no proven mouldboard, were known in third- and fourth-century southern Britain, and were probably the source of the similar implements attested in western Britain and Ireland in the second half of the millennium. Variants on the basic ard appeared regionally in parts of western Europe in the last century, possibly last two centuries, of the millennium, including southern and eastern England, where a coulter certainly, and possibly a mouldboard, marked the start of what on present evidence seems to be a very belated development into the full-blown 'English' plough, framed and with or without wheels, which had become common there by the medieval period. Until such is evidenced archaeologically before AD 900, the ard of Harley MS 603, fol. 66r (Pl. XXVb) and not the 'heavy plough' of the Luttrell Psalter

(Pl. XXVI, bottom) should be regarded as the principal cultivating implement of the Anglo-Saxons. While such ards eventually began to be superseded in the tenth century in England, however, they and various forms of digging implement continued to be used, in western and northern parts of Britain, well into modern times.

10 | Arable

> No agricultural system can be permanent that does not maintain an
> adequate soil structure.
>
> RUSSELL 1961, 432

Arable farming was clearly a continuum throughout the first millennium
but, like other aspects of agriculture, far from its history being a straight
line of progress it seems likely that it waxed and waned both in significance and in extent. It is already emerging in this essay that its extent
probably increased in the first two centuries AD and in the tenth and
on through the eleventh centuries, at least in southern Britain; while in
contrast local increases have been noted in the middle years of the millennium in northern Britain. The crops produced by the arable land, and the
numbers they had to feed, have also changed through time, and again the
evidence points to chronological and regional variety rather than steady
development on one particular trajectory. Simple models of 'progress',
resulting in matters being 'better' in AD 1000 than they were in AD 1,
are clearly redundant.

Using Russell (1961) as our starting point, he described (p. 432) methods for controlling the soil structure as falling into four groups: 'the proper
use of cultivation implements, of climate, of manures, and of growing
crops'. 'Cultivation implements' were discussed here in chapters 8 and 9,
'climate' in chapter 3. In this chapter we briefly discuss some aspects of
'growing crops', including the use of 'manures' and of the possible adop-
tion of an 'infield/outfield' system. We consciously avoid some topics in
this field, however, to sidestep repetition for, of course, many aspects of
arable farming have already been discussed or touched on. Indeed, such
a basic topic runs through the book, so this chapter is not meant to be
a stand-alone survey of it. We would stress two basic points. First, underlying any consideration of arable farming should be a recognition of
the distinction between normal maintenance of soil fertility – 'keeping the
land in good heart', or sustainability – and soil depletion, a situation when
all is not well and matters could run out of control if remedial steps, such

as changed land-use, drainage or manuring, are not undertaken. Second, especially in respect of Russell's point in the opening quotation above, the distinction made here between 'arable' and 'pastoral' in chapters 10 and 11 is too sharp in one crucial respect, for the animals of the latter are the most important means of retaining the soil quality of the former, either by dropping their dung directly on the land or by producing the prime organic constituent of manure which is made up elsewhere and then spread on the land.

Basic though Russell's science is, even without such scientific knowledge in the first millennium the fundamental importance of cultivation to survival was well recognised by realists of all persuasions. Caesar (*BG* V.12) noted as a matter of fact that the 'Belgic immigrants' of coastal south-east England, in contrast to the indigenous peoples inland, 'settled down to till the soil'. According to the *Anglo-Saxon Chronicle*, in 876: 'Healfdene shared out the land of the Northumbrians, and they proceeded to plough and to support themselves'; while 'the canons attached to the church of Llancarfan were supplied with 80 acres of arable, in order that "necessities" could be provided' (Davies 1989, 31). Davies makes explicit the direct association between the land and survival, 'arable land', not just any land, a critical distinction. Nevertheless, much depended on where that land was and what crops it was intended to produce. Hence, to continue with our Welsh example (Davies 1989, 7) though only as a metaphor for anywhere in Britain, 'In some parts of Wales, and certainly at higher altitudes, the summer is too short to provide an adequate growing season while even in the lowlands there is often too much rainfall and too little heat to guarantee an adequate ripening of cereals.' Nor do all crops have the same requirements. Oats, rye and barley all grow successfully at much higher altitudes than wheat, and indeed grow on a wider range of soil conditions. Localised increases in them could, for example, represent a change in planting regime as a response to nutrient depletion from over-exploitation of the permanent arable. It is a truism now and can fairly be assumed to have been one in the first millennium, but the basic rule for a farmer is 'Know your land, know what it can best do and make the most appropriate use of it.' In arable terms, that means grow wheat on the valley slopes and don't try to grow it on top of Snowdon. Another essential of arable cultivation was to do things in the right order and follow the sequence annually. Giraldus noted this in his *Description of Wales* (chapter 8): 'They plough the soil once in March and April for oats, a second time in summer, and then they turn it a third time while the grain is being threshed' (Thorpe 1978, 233).

Plate XXIX   Roman granary without its floor but with most of the floor-supports in place, Housesteads fort, Northumberland. Another granary is on the right, emphasising the importance of storing cereal at the end of a long supply-line on the frontiers of empire rather than relying on local resources which, though including arable farming, were likely to have been inadequate for a large, regular military need.

Even so, arable farming was inherently risky, always heavy work, often unrewarding and frequently disastrous. Land could flood, under both freshwater and marine inundation, as both a local incident and a regional disaster. Warner (1996, 54), for example, accepts in his authoritative synthesis of Suffolk history a 'major inundation of the fens in about AD 275' and a late Roman 'marine transgression', flooding large areas of arable land and causing the abandonment of many farmsteads. Plough-soil could be washed away – as the extremely wet autumn of 2000 reminded us; very wet or very cold weather could prevent the plough getting on to the fields; seed could fail to germinate or could be eaten by birds; young shoots could be overwhelmed by weeds or stunted by drought; crops could be diseased or be ravaged by raiders; harvesting could be blighted by bad weather; stored cereal could rot on the stalk, threshed grain could become mildewed, infested with weevil or the like, eaten by rodents or, as happened at Clonnard, Co. Meath, in 751, burnt in the drying kiln (Edwards 1996, 63). In other words, much could go wrong; that it did, and that the thought that it might was always in mind, is suggested by archaeological evidence such as alluvial deposits over occupation levels and rotten grain, and by the occasional records of such happenings in even the official annual 'national diary', the *Anglo-Saxon Chronicle*. In 893, for example, the countryside around Chester was ravaged of its cattle and corn, an incident likely to have occurred elsewhere many times in the preceding nine centuries when itinerant war-bands and armies were surely a near-continual threat to the sedentary arable farmer. Nevertheless, arable food production kept going throughout the millennium in Britain, and perhaps even kept Britain going; it continued as their sole livelihood, or a significant part of it, for most people.

Field management

Britain lies in the barley- and wheat-growing zone of European crops, entirely to the north of the vine and olive zones (Barker 1985, Fig. 18). Change was clearly occurring in these matters in the later twentieth century – vineyards, for example, were once more becoming successfully established – and similar changes occurred in the first millennium AD. Not only did particular species of crop wax and wane on a millennial pespective, but soils changed too, for example by being redeposited naturally as a result of both processes and events, e.g. in the Tyne and Thames valleys (Evans 1999, 93; Lambrick and Robinson 1979, 124). On the Berkshire and Marlborough Downs thin soils on chalk subsoil seem to have ceased to support arable farming, perhaps in part because of their deficiencies, and to have been used as pasture instead from the third or fourth centuries onwards (Bowden *et al.* 1993; Fowler 2000c). Ancient writers were much concerned about nutrient and structural deficiencies in the soil and gave plentiful advice about artificial methods of counteracting them (Spurr 1986, 126–32). Appropriate numbers of animals dunging the arable fields after harvest and during fallow provided the main antidote, while 'muck-spreading' and liming or marling were the most obvious human methods of replenishing soil quality. Pliny wrote that the Britons and the Gauls knew about 'feeding the earth with a kind of soil called marl' (Ryley 1998, 11). Midden material and natural organic material like

seaweed were used as manure in prehistoric times, and the practice continued in the first millennium AD (Appendix 1). At Shapwick, Somerset, for
example, it is typically assumed that a near-ubiquitous spread of Roman
pottery was 'manured in', evidencing 'that much of the study area must
have been under arable cultivation' (Aston and Gerrard 1999, 20). Indeed,
it could be argued that manuring rather than ard cultivation – that adding
to the soil rather than just turning it over – was the key element of good,
basic practice in arable farming which kept regularly cropped land in good
heart (Pl. XLII). Such generalities here are, however, based on Classical
sources and empirical practicalities, given that direct evidence of what was
actually happening in arable fields on most farms in Britain throughout
the first millennium is in short supply.

   Two other methods of soil replenishment are known ethnographically
and agriculturally in Europe and could well have been practised in the
first millennium in Britain. One was to import new soil on to a field. This
was a well-known technique in historic times in Holland, for example
a model used to interpret the replacement of soil within 'Celtic' fields
at Vaasen in the first two centuries AD (Brongers 1976). The technical
name for this was the '*es* system', envisaged as starting in the seventh century AD. Something similar may have been practised in rather different
environmental circumstances on Orkney where, at St Boniface church,
cultivation in mid-millennium may be 'represented by the formation of
the deep *plaggen* soil outwith and to the north of the enclosed Iron Age
settlement . . . These sediments consisted of *in situ* ash dumps, deposited
infrequently, with intervening periods of soil formation' (Lowe 1998, 205).
Elsewhere, and more whole-heartedly, 'Man-made soils in the vicinity of
the abbey on Iona were introduced to the site over some time within and
possibly continuing throughout, the period between the seventh century
AD and the medieval period' (Barber 1981, 359). The other method involved not shifting soil but growing a 'green' crop and ploughing it in
to refresh the existing soil. As Dark (2000, 82) remarks, 'Crop rotation
may also have been employed to reduce soil exhaustion and prevent the
build-up of pests and disease. Rotation involving legumes would have been
especially beneficial' to fix atmospheric nitrogen, as we now well understand. The average first-millennium farmer cannot be expected to have
known the chemistry which lay behind his action but he was doubtless
well aware, from traditional knowledge and personal observation, of the
likely future benefit as he ploughed in his bean stalks.

   A special ploughing such as envisaged there may in part explain one
of the more curious archaeological discoveries of the twentieth century,
plough-marks. They are literally the marks made by ploughs – or ards, in

which case they should strictly be ard-marks – in plough-soil or, more frequently as detected, the subsoil. Spade-marks are also known, but not yet apparently from a first-millennium AD agrarian context. Plough-marks are characteristically lines or linear grooves, sometimes in parallel lines alone, sometimes in a criss-cross pattern. Though known as archaeological phenomena for a generation in Holland and Denmark, it was not until the 1960s that they came to be recognised in British archaeology (Fowler and Evans 1967). A typical early discovery was during the excavation of Gadebridge villa (Neal 1974, 99 and Fig. 22), a small patch of three parallel lines just over a metre long without a convincing context or further details. From this it was somewhat questionably inferred that 'The ploughmarks of an early date tell us that crops were being grown from the earliest times.' Subsequently, such phenomena were commonly discovered, more fully recorded, and taken seriously as direct evidence of arable cultivation techniques with interesting implications for technology and land-use (Bowen and Fowler 1978).

Such marks, even if produced by an ard, could have been produced during site-levelling, for example as in the construction of Roman roads (Fasham and Hanworth 1978) or, even if agricultural, by just a one-off ploughing when, deliberately or not, the tip of the share bit into the subsoil. If deliberate, the action may have been to bring subsoil up into the seed-bed, another method of maintaining the quality of the soil. Marks made by the cultivating implement often go with ridging but they also occur alone, sometimes at the base of plough-soils and occasionally on their surface. In the dune system at Brighouse Bay in south-west Scotland, for example, 'a set of furrows impressed into the upper surface of the [buried] soil and covered by windblown sand . . . [was] aligned roughly north to south . . . [and] visible as low rounded parallel depressions 0.6 m wide and a maximum of 0.03 m deep . . . four furrows were [at least] 6 m long and approx. 1.3 to 1.5 m apart'. Dating is not precise but probably this 'cord rig' is of later prehistoric/early Roman date. Higher in the local sequence was another set of parallel ploughmarks 0.4–0.6 m apart, up to 7 m long and 150 mm deep which penetrated both upper and lower levels of another, higher buried soil associated with small shell middens, interpreted as a single ploughing in the second or third century AD to mix midden and soil (Maynard 1994). There, then, one author was interpreting his 'ploughing' as a special action to improve fertility.

Similarly, but in rather different environmental circumstances, scattered pottery, residual from organic manure, certainly indicated efforts in the first to second centuries to improve the quality of the much cultivated, shallow crumbly soil on the Upper Chalk of Overton Down, Wiltshire. A palimpsest of partly contemporary criss-cross ard-marks indicated cultivation of manured soil in a pattern which did not relate to the medieval (?thirteenth-century) ridge and furrow overlying it (Fowler 2000c, chapter 6; and 2000d). In contrast, the Hen Domen evidence (Fig. 7.8), chronologically coming within that date range on Overton Down, demonstrated cultivation of a field with associated plough-marks in the subsoil and narrow ridge and furrow on the ground surface. We should, however, recognise that, while it is a rare piece of archaeological evidence, that which it represents would have been a common activity in the tenth and eleventh centuries (Higham and Barker 2000).

Numerous examples also exist of marks and ridging going together in much earlier contexts, notably in the first to second centuries AD. In the first century AD, criss-cross ard-marks were made in the subsoil over which cord rig was created at Greenlee Lough, Northumberland, on land on which a Roman camp was laid out before the building of Hadrian's Wall (Topping 1989, Pl. 27, 177). Similarly, further east in the Roman military zone, many of the interpretative issues and some of the potential of ridging and the marks made by cultivating implements were illustrated at Denton on the western outskirts of Newcastle upon Tyne (Bidwell and Watson 1996). As in numerous other cases (Topping 1989, 171), Hadrian's Wall was the catalyst: its modern destruction in roadworks provoked an excavation, and its original construction had both preserved and probably destroyed earlier and perhaps contemporary agrarian evidence. Plough-marks – more correctly ard-marks – and furrows (though not actual ridges) occurred stratigraphically separated but each on both sides of the Wall foundations (only one ard-mark was below the Wall). All the furrows and some of the marks were on the same NW–SE axis; but some of the marks, the earlier of the two phenomena, were related to a ditch on their west, apparently a field boundary.

The whole complex is illumined by informed discussion of the soils containing these phenomena (see above for an example), but the discussion of the agrarian significance of the site is handicapped by treating 'ard' and 'share' as synonymous (Topping 1989, 12; cf. chapter 9). In fact, one intriguing aspect of the evidence may well be that it demonstrates in its earlier marks the actions of a cross-ploughing ard, perhaps fitted with a protective tip on its share, while the later 'furrows' could have been made by a plough with perhaps a flanged share and, if not a coulter, then some form of mouldboard, cf. Pl. XXVIII. The 'furrows' themselves suggested they may have been residue of cord rig, and such a plough could certainly have produced such ridges. This rather technical evidence nevertheless produced an admirably realistic agricultural conclusion:

> the furrows represent a single episode of cultivation after the land had been under grass for a long period ... probably in the year before the construction of the Wall. If this was autumn ploughing followed by seeding, then the farmer would never have had the opportunity to harvest the crop: at the beginning of the building season, when the line of the wall was laid out in the spring of the following year, the farmer would have been expelled from the land by the Roman army. (Bidwell and Watson 1996, 17)

Interpretation can also be pursued when considerable expanses of ard- and plough-marks are available, for example as attempted by Everton and Fowler (1978). Especially is this so when they are recorded in historically significant contexts such as, for the early centuries AD, at the building of Hadrian's Wall (above) or on questionably marginal Wiltshire downland (Fowler 2000c, chapter 6, 82–92), interleaved in the stratification of a Northumbrian proto-urban centre (Hill 1997), or related to the building of a motte soon after the Norman Conquest on the Anglo-Welsh border (Higham and Barker 2000).

Crop types

There is now considerable information about the crops that were grown in first-millennium Britain. The outstanding characteristics are, not very surprisingly, that there were indeed changes through those thousand years and that, throughout, there was also considerable regional variation (Greig 1991; van der Veen 1992; Dark 2000, 173–4). A summary based on their work indicates the following:

1. Cereals were grown in both upland and lowland areas throughout the first millennium AD.
2. Considerable changes in crop exploitation in the first millennium saw:
   (a) at the beginning, staple 'Celtic' crops of barley and spelt wheat with beans, peas and flax, possibly hemp too;
   (b) in the early centuries AD, in some areas, an increasing use of bread wheat, rye and oats, though with the late prehistoric staples – spelt wheat and barley – continuing strongly; some weeds such as cornflower, corncockle and stinking mayweed, abundant in first-millennium fields but not previously attested, perhaps indicating deep ploughing; the big change botanically if not economically being, however, the appearance of grapes

(and viniculture is now confirmed by vine planting terraces at Wollaston, Northamptonshire: Meadows 1996) and horticultural products such as ornamental and garden plants;

(c) bread wheat dominating the record at many sites after the fourth century, accompanied by rye, barley and oats, with flax and hemp strongly evidenced; plants used for dyeing, woad and madder, appearing at several Viking towns.

3. By the eighth century, in a pattern of what can perhaps be seen as a distinctively Anglo-Saxon crop husbandry compared to the early centuries AD, bread wheat (*Triticum aestivum*), rye (*Secale cereale*), barley (*Hordeum vulgare*) and oats (*Avena sativa*) were becoming the main cereals in England, supplemented by peas and beans, with different emphases between these components from region to region. Barley, however, remained important in Scotland and Ireland. With old-fashioned, *sensu* prehistoric, rye and bread wheat apparently favoured by the second half of the millennium in place of the traditional wheats, emmer and spelt, the palaeobotanical evidence hardly indicates innovatory change, such as new strains of plant, in cereal farming in the period.

Many studies underlie such generalisations, and different models for interpreting the evidence have also been used. Jones (1988b), for example, describes the arable field as 'a botanical battleground' in direct contrast to its conventional portrayal as the battleground between the farmer and nature. His real purpose, however, was 'to emphasise the ever changing nature of crop/weed communities' (Jones 1988b, 91), with some plants becoming dominant and others being removed from the communities with the passage of time. It is a useful metaphor, particularly in a thousand-year perspective. In that context, two changes stand out in particular. The first is botanical: a shift some time between 'the late Iron Age and the late Roman period' towards a new pattern of crop farming in which bread wheat, *T. aestivo-compactum*, consistently a minor component before the Romans, became increasingly common. Murphy (1994, 37) sees its importance consolidated in the early Saxon period in East Anglia. By the end of the millennium, bread wheat had become the most important cereal in Romsey, a relatively well-sampled town (Green 1994, 85) It is, of course, the most important of current wheats.

Furthermore, 'Alongside bread wheat, the frequency of rye, oats and legume crops increases in this period' (Jones 1988b, 90). Jones goes on to link this with his second major change, summarised in his own words as 'The plant evidence . . . provides us with a very direct record of the ecological impact of the transition from ard cultivation to deep ploughing' (p. 90). Such a broad generalisation is both a conclusion arising from evidence contemplated and a challenge for evidence to be sought. As we have already seen (chapters 7 and 9), and as we shall conclude (chapters 13 and 14), cultivation technology itself does not follow a smooth course of improvement through the millennium. However much of Britain may have been 'deep-ploughed' in, say AD 300, at most only patches of it were cultivated thus in, say, the eighth century when there is none but the most tenuous evidence that a proper, asymmetric plough capable of 'deep-ploughing' existed. On the other hand, we have already seen above that the evidence of ard- and plough-marks indicates that, on occasion, deliberately or otherwise, cultivating implements could be made to bite into subsoil. In any case, depth of ploughing may not itself be the most critical factor; the ability of a cultivating implement to turn the soil over, thereby burying weeds, is arguably as, if not more, important.

From that point of view, and standing back once more to appraise Britain in its north-west European context, some implements capable of truly 'turning the sod' – and therefore presumably fitted with the all-important mouldboard – were in operation in areas now within north-western Germany, the Netherlands and Belgium 'from c. 400 BC but mostly from the centuries around the birth of Christ' (Lerche 1995, 196). Arable was being similarly ploughed in Britain in the early centuries AD, as we have already seen, and it may well be that the situation there sub-sequently mirrored that in Denmark where 'signs of the use of the [real asymmetric] plough [with a mouldboard] appear sporadically from the early Viking period' (p. 196). In other words, while there may well be a broad and general truth in Jones' proposition that improved crop diversity resulted from the technological change from an ard to a deeper-cultivating plough, the actual situation varied enormously from place to place and throughout the first millennium to the extent that such variety simply cannot be explained monocausally. Neither can one ecological change be attributed to one technological change, particularly when the latter did not occur once and for all; though, all that said, undoubtedly the increas-ing ubiquity of the mouldboard plough by the eleventh century in much of England if nowhere else in Britain was making a significant impact on the landscape and its flora, wild as well as domesticated.

A mass of detail now lies behind generalisations about crops in the first millennium (Appendix 1). A sample of a large deposit of charred grain from an early/mid-third-century military granary at *Arbeia*, South Shields, for example, consisted of about half spelt, *Triticum spelta*, and half bread wheat, *T. aestivo-compactum*, with a little barley. Whereas the spelt could well have been a local product (and is now being grown again at *Gwyre*, 5 km away; Appendix 3), the bread wheat was probably imported (van der Veen 1989, 74, 154–5). On the one hand, the latter had not yet become quite so common in Britain at this time as argued by Jones above; on the other, and very positively, the former was virtually ubiquitous as a major component, often the predominant species, across the range of military, urban and rural sites in the first half of the first millennium in much of Britain south of Hadrian's Wall. It was, of course, primarily to feed the military garrison along the Wall (Pl. VIII) that cereals were assembled in the twenty-two granaries early in the third century at the fortified depot at *Arbeia* (Bidwell and Speak 1994).

For comparison, we use the data from a slightly later period in southern England, mindful, however, of Murphy's (1985, 108) warning in summing up his study at one of the classic sites in the mid-millennium: 'the cereal remains from West Stow must be seen as the product of an agricultural system adapted to a specific set of quite extreme environmental conditions . . . the results should not be extrapolated to apply to other areas'. At West Stow, Suffolk (chapter 5; Murphy 1985), spelt occurred in (pre-Anglo-Saxon?) contexts up to the mid-fifth century but not thereafter. Rye was in sufficient quantities in Anglo-Saxon pits to indicate its presence as a crop from the seventh century. This new prevalence of rye apparently continued: among large amounts of charred cereals from ninth-century pits and ovens at Stafford were considerable quantities of rye rachis, probably from use as fuel (Moffett 1988). Oats predominated in one oven, probably in a grain-processing area. In contrast, however, one of the main conclusions of a pioneer study in this field, of cereals in late Saxon urban contexts in central southern England (Green 1994), was that wheat and barley were most common, with rye rare. Great care has to be taken with urban contexts, however, for the samples in them may well be knowingly or otherwise biased. They might, for example, be part of a render from a rural tenant committed to provide a particular cereal – barley for beermaking would be a case in point. Urban deposits in fact often seem to represent the accumulation of cereals for specialist functions like grain-processing and cattle-feeding, or from special deposits like dung; so the relative proportions of species identified may reflect such a function rather than the emphases of crop husbandry in the surrounding countryside.

Overall, while a broad range of cereals seems to have been grown in most regions suitable to arable farming, more rye occurs where sandy soils best suit it and barley and oats were cropped more widely in less favourable regions. This was probably because of the climate/weather rather than because of soil quality as such; that is, those on the land adjusted their regimes to factors such as lengths of growing season and lower temperatures. The pointers are that they either tapped in to already well-known cropping singularities or quickly learnt from mistakes and observation in their husbandry. Their understanding may have been un-scientific but empiricism goes a long way in farming. Such conclusions are hardly earth-shattering: they could safely have been predicted, though the factual data produced by a huge research effort is useful support of theory and common sense.

The most significant point, however – though again not surprising – is surely that at the time in question crop husbandry was simultaneously the product and a reflection of natural environmental circumstances. In all significant respects, crop production in the first millennium AD was similar to that of the last prehistoric centuries. It may have produced more grain under duress during the imperial interlude but the palaeobotanical record does not demonstrate major, long-term improvement overall. In-deed, in promoting bread wheat and reverting to a more primitive favoured cereal, rye, and all but abandoning the well-tried insular staples of spelt and emmer, the crop husbandry of southern England in the eleventh cen-tury was arguably in some respects less well advanced than it had been a thousand years earlier. But then, though one can but speculate, perhaps it was feeding a population of only about the same size.

Mixed farming and infield/outfield

Though we have touched on animals as manure-producers, it is easy to regard cereal crop production as a self-sufficient process. In practice, of course, it usually occurred in conjunction with other food-producing activities. This involved different land-uses at the same time. Its general name is 'mixed farming'; it can take various forms. One of the most important ways of farming, very deliberately combining two different land-uses within an arable system, but closely linked to stock-husbandry, is called the 'infield/outfield system' (Dodgshon 1980, chapter 4). We could have discussed it under 'pastoral' farming (chapter 11), for animals and the use of their dung are key components; but essentially, the system was intended to utilise more arable land than was available in the permanently cultivated fields (Kelly 1998, 370). This system is now extinct in Britain, and it is bafflingly difficult to pin down in documents or archaeologically on the ground; but, away from the 'champion' lands of south-eastern and Midland England, with their emphasis on permanent, intensive arable, it is theoretically possible that 'infield/outfield' may well have been a common way of farming in much of Britain throughout the millennium.

In practical terms, it meant using outlying areas for extensive grazing and temporary cultivation while intensively using the older and more fertile areas central to an estate, township or farm. Dodgshon (1980, 100), using a fiscal rather than a processual definition, sees the system developing only after the first millennium in England. Aston and Gerrard (1999, 29), confronted by evidence of major local landscape change in the tenth century at Shapwick, Somerset, opted for an earlier origin within our millennium by suggesting that 'what had been a pattern of scattered hamlets and farmsteads, each with its own field systems of infield/outfield cultivation . . . was [then] replaced by concentrating population in new farms in a village in the centre of the parish'. In contrast, Whittington (1973, 571) suggested a late or post-medieval date for infield/outfield development in Scotland. Infield/outfield seems such a common-sense way of using land at a low level of investment and technology that, particularly with rising populations in the first four and last two centuries of the millennium, it would seem odd if such a practice, however informally, was not followed at times in some places. The methodology was neither backward nor primitive but appropriate in terms of human need, natural resources and the relation between the two. Such an interpretation, whether correct or not, is perhaps useful in bringing an ecological dimension to the workings of 'marginal landscapes' which does not necessarily spring immediately to the urban mind surveying the slight and temporary-looking impact of farming on such landscapes or the material poverty of its product.

Documentary evidence, certainly from Anglo-Saxon sources, gives little hint of infield/outfield or dispersed, low-density populations living in hamlets in much of first-millennium Britain; yet archaeology, while finding it difficult to prove infield/outfield systems in the Roman period or later, constantly indicates the presence of small settlements throughout the millennium over much of the landscape. Sawyer (1998a, 140–4) argues that Domesday Book itself obscures the presence of many such hamlets, anonymous as far as the great survey was concerned but named homes to tens of thousands of people. Formal description of an infield/outfield system in later documents may well be a quite separate issue from inarticulate practice much earlier; it certainly is from implications of archaeological and inferred settlement distribution patterns. Dodgshon (1980) writes with great understanding of precisely such aspects of the practice in second-millennium Scotland, and it is indeed not difficult to imagine similar activity elsewhere and earlier. Nevertheless, and not least in the light of Dodgshon's own conclusion (above), there is no proof that infield/outfield operated in Britain before AD 1000.

Arable farming as process

It is safe to recognise that farmers throughout the first millennium shared a common knowledge not just of how to do certain things but of the need to do them in a certain order and at certain times of the year. Columella, for example, was clearly not being original but usefully passing on received wisdom about farming in Italy in advising 'that on wet land the first ploughing was given in April, the second in June . . . ; whereas on rich land, on a declivity, the first ploughing was given in March, or even, if the season was warm and dry, in February' (as reproduced by Daubeny 1857, 123). In the later seventh century, St Cuthbert planted wheat at the right time in spring on Inner Farne when he decided to become self-sufficient, and he knew enough, when his first crop failed, both to suspect that the 'nature of the ground' was wrong and to replant with barley (Farmer 1988, 68). In the context of his own commentary on Roman husbandry, Daubeny (1857, 137) was giving advice in similar vein about a later stage in the food production process: 'With respect to corn, it should be reaped as soon as it is ripe, to preserve it from the birds, wind and rain. If cut early, the grain swells after it has been housed.'

Two illuminated documents from the end of the millennium illustrate our topic, both part of the Harley Psalter (BL MS 603 fols. 21 and 66r (frontispiece and Pl. XXVb). We will take them together, but using 21 as our lead, for it shows seven stages in the crop production process. These seven scenes are not shown graphically in a neat sequence but any viewer at the time, like us, would be able to recognise the order in which the scenes occurred. The first scene in both is ploughing (respectively, centre and right bottom), that is both artists begin by depicting well-established crop agriculture in which the farmer has neither the luxury of selecting his land nor the labour of clearing it. Nor does he have to do, as would certainly have happened variously in real life, any of the tasks of preparing the soil ready for cultivation, tasks like paring, burning to spread ash, or manuring. Anyway, having gone straight into ploughing, we then pass over any subsequent stages such as harrowing or otherwise preparing a seed-bed and move directly to sowing.

In folio 21 the sowing is being done apparently somewhat carelessly by a fellow throwing his head back. (Singing? Shouting at birds? Or just aghast?) His right hand broadcasts the grain-seed far too close together, almost dumping it on the ground. At the same time, grains spill out from what could be his pouch at his left hip. More probably what the artist is try-ing to show is that a long bib, on which the seed was kept, either tipped side-ways or slipped out of his left hand, spewing the seed out on to the ground.

To broadcast is a fairly inefficient method of sowing anyway, and requires care and attention, not the rather happy-go-lucky technique conveyed in 21's miniature scene. That this was recognised is as carefully
shown in 66r where the broadcast seed is very deliberately depicted, seed
by seed, in slightly concave layers in mid-air. This surely is an attempt to
show what actually happens as the sower's right hand moves horizontally
backwards and forwards quite quickly, releasing a trickle of seed which
becomes a layer through the air as he moves forwards at a slow but steady
pace. The result can be seen in a much better spread on the ground in 66r
than in 21.

The third stage arrives in 21 with no trouble (having omitted any
graphic reference to the continual tasks of weeding and bird-scaring). A
reaper in correct pose, left leg forward, sharpens with a whetstone in his
right hand the blade of an up-ended large, double-handed, broad-bladed
scythe. Again important steps are then missed: there is nothing about
stooking the crop in sheaves or carting it to stacks built in the field or in
the rick-yard (Pl. XXX); but the fact is that the harvest is by no means
'safely gathered in' until it has been partly dried in the field and directly or
in stages taken to where it is next going to be treated. Folio 66r recognises
this: it omits the reaping but rather graphically shows the harvest being
taken in, sheaf by sheaf, on the right shoulders of labourers bowed down
by their size and weight. Nor is this in any sense artistic licence: sheaves
are heavy, requiring some strength to lift and carry individually. It can
only be deliberate too that each sheaf is shown stalks to the front, ears
over the shoulder; long stalks too, also showing that here at least the cereal
was cut at the base of the stalk, not just at the ear.

The next stage on 21, which now takes the story through to the end, is
one not always shown, but here there is a brave graphic attempt to show the
movement involved in flailing. The implement used requires two hands,
one above the other, on its handle (Pl. XXIII, not illustrated from folio 21
on the frontispiece). The heap of grain is then gathered up by hand into a
wide-mouthed pot in scene five, after which it is stored in a large, vertical-
sided, horizontally ribbed bin. It is not clear what this is made of: it looks,
as it would be nowadays, as if made of galvanised iron, but was presumably
then of either wood, leather or sacking on a wooden frame.

The last scene is a composite, a sequence of activity rarely drawn and
not always at the forefront of the agrarian mind. The grain is taken in a pot
out of the bin and tipped into a sack of which the mouth is held open by a
second man. He then walks away with the sack over his left shoulder, and
takes it to a third person who receives the sack, possibly having bought it.
The last incident is not absolutely clear but it is probable that the third

Plate XXX   Harvest wagons and oxen, earlier twentieth century, Causse Méjean, Lozère, Languedoc, France: scenes like this must have been common each year in the first millennium AD.

person is selling the grain to others. Certainly a crowd is indicated, and certainly the last episode as a whole is about distribution and marketing. Overall, there is no doubt whatsoever that the artist (or artists?) knew what he was depicting stage by stage, detail by detail, and that he was demonstrating a process that his viewers fully understood too.

This graphic description of the story is itself right at the end of the first millennium, but its essence and many of its details would have been found at any time earlier in those thousand years. This, after all, was daily life for most people: inevitable, arduous, but already beginning to acquire that quality of virtue which so becomes one of its characteristics in later literature. Bede (in Farmer 1988, 192–3), for example, sought to emphasise the humility of Eosterwine, second Abbot of Monkwearmouth and Jarrow, by stressing how he took a positive delight in sharing the ordinary work of the community, 'taking part cheerfully and obediently in every monastery chore'.

Aelfric's *Colloquy* is another, very different and later written source of more general application. It gives us a ploughman's perspective of the tenth century (Swanton 1993, 169–70). 'How do you carry out your work?', the ploughman was asked. His reply told of how he was accompanied by 'a lad driving the oxen with a goad, who is now also hoarse because of the cold and shouting'. And, as well as the work in the fields, 'I have to fill the oxen's bins with hay, and water them, and carry their muck outside.' But overall 'It's hard work, sir, because I am not free.' At the personal level, it was not the labour itself which was hard, but the absence of choice about performing it which hurt.

11 | Livestock

> A series of harsh winters or an outbreak of bovine disease or of war may
> cause the death of large numbers of cattle with a consequent increase in
> the price which can be asked by sellers of the surviving cattle.
>
> KELLY 1998, 57

The sentiment at the end of the last chapter is, if anything, even more
the case with stock-farming, for then there are two masters – the lord
and, immutably, the stock. The critical importance of animal husbandry,
for actually getting work done never mind the economics of the market
place in our opening quotation, is illustrated by the situation as recorded
by William I's clerks at the two Overtons in the Kennet valley, Wiltshire
(Fowler 2000c, chapters 8, 9). We assume that oxen, their needs and their
care were similar whatever the century until their replacement by horses
and tractors.

In 1086 West Overton had land for four ploughs, East Overton for
seven; the two estates were worked by about thirty-five men out of a
population probably approaching 200. Apart from feeding nuns, monks,
other animals and themselves, the workers also had to feed all twelve
months in every year the oxen which pulled the ploughs for perhaps only
two or three months each year and worked only sporadically for the rest of
the time, e.g. at harvest (Pl. XXX). Each plough with its team of trained
oxen was the equivalent of a modern farmer investing in a multi-purpose
tractor and fittings (Pl. XXXII). Eleven ploughs on the combined estates
at Overton could have meant, assuming the maximum of eight oxen per
plough in simultaneous use, eighty-eight oxen in residence. Allowance
should probably also be made for 'spares', because animals do not, any
more than machines, work every time they are needed, so it would have
been necessary to keep a 'bovine squad', rather as a football club keeps
twenty-five squad members for an eleven-a-side team game – against the
day when it is right to start ploughing but two of the first team are down
with fetlock injuries. Perhaps, therefore, about one hundred oxen had to
be fed every day. The figure is clearly so ridiculous that either oxen must
have been shared, or teams were less than eight, or the work was staggered

so that, say, one team on each estate could manage. Even half that number emphasises, however, the demand that traction power in arable farming made on an estate's pastoral resources.

In montane Galicia in the 1970s the family ox was kept indoors continuously except during the few hours it was working from time to time (Pl. XXXI). Each day the farmer cut grass for it, bringing the feed back to the house to minimise the ox's energy expenditure and food intake, and facilitate the collection and stock-piling of its static output, manure – a form of 'zero grazing'. The principles in these two anecdotes probably applied more or less in Britain in the first millennium AD.

Stock and landscape

Throughout the millennium, the domestic stock consisted overwhelmingly of cattle, sheep and pigs. There was no abrupt or significant change in their types or sizes, suggesting that no major breeding programmes or import of foreign stock occurred over a thousand years. Indeed, it is unlikely that different breeds of cattle and sheep equivalent to those now familiar on British farms existed, though evidence of increased wool production in the third/fourth and ninth/tenth centuries could indicate the exercise of some selection as much as an assumed raising of greater numbers of animals. Similarly, the fact that cattle were kept for traction rather than milk and meat could well have influenced slaughtering practice if not breeding habits.

The study of animal bones from modern excavations not only shows us the range of animals being kept – and eaten – but also points to both changes in proportions of stock through time in one area and differences in proportions of cattle, sheep and pigs in different regions at the same time. Emphases in local economies varied, between sheep and cattle usually, depending for the most part on changing demand for wool and meat. Such emphases could also reflect the nature of long-term husbandry in one area, for example that it was basically an arable, wheat-producing area, and also economic shifts as time passed. A decline in sheep and pig and an increase in cattle might well be the result of a phase of arable expansion. Cattle, for example, generally increased in number in proportion to sheep in the early centuries AD, representing an increased demand for beef but also probably for traction, hides and horn (Grant 1989). Domestic pigs may in their turn have increased in the third and fourth centuries, but whether that represented a fashion for pork or something more profound is uncertain.

Particularly for the earlier part of the millennium, such generalisations come from detail retrieved in the field. One such detail is part of a six-tined wooden hay-rake from a third/fourth-century context at Stonea Grange, Cambridgeshire. This underpins a generalisation about the cultivation of grass in the Fens, linked to the introduction of scythes for grass-cutting and hay-making (Stonea display, British Museum). Dark (2000, 84) conjures up hay-meadows in the Thames valley indicated by waterlogged plant remains of such as ox-eye daisy, yellow rattle and knapweed (Robinson 1979). Greig (1988) gives other examples, including one at Lancaster 'where horse droppings contained seeds of fairy flax, clovers and knapweed'. Palynology shares the spotlight, however, with many other sources in this matter. Place-names are a case in point. For example, the distribution in eastern Scotland of the word 'pit', here meaning a share or portion of land and thence a variable land unit, like an 'estate' or 'hundred', is on slopes, sheltered and on loamy soils, generally agreeing with that of best soils, that is, those best suited to arable. Contrary to perceived wisdom, therefore, it seems likely that crop-production, not pastoralism, was probably the mainstay of Pictish livelihood in a mixed farming economy (Whittington 1974–75).

Arable attracts attention in the historical landscape, and it is an intensive use of land; yet it is seldom the widest in extent. In four open field parishes in Lincolnshire, for example, out of a total of 10,700 acres, exactly a third was not arable (Russell 1974, Fig. 1). Two thirds of the parish of Little Wenlock, Shropshire, were common waste and woodland, that is areas available for grazing (Gelling 1992, 174–5). Such ratios are critical, for stock has to be fed; and it is generally most efficient if the animals munch, chew and nibble their way day after day extensively across landscapes which have to be managed in such a way that the food on them continuously renews itself. To produce food, arable is sown; pasture is sustained. In terms of the agrarian process going on, in addition a significant proportion of the arable was available in any one year for temporary grazing.

Animal husbandry looks casual; but of course, it is not. Pasture requires as much management as arable land. Arrangements for grazing stock were by and large made locally; but the practice does not necessarily leave structures or even just marks on the landscape as is often the case with arable farming. Nevertheless, feeding stock out of doors was very much an organised process, not least because the land involved often lay distant from the stock-owner's community or farm. Inter-community negotiation was necessary to sustain the system. For much of the period it seems that pasture was defined as much by the right to feed animals over certain areas of land as by definitions of land itself. This arrangement still persists over much of the Lake District, for example, where characteristically small farms with only a few acres of owned ('in-bye') land are viable economic

Plate XXXI Hay harvest: could this possibly be a photograph from Britain in the first millennium AD? No, because of the growing maize crop; but otherwise it is plausibly a version of a common agrarian scene in the first millennium, with the hay stooks, wagon with two solid wheels, a pair of yoked oxen, the manual labour with wooden, two-pronged pitchforks, strip fields in an open landscape with distant boundaries, only a few trees and a patch of scrub. Galicia, Spain, 1974.

units because with the property goes rights to graze sheep over thousands of acres of fell (upland moors). This manner of farming in a largely pastoral economy dictated by the natural conditions, notably of mountains, narrow, steep-sided valleys and high rainfall, is the significant factor in giving the regional landscape its particular short-grassed, treeless appearance, and there is little reason to think it was otherwise 1000 to 2000 years ago (Pl. II; see generally Winchester 1987).

Yet in every case caution must be exercised in extrapolating backwards like that: what seems 'reasonable' can so easily be thrown by one unconsidered factor in the equation. Forbes (1998, 27–31), for example, provides, admittedly in a somewhat unexpected context, some useful data about feeding stock in 'pre-industrial Britain'. A case in point is his reminder (p. 28) of Tusser's (1573) advice that 'oxen that draw' should 'have hay and not straw', advice which relates both to our West Overton medieval example earlier this chapter and, with some confidence, to matters in the first millennium AD when neither oxen nor their tasks, as far as we know, were significantly different. Similarly, advice about folding sheep on the stubble of fields in the few weeks between harvesting and autumn ploughing, to feed the animals, reduce the stubble and manure the ground (p. 29), is common-sense practicality likely to span the centuries whether they be medieval or pre-Norman. On the other hand, the fact that 'to keep a milking cow over winter demands at least a ton of hay' (p. 27), while doubtless valid and interesting in itself, cannot be transferred to the first millennium because, again as far as we know, cow's milk was not the main reason why cows were kept. Similarly, Whittle (1982, 195–6) sum-marises a great deal of data about the sheep-carrying capacity of different land-types, the gist of which for our argument here being that, again, modern or even historic rates for sheep-per-acre in one place at one par-ticular time simply must not be applied elsewhere to illumine other times without considerable circumspection. Nevertheless, such studies can help understand agrarian process – important with such an often evidentially insubstantial practice as pastoralism - even if conclusions seem to be 'obvious'. In the case of Whittle's summary, such are to do not with stock-ing ratios in open country but with a 'timeless generality' like 'the poorer the pasture, the greater the energy expenditure needed by the animal to exploit it' and 'variety of pasture sufficient to include reasonable winter–early spring grazing is an advantage' (p. 196). Such can be used of the first millennium.

Grazing was also widely practised in woodland. Its characteristic effect was to reduce secondary growth so that a woodland pasture tends to have little understorey and short-grassed sunny glades beneath a high canopy. Though this sort of use seems to be casual in the extreme, it has to be highly regulated, for wood-pasture is a fragile resource in ecological terms. In general, as now, quite large areas of countryside which appeared to be doing nothing most of the time except grow trees and rather poor grass were in fact deliberately managed to be like that because they were important resources in the rural economy. They were also particularly important for poor people who, with or without legal rights, could graze a few animals and collect enough fuel to scrape a living on the fringes of agrarian society as well as of the ordered agrarian landscape.

Within that ordered landscape, however, changes could occur, and one consequence could be to push ever more stock to the margins. Change could affect pasture as much as cultivated land (chapter 10). In fact, in an expanding agriculture, the two were interconnected, for pasture was bound to decrease if arable expanded. That was what probably happened in the first and second centuries AD and is documented in the tenth/eleventh centuries AD. Place-names seem to tell the same story (chapter 4); a local example takes us down to the level of field-names. On the late Saxon estate of West Overton, Wiltshire, the field-name *Southfield* first appears in 1311. From the references in the tenth-century charters to this area as *dune* (S449) and *scyfling dune* (S784), we can infer that between 972 and 1311 this land south of the settlement of West Overton was turned from pasture into arable. Thus, although the area continued to be referred to as *Schulflydon* (1312), the land was under the plough and called *Southfield*. Was this transformation of rough pasture to arable due to the introduction of some new techniques, increased manorial demands or the need to feed and employ an increasing population rather than stock?

Our example there uses a real case of pasture being converted into arable, making the point that we have to be very careful in using those two concepts: clearly one sort of land can become the other, and *vice versa*. That we have done so with our chapters 10 and 11 is a matter of organising our material rather than representing the realities of farming except at the two extremes of total crop-farming and total stock-farming. In particular, no total divorce was possible in arable farming before the arrival of chemical fertilisers because animals were essential to manure the cropable fields; so an element of pastoral farming was always needed by arable farming. We love classifying land, and indeed much land management now flows from that; but we must not assume that such labelling of the landscape, giving different functions to different land areas, was the way that first-millennium people thought about their land. It is only a guess, but the first-millennium mind-set was probably neither so absolutist in its thinking nor so rigid in its practice. No doubt it could think of distant upland pasture as suitable for traditional, annual summer grazing, but not hesitate to plough up some of it one year opportunistically.

Transhumance

Stock-farming is now systematic in its breeding, though this was not apparently so in the first millennium when there was no scientific basis for anything other than chance, farmers' choice and animal chemistry; but the use of the landscape was organised, though the signs of that are not too evident in field or document. As with arable, however, it is reasonable to look for enlightenment to recent, possible analogy. An example of one type of pastoral system in operation is provided from Donegal early in the twentieth century (Watson 1998). There, because of the accident of

documented change, we are given a glimpse of an old, even archaic system of land and animal management called a 'run rig' or 'rundale' system
of land-holding and seasonal transhumance. This was a practice which,
doubtless with variations in detail, may well have already been traditional
in the first millennium. The basic components of the system were relatively intensively grazed patches of pasture, perhaps enclosed but usually
not, lying near the homestead and used for overwintering and young stock;
and rights to graze extensively over unimproved rough pastures distant
from the steading, indeed sometimes so distant that transhumance was
necessary.

In this case in the mid-nineteenth century the changes were the direct result of the landlord's intervention in the running of the estate, an
event which may also have been paralleled many times elsewhere without
being documented as it was in this case. Unenclosed patches of ground
were consolidated into marked out areas permanently associated with one
holding; and hill land was improved for the overwintering of cattle there.
Without documentation, the only evidence of such a radical change could
well be nothing more now than a pattern of abandoned banks in an un-
farmed landscape; and even if such were found and surveyed, and even
dated, it would be difficult to discern their significance, not only in terms
of local economic history but also as witness to both a specific event ending
a traditional pastoral practice and a change in tenurial relationships. The
paper we quote was pertinently called 'The facts do not speak for themselves', and concluded that 'it was the landlord who moved the people
from [the village] to the hill slopes for social and economic reasons, not
environmental pressures'.

'Transhumance' is an aspect of animal husbandry now almost completely forgotten in Britain; yet once it was widely practised as an essential
part of raising animals for food and their products. Essentially it involves
taking animals – a herd of cattle, or more often a flock of sheep – to graze
during the summer on distant pastures away from the 'home' fields. May
to September or October were the 'away months', and if the full five to
six months were spent on far-distant pastures, then whole families could
move there. The summer grazing might then be in a further part of the
local territory, using marginal land otherwise unproductive, or in really
distant lands where grazing was allowed by custom or precedent. But
distance laterally was not the only factor; altitude could also be a crucial
factor, for mountain pastures high above the valley fields could also make
it impractical to return home every night or even every week.

The point of these manœuvres was to seek cheap and often very healthy
grazing while resting the pastures which would have fed the stock in

the spring and from which a hay crop was essential in June/July. Such pastures might also have to provide space and often animal feed during the early winter before the expensive business of folding stock indoors began. The practice is well evidenced in medieval England and was widely practised in slightly different forms in Wales and Scotland; undoubtedly its roots lay in the first millennium and earlier, but as with so much about stock-farming, its early existence is difficult to prove. It was widely practised, however, in temperate Europe until recently, and still is to an extent, though on a declining scale. It died out, for example, as a long-distance phenomenon in Languedoc in the mid-twentieth century, though formerly tens of thousands of sheep were walked the 150 km and more from the coastal winter grazing along the Mediterranean to the montane pastures of the Causses and Cévennes (Fowler 1998). There too the uplands are dotted with the archaeological remains of long-used settlements temporarily occupied each year by local families moving up for the summer from narrow valleys with very little grazing. The same phenomenon can still be seen, with cattle in the Alps and the Pyrenees, and sheep in usually more remote parts of Italy and Spain (Jarman *et al.* 1982). Very similar scenes would have been the seasonal norm throughout the first millennium in Britain, lowlands as well as uplands (Hooke 1998). And, once again raiding Ireland for analogy, it is likely that human scenes and activities occurred in this context similar to the generality recorded (slightly romanticised, one senses) by Evans (1957, 208): 'Among the many toys and playthings made of rushes we find baskets for wild strawberries and blaeberries, rattles, butterfly cages, fishing nets, caps, bracelets, belts, hatbands, mock-ceremonial whips, canes and swords and imitation birds' feet and flowers . . . in general they are the products of the infinite leisure of long summers days of cattle-tending in field, bog or mountain.'

Uplands

Upland pastoral farming persists in Britain today in its own right rather than merely as recipient of stock from elsewhere; as was indeed always the case. It may be misleading to use much later documentation pretending that it may illumine farming in the same area at any time a thousand and more years earlier. Yet the resources of a Cumbrian 'statesman's' farm and the quality of its subsistence economy indicate, as well as the particular, the general nature of Pennine upland husbandry within the present climatic zone (Marshall 1971, quoted by McDonnell 1990, 39; see also generally Winchester 1987). The farm consisted of 20 acres, 1 acre producing oat-meal for human use and 1/2 acre providing potatoes for people and pigs (what was the first-millennium equivalent?). Two cows produced butter and milk mainly for sale; female calves were raised, bull calves sold. One or two sheep and a pig provided enough meat for a year; wool was spun for sale and home-made clothes. Doubtless details differed from area to area and time to time, but that description seems to possess an elemental credibility for many places at many times in Britain's uplands. It conveys the flavour of a way of life which, through continual labour, perseverance and patience, produced a sustainable livelihood largely independent of external inputs except for restocking through use of the cash from periodic but vital sales. It is not fanciful to imagine something very close to that sort of life being lived by many upland households – probably the better-off ones – in the first millennium AD. Stable in its way, this way of life is nevertheless always on a narrow resource base; its consequential economic fragility in the face of external change is sharply exposed in the early twenty-first century. Were it not for external support, for reasons largely not to do with economic viability alone, the uplands would be seeing another phase in their long saga of habitative abandonment.

Stock

Stock is now reasonably well known from archaeological contexts (Maltby 1981; Crabtree 1985; 1989); we best know from the later part of the millennium that it was held very high in the esteem of contemporary farmers. It was no accident, for example, that the *Anglo-Saxon Chronicle* recorded that in 909 Edward's army 'ravaged very severely the territory of the [Danish] northern army, both men and all kinds of cattle', and in 917 'captured no small number of men and cattle, between Bernwood Forest and Aylesbury . . . and went to the borough at *Wigingamere* and beseiged and attacked it long into the day, and seized the cattle round about'. We see cattle in particular being noted not only as of major concern but almost on a par with men.

In 896, for example, the *ASC* records that the English 'were much more seriously afflicted . . . by the mortality of cattle and men' over three years than they had been by the Danish army. Other epidemics were recorded in the ninth and tenth centuries, times when sufficient numbers of animals died from disease to cause at least a local disaster. An implication is clearly that epidemics occurred at other times throughout the first millennium but have not been recorded. Dramatic though such may have been, they were not perhaps the main threat in stock-husbandry, for it seems a reasonable guess – the subject seems poorly studied – that disease was fairly common among animals. Their bones in general suggest reasonably

Plate XXXII A team of oxen with neck yoke, earlier twentieth century, Causse Méjean, Lozère, Languedoc, France.

good health, but few diseases leave distinctive evidence on bones. Through transhumance, and in particular the taking of animals to urban markets in Roman and later Saxon times, mechanisms for transmitting disease existed even within the generally small-scale and localised stock-farming side of British agriculture (Pl. XXXV).

To some extent, we can still see in the twenty-first century animals similar to those eating their way across the pastures of the first millennium. Then, in general, they were smaller than today, a cow, for example, being about 115 cm high and a sheep about 60 cm high at the shoulder. Pigs were, in Payne's pithy words, 'small, dark and hairy' (*EASE* 39); their characteristic alert ears, long legs and U-boat shaped bodies are retained by their modern, half-breed descendants (Pl. XXXVII). These animals often now come with names given to them relatively recently, telling of aspects of their modern history. So for cattle we have the Chillingham White Cattle, named from the Northumbrian park where they still live; Highland cattle, so-called to indicate their Scottish origin, now with overtones of certain qualities such as hardiness arising from their home pastures; and Dexter Cattle, product of a nineteenth-century cross but in size and shape similar to cattle of the first millennium, BC as well as AD, and therefore much favoured for public show at various 'ancient farms' (Pl. XXXIII). They can be compared physically with cattle in Roman Britain which averaged about 1 m high at the withers. Other bovine stock with, in one or more ways, characteristics of 'early' types include Belted Welsh, Chartley and Polled British White cattle.

Comparable sheep include Manx, Orkney, Morrit Shetland, Soay, St Kilda and Portland types, all named after islands. Their principal virtue in this context is that their insular isolation as 'island survivors' – as Jewell *et al.* (1974) called the Soays on St Kilda – meant that during the

'Agricultural Revolution' of the eighteenth and nineteenth centuries their predecessors escaped the effects of breeding improvements. As a result, the present-day sheep are to a large extent 'unimproved' and similar, genetically as well as physically, to those of the first millennium (Pl. XXXVI). The fleece of the Soay, for example, a slender-boned and extremely agile beast, is plucked, not cut. The Herdwick, a hardy, long-woolled breed from the Lake District, and the Jacob, a sheep of many colours, have similar 'ancient' characteristics. Their comparators among the pigs are the Tamworth (Pl. XXXVII), Gloucester and Woodland White, and among the horses the Exmoor pony. Old Pilgrim geese are the poultry equivalents.

No one is claiming that any of these animals today are exactly like those of 1000 to 2000 years ago, for it is truly difficult to avoid the effects of breeding during the second millennium and in particular deliberate, man-induced breeding over the last three centuries. On the other hand, breeds like those mentioned collectively give some idea of the livestock in the first millennium and there seems no good reason to doubt that a shepherd in Roman Britain would feel at home with the ovine survivors, particularly the Hebridean types (Pl. XXXVI). They and other relevant animal breeds such as those mentioned can been seen *par excellence* at the Cotswold Farm Park, Butser Ancient Farm and *Gyrwe*, Bede's World (see Appendix 3).

Relatively detailed summaries of two modern studies arising from later twentieth-century excavations illustrate how the dry bones of such animals can tell us about the animals themselves and the ways in which they were used in the first millennium.

West Stow (Crabtree 1989; for the site itself, see chapter 5)

One of the more detailed studies of animal bones now available is that from West Stow. The faunal remains (175,263 mammal bones and fragments) were found in sunken-feature buildings (SFBs), pits, ditches, post-hole fills, hollows and layer 2, the main occupation layer. It is likely that many small bones such as tarsals and carpals and the bones of smaller animals (fish and birds) were underrepresented.

In Phase 1 of the site's occupation the presence in the basements of timber buildings of all the skeletal elements of cattle, sheep, goat and pig, and to a lesser extent of horse, indicated that they were slaughtered, butchered, consumed and disposed of at the site. They probably represent the bulk of the Anglo-Saxon diet. Dogs, presumably not as food, were present throughout. Goats, present on a 1:100 ratio compared to sheep, were perhaps kept primarily for milk (and therefore cheese?). Red deer and roe deer were also occasionally hunted for food. Wild species seem to decline in number at the site in Phase 2, indicating the minor role that hunting played in the economy. The species represented remained the same, with the addition of badger, as did the sheep to goat ratio. The data and trends continued similarly in Phase 3.

Sheep/goats were the most common species, followed by cattle, pigs and finally horses. Sheep increased in importance during the course of the occupation at West Stow, apparently as part of a long-term local trend which in fact saw them established as generally the predominant species in Suffolk by the time of the Domesday survey. A corresponding decrease in cattle up to the mid-millennium at West Stow contrasts with coastal North German sites where cattle were predominant. They were, however, never a negligible component of West Stow farming and diet: in Hall 6, for example, cattle bones made up 27 per cent of the assemblage even on a low count, and they constituted 42 per cent in Hall 1.

The importance of pigs was particularly marked early in the 'Anglian' settlement's life. They made up 9.8 per cent of the late prehistoric assemblage, 14.3 per cent of the assemblage in the early centuries AD, and 23.4 per cent in the early fifth century, declining to 12.3 per cent in the late fifth century. They 'seem to have played an important role in the establishment of the farming village at West Stow in the early part of the fifth century' (Crabtree 1989, 11). Halls 3 (SFB 36, 48 and 52) and 6 (SFB 61 and 64), for example, used in the decades after AD 400, showed high percentages of pig bones (23 per cent and 26 per cent respectively) in comparison to other Halls (13–15 per cent).

The increase in pigs' relative importance contrasts with their 5.3 per cent presence in the assemblage at Feddersen Wierde, Germany. If the 'Angles' who settled the village were Continental immigrants it is possible that a high proportion of pigs may have been used as an adaptation to the colonial situation, as settlers had to establish farms in areas quite unlike their homelands. Pigs reproduce rapidly and enable herds, and a good supply of meat and usable animal products, to be quickly established. Large numbers of pigs require pannage, however, and the Breckland habitat around West Stow is not ideal for this purpose. Some low-lying parts of the river terraces may have provided pannage locally, but perhaps it had to be sought by swineherds taking the animals to the more heavily forested areas of the central East Anglian clay belt, archaeologically notable for its heavy Romanised occupation. It is possible that once the establishment of the farming community was completed pig numbers may have decreased because of the limited availability of pannage in the immediate area of West Stow. In any case, it seems that their role declined as that of sheep increased in the later fifth century and afterwards. By then too, the horse had almost disappeared, but a relatively high percentage of horse bones in Hall 7 (2.3 per cent) in the decades around AD 600 parallels the overall high frequency of horses in Phase 3.

Other Anglo-Saxon features such as pits, ditches, hollows and the general occupation layer produced comparable evidence on much lower bone counts. Pits contained 45.5 per cent ovicaprids, 37 per cent cattle, 14.6 per cent pigs and 3 per cent horses. Most of the ditches dated to the seventh century and yielded 44.8 per cent ovicaprids, 37.5 per cent cattle, 16.1 per cent pigs and 1.7 per cent horses alongside dogs and roe deer.

Overall, West Stow shows a remarkable consistency in its animal husbandry over some three centuries as an Anglo-Saxon settlement, though it has to be – and can be – seen in a longer-term perspective both environmentally and economically. While trends can be detected, no major change in the site's stock-farming and, more accurately, its meat consumption and animal-bone disposal practices in the period *c.* 400–700 AD were apparent. In several crucial respects, notably the pastoral component of its economy, it seems to have been largely self-sufficient and not dependent on a wider network.

Hamwic *(Bourdillon and Coy 1980)*

For comparison, we now turn to a later site, *Hamwic*, on the eastern side of the Solent across from Southampton. Our data come specifically from its Melbourne Street site. The place was urban in some respects but was primarily a trade centre. Lest such a context be thought irrelevant to agriculture, let our assumption be overt: that the great majority of animals consumed in *Hamwic* were bred in the country and, either on the hoof or dead, were taken to *Hamwic*.

A total of 48,214 identifiable bones and fragments were recovered and studied from stratified middle Saxon levels on five areas of the Melbourne Street site. They almost certainly represent less than 10 per cent of the total number of bones that they indicate were once on the site. The majority of the bones were recovered from pit features. Again, no routine sieving occurred. Only a few large bones were found, but this stems directly from deliberate Saxon activity and not from later decay. All bar 0.07 per cent of the mammal bones were of domestic species; 96.08 per cent of the bird fauna were also of domestic species. These figures indicate that the *Hamwic* occupants depended almost exclusively on domesticated mammals and birds for their meat. This would not be uncommon for the period. At Haithabu, for example, a contemporary trading-port in Denmark, 99.7 per cent of the assemblage was of domestic species, even though deer and wild pig were almost certainly available in the area. Ample provisioning and the production of food were likely to have been achieved with a comfortable margin of ease. Pig tibias and femurs were not at all common, for example, perhaps reflecting a retail or provisioning business in which *Hamwic* hams were prepared for consumption elsewhere.

Cattle were the predominant species; about 70 per cent were female. Their estimated withers height of 1.162 m places them centrally in the heights of Roman cattle, perhaps suggesting breed continuity in the region. They were probably brought to *Hamwic* on the hoof for slaughter, unless considerable grazing was available nearby. Evidence for hay may indicate that at least some were stalled for fattening. The mature cows probably represented the breeding population, but they would also have provided milk, traction for ploughing and transport as well as dung used in arable farming, as a mordant in dyeing and as an ingredient in daub or cob.

Mid to late adolescence, when many of the cattle were killed, is a sound time for slaughter, ensuring that the optimum amount of meat will be received in return for foodstuff consumed. The waning of death rates thereafter may indicate that cattle were kept for alternative reasons. In fact a substantial core of old cattle were seemingly kept among the *Hamwic* herds. As well as providing meat and bone marrow, dead bovines could also provide bones for working and possibly skins for tanning or parchment, though no evidence of such processes was found.

The mean withers height for sheep was 0.614 m, which was larger than late prehistoric Wessex sheep but smaller than those at Haithabu. The animals were lightly built, and no individual would have produced a substantial amount of meat; 19.2 per cent of sheep were killed before the end of their first year, presumably for meat; another concentration including rams and wethers occurred at 3–4 years old, presumably after several wool–clippings. Perhaps as many as 9 per cent were kept to an advanced age, probably for milk, skin for parchment, and dung in addition to wool. A variety of nearby habitats such as chalk downland and saltmarsh would have been suitable for rearing. Many sheep were killed at 28 months and $3^1/_2$ years (in modern terms). This peak could correspond to animals deliberately chosen for meat, but could also be representative of animals rejected at the end of a first breeding season. Thirty per cent of goats were killed by 2 years old in modern terms.

Domestic pigs made up 15.3 per cent of the faunal assemblage; most died young. The *Hamwic* pigs were large, in fact larger, stronger and more heavily built than the sheep so they would have been a great source of meat. Nearly all were killed before reaching full size. Females made up about three-quarters of the porcine population.

Plate XXXIII Dexter cattle, Bede's World, Jarrow, South Tyneside. The pair have been trained to provide pulling power, somewhat reluctantly, on the 'Anglo-Saxon farm'.

The *Hamwic* horses were about the same height as modern-day large ponies (14 hands, 1.37-1.4 m). They were strong and heavily built, larger than late prehistoric Wessex horses, and lived to about age 20 in modern terms. They were probably bred away from the town and imported when they reached a useful working age. Their work was probably as mounts, packhorses, and possibly for carting. *Hamwic* horses died old.

Pathological reactions to age and hard work can be arthritis, spondylosis, ankylosis and similar conditions. These conditions were commonly displayed through some form of exotosis or accretion of the bone. The horse specimens showed a high incidence of arthritis, probably reflecting hard use and great age. A few cattle bones also displayed arthritis. Cattle may have been worked long and hard, although the proportion of unhealthy bones is less than in horse. Some sheep bones indicated the animals had been firmly restricted (either hobbled or tethered), perhaps to prevent movement during milking. Malnutrition among the domestic stock was virtually non-existent.

The assemblage lacked evidence for slaughter, so perhaps killing was by simultaneous and instantaneous severance of the carotids, with or without prior stunning. Or perhaps much of the meat came as deadweight. The pig and ovicaprid skulls were frequently cleft for brain extraction.

Plate XXXIV
Scraping an animal hide, stretched on a wooden frame, in preparation for making parchment at a display by the Dark Age Society, Lindisfarne Priory, Northumberland.

Cooking was by stewing rather than roasting. Salt-producing areas were accessible on the Hampshire coast and therefore salting all of the domestic species and fish would have been possible for preservation and taste. Some bones were sawn for bone-working, perhaps to be sold to seafaring traders. Cattle, sheep and goat horns were used. Goat horns, or actual goats, may have been imported. Red deer antler was extensively worked.

Plate XXXV   Flock of unimproved sheep, locally called *brébis*, being led out into forest pasture early in the morning on the Causse Méjean, Lozère, Languedoc, France. These sheep are kept primarily for their milk, used in cheese-making, and secondarily for their meat. The purpose of their grazing is not merely to enable them to feed to produce milk but also to dung the land.

Plate XXXV   Flock of unimproved sheep, locally called *brébis*, being led out into forest pasture early in the morning on the Causse Méjean, Lozère, Languedoc, France. These sheep are kept primarily for their milk, used in cheese-making, and secondarily for their meat. The purpose of their grazing is not merely to enable them to feed to produce milk but also to dung the land.

The *Hamwic* study illustrates with clarity the generality that the overwhelming product of stock-farming was food; but that animals had all sorts of other uses too, and very little of them was wasted. Some may even have been kept primarily for other purposes. Nor was a need to meet the demands of a specific market unknown, and the logistics of satisfying a large demand may have been worked out in non-urban contexts. Some cattle, for example, may have been encouraged to produce skins with qualities needed to make good parchment (Pl. XXXIV); and the sheer numbers involved suggest special herds. The *Codex Amiatinus* for example, a copy of St Jerome's Latin Bible produced in the scriptorium at Jarrow under the monk Bede about AD 700, required some 515 calf skins to make – and three copies were produced in very few years. Where nigh on 1550 calves came from, where they were bred, kept and slaughtered, raises interesting questions, not least about the management of St Paul's monastic estate if, as one suspects was the case, the need was supplied locally. Given such monastic output from several establishments from the seventh century onwards, the demands of scriptoria and literacy may well have been a not insignificant demand on stock husbandry over the last four centuries of the first millennium. The demand was at any rate sufficiently in the popular consciousness for it to generate its own riddle:

I am the scalp of myself, skinned by my foeman:
Robbed of my strength, he steeped and soaked me,
Dipped me in water, whipped me out again,
Set me in the sun.
I soon lost there
The hairs that I had had.

By and large, however, looking after animals was not always fun, be they cows, sheep or pigs and whatever the period. Round about AD 1000, the 'oxherd' in Aelfric's *Colloquy* (chapter 9; Swanton 1993, 170) exclaims:

> Oh, I work hard, my lord. When the ploughman unyokes the oxen, I lead them to pasture, and I stand over them all night watching for thieves; and then in the early morning I hand them over to the ploughman well fed and watered.

The shepherd speaks similarly:

> In the early morning I drive my sheep to their pasture, and in the heat and in cold, stand over them with dogs, lest wolves devour them; and I lead them back to their folds and milk them twice a day, and move their folds; and in addition I make cheese and butter; and I am loyal to my lord.

The work and sentiments of a farm-labourer in 1930s Wiltshire are similar, echoing the daily experience of many a herdsman through the ages (Street 1932, 21):

> All we do do is run about and sweat atter they blasted sheep. We be either lambing 'em, runnin' 'em, marken 'em, shearing 'em, dipping 'em, or some other foolishness. And they can have all the grub we do grow, and God knows how much it do cost the Guvnor fer cake.

12 | Food and diet

> The food was there, in England, at the hall door.
>
> HARTLEY 1999, 21

It would not require much imagination to guess accurately the range of main foods available during – and in many cases throughout – the first millennium AD. They are in any case remarkably well attested in documentary and archaeological sources. Here, we touch on those foods other than those from the mainstream agrarian activities of arable and animal farming for, as well as producing food from cereal fields and grazing stock, people foraged and collected, and grew food round about the home in gardens and orchards. We also look at food, diet and nutrition as a whole. People ate to live, and few could afford to live to eat; though feasting, on holy days and at key times in the agrarian calendar, was a broad-based social activity of considerable significance.

Food from the wild

All around the towns, villages and farms of the first millennium was, as many a wise enthusiast still preaches today, a veritable larder of food waiting to be hunted, trapped, fished, poached, picked and generally collected in a countryside far fuller of edible species than is the case now. Again, the point is obvious, so need not detain us except in three aspects, but the brevity of this note should not be allowed to detract from the importance of this natural food source in terms of quantity, diet and nutrition for a population often on the breadline and below.

Wild deer, red and roe, and other animals like hog/boar and hare, together with birds, were a significant part of the meat diet for many. Since such a resource was indeed precious for the formalities of social hunting as much as to supply food, it was protected from all but the privileged, certainly in the later centuries of the millennium in England and by inference earlier. Deer antlers, for example, are not unknown on

Roman sites, and among Roman introductions were fallow deer as well as the game birds guinea fowl, pheasant and peacock. The documentary and other evidence for Anglo-Saxon hunting is unimpeachable (*EASE* 1999, 244–5). The huntsman was indeed a person of some stature late in our period: he comes fourth after ploughman, shepherd and oxherd in the 'Master's' inquisition of various people in Anglo-Saxon society in Aelfric's *Colloquy* (Swanton 1993, 170–1). 'Whose huntsman are you?', he is asked. 'The king's', he replies. He later describes how he hunts with nets and dogs, catching stags, wild boar, roe-buck, does, and sometimes hares. Birds, and wildfowl in particular, both in their eggs and as meat, provided less visible alternatives to quadrupeds for the fowler – and doubtless for the hungry subservient too, for it is easier and less obvious to steal birds' eggs than to dispatch a stag. It is no surprise, then, to find such items as duck, pigeon and goose evidenced on archaeological sites: at the Gorhambury Roman villa, Hertfordshire, for example, the birds represented included goose, duck (mallard and teal), woodcock, pigeon, blackbird, finches, rook, crow and jackdaw as well as the domestic fowl (Neal *et al.* 1990, 211). Elsewhere, skylark and swan were doubtless taken too. Another example of the range of food presumably hunted and eaten at one site, later than Gorhambury, is provided at 'Anglo-Saxon' Wraysbury, Berkshire (Astill and Lobb 1989).

Fishing, another obvious source of food, was probably even more common than hunting. Fish were eaten fresh, dried, smoked and salted, from marine and riverine habitats, local and imported. They were a major part of the diet. At Gorhambury, eels were overwhelmingly the favourite, especially in the first century AD, with only small quantities of other species such as herring, dace and plaice represented (Neal *et al.* 1990, 212). In the second half of the millennium there is abundant documentary as well as archaeological evidence (*EASE*, 185–6). It is unclear whether fishing was a sport. That it is specified in some Anglo-Saxon laws, with fines, implies that it was reserved at least in some places for the landlords in the same way as hunting was for sporting purposes. Fish were caught by rod and line with fishhooks, and they were netted *au nature*; but they were also to an extent 'farmed' in that fish-ponds were certainly in use from the seventh century if not earlier, fish-weirs were being built a little later, and systematic 'fish-drives' may be suggested by the elaborate structures found in the River Trent at Colwick (Salisbury 1981).

The degree to which Classical evidence can be used to illumine life in the first millennium in Britain is a moot point, but is an account by Ausonius of fishing on the Moselle different at all significantly from what it would have been like on a British river?

[A] throng of predators scours all the deep places for fish, ill-protected –
alas – by the river's sanctuary. This man, far out in midstream, trails his
dripping nets and sweeps up the shoals, ensnared by their knotted folds; this
man, when the river glides with peaceful flow, draws his seine-nets floating
with the aid of cork markers; while over yonder on the rocks another leans
over the water that flows underneath, and lets down the curved end of his
pliant rod, casting hooks baited with deadly food. (quoted by White 1977,
126)

Eels, traditionally the poor man's food in later times, seem to be far and
away the commonest catch, judging from both archaeological and documentary evidence. We have already noted them as enjoying an early
dominance at Gorhambury; Wraysbury provides an archaeological Anglo-
Saxon context for them, together with other fish (Astill and Lobb 1989).
Oysters were an archaeologically obvious part of the Roman diet, less so
later on. Otherwise, from various sources, we know that the people of the
first millennium were eating salmon, roach, burbots, lampreys, pike, trout
and sturgeon, probably with shell-fish, octopus/lobster and squid sometimes on the menu. Dried herring and probably cod were being imported
at the end of the period.

Nature provided yet more, just for the collecting, as had indeed been
the case since Palaeolithic times. Honey was a crucial natural product
to be gathered, though domestic bees were kept by some: it was used
for ink and medicine as well as sweetener, and beeswax was used for
writing tablets and for candles. Seasonally, but mostly in the autumn,
a host of food on trees, shrubs and bushes and among the fungi was
available – as indeed is still the case. Among berries were wild strawberries,
juniper, sloes and elderberries, all useful too for making drinks. Among
the wild fruits were crab apples, quinces and hazel nuts. Down among the
grasses were numerous fungi, some edible and some, as is the case with
berries, distinctly inedible. A pragmatic knowledge of such matters can be
assumed. And then there were also many other wild plants adding to the
natural larder – dandelion leaves to be collected, for example, and fennel
to be dug up.

Herbs (Appendix 4)

During much of the millennium in many places there were 'Abundant
fruit, cultivated and wild, imported and local, and some herbs and spices',
with 'plants being used for drink, for dyeing, for their fibres and as possible medicines' (Greig 1991). Special among the beneficial plants were
herbs, present in prehistoric times as exemplified by coriander and poppy

seeds, and then grown and gathered throughout the millennium after their number was considerably added to in the early centuries AD. Not a mainstream food as such, they were appreciated for flavouring and were essential for medicinal purposes (see generally Bown 1995).

By the first century AD it is likely that a profound empirical knowledge of herbal properties generally existed, continuing through the millennium. Locally, the places where particular herbs grew in the wild would be well known. To such indigenous knowledge was probably added, at least in the higher levels of society, an imported and slightly more scientific Mediterranean knowledge in the early centuries AD. The Classical world was fascinated by herbs (Ryley 1998). Aristotle created a garden with more than 300 species of herb, and he and his school wrote about plants and their medicinal properties. Dioscorides, another Greek, lived in Rome in the first century AD, producing *De Materia Medica*, a great work at the core of European understanding of these matters for the next two millennia. With illustrations drawn from life, he discussed about 600 plants and their healing properties for a range of ailments. This sort of knowledge, partly through military contexts and doubtless through other secondary sources, may well have circulated at least among the garden-owning classes in southern Britain. Numerous herbs were introduced to Britain by the Romans, e.g. parsley, borage, dill, mint, garlic, rosemary, rue and sweet marjoram. A herb garden existed at Fishbourne (Cunliffe 1971), and others among the elaborately decorative villas of the third and fourth centuries in the Cotswolds are probable.

Therapeutic treatments were widespread in post-Roman Britain, based on a Classical knowledge adapted to the flora and fauna in north-western Europe (Cameron 1993). As a continuum or not, herbs were certainly being grown at early Christian monasteries, places which after all were caretakers of other aspects of Mediterranean culture. Some of the best evidence for this comes from the excavations at St Paul's church, Jarrow, site of the monastery that was home to Bede in the later seventh and early eighth centuries (Cramp 1969), and more recently from late fifth- to sixth-century contexts at Whithorn in Galloway (Hill 1997). That herbs were being grown to be used for their medicinal properties cannot be proved, though some of the Whithorn evidence is suggestive (below). At Fishbourne and Jarrow a range of appropriate herbs across the first millennium is now being grown, respectively in a 'villa' and a 'monastic' herb garden (Ryley 1998; Marsh nd). Indeed, at the latter, they are used daily in the museum restaurant (below). Cultivation and use was not, however, confined to monasteries. At *Hamwic*, for example, in the middle Saxon period a range of plants probably used as flavouring rather than medicinally included celery, thyme, mustards, sweet cicely, caraway, oregano, sage, coriander and hops (Green 1994, 87).

It is likely, however, that the main monastic use was medicinal, adminis-tered to the poor and the sick who doubtless daily came to the doors for succour (see Whithorn below). Herbs for therapy were of vital import and interest in the daily life of people who, like us, did not want to die and were anxious to keep well or 'get better'; people who, unlike us, did not have resort to treatment by modern medicines and facilities. Herbs were probably as basic to the monastic medicine dispensed to the suffering as they were among the 'medicine-men' and 'witches' out among the vil-lages and farms (*EASE*, 298–9). Their 'green pharmacy' (Griggs 1981) was a crucial ingredient in the reality of first-millennium life, and, more generally, 'the Anglo-Saxon seems to have been far more knowledgeable about medicinal plants than anyone on the Continent' (Griggs 1981, 21). In Appendix 4, therefore, we list some herbs and medicinal plants, with their properties and uses, which could have been used in first-millennium Britain. It includes, for example, agrimony, usable as a digestive tonic and for treating wounds because it improves blood coagulation; greater plantain, again a multi-purpose plant, usable as a styptic and to soothe stings and bites, and as an infusion to relieve bronchitis, coughs and lung problems; and the wonderful nettle, one of the most wide-ranging of multi-purpose plants, usable for everything from treating dandruff to making beer!

As a result of environmental deterioration, some medicinal plants are difficult to find today. Modern society also tends to spurn this resource. Neither fact should blind us to the basic importance of that resource to people in other circumstances. As a specific example, a clay-lined pit filled with organic soil at Whithorn, confidently dated to the late fifth/early sixth century, was identified as a latrine pit. A sample from it contained seeds, fly puparia, mosses and abundant bran from human faeces. The plants represented were coriander, dill, fat hen, sedge, blackberry, black mustard, red shank, dog rose, chickweed, bracken and five mosses. The bracken and mosses had been presumably used for wiping and cleansing purposes but the others, by definition probably eaten, included a number which suggested treatment for digestive problems.

In particular, wrote the excavator (Hill 1997, 124), 'four edible species (coriander, dill, blackberry and black mustard) and two (red shank and fat hen)...have sometimes been used as food. Neither coriander nor dill is native to Britain, and both may have been introduced as herbs or spices by the Romans' (though coriander is known in pre-Roman Britain; Godwin 1975, 223) or brought over by traders with Mediterranean pottery around AD 500. They may have been used for cooking, but 'both are acknowledged cures for wind and flatulence' (p. 124). Other medicinal plants – mustard, chickweed and dog rose – have similar properties so it seems reasonable to infer that this pit is silent witness to a communal digestive problem. Completely independently, Pearson (1997, 22–3) noted that a diet containing high levels of insoluble fibre, primarily in grains and in vegetable and fruit skins – very much on the monkish menu – can produce 'severe flatulence and abdominal cramping, coupled with chronic diarrhea and dehydration'. Pips and seeds may well be pointing to an uncomfortable consequence of the relatively well-fed monastic life which more high-minded studies are far too fastidious to consider.

'Whether culinary or medicinal, the coriander, dill and mustard are likely to have been cultivated, and imply that there was a herb garden at Whithorn in the earlier sixth century', just as there seems to have been at Jarrow in the later seventh and eighth centuries. 'The other species [at Whithorn] are not all natural neighbours, and were unlikely to have been growing in the vicinity of the pit. Sedges prefer wet ground, dog rose favours woods, hedges and scrubland, while bracken needs light acid soils. Fat hen, chickweed, and red shank are all weeds of cultivation, and could have been included accidentally with the cereal. The mosses show a similar diversity of habitat and would have been gathered from scattered sites' (Hill 1997, 124).

In contrast, the floor of another, somewhat later pit was 'covered by a thick deposit of blackberry pips' (Hill 1997, 127). Elder, woundwort, hemlock, small nettle and meadow buttercup, plus hundreds of fragments of wood, bark and roots and stems, were also present. The blackberry pips, the heather and the bark were probably debris from dyeing; the other plants may have been just growing around the pit but seem more likely to have been medicinal waste. If so, despite there being only five species (four in practice, for meadow buttercup is poisonous and has no medicinal properties), they cover a wide range of illnesses and disorders (see Appendix 4). Hill (1997, 128) notes the use of elderberry in treating colds, influenza, other respiratory disorders and rheumatism; of woundwort in treating wounds, cramps, joint pains, diarrhoea and dysentery; of hemlock as a sedative; and of the 'astringent, diuretic and tonic properties' of nettle, for eczema and haemorrhage. These medicinal herbs 'were perhaps the remains of compresses for wounds or inflammations, combining the vulnerary virtues of woundwort, the astringent properties of nettle, and the sedative qualities of hemlock'. 'These two pits complement the historical evidence of healing at Whithorn' (Hill 1997, 124).

Domestic food

We can next look briefly at two further archaeological sites to exemplify the sort of information about food, primarily domestic but with wild ingredients, which actually survives in the ground. Here we are particularly concerned with animal bones, common on most habitation sites of the period, and usually, but not always, informative about the preparation or consumption of food.

Watkins Farm, Oxfordshire (Allen 1990)

The site was occupied either side of AD 1 (see chapter 6), and showed evidence of an animal husbandry which was probably part of a relatively self-contained subsistence pattern. It concentrated on animal rearing and dairying, with sheep playing a secondary role for meat and wool to feed and clothe the inhabitants of the farm. Horse was well represented, hinting perhaps at some form of specialised function or high status bound up with equine breeding and training.

In the early centuries AD, butchery at this site conformed to late prehistoric patterns at other Thames valley sites such as Ashville and Abingdon rather than to Roman sites such as Claydon Pike, Lechlade. During both periods at rural sites, however, the butchery of large carcasses at least was probably carried out on the ground. A cattle sacrum chopped through the side from the anterior provides evidence that in the Roman period carcasses were not hung by the back legs and cut down the middle from the posterior. Skinning for meat removal and bone working were evident on the horse bones. Two sets of articulated cattle vertebrae could indicate nearby slaughtering areas. Articulated limb bones, notably of horse, were occasionally found on the settlement periphery and in the entrance ditches. Moderately complete crania were spread more widely. A probably 'Roman' horse had been buried in the middle of the central house. Dog skeletons in the main enclosure were most likely to be either Roman or late prehistoric.

Wild species represented here were not necessarily food: occasional red deer, hare, cat (possibly wild), water vole, field vole and frog. A group of pike bones lay in an Iron Age well; herring was also eaten. Mallard, one buzzard and two greylag or domestic geese were also present. These uncommon wild animals show that fishing and hunting were part of the Watkins Farm economy in late prehistoric and possibly later times.

The pattern of distribution of plant remains seemed to suggest a relatively small-scale processing of cereals for immediate domestic use. The processing of glume wheats (such as spelt) when practised on a large scale generates a large amount of the chaff/weed by-product; but when the process is undertaken on a small day-to-day scale the chaff might go back into the hearth or oven used during the process, and that is what appears to have been going on here during the site's Roman phase. It is not clear, however, whether the settlement was primarily a producer or a consumer of crops.

Wharram Percy, Yorkshire (following Richards 1999, 52–4; Beresford and Hurst 1990)

Wharram Percy is best known as a deserted medieval village, but its Middle Saxon phase as represented beneath the South Manor is of considerable interest in the context here. The local environmental evidence for the pre-Conquest period suggests an area of mixed arable farming and grazing land, with very few trees. The principal crops were wheat, barley and oats, with small amounts of rye. Peas were important and flax cultivation was likely. Wild fruits and nuts were probably obtained from further afield, on the woodland margins. Rushes, hay and heather were also probably brought from some distance, for example from the moors some 15–25 km away.

Otherwise, overall, the diet was sustained from the site's own resources. The animal husbandry looks like part of a self-sufficient economy based on sheep, the most numerous animal, with cattle supplying most of the meat in cuts which, unlike some other contemporary sites, were apparently from all parts of the beasts. Pig was insignificant; oysters were the most exotic dietary element.

Animals were not just for food. The cattle provided dairy products but also traction. The animals together supported small domestic textile and bone-working industries producing presumably wool and certainly combs and pins. The range of iron objects indicated the working of wood, textiles and leather, as well as agricultural activity (Stamper and Croft 2000). There seems, however, to have been very little in the way of luxuries, for example imported fruits, herbs or spices. Nor, one suspects, was there much spare capacity or margin for error. Everything suggests quite a low level of subsistence, with little if any 'trickle-down effect' from the nearby *wic* of early York.

Food, diet and health

These two cases, selected from hundreds, provide a sample of the detail of archaeological evidence and its interpretation in first-millennium Britain. We now look at various aspects of food, diet and nutrition more

Plate XXXVI
Unimproved sheep
breeds, Soay to the rear
and a Portland to the
fore, at Bede's World,
Jarrow, South Tyneside.

generally. As we begin, modern practitioners of the food-quest accustomed to the hygienic cleanliness of cellophane-wrapped food-packages on supermarket shelves might care to note one of Pearson's (1997, 31) conclusions: 'The food supply may have been natural, but it was certainly not pure. Contaminants included insects, rodents, fecal matter of various sorts, poisonous weeds harvested along with the crops, dangerous herbs, molds, and viral or bacterial diseases resident in the animal populations.' She was describing the early medieval situation but there is no reason to doubt her accuracy for earlier times (and doubtless later too).

Food preparation was not intrinsically different from modern practice and common sense. Raw materials were cleaned, ground, chopped, dried, seasoned and cooked. Some of them may previously have been dried, smoked or stored, or preserved, by fermentation or in fat but commonly in salt, one of the essentials, both as food-ingredient and preserver of food. It came from coastal salt-pans in places such as Lincolnshire, Essex and Hampshire, either outside sea-banks as at Fleet (Stafford 1985, 6) or as part of simple dyke and drainage works designed to produce very shallow sea-water which wind and sun could evaporate. Salt was also mined, notably at Droitwich (Gelling 1992; in general see Woodiwise 1992).

Domestically produced foods were prepared, as until the early twentieth century in much of Britain, in the kitchen, where flour for example was turned into bread, biscuits and 'cakes'; from the dairy present on many farms whence came milk, butter, cheese and cream; from the farmyard which produced poultry, eggs and some meat; and from the garden where, following a significant number of Roman introductions, cabbage, turnip, carrots, parsnips, leeks, onions, shallots, radishes, asparagus, celery, lettuces, endive, globe artichokes, marrows and cucumbers, and pulses (beans and peas) were commonly grown. Ryley (1998, 8) summarises for the early centuries AD by remarking four types of garden based on Italian models: 'the formal, the semi-formal, the "natural", and the kitchen garden', only the last of which was entirely utilitarian. An outstanding formal garden in what is now the City of London links country and town and reminds us that we need not go further up the garden path in the pursuit of food: it lay beneath what is now Cannon Street station.

Other former food-plants now exist only in the wild, e.g. fat hen, mallow, orache and corn salad. A taste for imported luxury foods, with wine pre-dating the Roman Conquest and flourishing in the upper levels of society in the millennium's early centuries (Salway 1981, 57–9), was never totally lost and, like other elements of the Classical tradition, was later maintained in monasteries. There edibles like dates and almonds, spices like pepper and cinnamon, and olive oil, and of course wine, were, if only occasionally, elements of the holy life. Secular as well as monastic diets could also include fruits such as apples, damsons, cherries and plums which could have come from orchards. They were certainly cultivated at the grander houses throughout much of the millennium; and grapes and, later on, wines from vineyards were again certainly present in a similar social milieu at least in southern England in both the early and later centuries of the millennium. Roman culture introduced to Britain vines, figs and walnuts, sweet chestnuts, medlars and mulberries. Wine was being imported before AD 43, became a hallmark of 'Roman lifestyle' in Britain, and, judging from fragments of Mediterranean wine jars in western Britain, was not thereafter confined to holy tables. It continued to be consumed at secular sites, notably Tintagel island and various hillforts, on both sides of the Irish Sea in the sixth century. Monasteries characteristically possessed vineyards in the remaining four centuries of the millenium. Some forty-eight vineyards were disposed in a band from Somerset to Suffolk across late Saxon southern England (Hill 1981, map 196).

Food consumption

What was actually eaten at any one meal depended, in the first millennium as now, on three factors: the social class of the eaters, the time of day, and – though this now scarcely affects modern urban Britain – the season of the year. Nevertheless, there must have been millions of meals eaten in those thousand years which consisted of one or more of a soup (leek, cabbage, nettles, some herbs and some bones), something cereal-based – porridge, bread and/or 'cakes' (biscuits), perhaps with a sauce, condiment or jam – and water or (barley) beer. A favoured Roman delicacy, however, fermented fish sauce, fortunately found no future on British or Anglo-Saxon palates.

At the highest levels, socially and gastronomically, were banquets and feasts and, for many throughout the millennium, after the day's labour the main meal in the evening. We must remember, however, wise words a long time ago: 'To picture the *cenae* of the Romans as so many eating orgies would be like . . . supposing that the long, lavish, hospitable meal offered at a country wedding represented the peasant's normal standard of living' (Carpocino 1956, 263, in a book which puts dining and food in their Roman social context). The same applied to the legendary Anglo-Saxon and 'Celtic' feasts, occasions as much about status and social statements as about food and drink. A Roman banquet could have included some delicacy to begin with, such as green and black olives or, quite exceptionally, dormice seasoned with poppy seeds and honey; main courses, of one or more of beef, pig, goose, chicken or hare, with vegetables and sauces; a dessert of fresh or dried fruit, or fruit in pastries or honey cakes. Wines doubtless flowed. (Based on Renfrew 1993, 59–61.) Meals in real life for most people would have been a mere shadow of such a feast but special occasions could have included elements of it and doubtless many a villa-owner had such models in mind when entertaining as best he could in southern Britain in the first to fourth centuries AD.

A cereal-based recipe which, give or take the odd ingredient, could easily have been used across the range of society in the early centuries AD was for 'Julian pottage' (Renfrew 1993, 91):

8 oz. whole wheat grains, soaked overnight

1 tbl olive oil

2 cooked brains

8 oz. minced meat

a pinch of pepper, lovage, fennel seeds

1 tsp anchovy essence

1 tbl wine

2 pt stock

Drain the wheat grains and bring them to the boil in a pan of water. Simmer until soft, add the olive oil and continue to cook until thickened to a creamy consistency. Pound the brains and minced meat in a mortar, then put in a saucepan. Pound the pepper, lovage and fennel seed, and moisten with anchovy essence and wine. Add this to the meat in the pan. Bring gently to the boil and add the stock. Add this mixture gradually to the wheat, mixing it in by the ladleful, and stir until smooth, to the consistency of thick soup.

The menu at an Anglo-Saxon feast might well have included some or all of the following (based on menus as served at Bede's World, Jarrow, in the 1990s):

Broad bean and spinach broth
Saffron bread
Smoked fish with buttermilk sauce
Honey glazed chicken with fennel
Roast pork with apricots
Leeks in almond cream
Yellow pea and honey pottage
Green salad of the fields and hedgerows
Braised caboches with juniper berries
Berries and honey crumble
Nettle tea

Common sense and imagination have to be brought to particular recipes because we do not have a book of Anglo-Saxon recipes as we do for Roman dishes. A typical, non-cereal dish, also served at Bede's World, could well have been cabbage with juniper berries, requiring:

8 oz. butter
8 chopped onions
8 cloves garlic, crushed
48 juniper berries
8 lb cabbage
salt and pepper

Melt butter in large pan. Add onion, garlic and juniper berries. Cook lightly until onion is soft. Add cabbage, stir until well-coated in butter. Cover and cook for 10 minutes, stirring occasionally. Season. NB. Cabbage should be slightly crunchy and not soft.

But perhaps that last point was a nicety lost on an Anglo-Saxon girl slave poring over the dark recesses of a black cauldron as she knelt on the earth floor in the smoky gloom of an unlit hall.

Perhaps beer rather than wine would have accompanied such a dish in the mid to later centuries of the millennium. Both provided carbohydrates as well as alcohol; the latter was also used to preserve grains and fruits (fermentation).

Diet and nutrition

Most of the European population 'lived routinely at marginally adequate or outright substandard levels of malnutrition' (Pearson 1997, 1). The alternative view, which Pearson acknowledges, is that 'Anglo-Saxon peasants were reasonably well-fed.' She argues (p. 3) for an increasing grain dependency spreading out from the Rhine valley from the seventh century, leading to a basic diet of 'bread, beer and various gruels'. Obviously, lacing such fare with vegetables and herbs from the garden, and with wild produce, was important in dietary and nutritional terms. Kootwijk on the lower Rhine is offered as affording a glimpse of such a mix. There the inhabitants of a Carolingian village were eating a diet dominated by rye, with oats and barley too, mixed with edible seeds and flax for fibre (Pals 1987). The last two constituents were not present at Wraysbury, Berkshire (Astill and Lobb 1989), a rural settlement of the late ninth to twelfth centuries. A wide range of plant evidence suggested that bread wheat may have been grown with barley as a maslin crop, that the cleaned and charred state of much of the grain may have been because it was either being processed or had been bought in for eating, that the oats may have been animal fodder, and that the high proportion of legumes may have represented both food and nitrogen-fixing. The diet also included meat from pig, deer, hare and wildfowl, a lot of freshwater fish and eel, and hazel nuts but no fruit.

Such diversity would have been supplemented by a range of other foodstuffs available seasonally, so diet and nutrition need not have been monotonous. Wheat was nevertheless desirable, for it possessed a high ratio of harvest grain to sown grain and made gluten relatively easily available in bread and other forms of food. It was, however, always a demanding plant in the field and impossible to grow in some places. Ideally, it would be balanced or replaced by rye as the autumn-sown crop and barley and oats in the spring. However unvaried a cereal-based diet may have been, it was these grains which provided vitamins K, B1, B2, niacin and B6, plus folic acid, potassium, phosphorus and magnesium, and fibre – the arguments for a first-millennium muesli were nutritionally as strong then as they are now!

Well-off people undoubtedly ate a lot of meat throughout the millennium, but it is not clear how far down the social hierarchies regular meat-eating descended or even if it was everywhere preferred. Kelly (1998, 316), for example, states that 'the staple diet of the early Irish consists of bread and milk'. Certainly, however, most people would have had occasional meat-feasts at the very least – the days around 'bone-fire time' are noted as one such below (chapter 13) – even if meat was not a

regular part of their diet. This is important, for both animal and poultry meat provided complete protein, and vitamins K, D, B1, B2, B6 and B12, niacin, iron and zinc. Cattle, pigs, sheep and goats, however, produced scrag-ends and the like, probably unwanted at landlordly tables, with plenty of bone-marrow, offal and other 'waste', so the nutritional benefits of meat and its products are unlikely to have been totally denied to many. As a living example of how desirable or otherwise such may be, however, serious students should meal-test appropriate 'products', characteristically in the form of numerous varieties of local 'sausage' basically consisting of animal fat and whatever else is left after everything else has been eaten. The Caussenard 'sausage' of Lozère in central southern France, its heavy herb coating totally failing to disguise its true nature, is a classic example. Fish, however, were and are an alternative; they too are high in protein. The most balanced form of dietary protein was obtained from eggs.

Vegetables and fruits, then as now, provided vitamin C, plus carbohydrates and dietary fibre. One suspects that much of that nutritional benefit came from cabbage and onion, forever simmering in a soup or stew; and that, though a wide range of vegetables and fruits was present in Britain, their availability and accessibility to many people was limited.

Plate XXXVII
Half-Tamworth pigs in confrontation and mud, glorious mud, at West Stow, Suffolk.

Fruits, however, as with eggs, could be collected from the wild, so good nutrition did not necessarily depend on a family possessing a garden or, in towns, having access to a market. Legumes provided a range of nutritional desirables: peas and beans provided protein plus complex carbohydrates, vitamins B2, niacin, B6, minerals potassium, magnesium and iron, plus dietary fibre.

Relatively minor components of the diet were fats and oils like butter and animal fats providing calorific density for energy, and seasonally available items like mushrooms whose nutritional level made it worthwhile finding and picking them. They provided significant levels of protein and vitamins D, K, B1, B2, niacin, folic acid and various mineral elements. Wild berries were high in vitamin C. Honey was the only sweetener in the diet, and was of course also used to make mead.

Much of the above is taken directly from Pearson (1997). She concludes that all the ingredients mentioned would have made a good diet if they were *all* available *much* of the time; together they provide good nutrition. But she doubts whether they were accessible to many people in adequate quantities, specifying that vitamin C was probably in short supply. Excessive fibre may also have been a rather different problem. She also suggests of pastoralists that, while their protein intake is likely to have been sufficient, they may have lacked adequate intakes of complex carbohydrates.

In medical terms, the Anglo–Saxon diet was in general adequate in proteins but iron-deficient, a serious matter for females (Cameron 1993); it is unlikely to have been significantly different for most farm-workers earlier in the millennium. Rheumatoid arthritis was common, malaria was present and, uncommonly, so was cancer. In general medical practice was based on insular adoptions of earlier methods, some derived from a knowledge, perhaps at second hand, of Classical medicine. Blood-letting was a common treatment and surgery was ill-understood in the second half of the millennium (Cameron 1993). Skeletal evidence not uncommonly shows bone-dislocations or breakages which have been poorly set or not set at all. Such dislocations and breakages as well as the results of dietary deficiencies and malnutrition must have taken a very visible toll on people in the first millennium.

Diet and nutrition were not, however, the only factors in personal and social health: hygiene was obviously important too and, on the face of it, an area where big differences between the first and second halves of the millennium seem apparent. Roman culture not only included an emphasis on personal cleanliness, with a range of preparations in oils and scents and

Plate XXXVIII
Typical 'Anglo-Saxon' food ready to eat: eggs, cheese, pulses and herbs displayed by the Dark Age Society, Lindisfarne Priory, Northumberland.

of implements to apply and remove them; it also provided an infrastructure of sanitary, bathing and drinking hardware to achieve certain levels of public hygiene and recreation. It is, of course, highly debatable how far down the social hierarchy in Britain such benefits flowed, and in any case we are moving well outside our agrarian remit; but the point is that such private or public works and, as far as we know, habits did not prevail in the same way in the post-Roman world. Perhaps people then were healthier because they were hardier and, possibly, dirtier; but such speculation merely underlines the reality that, however well or otherwise societies fed on the products of their farming, food alone did not produce good health. The products of all the work of farming, and of taking from the bounty of nature, were neither equitably distributed nor adequate given the state of medical knowledge, nutrition and hygiene at any time in the millennium. Malnutrition and physical deformity were almost certainly common conditions, and common sights too, in the agrarian societies of those one thousand years.

13 | Agrarian society in the first millennium AD

'What do your friends do?'

'Some are ploughmen, some shepherds, some oxherds; some again, hunts-men, some fishermen, some fowlers, some merchants, some shoe-makers, salters, bakers.'

AELFRIC'S *COLLOQUY*, TRANS. SWANTON 1993, 169

It is salutary to think that most people engaged in agriculture in Britain in the first millennium AD had no scientific knowledge of how farming 'worked'. They – the range of people known to Aelfric – enjoyed, of course, considerable practical knowledge inherited from prehistory and daily reinforced. That the conversation in Aelfric's *Colloquy* continues in this vein for several pages (see examples in chapters 8–11) illustrates just how close, at least in their modes of speech, metaphor and thought, even the 'elite' in a monastic school were to the agrarian way of life. Similarly, while Bede's *œuvre* gives us little direct agrarian evidence, his prose is alive with farming allusion and imagery. While individual communities may have learnt the hard way that the best crop for the upper fields was barley, that emmer wheat grew particularly well when it followed a crop of beans, and that most crops did better after fields had been manured, society as a whole had no testable, rational idea why these things were so. Arguable elements in that generalisation relate to the degree and relevance of Classical knowledge directly during the first four centuries AD and more distantly thereafter (chapters 1, 12; Fussell 1972); but in any case farming in Britain in the first millennium could hardly be 'scientific' as that term is now understood.

The sheer inertia of scientific understanding was more bluntly called 'failure' in an early exploration of the backwardness of medieval science (Postan 1973, 81–6). Writing in the later first millennium BC but influen-tial in the early first millennium AD, Virgil (*Georgics* II.207) observed that [what we would call the] fertility of the soil decreased when successive crops were taken off the same plot. Writing two millennia later, Daubeny (1857, 80), Professor of Botany and Rural Economy in the University of Oxford, blustered that 'The notion of the soil being worn out by fatigue may appear to us too absurd to require the trouble of refuting . . . the error is committed [by Virgil and modern farmers] of attributing to inert matter properties belonging only to living substances.' Presumably if neither of those worthies knew of the soil as an organic matrix, then neither did farmers in Britain throughout the first millennium. Russell (1961, 1, which inspires much of the rest of this passage) memorably underlines that particular point in quoting an 'ingenious speculation' of 1563: 'when you bring dung into the field it is to return something to the soil that has been taken away'. His was an articulation of an observation which had blindly motivated farmers since the early days of agriculture ten millennia previously but which, as a best-guess, still represented the bow-wave of understanding in Elizabethan times (a guess which experiment later showed to be right in principle though wrong in detail: the improvement was ascribed to salt).

Despite the lack of scientific understanding, throughout the millennium, as Stafford (1985, 15) remarks of its later centuries, 'Agriculture dominated the lives of most of its inhabitants . . . The importance of the land and its agricultural exploitation recurs throughout the documents of the period, sometimes explicitly described, more often an unconscious element in the ideas, assumptions and concerns of the writers.' This is implicit throughout Domesday Book, itself a monument to how one agrarian society thought about itself and its land, but it is there much earlier too, in the first laws to survive in written form from the later seventh century and, sometimes explicitly, in the surviving land charters from the late seventh century onwards. The mere fact that a man of property – a king or noble – maybe out of kindness, more probably for political reasons but most certainly in many cases to ease the opening of the Gates to Heaven and thence to Eternal Life, chose to grant land rather than anything else gives a very clear signal of the scale of values in his society. The problem is that we do not know how early in the millennium that attitude existed.

History seldom, and archaeology almost never (cf. chapter 10), tells directly of labourers in the field. An archaeological exception could be the ploughman in the Piercebridge model (Fig. 9.2a) for, even if his field was Continental and his task ceremonial, his bearing and clothing suggest a realism it seems reasonable to take as authentic. He leans forward at a realistic angle of effort, thrusting hard off his right foot while pushing his left knee against the stilt; the now-broken goad in his right hand would doubtless have sought to induce a reciprocal effort on the part of his team. The toss of the bovines' heads does indeed appear to suggest they may be about to convert recalcitrance into action. The whole scene would have resonated with those who laboured in all weathers at this essential but exhausting and tedious task. They would have recognised the 'common touch' of the ploughman's clothes, an interesting combination of hooded cape, sleeved tunic, leggings and boots. The cape covers his head and shoulders, framing the fine detail of a rounded, slightly chubby face, 'Classical' rather than 'Celtic'. Fastened below the neck in the centre of the chest, the cape at the back drops down to a point below the shoulders, with what looks like a seam along its midline. Its stiff appearance probably indicates it was made of leather. The folds of the tunic, in contrast, indicate that it was made of cloth, pulled in by a belt around the waist and ending mini-skirt fashion just above the knees. Protection for the legs which would otherwise be exposed to the elements was apparently provided by winding strips of cloth around them, a technique still in use among farm-labourers until recently. His feet were covered by what appears to be a sort of unlaced, leather, ankle-length boot, akin perhaps to a modern moccasin. This detail here is provided because there seem very good grounds indeed for believing that we are able to view not just a typical aratral scene but an archetypal ploughman at work in characteristic labourer's clothing.

Another exception to the lack of evidence about individual labourers in the field comes occasionally, and perhaps surprisingly, from ecclesiastical sources late in the first millennium. Aelfric's *Colloquy* is noted above. Another example is Bede in his *Lives of the Abbots* (Farmer 1988, 193): he describes Eosterwine taking 'his share of the winnowing and threshing [is it indicative of the author's hands-off experience of farm work that Bede puts these tasks the wrong way round?], the milking of the ewes and the cows; he laboured in the bakehouse, garden and kitchen, taking part cheerfully and obediently in every monastery chore'. Nevertheless, in general, history and archaeology are more concerned with agrarian society than individuals in the first millennium, even though that society, however internally arranged, was not totally synonymous with everybody living in the country. From the first century AD onwards, many were living elsewhere, for example in towns and ports, and furthermore non-rural factors were significant; both were influential in the agrarian economy. Similarly, there were economic and social activities in the countryside which were not agrarian. Nevertheless, overall Britain was deeply agrarian in its way of life, the more so the further from London. Even by AD 1000 there simply was no industry in northern England, Wales, Scotland and Ireland, for example, of a scale to dilute the overwhelmingly agrarian nature of the societies of those parts of Western Europe's offshore islands. Overwhelmingly, consumption of the agricultural product was local; by and large, people ate what they produced, and their food depended very much on their own efforts. The economic model of 'direct agricultural consumption' proposed for western Europe (van Bath 1963, Part II) seems to apply to those offshore islands too.

Yet developments during the millennium profoundly affected for all time that agrarian society; and, it can be argued with the benefit of hindsight, set it on a developmental trend which began to prepare it for transformation a thousand years later into the world's first modern industrial society. In the early centuries of the first millennium, the establishment of towns and cities, connected by a road system – indeed the whole idea of a materially more advanced form of living – was something never completely forgotten, let alone reversed; nor was the experience of being part of a wider world of Europe and beyond. At the time, for the first time, a small but significant part of the otherwise agrarian population was consuming indirectly, not directly.

Five processes in train during the second half of the millennium were revolutionary in their British context. Paganism gave way to Christianity, and a large religious organisation, the established (Catholic) Church, was a major player in the agrarian life of the country by the end of the millennium. Previous power and administrative structures were largely swept away by the tenth century when they were replaced by a uniform system based on shires and hundreds (or their equivalents by other names). At a more local level in England, and specifically in the tenth century, the management and cropping of the land itself was generally changed into a new communal system. English speech was superseding Welsh throughout the area that was identifiably England by AD 1000. And by the same date, mirroring in many respects what had happened by the second century, towns were securely established and were growing individually as a recognisably urban network developed throughout southern and Midland England with outliers – some significant – beyond. All these processes had agrarian implications which we need to consider in the context of concepts of 'agrarian society'.

In addition, and if correct directly related to agrarian affairs, subregional distinctiveness could well have been developing as an effective matrix within which agrarian societies, not just one society, were evolving a healthy diversity in terms of agricultural practice, material culture, speech patterns and identity. Several commentators have independently observed this phenomenon in their own areas of study: north and south of the River Wear in north-east England, the West Midlands compared to the East Midlands and the Fens as distinct from the rest of the East Midlands, the Weald as different from the rest of Kent, south-east Wales as different from the rest of Wales.

Land and society

Land remained basic, and the constant refinement of definitions of its extents, worth and functions was a social preoccupation. William's Domesday, thorough and innovatory though it was in intent and execution, actually lay well within a continuing tradition. Ninety years earlier a predecessor, King Ethelred 'the Unready', was busy defining a piece of land in Kent which he was giving to his mother – again a mark of respect with land at its core:

> These are the boundaries of the three ploughlands at Nackington: first to Leofsige's boundary, from Leofsige's boundary to the emperor's (?) paved road, along the paved road to the cross, from the cross on along the emperor's paved road to the hill at *Hlothgewirpe*, from *Hlothgewirpe* to Wulfric's mill at his borough-gate, from the mill, along Wulfric's paved road, out to *Sethehlinc*, from *Sethehlinc* out to Hardres, from Hardres to South Nackington, to Siweard's boundary, back again to the boundary of Leofsige the Black. This is the house that belongs to Nackington; [that] which Leofstan built within the queen's gate. This is the swine pasture belonging to Nackington: *Widgreding* acres; and at *Wirege* [Perry?] there is one ploughland which Wulfstan of Saltwood has. (*EHD*, 534)

Immediate purpose of the document apart, such graphic description speaks volumes about attitudes of king and subjects to their land. Detailed comment is unnecessary: the deep, almost loving, familiarity with a local landscape, some of its history and some of its people, is apparent and impressive. This was far more than bureaucracy in action; it is an exemplary manifestation of a long, successful relationship. That relationship certainly existed at the beginning of the millennium but unfortunately we have no verbal description illustrating how British people regarded their land then. We can but share outsiders' views (chapter 1).

For the second half of the millennium, we can then infer from written evidence how people saw their land and combine that inference with our own interpretation of the same evidence to give us some idea of what they were looking at, especially in the tenth and eleventh centuries. This example involves the modern civil parish of West Overton, Wiltshire (Fowler 2000c, chapters 10 and 11, with references). A millennium ago almost exactly the same area now within that parish was embraced by two estates side by side straddling the River Kennet; they were probably formed about 500 years earlier by the subdivision of a single estate which had existed early in the first millennium if not earlier. In 1086 *Overtone* (that is West Overton, the more westerly of the two estates) was worth 100 shillings and paid geld for ten hides as part of the large estate of Wilton Abbey

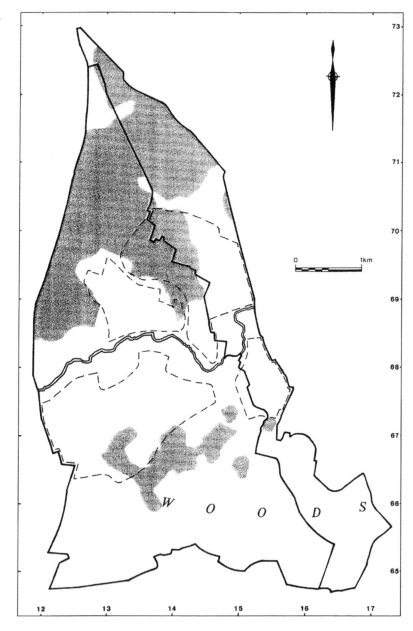

(231 hides). Land, in other words, was seen as a resource to produce revenue, in this case to support nuns, economically non-productive members of society. The estate's gross income was £246 15s, the highest recorded for any nunnery in England. In the Domesday record, seven hides and half a virgate were in the West Overton demesne, worked by two serfs with two ploughs, while elsewhere on the estate three villeins and eight

bordars had two ploughs to farm the remaining two hides and three and a half virgates. The local economy critically depended, therefore, on four ploughs, a reality recognised by the fact that it was they, not the land they worked, which were taxable. The estate's small but typically diverse resources included 2 ha of meadow, 8 ha of pasture, 8 ha of woodland, and a mill, worth 10 shillings, which dealt with the cereal product of all those resources combined.

Domesday Book also records that the Bishop of Winchester held *Ovretone*; but this was the other estate, East Overton, an area of land paying geld for fifteen hides, half as many again as West Overton. The land in this case had changed hands at some point in the century and a half before 1086, from a lady Wulfswyth, or her predecessors, to Winchester; its demesne had fallen in value by 25 per cent between 1066 and 1086. The estate contained enough land to need seven ploughs, with eight and a half hides and two ploughs in demesne, thus leaving the villeins' five ploughs to farm the remaining six and a half hides. The arable was immediately south of the village and, across the floodplain where lay the 6 ha of meadow, to the north, in both cases on valley slopes. Pasture and woodland were further out, respectively to north and south. The pasture, probably still far to the north on Overton Down where it had been in the tenth century, covered some 130 ha, roughly three times the area of woodland. The woodland, perhaps covering an area of about 40 ha, in contrast lay in a long, fairly narrow area at the very southern tip of the estate. The size and shape of the woodland within the tithing of East Overton today reflects fairly closely the Domesday record (Pl. III, Fig. 13.1).

It is likely in fact that something very similar to that list could have been drawn up for all the resources at any time during the preceding thousand years. Probably, too, the attitudes implicit in such a list would, at ground level anyway, not have differed all that much among the people actually living and working there. We, however, tend to obscure that reality by attaching different labels to groups of such people by virtue of their period ('Romano-British'), race ('Anglo-Saxon') or nation-state ('Anglo-Norman'), rather than by their function, farmers. Giraldus was not a farmer, admittedly, but does it really matter in this context what label we give him? There is surely a recognisable familiarity for the modern reader in his description of the mountains as seen from Anglesey: they 'are called Eryri by the Welsh and by the English Snowdon, that is the Snow Mountains' (Thorpe 1978, 194). He shows in that one short sentence an awareness of physical geography, climate and linguistic and racial difference. He also notes elsewhere that the brick walls of (Roman) Carmarthen are partly still standing on a riverside site 'surrounded by

woods and meadowlands' while to the east is 'Cantref Mawr . . . a safe
refuge . . . because of its impenetrable forests' (following Davies 1989, 11–
12; Thorpe 1978, 138–9). It is difficult to see any significant difference in
attitude between such topographical writing and the best of today's, and
it seems not unreasonable in this case to infer a similar attitude in at least
the later centuries of the first millennium.

Values

The production of cereal was the only operation involving a one to one
relationship between a particular man, the ploughman, and an animal, or
the four, six or eight individual oxen which made up his team. Each ox
represented a large investment. It is tempting to say that a team of them was
priceless, but in fact it was valued down to the last equivalent of a nut and
bolt precisely because an ox was such a valuable asset in a basically agrarian
society. Each part of an ox had a sort of price-tag, just as with a tractor
today as the farmer finds when he goes to the agricultural engineer's to buy
a replacement part. So important was that matter that, round about AD
690, it is documented as of kingly concern: Ine decreed that 'The horn of
an ox is valued at tenpence . . . the tail of an ox is valued at a shilling . . . the
eye of an ox is valued at fivepence' (*EHD*, 370). Four hundred years on
and the Domesday surveyors, quite as much as their witnesses, would
have known all that. No wonder they listed their resources!

And no wonder that, from the earliest surviving English documentary
evidence, not only was everything valued but remarkably detailed lists of
fines and punishments were drawn up to deal with those who transgressed.
'If anyone kills [my] smith . . . he is to pay the ordinary wergild' decreed
Ethelbert of Kent within a year or two of AD 600. Two implications of
this specification of a particular class of person, perhaps even an individual, follow: one is that royal blacksmiths are absolutely so important that
they need legal protection; the second is that a royal blacksmith – and
the same surely went for a village blacksmith too – was relatively more
important than quite a lot of other people just as one crime, murder, was
more heinous than another, fornication. For example, Ethelbert continued, 'If anyone lies with [one of my] maiden[s], he is to pay 50 shillings
compensation' (to the king, of course, for he was the slighted one), about
half the fine for killing a blacksmith; but if a 'grinding slave' was the sexual (but it was really social) offender he had to pay only half as much and
a 'third-class' slave only 12 shillings, half as much again (adapted from
EHD, 357).

Clearly, sin was relative and its punishment as hierarchical as the agrarian society in which it occurred. In such Laws we are clearly hearing the concerns of an agrarian society. Social stability (including deterring bastard births as a social, not moral, issue), security of property, protection of important members of society: these were the things that mattered. In a world where the circulation of information depended on word of mouth and visual impact, society had to ensure as far as possible that a metaphorical Aelfrisc could anticipate accurately what would be his fate when he burgled your farm or stole your sheep. He would also be punished for sleeping with your wife, not with a set fine but only in degree relating to your status in society.

Later, royal laws tended to be more concerned with the niceties of regal relationships with subjects, the rights of clergy and ecclesiastical observances, for example in taking communion and observing feast-days. Their explicitly agrarian tone and content diminished while other themes continued. On the illicit sex issue, for example, Cnut, in or just after 1020, maintained the tradition of royalty, on behalf of society, trying to regulate personal behaviour when he decreed that 'If anyone commits adultery, he is to pay compensation for it in proportion to the deed.' The relativity is partly explained in his following statement that 'It is a wicked adultery that a married man should commit fornication with a single woman, and much worse if with another's wife or with a [nun].' Sex with relatives, widows and maidens was punishable at the wergild level. If, in contrast, a married woman was known to have committed adultery (being found out, not the act, was apparently the crime), she lost her material possessions, her nose and her ears; but in the same Laws there is now nothing about five-penny ox-eyes.

In society as a whole, doubtless the agrarian concerns remained, at communal level certainly but also at the pinnacle of society as Ethelred's charter of the late tenth century illustrates (see p. 261); but by the turn of the millennium, those concerns had ceased to be pre-eminent, or to be articulated, in the laws promulgated centrally by the ruling power of King in Council. Cnut, as the king of a divided country, was primarily seeking to reinforce traditional regal authority while creating a national entity in which personal rights and duties were clearly spelt out. His Laws show him particularly concerned to underpin the position and status of the established Church and protect clerics; they speak of horses and personal weapons, not oxen and stolen meat. He descends, however, to one rural detail, comparable to the detail about sex, and clearly a matter of great personal interest. 'It is my will', he declares, 'that every man is to be entitled to his hunting in wood and field *on his own land* ', but 'everyone is to avoid trespassing on *my* hunting, wherever I wish to have it preserved' (author's italics; *EHD*, 426, 427, 430; 'stolen meat', 366).

Conservatism

In the same spirit of conservative regulation, and certainly for at least 400 years before Domesday Book, the bounds of property in the countryside were beaten to ensure that a property transferred was a property defined in detail. The progress of the jury around the bounds was also to make sure that neighbours had not filched a furrow's width or a strip of grass alongside a wood. The act of beating the bounds is shown in progress on the Norman font in Burnham Deepdale church, Norfolk (Hill 1998, 34). The excruciatingly detailed lists in Domesday were themselves basically heir to many centuries of measuring the land, listing its resources and counting its worth. Agrarian societies are often regarded as conservative; there is indeed little incentive to change when to survive is to be successful and success is judged by survival.

To say as much is in no way to imply that this society was only sub-sisting: for one thing, its farming economy throughout the millennium except possibly for a short period in the middle was always supporting a non-productive element in society, an element which became larger and more precise in its demands as the later centuries unfolded. In social and agrarian terms, neither the state nor, later, the Church in particular was cheap. So, after paying their dues yet still gaining a livelihood for another year, the prime concern of many of the members of the agrarian societies of the first millennium AD would be defensive, that is in keeping things as they were, exactly. It is not unreasonable to assume that such was the general approach to life throughout a deeply agrarian Britain, not just in England where it happens to have been documented in the later centuries of the millennium.

This assumption has some backing in the form of both written and graphic representations. They show the unending agricultural cycle, their images associated with seasonality and the importance of doing the right things in the right order at the right time. In a discussion primarily con-cerned with source criticism, Hill (1998) adduces a basic English cycle of 'labours of the months' sufficiently well known at the time to underlie the sequence of illustrations in two illuminated manuscripts of the first half of the eleventh century (BL Cotton, Julius A.VI and Tiberius B.V) and the near-contemporary *Gerefareeve*, in his own words 'not a poem but a homiletic account of the duties and needs of the steward of a large estate'.

Plate XXXIX
Overgrown hazel on the Chiltern Hills, Oxfordshire, showing the clear signs of having been formerly coppiced, i.e. regularly cut back, to produce firewood, wands for wattle, and all sorts of useful sticks. Properly managed, woods of such trees would have been an essential resource near most settlements in first-millennium Britain.

Table 13.1 here adopts Hill's (1998) Table 1 to indicate the monthly and seasonal routine likely to have been followed at the end of the first millennium by all those working the land in at least southern Britain. Plus or minus a few adjustments for changing climate and crops, and different agrarian emphases in different places, such a cycle not only was probably followed in much of Britain throughout the millennium but was part of the mind-set of much of the population.

Rather surprisingly, the reeve's duties do not include hay-making, a crucial task in June/July for any farm or estate with domestic animals to keep during the winter. Otherwise, the main difference between the two sources seems to be that the reeve's life – or the author's view of what that life should be – does not include recreation, namely the feasting in April and hunting in September of the more hedonistic (or socially superior?) graphic artists. This is particularly marked given that the reeve's duties are spelt out in much more detail than the tasks depicted in the more limited illustrations; but clearly a man of such year-round responsibilities was not allowed to enjoy himself. That said, a good correlation exists between the graphic and written sources, with the main tasks in each season being common to both.

Perhaps the *Gerefa* should be regarded as a traditional document rather than a conservative one. For one thing, its origins may well lie earlier than *c*. AD 1000, for existing eleventh-century texts seem to include intrusions if not actually be copies (Harvey 1993, which this paragraph follows). While the farming calendar and the actual work it describes are indeed

Table 13.1 The labours of the months in England *c.* AD 1000 (adapted from Hill 1998, Table 1). The left-hand column indicates the agrarian activities depicted in each month in the illustrations in two eleventh-century documents, BL Cotton, Julius A.VI and Tiberius B.V; the right-hand column gives the instructions by season and month of the *Gerefa*, a late Anglo-Saxon document. Activities on the left in bold are those listed in the *Gerefa* as necessary at the same time.

IMAGES OF	MONTH	DUTIES
Ploughing with oxen, sowing	JANUARY	*Winter* see Nov./Dec. below
Pruning vines (?)	FEBRUARY	*Spring*
Felling trees, **digging, sowing**, raking in seeds	MARCH	Plough, dig ditches, hew wood for deer-hedge, set a vineyard, set madder, sow beans,
Feasting	APRIL	linseed and woad-seed, plant a garden
Shepherding	MAY	*Summer* Harrow, weed, carry out manure, set out sheep
Felling timber	JUNE	hurdles, make folds, shear sheep, build up,
Haymaking, mowing	JULY	repair, build with timber, hedge, cut wood, and make a fish-weir and a mill
Harvest, reaping	AUGUST	Harvest, reaping, mowing
Hunting	SEPTEMBER	*Autumn* Set woad, gather home many crops, thatch and cover them, cleanse
Hawking, wild-fowling	OCTOBER	the folds, and prepare cattle-sheds, shelters and soil for winter
Keeping warm with a fire	NOVEMBER	*Winter* Plough, cleave timber, make an orchard, do
	DECEMBER	many things indoors
Threshing (barefooted), sieving, counting the grain and storing it		such as thresh, chop wood and stall cattle, put pigs in sties, and make a fire

unavoidable and in that sense traditional, its content and style tell of other matters. It spells out the qualities required of a reeve and remarks on the management of workers. As well as laying down the cycle of seasonal work, it lists the equipment needed to perform it. And it returns at its end to the quality of, in effect, the estate manager by stressing the importance of the reeve's attention to detail. As others have remarked, its structure and tone carry echoes of Classical manuals on how to farm, notably Cato and Columella, while to English scholars, far from being a down-to-earth record of the rights and obligations of workers and tenants, it 'belongs to the literary, cultural and scholastic world of the late tenth and early eleventh centuries' (Harvey 1993, 11).

Associated with it, at least in the manner of their physical survival and treatment by historians, is another, similar manuscript known as the *Rectitudines Singularum Personarum*. This, in contrast, reads like a practical text, defining what the estate manager could expect to receive from others – the freemen and the servile labourers – working on an estate. Perhaps in origin the text relates to a particular estate – Harvey (1993, 21) suggests that of St Peter's, Bath, on its resumption of a monastic role in AD 963 – but, again, it has been modified. Nevertheless, a range of estate workers is in effect listed: sower, oxherd, cowherd, shepherd, goatherd, swineherd, beekeeper and cheesemaker. Nothing unusual in that – except where is the ploughman? – but it reminds us of the variety of activities that had to be carried out on a farming estate, in a ceaseless round of both never-ending and seasonal work, if the lord was to feed himself and his household. At the same time, the same resource had to be able to meet obligations both above in the social scale – say, the king or a bishop passed by – and below for the people on his own estate, for example, as the *Rectitudines* define, with his *feorm* to specified classes of person at Midwinter and Easter. Perhaps the most significant development here, however, in both the *Gerefa* and the *Rectitudines*, is the historical implication that agrarian society in England was more and more being localised within thousands of such estates. For many there was doubtless little change from the way their grandparents had lived, but for all how and when they worked was increasingly tied into a vertical system of rights and obligations which were now being written down and formalised, not just by the king at the top as we have seen earlier (chapter 4) but by the local lord who was employing good men as managers with 'performance targets' to achieve as specified in a written brief. The evidence from these documents, from Aelfric's *Colloquy* and from many local sources is overall unambiguous on this score. The only argument is the degree and extent to which it was new in the later tenth century. Was it the written evidence which was new, merely telling of something

Plate XL Pollarded beech tree of some considerable age on the Chiltern Hills, Oxfordshire, showing that it too was cut back in early life to make it more productive of useful timber (perhaps in this case, near High Wycombe, for furniture). Such management of trees like beech and oak must have been practised widely in the first millennium to provide one of the main raw materials for buildings, roofs, fences, bridges, boats and ships.

which had been developing over centuries? Or was a major social change actually being documented as it happened? Either way, English society seems to have reached a stage of more overt sharing, of both the work and its product, in good times and in bad.

'Spreading the load' and risk-sharing were strategies to help lessen the worst effects of what could so easily happen, for example if such a cycle was not followed or, more randomly, if God in his Heaven was displeased by mortals' misdemeanours down below. Paradoxically, as is the case in poor societies today, a large family could share the work and reduce the risk to the young and to parents in old age by looking after them in large households; while at communal level, evidence for farming co-operatively on some matters, and even in common, appears almost as soon as documents become available. King Ine's famous Laws of *c.* 690 (*EHD*, 368–9, para. 42), for example, may be ambivalent in an aratral sense but there is no mistaking the principle of co-operation in some form which underlies some of the constraints on subjects' field behaviour. For early in the same century but among the North rather than the West Saxons, Alcock (1988, 25–7) firmly addresses the practicalities of farming on a royal estate without such specific documentary evidence, but his argument could also hint at a top-down, implicitly co-operative mechanism which might have been used in the collective interest. Alcock seeks to identify agricultural buildings, such as barns, among the many well-excavated timber structures with regal associations in the region. His point is not merely morphological but functional, for he is seeking the archaeological reflection of 'the administrative arrangements for the receipt and safe storage of food-renders, especially grain'. The concept of 'food-render' may not be very democratic, and grain collected autocratically and stored centrally was not primarily intended to do other than support, in this case, a regal life-style; but here and in general – for it was a mechanism long practised – is a hint of another potential strategy which could be turned to the common interest through communal distribution in time of need. In general, however, we do not see through the millennium a general practice of agriculture formally based on principles of co-operation right through the farming year, though such was becoming the case more widely by AD 1000 in England and perhaps further afield. In Ireland, for example, tenurial arrangements had existed much earlier for dispersing the land of the kin into portions held by each adult male, and specific tasks such as ploughing and pasturage could be carried out co-operatively within a neighbourhood or familial group (Edwards 1996, 53; Kelly 1998, 445–6).

Trade and agricultural products

In contrast to such common-sense, locally controlled devices to alleviate the rural lot, two or three of the most significant developments for agrarian society were externally generated and outside its control. One was the reappearance and then growth of towns. The urban phenomenon occurred on many old Roman town sites, using some of their attributes, like holy places at Canterbury, or near such old towns which were used as quarries for building materials as at early medieval St Albans across the river from *Verulamium*. Completely new urban sites emerged as well, responding to new demands of the post-Roman world. Chief among these demands were, again, defence and trade. With the threats coming from different directions and of a different nature from imperial needs some new sites were required, particularly after the mid-ninth century; and similarly with trade, but somewhat earlier.

Economic orientation in the seventh and eighth centuries shifted more to the east and north-east from southern England, rather than the traditional southern and south-eastern routes to the old Mediterranean world. Now, a new, non-Classical, western and northern Europe began to emerge from the upheavals of the collapse of empire. And one response was in the form of new small sea-ports, using river-banks and beaches, rather than major capital projects producing engineered constructions like quaysides. Tentatively at first, traders, encouraged in all likelihood by royal and noble interest, reached out from a growing stability in England across the North Sea and the Channel, perhaps in the seventh century – as has been strongly argued for Ipswich (Wade 1988) – and certainly in the eighth century (Hodges and Hobley 1988). These are places now known collectively as the '*wic* towns', the Norwich, Ipswich, Dunwich, Sandwich and Greenwich of current place-names; but others, like London's *wic*, Aldwych, along the eponymous Strand, and Southampton's predecessor, *Hamwic*, came and went after a significant but brief appearance.

'For some 150 years *Hamwih* was the centre of economic activity on the south coast of England, acting as a redistribution centre for goods imported from the continent, and exchanged for the products of the English kingdoms' (Holdsworth 1980, 1, and on which the following account is based; for *Hamwic*'s significance in terms of animal husbandry, see chapter 11). This early urban site was placed on low-lying flats of brick-earth by the western bank of the River Itchen and on the eastern side of the Southampton peninsula. It was not a reused Roman town (though the walls of Roman *Clausentum* stood but a kilometre to the north), and had never been intensely occupied before the Saxon period; nor did it become the site of a major medieval town. Its advantages in the later first millennium included being protected by the river bend, being beside mud flats where ships could beach, and having good communication with one of the old cities, Winchester, re-emerging in the eighth and ninth centuries as one of the pre-eminent urban centres in Britain. *Hamwic* was an enclosed settlement, covering 33 ha with a network of parallel and interconnecting streets. Houses were aligned with the streets, and often had property boundaries which enclosed latrines, rubbish pits, wells and ancillary buildings. Site IV, for example, contained three wells and an unusually large quantity of fish bones, possible wooden well-lining, and crucible fragments, iron and slag indicating a nearby metal-working area. Another example, Site V, as well as producing material with an uncalibrated radiocarbon date of AD 750–870, provided an unusually high number of bone fragments, and loom weights suggesting textile manufacture; while on Site VI generally the pits were filled with household refuse, animal bones, shell and pottery. Among a range of material from the site as a whole were stone querns including a number of pieces of imported Mayen (Germany) lava, and bone and antler artefacts including a red deer antler pottery stamp and a flute made from a goose ulna.

Hinton (1998, 57–8) summarised the *Hamwic* evidence by suggesting that overall it indicated 'a substantial but not flamboyant lifestyle'. Meat came mainly from cattle: 'almost half of these were elderly, no longer useful for hauling ploughs and carts, and getting too old for calf-bearing'. Though more of the sheep were younger, many 'were eaten only after they had outlived their usefulness as providers of fleeces . . . [which] suggests a significant economic trend to production to meet demand for textiles'. Similarly it was older rather than young pigs that supplied the pork. One of the most significant demonstrations from the *Hamwic* bone evidence was, again in Hinton's words, that 'The animals were being culled and driven in for slaughter from some distance away, for there are fewer young animals in the bone assemblages than there would be if breeding herds were represented.' Whereas stock could hoof it into town, cereal had to be hauled. It arrived ready for grinding into flour on Rhenish lava querns. All this seems to bespeak an increased, urban demand for food, and a gearing up of rural production in response to the new market (Fowler 1981b). A growing influence of the market, in the modern sense, on the nature of later Anglo-Saxon farming is suggested by the contrasting information from Ramsbury, where pigs fattened in the local woodland seem to have been consumed on the spot.

Despite the mundane nature of such material, at *Hamwic* it came from a highly developed urban community composed of merchants, artisans and other specialists who were supported by the efficient exploitation of the agricultural capacity in the surrounding region. *Hamwic*'s population seems to have been reasonably healthy on a coarse, fibrous diet, with childhood infection absent and very little prolonged or terminal illness. For a time, around AD 800, it prospered economically. It was probably minting its own coins in the eighth century and may well have been acting as 'gateway port' to Mercia as well as Wessex before *c.* 730. Its external contacts were with central and northern France and with Frisia and the Rhineland, probably through Dorestad, a comparable site on the Rhine estuary in what is now Holland. The *Anglo-Saxon Chronicle* records the destruction of *Hamwic* in 842 but its end as a European port may also have been due to the need of such places increasingly to be defended and to possess quays or wharves for vessels of deeper draught. Economic decline was advanced by the end of the ninth century, though the site was never fully abandoned. Trade effectively ceased, however, and people moved away, leaving this maritime centre to revert by the tenth century to countryside.

Elsewhere similar coastal developments, not necessarily urban, met economic needs, drawing on a region's agricultural produce. Lead and pottery at Flixborough, for example, reflect 'the role of the Humber estuary as a trading interface with south eastern England during the 8th and 9th centuries' (Loveluck 1998, 157). But it too may well have passed a peak for 'Links with continental Europe were evident throughout the Middle Saxon occupation but after the mid-ninth century continental imports no longer seem to have been available' (p. 157). Perhaps Viking ships in aggressive mode were sufficient to have disrupted trade to and from Britain. Nevertheless, Flixborough was one of a group of non-urban settlements benefiting from integration within the same long-distance exchange networks which ran along the North Sea coast to the Humber estuary and well back into the agrarian hinterland through its feeder rivers (Loveluck 1998).

Towns were nevertheless clearly significant for an agrarian society throughout most of the millennium: they consumed and distributed the agricultural product, providing some return, however small, to a population predominantly tied to the soil. One element in the distributive mechanism was the market, often associated with a fair, occasions as much as places. They were not necessarily in a town like *Glevum* or *Hamwic*; throughout the millennium, judging by documented later examples, we can guess that rural meeting-places at which goods and gossip were exchanged played an important role in agrarian life. 'Some of the fairs and markets mentioned in Domesday Book and later sources existed already in the early eighth century' in eastern England (Sawyer 1998a, 270). Their equivalents almost certainly existed elsewhere in the first four centuries of the millennium too, and also, as the framework of a more firmly established society and economy evolved, in the last 300 years.

Belief

Despite such features of a developing society, the population remained essentially non-urban. It was also ignorant of agricultural and environmental science, yet possessed of a range of powerful religious beliefs, some of which related directly to farming success – or at least the prevention of failure. In the early centuries AD, 'official' Roman gods, and some goddesses, dominate the record, though there was little direct connection between them and farming; but in reality, locally powerful deities, very much part of daily life and occasionally glimpsed in surviving 'native' sculpture, probably dominated the religious life of much of the farming population (see Appendix 1). In the second half of the millennium the beliefs of an increasingly dominant Church similarly held the recorded high ground, though society persisted in being particularly prey to superstition, auguries and the like. As illustration, we could have selected one of the great themes, from among the several stories of ethnogenesis for example, which provided the frameworks within which people lived during the first millennium; but we select a relatively minor aspect which nevertheless, from the point of view of those working the land at the time, would have been particularly welcome because it led to breaks in the fairly boring routine of agricultural life.

Deep-rooted in pagan religions and remnant for centuries thereafter were various festivals entrenched in the cycle of the agrarian year. Christianity invented some new ones but, in line with St Augustine's advice to his missionaries to England about sacred places, colonised existing dates where appropriate. This led to considerable overlap, as with what is now Christmas for example, for both old and new were practised in what remained basically an agrarian society, whatever its beliefs. Festivals in such a society could involve feasting – and fasting (1999, 414–15). We exemplify with a deeply agrarian time of year which, in a way paradoxically, led to a prolonged binge as food shortage could, at the start of winter, confidently be anticipated.

All Saints' Day was and is on 1 November. Its alternative name, All-Hallows, fairly plainly indicates that the occasion was a Christianisation of the pagan Hallowe'en, a celebration of witches and things of the dark conjured up by the thought that now was the real onset of winter, the beginning of 'the thinnest time of the year' (Toulson 1993, 21). Two thousand years ago the moment was of great significance to an insular, agrarian society dependent for its food on what it could itself grow. It was metaphorically important also, as the end of the pagan year, the end of Lammas; and consequently it was important too as the beginning of the new year, Samhain. By the end of our millennium, the same moment was marked by Christian iconography.

The time was also functionally important because, whatever the gods and saints were promising, the pragmatic farmer had to make preparations with his farm, his family and his stock for the long, cold nights ahead. Agrarian society in Britain slaughtered its livestock that it could not afford to feed during the non-productive months ahead. November in the pagan English calendar was 'Sacrifice month' (Herbert 1994, 47). Some stock had to go; some could be eaten but, so perhaps the pragmatist attitude suggested, we might as well appease the gods too, for there is nothing to lose. Everybody knew that from now on the world of nature stopped growing; but no one knew for certain whether that world had died or merely slept. All that humans could do was to pray a bit, survive the winter and hope, in an unscientific way, that nature would once more mysteriously stir and restart its magical cycle of rebirth in Imbolc in three moons' time, and thereafter fructify in Beltaine.

Much of this sort of belief and activity related to the changing seasons, the sun and the moon and the agricultural cycle, hardly surprising in a society which, as commentators from Tacitus to the present have remarked, 'looked on the earth as their mother' (Herbert 1994, 12). It was natural that portents should be sought in them about forthcoming weather

(cf. Pearsall and Salter 1973). Much more than now, weather was crucial to an agrarian society: it decided what could actually be done on the
land week to week and day to day. It is not fanciful to imagine the eager,
sometimes anxious look directed up at the weathercock first thing in the
morning, for the wind–strength and direction could well indicate what
sort of work was going to be possible that day. The artists apparently
distant from life's realities in Canterbury and other monasteries actually
well knew what they were at in showing weathercocks in their pictures
and could even have been drawing from life (Carver 1986, Table 1).

Knowledge of what the weather was going to be like over the next few
weeks decided whether or not what was physically possible was actually
carried out. There was, after all, every reason for not taking advantage
of a warm, dry day in late March to plant your precious, irreplaceable
seed–corn if you knew that next week was going to enjoy hard frosts and
freezing rain followed by early April days of torrential rain. So any way of
finding out what the weather was going to be like over the next few weeks
was as important as knowing what was going to happen today. Hence
proverbs such as the well-known one about the weather on St Swithun's
Day (15 July) indicating what it will be for the following month. Another,
similar gem of rural wisdom is that appropriate to Hallowe'en:

> If ducks do slide at Hallowtide,
> At Christmas they will swim;
> If ducks do swim at Hallowtide,
> At Christmas they will slide.

That is not just quaint. Its point is to help judge whether or not to get
on with autumn ploughing, and perhaps even an autumn sowing in the
milder south – a particular example of the sort of folklore likely to have
underpinned farming practice in the first millennium. Such lore was
obviously uncertain in its forecasting but must at least have offered hope,
particularly in the late autumn/winter when many a first-millennium
farmer would have been anxiously seeking signs that nature was not dying
and merely slept before another life-saving reawakening.

Eleven days after All-Hallows came Martinmas, a Christianisation in
honour of St Martin of Tours of the feast of the Roman Bacchus; the
common factor may well be the feasting traditional at this time of year
when fresh meat was readily available as weak and excess stock was killed
off. Another connection with agrarian life is that St Martin became the
patron saint of blacksmiths, 'most probably because of the association with
the fire festivals of this time of year' (Toulson 1993, 34; according to this
author, following *OED*, 'bonfire' is from 'bone-fire' as animal carcasses

were consumed). Through the blood and smoke of Martinmas, we can observe whether the leaves have fallen off the trees or not. If they have not, then we can expect a cold winter. And we should also note the direction of the wind that day for its direction then will at least foreshadow whence it will be blowing – and therefore give us some idea of the likely weather – for the rest of the year. That will give us something to be holding on to as we approach the nadir of the year at the Winter Solstice.

All this sort of thing may well sound nonsense to the twenty-first-century mind; but to dismiss it because of that would be to miss its point historically. It does not matter whether it is scientifically correct or not; its significance is that, in a pre-scientific time when there was nothing better to go on, people believed it; or, at the very least, struggled to make the best they could of such nuggets of empirical observation in lives that were for most a constant struggle against, at best, uncertainty. During the second half of the first millennium, time-honoured pagan beliefs and practices of this sort tied to certain days were replaced or adapted by a Christian iconography, in particular a littering of the calendar, and therefore the agrarian year, with saints' days. Most of such saints were specific to one place, or just a few places, some of which became places of pilgrimage. Canterbury, as Chaucer was later to recount, is the obvious one.

Much of the landscape, however, came to be dotted with saintly desti-nations (Hill 1981, map 245; Sawyer 1998a, Fig. 10, both clearly showing a north–south divide in religiosity, with distributions remarkably similar to those of Roman villas). Suffolk provides an example of the phenomenon in one area at one time, ranging from major cult centres like that of the powerful St Edmund at Bury to minor places like Blythburgh whence the now obscure St Iurmin was removed to lessen the saintly competi-tion (Warner 1996, 136–43). Taking a sample almost at random, Whitby, Whitchurch Canonicorum, Whithorn and Wilton provide an alphabet-ically adjacent but geographically scattered list of place-names that be-tween them cover 8 February (St Aeflaed); 10 February (St Trumwin); 11 February (St Caedmon); 9 March (St Bosa); 29 April (St Wilfrid); 7 May (St John of Beverly); 18 May (St Elgiva); 1 June (St Wite); 5 July (St Modwenna); 26 August (St Ninian); 9 September (St Wulfhild), 13 September (St Wilfrida); 16 September (St Edith); 8 October (St Iwi); 12 October (St Edwin); 20 October (St Acca); 31 October (St Begu); 17 November (St Hild); 24 November (St Eanflaed); 25 December (St Alburgh) (Phillips 1997, 63–4). Most of such detail would, of course, be a world away from the ploughman in the furrow and the shepherd on the hill, but there would surely have been a general awareness of such a saintly crowd, as there surely was of differently named gods and goddesses in pagan times; and every so often, in many a locality, the local saint's feast day would have come around, perhaps on the same day in Christian times as for long before. In one of our examples, Whitchurch Canonicorum, not only were the relics of the anchoress St Wite still venerated at the end of the twentieth century but a holy well 'dedicated to her', in the language of the Church, exists nearby; but one wonders whom the lady ousted.

Though people's beliefs were doubtless sincere, in an agrarian society always close to uncertainty about next week's food, any straw in the wind about the future was worth grabbing. Tomorrow was a foreign country which, like Heaven, offered no guarantee of entry. It was not just enough, therefore, to observe certain days and honour certain names, whatever the religion. Even as Christianity spread, such was the nature of farming rather than anti-Christian feeling, specifically agrarian ritual and even ceremony persisted, for there was nothing to lose and some anecdotal evidence indicated to pragmatic minds that it might work. To such minds in any case, magic or not, there were strong reasons for doing things the way they always had been done, so affording 'a quasi-ritual atmosphere' about turning out for ploughing in Suffolk as late as the twentieth century (Evans 1960, 28, and esp. chapters 23 and 24). Similarly pragmatic, though more overt in religious association, were plough rituals, illustrated in petroglyphs in the Europe of the second and first millennia BC (e.g. Coles 1990, 30, fig. 16a). Despite their very obvious pagan origins and sexual thrust, they continued, according at least to one account, with the participation of the early Church: as the first furrow was cut by an anointed plough, so was recited 'Hail to you, earth, mother of mortals, may you grow big in God's embrace, filled with food for the use of humankind.' (Herbert 1994, 14).

Language

We have from time to time in this essay touched on how people spoke. Any elaboration of the linguistic dimension in the context of developing British agriculture up to Norman times would have to take into account the separate, and no less widespread, agrarian terminology of the Germanic languages. The British Celtic background with its long enrichment from Vulgar Latin, in the mouths of a great many ordinary people busy with a primary industry, takes us back to an interaction that was technological rather than linguistic. The experience of parallel societies elsewhere enforces a belief that innovations in British farming must have demanded innovations in nomenclature. If the evidence for such changes survives at all, then it would seem to lie far below the horizon represented by place-names, even by field-names and charter-bounds. It has nevertheless a relatively unexplored potential for improving our understanding of farming in the first millennium, perhaps as significant as further discoveries in the material culture of the agrarian societies then populating Britain.

14 | Farming in the first millennium AD

– fold, fallow, and plough;
And áll trádes, their gear and tackle and trim.

GERARD MANLEY HOPKINS, *PIED BEAUTY*

A conventional historical framework for the first millennium is of course constructed around several supposedly key dates such as AD 43 ('Roman invasion'), 313 ('Imperial Christianity'), 410 ('End of Roman Britain'), 449 (start of 'Adventus Saxonum'), 597 (reintroduction of Roman Christianity), 789 (first attack by 'Northmen'), 855 (Vikings first over-wintered), 899 (death of Alfred) and 960 (Dunstan, Archbishop of Canterbury), with 1066 and 1086 (Norman Conquest and Domesday Book) added as relevant and memorable dates.

Apart from the first and last, the dates do not appear to be of particular relevance to agrarian history. Perhaps there is not much correlation between political and military events on the one hand and developments in agriculture on the other. An agrarian perspective might well choose not to shape itself within a chronological framework and, even if it did, in however short and deliberately selective an overview as here, would pick out different dates or times as 'significant'. Ours are around eight points in time that we think of agrarian significance in the 1100 years to the end of the eleventh century: *c*. AD 50, 180, 270, 450, 625, 800, 1000 and 1086. They define eight phases, though clearly all phases are a continuum in more than one sense and change occurred either side of each date. The dates provide the nodes in a chronological framework of phases for our brief discussion, phases suggested by significant developments in farming and its contexts.

1. Before the mid-first century AD: the prehistoric inheritance

Britain had already been farmed for thousands of years as we pick up the narrative of agrarian history in the century or so between the invasions of

Caesar (55–54 BC) and Claudius (AD 43). The landscape was littered with remains of ancestral farmers (Pl. V) and, less visibly, bore the signs of the environmental impacts of that long process (Pl. IV). Much of the uplands, for example, was already podsolised into low-fertility, treeless moorland, suitable only for extensive stock-farming; some of the lowlands, notably the chalk downs, were also almost treeless, pedologically exhausted but available as permanent pasture. Along the broader valleys of the lowlands, but similarly in their often narrower counterparts to west and north, in-tensive cropping on permanent arable was proceeding (Pl. II). A whole range of other varieties of farming was being widely pursued, for exam-ple along the upper edges of valley slopes, on marshlands, and around and within naturally wooded areas where tree-cover still dominated. The Weald, the New Forest and Savernake Forest (Pl. I), exemplify the latter in the lowlands. Particular adaptations and exploitation included shifting cultivation, wood-pasture and grazing on seasonally available wetlands such as those around the Severn estuary.

Similar farming patterns were being followed in parts of the climatically slightly harsher uplands, and there a wide range of adaptations to natural and anthropogenic circumstances was variously in operation. Systems of stone-hedged, enclosed fields were being laboriously created throughout the Highland Zone, many permanently to mark the historic landscape and some to be still in use 2000 years later (Pl. VI). In contrast, transhumance and variations on what later came to be called run-rig, for example, were widely practised as people in areas more markedly constrained in agrarian terms than was the case in southern Britian sought by different methods to solve the ever-present problem of feeding themselves. Travelling long distances to feed their stock in summer while intensively manuring and cultivating a precious small area around the farmstead (later 'in-bye land') were worthwhile mechanisms to that end when the alternatives were the uncertainties of abandonment or the certainty of death.

Much of that general picture continued over much of Britain right through the first millennium and later. Change, and a quickening in some aspects of those age-old practices, was, however, already happening in the first centuries BC/AD. Population was increasing, probably rapidly. Po-litical power, and consequently in some respects settlement nodes, were tending in much of Britain to become centralised in fewer, particular places – not just in the obvious 'Belgic oppida' that both Roman invasions encountered in south-east Britain at Colchester and Wheathamstead but also in the west and north at old tribal headquarters like Maiden Castle, Dorset, and Traprain Law, Lothian. Coinage was circulating in southern Britain, introducing a new concept into agrarian affairs for some. New markets, for example, were opening up for agrarian products on the Continent, reputation came to be recognised, judging by Tacitus' remarks, and the value of a 'British brand-image' for insular cereal, wool and hunting dogs perhaps began to be appreciated. And these latter developments all arose because of a closer relationship, within a Roman Imperial framework, between Britain and Gaul.

All this, completely outside the control of peasant farmers and even any general concern about farming that may have existed among political leaders, nevertheless impacted directly and indirectly on farming. Agriculture was clearly operating in very different circumstances by the mid-first century AD than from those prevailing in the mid-first century BC; and indeed considerable change was already in train in the decades immediately before the Conquest began. By AD 40, agriculture was, in part at least, already operating in a market economy of cash, cereal surplus and export, circumstances which were emphasised rather than created by the Conquest. Similarly and simultaneously, new demands were also growing internally. These came not just from a larger population, perhaps now approaching 2 million, but from more people living in proto-urban communities and working in activities like trade and what we would now call 'service industry'. The significance here, in a development which has seldom subsequently been reversed, was that this growing segment of the population was not directly involved in food-production as had been the case in 'the good old days BC'. Major changes were, then, already in train concerning agriculture and farming communities at the time of the Roman Conquest of Britain from AD 43 onwards.

2.   Mid-first to late second centuries: Roman impact

Such changes continued and were exaggerated by the Conquest, and new developments were both directly occasioned and stimulated. That, at least, is the interpretative model to be favoured here, so it is important to remember that other interpretations have been proposed. For example, while he accepted that 'In terms of crop production . . . the Roman period falls into a longer period characterised by expansion and diversification onto new types of soil', Jones (1982, specifically 97, 101) notably proposed that 'In the Roman period a phase of stagnation, when innovations are confined to the sphere of crop redistribution, may be detected from the conquest to the late third century' (at least we agree about the late third century as a defining period! – below, Phase 4). Farming practice to a large extent and over much of Britain indeed remained much the same, but in both an immediate and a longer-term perspective agriculture was changed for ever. The environmental impact of the Conquest in a military sense is debatable but its consequences on the landscape are reasonably clear, at least at a primary level. First there was the direct and immediate impact of military activity and the establishment, eventually over all of Britain except northern Scotland, of military installations. They required manning and provisioning; much was acquired locally. More long-term, Britain as a province of the Roman Empire was expected not only to feed itself and the army of occupation but also to continue to supply cereal and other exports to the provisioning of the greater part of that Empire across the Channel. A widespread, state-led agricultural revolution therefore occurred during the second half of the first century AD, concentrating on making existing arable more efficient and breaking in more land to increase the area under cultivation. Marginal lands on the Wessex downs, for example, were therefore put to the plough, often in newly reorganised and newly created field systems; wetlands as around the Severn estuary and the Wash were drained and made efficient corn-producers. Overall, farming was made a more efficient, demand-led operation, and doubtless both the land and its workers suffered as a result. Such a general impression, however, must be tempered by a recognition of a reality on the ground about the individual circumstances of change from 'Celtic farm to Roman villa': 'every farm was subject to the changing whims and fortunes of its owners, of their neighbours, and of the local and imperial governments. The widespread effects of government or tribal policy and actions may have created broad patterns, but personal circumstances will often have disturbed such patterns in individual cases' (Branigan 1982, 83). In any case, as Branigan (p. 95) pertinently concludes: 'the laying out of thousands of acres of new fields, droveways, and enclosures represents a far more profound change in the British landscape than did the thinly-spread buildings of a thousand or two fashionable, Romanised bungalows'.

While a government drive for increased production may in the first place have been designed to provide food for an army of occupation and export, five other post-Conquest innovations also had a direct effect on farming. The growth of towns, small and large, both created demand and provided a market; the construction of a road network provided a means in due course for distributing at least some of the agricultural product. They, with military and political change, induced a socio-economic development which saw, at least in southern Britain, the creation of a materially rich class of landowners introducing or aping Classical *mœurs* and life-style. On their estates new agrarian methodologies, cropping regimes and livestock appeared; and in their houses, new foods appeared. Such generalisations reflect the presence of a small upper class in southern Britain which effectively consolidated, or at least re-emphasised, a trend which had been present in late prehistoric Britain; but now it was overt, materially obvious. This prosperity and social status were nevertheless echoed elsewhere in, for example, house plans in the south-west and in Anglesey; and, in however humble a way, in manufactured material possessions – a few wheel-made pots and a bead of Roman glass – even in 'native hutments' in the hills.

3.   Late second to late third centuries

If there was a period of greatest prosperity in the first half of the first millennium, this was probably it. Now there was a phase of consolidation rather than continuing change, though after five generations of Roman-ising initiatives and influence landscape and agriculture were widely different from what they had been in the last decades of pre-Roman Britain. Essentially that most vital of agrarian necessities, peace, now prevailed. Even in the far north, confrontation had diminished, however uneasily, once the Romans had finally adopted a sensibly limited rather than an expansionist frontier at the north-western limits of Empire. Though external threats existed, at this time the army of occupation was also Britain's defence, a defence moreover which incidentally provided, not least in its civilian appurtenances, a ready market for agricultural produce. Towns prospered too, even those which had not at first 'taken' when planted out in alien country; most of the thousand or so villas existed in some form or other, from a few veritable palaces to single-house, timber-framed farms; and for a time at least it seemed that the very considerable structural investment in the countryside a century or so earlier was paying off in sustained mixed-farming production. Applebaum's (1972) summary 'deserves extensive quotation' (John 1973, 135):

> The factors making for the adoption of larger fields . . . extended beyond the operation of a larger deeper-cutting plough. They arose with the multiplication of man-power not restricted to the family (slaves, wage-labourers, and tenants), with the availability of markets which led to the development of commercial farming; and in response to the demands of the armed forces and of taxation. From these factors were [*sic*] born the capitalist estate, with its exploitation of new imported techniques . . . all these methods demanded controllable enclosed fields which needed to be larger in order to be profitable.

Much of that quotation could apply in both the previous and the next phases. It omits to mention, however, that overall this successful but basically agrarian economy was reinforced with successful, locally large-scale industry and European trade under, disliked or otherwise, a relatively stable political system.

4. Late third to mid-fifth centuries: change and disintegration

In agrarian respects at least there seems some merit in thinking in terms, not of 'late Roman' as meaning the third and fourth centuries, but of a third period of change beginning *c.* AD 250–70 and lasting for two centuries or so. The change in mind here is essentially the breakdown of the Roman economic system in Britain within which agriculture had expanded and with which it retracted to come to rest in an almost pre-Roman state of operation by about 450 (but cf. Jones 1982 who sees this as a period of 'innovation', and Dark 1994, xii, who argues that 'Roman Britain ended not in the fifth century, but the seventh'). Of course, within our broad generalisation, there were many upsurges, some local and some of provincial significance such as the growth of luxurious country houses of Georgian and Victorian magnitude in the Cotswolds and Kent. They can only have been sustained by large and productive estates, perhaps expanding to their physical limits in terms of land being intensively cropped and intensively grazed – not totally dissimilar, perhaps, to our view of the tenth century, Phase 7 below. Innovations also occurred, such as the new field system noted at Heathrow, and probably the development of a genuine heavy plough, itself as likely to be indicative of increased intensification of cultivation on productive fields rather than necessarily of an expanding arable regime. But overall, while one can argue about when the process started, a long-term downward economic trend long before a fourth-century 'decline' appears to be reflected in a farming industry which, from well within the third century, seems to lose its expansionist mode while moving from arable and mixed farming to one concentrating very much on stock, and wool-production in particular. It must, however, be emphasised that such is very much a view of and from the Civil Province. It is a conventional view too, one which could easily be replaced. Lambrick (1992, 101–3), for example, has picked out the potential significance of horticulture and hay-making on low-lying, fourth-century sites (Farmoor and Claydon Pike) in the Thames valley. The older, non-improved farming and ways of life in west and north were much less sensitive to Imperial economics and doubtless continued largely unchanged with their ards and extensive grazing (though elements of agricultural conservatism, even in the Thames valley, are implied by the Abingdon ard, chapter 9 above). But even places with more traditional economies would have suffered severe local economic shock when the garrison withdrew, leaving no market for their produce and no cash to buy life's little luxuries like a bead necklace.

One area which seems to encapsulate much of the foregoing is indeed the Upper Thames valley. There the extent of land under arable was increasing from later prehistoric times into the first centuries AD. Thereafter, however, of thirty-seven excavated rural settlements tabulated by Lambrick (1992, Fig. 27), only ten unambiguously continued in use after AD 250 into the later third and fourth centuries. Though three restarted after 250, there was not a single new settlement after 250. In crude terms, thirteen – about one third of the total tabulated – were occupied in the fourth century; but those thirteen settlements still occupied in the fourth century were only just over half the number (twenty-three) of settlements present in the first century. Another 'local' example both bears on our hypothesis and brings out how change can produce different results in the same area, in this case a big one, Wales. Davies (1989, 2) remarks that

> Such Roman military garrisons as remained in Wales after the second century, which were not many, appear to have been withdrawn by the late fourth century and the formal contacts of central Roman government with the provincial administration of Britain appear to have ended in the first decade of the fifth century. Membership of the Roman Empire left an uneven impression on Wales, however, and by the fourth century the character of the South East – with its many villas and well-worked estates – was in many respects distinct from the rest of Wales. This Roman background, and in particular the experience of having been part of a wide network of economic relationships, continued to mark the South East, conditioning development over the next three centuries in particular.

Similar arguments could be advanced for south-west Britain beyond Exeter and northern Britain beyond York. Disintegration was happening long before AD 400 and the official end of Roman Britain in 410 – a failed cry for help, let it be noted, which was urban, not rural. Clearly farming continued, for, whatever the political and military situation, perhaps as many as 4 million mouths still needed to be fed even at the end of this phase. The fact that in many places farm buildings, even farm houses, were not repaired and were eventually evacuated could be interpreted as an indication of how great was the struggle simply to keep farming going: maybe there was little spare energy, never mind cash, to give to such repairs. The appearance of corn-drying ovens on many sites in the fourth century may also be indicating a climatic change to wetter conditions – a parallel with a similar phenomenon in the thirteenth and fourteenth centuries is suggested by the archaeological evidence. Yet circumstances can be viewed quite differently: Dark (1994, 68), for example, argues that, 'instead of economic decline following the "end of Roman Britain" in AD 410, we might see a period of rapid economic growth in the early fifth century'. We cannot see the organisation which would drive such growth, though our interpretation does not require an agrarian collapse, in terms of activity and food production, on a par with a collapse of centralised power and other economic activity for which evidence seems fairly convincing. Rather do we see, towards the end of this phase, people – land labourers, former tenants and perhaps even slaves – continuing to work the land, but probably increasingly for themselves rather than a landowner in lowland Britain. In arable farming, such were tied to particular lands, for whatever the tenurial circumstances fields are not portable and do not move. While livestock-farming has the big disadvantage that the animals need attention of some sort every day, it has the major merit that you can take your livelihood with you, so stockmen and shepherds could if necessary move on without leaving everything behind.

5.   Mid-fifth to early seventh centuries: continuity and some disruption

This was the period of about one and a half centuries, slightly more, in which a conventional history would see large numbers of Teutonic invaders conquering and colonising England. Given that the particular characteristics of Romanised farming in Britain had largely faded by the mid-fifth century, it is actually quite difficult to see any significant agrarian change in that situation until the early seventh century (see Phase 6 below). Documentary evidence is virtually useless in illuminating an agrarian perspective on this period, but we now have a number of well-excavated archaeological settlements which span it. One example is at West Heslerton where 'Plant macro-fossil evidence initially indicates a wide range of species including crops as well as fruits and berries. The majority of crops appear to have been grown on the broad flat margins of the Vale of Pickering to the north of the site. Charcoal evidences dominant oak and hazel plus lots of fruit woods, perhaps indicating orchards.' Agricultural activity at the foot of the Wolds increased during the Roman period and some of the enclosures were used for stock, 'perhaps including over-wintering of animals within the immediate vicinity of the settlement core to the south. The presence of a possible mill in one area was indicated by clear signs of water-course management, the distribution of quern fragments . . . ' (Powlesland 1999, 61–5). In essence, that could be a description of a Roman villa and its lands in the fourth century; yet it is a situation which seems to have been reorganised internally by newcomers, arguably Anglians, arriving *c*. 500. It is a metaphor for what seems to be the case during this phase: there is nothing, culturally, technologically or environmentally, to indicate major agrarian change. Indeed, Dark (1994, 68) goes further, arguing that such documentary sources as are available 'all seem to indicate that fifth-century lowland Britain was a wealthy society'. That could well be true of middle and western Britain, since in agricultural terms there seems no reason to predicate a major change for the worse; but there may well have been problems of food supply among both incomers and their new, indigenous neighbours from the later fifth century onwards.

Of course, different localities would have seen their local changes: a new farm being created for example, even a new settlement coming into existence along a river bank rather than along a Roman road. It is likely some land reverted to scrub and perhaps even became young woodland if untouched for a century or more; the amount of such land depends on whether or not disease brought about serious demographic decline during this period. On the other hand, a large number of newcomers could have offset such indigenous population loss, particularly in the sixth century. Overall, such evidence as there is suggests that arable areas continued much as before, and even expanded in some places in north Britain. There appear to have been no technological developments, though remnants of what were by now the 'old' technology – ideas about ploughs with coulters and asymmetrical shares for example, or knowledge of how to construct a water-mill – probably survived in the British, Christian west. By the early seventh century, the oral naming of parts of the landscape had developed to the extent that it was ready to be written down and, in some cases, transmitted as place-names in the present landscape.

6.   Early seventh and eighth centuries: an organised land

While the land held on to its various pre-Roman nomenclatures to west and north, permanent renaming in a Germanic tongue ('Old English') of the landscape of what was about to become new England was virtually completed. In England, too, a settlement pattern of first-generation pagan Saxon villages was consolidated, with new trading as well as ecclesiastical centres developing, particularly at river crossings and on estuaries. Furthermore, throughout Britain, at the same time the land was organised into estates many of which, in one form or another, are reflected in present-day arrangements. Blair (1991, 162) refers with apparent admiration to 'the startlingly thorough local organisation of the early to mid Anglo-Saxon

Plate XLI Reconstructed Anglo-Saxon *Grubenhaus* at Bede's World, Jarrow, South Tyneside, based on the ground plan of one excavated at New Berwick, near Wooler, Northumberland. The structure models only one of several possible interpretations: a simple A-frame structure with wooden-pegged oak planks and a heather thatch is pitched over a rectangular pit with steps down into it inside the door. The fence in the foreground is of wands interwoven between upright stakes and posts, three types of wood which, in its prime, the hazel in Pl. XXXIX could have been producing.

period, which left a framework so comprehensive that all future developments . . . were moulded by it'. Some of these estates were old tenures newly made overt; others were new creations, albeit from older arrangements. Some estates, probably of scattered areas of land quite as much in England as in Wales and Scotland, were secular, and as much to do with status and power among local lords and chieftains as with the production of food. Others of these newly recognised territories came, for reasons of piety and self-interest, as grants into the hands of the embryonic Church, a trend that continued throughout the rest of the millennium. Bede's monastery on the banks of Wear and Tyne, for example, was founded in the late seventh century on grants of land from the royal estate, a typical arrangement designed not just to produce food and rents but also to act

on behalf of the king as an insurance policy for the great Hereafter. It
was on such estates that, we largely infer, farming slowly returned to an
organised and more productive basis, reflected, for example, in new crops
and changed emphases in agricultural production. Of new technology,
however, there is as yet no sign, though typically in an estate context at
Tamworth the horizontal mill was reintroduced.

In rather different monastic circumstances about the same time that
Bede was writing, Adomnan wrote his *Life of Columba* on the island of
Iona off Scotland's western coast. He mentions 'milking, butchering,
threshing and ploughing'. Cogitosus' *Life of Brigit* refers to 'the difficulties encountered in the transportation of newly-quarried millstone to the
monastery' (Edwards 1996, 4). The first of those quotations tells us of
ploughing in a part of Britain where it is all too easy for our perspective
to be seduced by a dominance of pastoralism; the second is valuable in
exemplifying the insertion of the new into the landscape, one of the two
key points in this section. All over Britain, ecclesiastical buildings from
small to relatively large were becoming a landscape feature during the
period; so too were secular centres, sometimes with the early churches.
But both our quotations are used here primarily because they remind us
of the ordinary daily lot of most people throughout this millennium. In
looking for change, we must never forget that reality.

7.   The ninth and tenth centuries: war, colonisation
    and innovations

In an agrarian perspective, this was probably the most significant phase in
the whole of the first millennium, both in terms of change itself (though
Phase 2 might well have matched it) and in terms of changes which created
significant elements in farming throughout medieval times and, in some
respects, up to the present. Blair (1991, 162) concluded his study of Surrey
by remarking on 'the dramatic effect of growth between the late 9th and
mid 12th centuries, when the whole basis of exploitation changed . . . into
the self-contained, internally focussed entities which we think of as classic
manors and classic parishes'.

Yet it was a time of considerable, at times continuous, disruption and
political instability. If it was so innovative, perhaps it was a case of response and reaction to adverse stimuli, and perhaps there is after all a
connection sometimes between farming and military and political affairs.
Some changes were in train, however, in the earlier ninth century, before
the Vikings began to transform themselves from raiders to invaders and
settlers in mid-century. Many of the early Anglo-Saxon settlement sites
in particular were abandoned early in this phase (if not at the end of the

previous one), and it is during the ninth century that much of the rural settlement pattern of pre-industrial England came to be stabilised in the landscape. Of course, many settlements have since died or moved, but essentially most of England's 'medieval' and present-day villages were located during this phase. Anglo-Saxon communities sometimes simply shifted to a new site; elsewhere, in north-west England for example, new settlers, Norse in this case, formed new settlements. Much the same is true of many towns, clearly an important development from an agricultural point of view: places like Tamworth, Hereford, Wallingford came into being as small towns, and several former, even 'dead', Roman towns took on a renewed lease of life which they have subsequently not relinquished, e.g. Exeter, Winchester, York.

York's revival was very much within a Scandinavian orbit, a political development with major implications for North Sea trade and, therefore, for the agrarian economy of eastern England. Much of this area became the Danelaw and was settled by colonising Scandinavians who gave new names to villages during this phase without necessarily creating new villages. Behind the fighting and the massive payments of Danegeld, it may well have been here, in the encounter in the ninth century between immigrant, politically dominant stock and traditional farming communities, that some of the processes of social and agrarian change which became such a hallmark of the tenth century were triggered. That context may not have been alone as a seed-bed for basic changes; and the fact of other possibilities emphasises the potential of this phase as one of significance. Other contexts could have been in the new circumstances in Midland England created by its reconquest in the first half of the tenth century; and in the re-formation of monastic life and the estates which supported it from the mid-tenth century onwards. Certainly it is no coincidence that so many of the Anglo-Saxon land charters are of mid-tenth-century date and later. Interestingly, overall they depict a landscape of established estates with clearly recognised, often ancient, boundaries. They do not speak of an agriculture ravaged by marauding armies nor of a tenure disrupted by new and disrespectful disposition of land. That certainly seems true of Shapwick in Somerset where Aston and Gerrard (1999, 29) write easily of the possibility that 'on selected arable estates, a deliberate decision was made by some large monasteries to re-order both landscape and settlement on an impressive scale . . . The context . . . might be the re-invigoration of monastic life under Dunstan in the 940s and subsequent monastic reforms.' We had indeed wondered ourselves whether this Phase 7 in our division of the first millennium should not have ended before the mid-tenth century rather than at its end, so that it ran from *c.* 800–940, allowing Dunstan and monastic reform to fall into a last, dynamic Phase 8 of another century and a half of agrarian history up to Domesday Book.

In the English countryside generally, arable expanded as population grew and demand probably led either to a remembrance of the heavy 'Roman plough' which may just have survived in Wales and Cornwall or – much more probably – to technological experiment with bits and pieces on an ard from which emerged the one-way, wooden-framed plough with coulter, asymmetrical share and fixed mouldboard. This may have happened in the ninth century but, in the absence of conclusive evidence, seems more likely to be a tenth-century development. Whatever the date of origin, if such there was, actual application is likely to have varied region to region, even estate to estate, over several generations in England, never mind the rest of Britain: 'Intensive study of Anglo-Saxon settlements and field systems . . . has shown that there were many forms of both, with regional variations, and that there were major changes in the period. It is becoming increasingly difficult to generalise' (Sawyer 1998a, 266).

One generalisation remarked by contemporaries, and many subsequent scholars, was the widespread felling of woodland, the claiming of the waste, 'assarting' to use a later term, during this phase. The converse was the loss of grazing land, and of common grazing practices if not actual, legally established rights. In these circumstances, driven by both consumer demand – more mouths to feed – and a proprietorial desire not just for adequate but for profitable farming, estate management would seek to improve efficiency. This created consequences, summed up as 'a general principle' that 'the shorter the supply of common waste during the 9th to 11th centuries, the more integrated local communities were likely to become, and the more susceptible to the hand of lordship' (Blair 1991, 162). Whether the new plough developed as another consequence of proprietorial initiative or as the tool of clearance and new land-use arrangements is unknown and probably unknowable, but we can infer, and in some cases actually see, new arrangements of large arable areas – physically 'open' if not necessarily 'common' fields – coming into effect during this phase. A one-way plough would suit large fields, and given that it seems in general that field shape and size follow the available technology, that is probably the way to express the development. In any case, it is somewhat implausible to envisage that a new plough was invented to fit a new type of independently created field system.

8. Eleventh century to Domesday Book

Our survey should, strictly speaking, end in AD 1000, but nothing partic-ularly important for present purposes happened then: 'the king went into

Plate XLII Manure heap, produced in three months by about 400 sheep, some of them in Pl. XXXV. The creation of such middens, and the distribution of their contents across the land, pasture as well as arable, were both major pre-occupations and a fundamental of successful husbandry throughout Britain during the first millennium.

Cumberland and ravaged very nearly all of it . . . Then [his ships] ravaged the Isle of Man' (*Anglo-Saxon Chronicle*) – for the time, a normal sort of year in official eyes. William I's survey eighty-six years later is, moreover, irresistible as a landmark in agrarian history, so we add an eighth phase. During it, fortified centres, perhaps knowingly 'manor houses' or even proto-castles, began to appear in the landscape, a trend of course accentuated in the twenty years between Conquest and Domesday by the appearance of numerous mottes, some with baileys. Other new settlements appeared too, and some existing ones were razed, as was some countryside, during the same period. Before the Conquest, however, and in some respects throughout the eleventh century, this phase's main characteristic seems to be an intensification of the processes and trends of the tenth century rather than further innovation. It was a time, at least in the view of the *ASC*, dominated by wars and politics, yet even the numerous military comings and goings cannot disguise that they were occurring in an agrarian landscape which was being cultivated, grazed and managed.

Probably, however, the developments of greatest significance were not so much in technology or in the field as, silently, in the land-owning and social infrastructure. We turn once again to Blair (1991, 162), who articulates in his conclusion precise observation of 'the ever-present influence of seigneurial demands from the king downwards, defining local communities, moulding the expanding economy, and giving an ordered stability to the new patterns of rural life'. Such significance is not of course picked up by the *ASC* which, rather like a daily paper, frenetically records the doings of royalty and its opponents without seeing what is really happening in the land. Later historians have been wiser. John (1973, 138), for example, seeing some stability there where chaos seems to rule, refers to 'a much greater degree of continuity at the grass roots level' than has been supposed. Such continuity underpinned what was by the early eleventh century a revolutionary agrarian situation compared with a hundred years earlier. The population was growing, perhaps at a faster rate in this phase than in the ninth century; the climate was improving. A seigneurial stranglehold on the land and its workings was firmly established, with all its implications for social structure and agricultural productivity, an increasingly market economy was in place in the sense that farming had moved on from mere subsistence to profit-making, and most of the technology – critically the plough and the water-mill – was in place as the technical infrastructure of British agriculture for much of the next millennium. We can now strongly suspect too that the critical time for the formation of so much of the rural English landscape familiar to us today was not the Migration Period or the seventh century but the last 200 years of the first millennium (here Phase 7) and perhaps specifically the century before Domesday Book (Phase 8). That Domesday Book should have been compiled so quickly speaks volumes about the highly organised state of English agriculture, quite as much as the bureaucratic efficiency of William's scribes; and the survey shows the system operating well, apart from some local difficulties in a few places immediately after the Conquest. The whole, from king to landholder, from kingdom to ploughland, from status to service, seems to be held together by a concept of 'worth', or 'value' in modern terms, quite as much as by legal ties and social duties.

Our initial belief is that not a little of the existing landscape, its working and the attitudes of societies in Britain to it now, derive significant characteristics from the farmers and their farming of 1000 to 2000 years ago. In particular, long-established principles of good husbandry which seem to develop in that millennium underlie the contemporary creation of 'the conservation ethic'. And what is that modern mantra, 'sustainability', but good husbandry writ large? Respect for the workers on the land in the first millennium AD is balanced by respect across ten centuries for the agrarian achievement during a thousand years of unremitting and largely anonymous endeavour. AD 1000 may actually be just when, after much travail and years of relatively slow development, farming as we know it was really well founded and about to move into long-term expansive mode.

That is certainly an impression conveyed by Domesday Book, a survey which after all relates as much to what had been as to what was in 1086. Either about then, or more particularly nearly a century earlier at the official end of this essay, in terms of British agrarian history we stand both in the mainstream of a long tradition and at another beginning rather than an end.

Main printed sources and further reading for each chapter

Much material on the first millennium is available electronically. Indeed, in some respects, such as academic discussion about aspects of the period as well as data-bases, the web is now a more up-to-date medium than conventional publication and libraries. General archaeological enquiries can begin with sites such as the Council for British Archaeology's http://www.britarch.ac.uk. A search starting with a simple key word like 'Roman' will easily engulf an enquirer; good archaeological and historical entry points can be found by just keying in similar words like 'Anglo-Saxons' and 'medieval' subtended to 'Britain' or 'UK'. 'Anglo-Saxon literature' and 'Anglo-Saxon bibliographies' are particularly useful; the latter leads to a bibliography on 'Agriculture and Food History'. The most comprehensive agrarian electronic source, though weighted very much to the second millennium AD, is the Rural History Database of the Rural History Centre, University of Reading, UK, approached through www.rdg.ac.uk. *Anglo-Saxon History: A Select Bibliography* by S. Keynes is available on request from the Department of Anglo-Saxon, Norse, and Celtic, 9 West Road, Cambridge CB3 9DP.

The rest of Appendix I concerns printed publication. It effectively serves as the academic underpinning of the text which, as explained in the Preface, has been relieved of many in-text references in the interests of readability. It might also help as a starting point for those setting out on their own work, and is organised accordingly. Neither the Bibliography nor this Appendix attempts to be comprehensive for the first millennium, though together they are reasonably full (up to late 2000) as an introduction to mainly secondary sources in print, either by specific reference or by earlier references therein. This Appendix includes some items not cited in the text, where space constraints forced the exclusion of some even directly relevant material. Throughout, subjective indications of worth are intended to be helpful, not prescriptive: it really is for students to make their own evaluations.

In general we have found that, historiographical interest apart, few published sources before *c.* 1970 are of much value for present purposes. Exceptions are, of course, some basic catalogues, e.g. Glob (1951), Sawyer (1968), White (1967), and a few seminal texts, e.g. Maitland (1897), Hoskins (1955). The Bibliography and the sources indicated here are accordingly weighted towards recent, in many cases the most recent, references, many of which themselves give earlier sources not listed here. Wilson (1976), for example, is archaeologically a good bibliographical horizon since it represents what was available and in use up to the mid-1970s. The chronologically later entries 'Salway 1981' and 'Smith 1997' carry with them a huge bibliographical resource for the first half of the millennium; 'Hingley 1989' does likewise for rural settlement then, and 'Graham-Campbell and Batey 1998' similarly covers Scotland later in the millennium. 'Higham 1993' is a useful bibliographical entry for northern Britain. 'Hooke 1998' contains ten pages of largely modern references central to this book which are not, except selectively, duplicated here.

The new student is best introduced to the period in shorter, modern general histories, such as Millet (1995), Loyn (1991) and Sawyer (1998a), following up with such standard, substantial works as Frere (1987), Salway (1981) and Stenton (1971). Older general works are not worth much attention because they were written within now anachronistic paradigms; but of course most contain references to specific information, such as an archaeological item not otherwise published, or a flash of insight – Hodgkin (1935) is a good example. Apart from the short and scholarly Salway and Blair (1992), there was no modern 'student's introduction' to the whole of the first millennium in Britain or to the whole of Britain throughout the millennium, but James (2000), published as this text was completed, could meet the need; similarly, Arnold and Davies (2000) could do likewise for Wales alone. Smyth (1984) already exists for Scotland. Otherwise, of the currently available paperbacks covering either the first or the second half, and varyingly the middle, Hinton (1998), Sawyer (1998a) and Welch (1992) are sound introductions. Dark (1994), though contentious and non-agrarian, and now Knight (1999), scholarly but also non-agrarian, interestingly try to synthesise five centuries around the millennium's middle as a unity.

Much of general agrarian interest as well as of regional synthesis is included in the nine volumes 'to AD 1000' of Longmans' twenty-one volume *A Regional History of England* series, edited by Cunliffe and Hey.

Similar remarks apply to two other series: *Studies in the Early History of Britain*, Leicester University Press, under the editorship of Brooks, several volumes of which are much used here; and Manchester University Press, *Origins of the Shire*, edited by Higham. Some regions have good stand-alone studies on some or most of the first millennium, e.g. Higham (1993) on Northumbria.

British agrarian history of the first millennium AD as such has not enjoyed its own work since Finberg (1972a), but well-informed if chronologically limited treatments of the topic, up-to-date at their time of publication, appeared in some general works, notably Hinton (1998), Loyn (1991) and Dark and Dark (1997). Hingley (1989, 199–206) helpfully lists with bibliographical references all the Romano-British sites mentioned in his text; Reynolds' (1999) bibliography, useful in itself, can be used to access much of the recent site literature for the second half of the millennium. A major, directly relevant study in terms of its methodology, results and location (between the rivers Rhine and Meuse) is Kooistra (1996).

The key specialist journals are *Tools and Tillage* and *The Agricultural History Review*. An important general point for the student 'working' the period is that, while international and national journals such as *Antiquity* and *The Archaeological Journal* are obvious sources to search, a huge amount of archaeological information is annually published in specialist national journals and in regional and local summaries, reviews, newsletters, etc. *Britannia*, for example, annually catalogues and summarises work in 'Roman Britain'; the public sector archaeological services for England, Scotland and Wales also produce an annual roundup of how they spent the tax-payers' money. Most CBA Regional Groups publish annual reviews; some have grown to be respectable journals, e.g. that for Wales. Much of this material is not otherwise published. Very little of significance for present purposes has been published in recent years in historical journals – perhaps 'historians' journals' would be more accurate – with *Anglo-Saxon England* being the most likely exception.

Students should be aware that there are many unsound, and indeed fantastic (some knowingly but most, sadly, unconsciously so), books about aspects of the first millennium, notably concerning Roman roads and legions, 'King Arthur' and his genre, and bloodthirsty, battle-axe wielding, horn-helmeted Vikings. For academically sound historical fiction, read Rosemary Sutcliffe's novels.

Chapter 1 The first millennium AD

The wider background to Britain's brush with the development and decline of the Classical world is provided in the current and forthcoming

Cambridge Ancient History, volumes X–XIV, particularly for present purposes in the works of Garnsey. Randsborg (1991) provides an all-embracing perspective of first-millennium Europe and the Mediterranean from a non-Classical viewpoint; van Bath (1963) remains authoritative for European agrarian history after AD 500. Knight (1999) places Britain firmly in its European context between the third and seventh centuries.

Essential sources and useful background works on the first millennium AD in Britain itself include: *EASE*, Roberts (1977; 1987), Salway (1981, 1993), Taylor (1983) and Smyth (1984). Relevant books seemed to pour off the presses as we wrote and, short of stopping production, it was impossible to note, let alone study, all of them. One of the most welcome, but too late to absorb, was Richards (2000).

Good entry points to specifically landscape and agrarian matters are: *pre-AD 1*: Fowler (1983a), Mercer (1981), Piggott (1981) and Pryor (1998); *1st millennium AD*: Finberg (1972a) and relevant entries in *EASE*. The 'bibliographical horizon' *c*. 1970 would include Fenton (1968), Gailey and Fenton (1970), Alcock (1971), Finberg (1972a), Fowler (1972, 1975a), Fussell (1972), Baker and Butlin (1973), Postan (1973), Grigg (1974).

On the population question, see e.g. Arnold (1982, 456–7), Cleary (1995, 12–14, 19), Cunliffe (1978), Higham (1992, 8–9), Hingley (1989, 3–4), Jones (1996, chapter 1), Kerridge (1992, 37); while for agriculture and population change in general, see Boserup (1994) and Grigg (1980).

The following, in themselves and in the references they provide, underpin the section in the text on 'agriculture in the history of the first millennium AD': Bowen (1961, 67), Chadwick (1907), Fussell (1972), Hoare (1820, Iter III), Hoskins (1955), Jones (1964), Maitland (1897), Postan (1966), Randsborg (1991), Seebohm (1890), Tusser (1573), Vinogradoff (1905; 1908), White (1970a). The last paragraph of this section is based on: Dark (2000), Finberg (1972a), Fowler (1976a; 1981b), Hallam (1988), Hooke (1998), Loyn (1962, [1991]), Rackham (1994), Reynolds (1999), Rivet (1958), Stevens (1966), White (1967).

Oppida, still an ambivalent phenomenon in the southern British landscape, are best approached through Collis (1984) and Woolf (1993), and Evans' (1999, chapter 8) recent environmental discussion (with references). Cronon (1983) unconsciously provides some challenging models of what may have happened in Britain in the fifth–seventh centuries.

Chapter 2 Evidence

Rivet (1958) remains an authoritative and handy introduction to Classical written sources for Britain, otherwise displayed and used throughout the

œuvre of K.D. White and, for Britain, embraced in the major bibliographies
such as in Salway (1981). Morris (1973, 522–46) displays an enormous
range over Britain; for English early medieval written sources, Whitelock
(1955 [1979]) is fundamental, Stenton (1971) is comprehensive and Sawyer
(1998a) is bibliographically a useful starting point. Holdsworth and
Wiseman (1986) enlighten with informed discussion .

With primary archaeological evidence in continuous and rapid production, the best sources of up-to-date information are the web, lectures, conferences, new museum exhibitions, and the learned societies' main annual
journals such as *Britannia* and *Medieval Archaeology*. The journals *Anglo-
Saxon England, Anglo-Saxon Studies, Landscape History* and the *Journal of
Historical Geography* also publish key papers on methodology and current
research, e.g. Fulford (1990). *British Archaeological Abstracts* are essential
to keep these outpourings under some sort of bibliographic control; so
too, used selectively, are societies' newsletters and other ephemera, and
the popular publications *British Archaeology* and *Current Archaeology*.

Historical evidence and its uses are discussed by many historians, e.g.
Carr (1990), Marwick (1989); archaeological evidence and its uses has similarly spawned a library of its own, e.g. Renfrew and Bahn (2000). Many
have commented on the relationship of archaeology and history, cf. the
percipience of Collingwood (1989) and two discussions specifically on the
topic, Wainwright (1962) and Dymond (1974). Davies (1989) was writing
in the later 1970s for an initial publication date of 1982; her 'Appendix: the
source material' discusses with clarity and sensitivity the realities of using
eight categories of evidence in a particular case, early medieval Wales.
Fulford (1990) discusses four types of evidence for 'Roman' landscapes
in Britain. 'Oral history, memory and written tradition' are explored in a
series of papers in *Trans. Roy. Hist. Soc.* 6th ser., 9 (1999), 161–301. Hill
(1998) builds on Carver's (1986) appraisal of manuscript illumination as
a valid source of agricultural evidence, independently of our discussions
here and in chapters 8, 9 and 13 (see note on chapter 13 below). Anglo-
Saxon land charters are catalogued authoritatively in Sawyer (1968) and
both used and discussed throughout Hooke's work. Hooke (1990) in particular is an outstanding and illuminating example of charters worked out
on the present landscape.

'Landscape archaeology' has generated its own literature since *c.* 1970,
discussed as it emerged in Fowler, E. (1972), Fowler, P. J. (1972) and
Rahtz (1974), and *post hoc facto* in Aston and Rowley (1974), Barker and
Darvill (1997, esp. chapter 1), Higham (1992, chapter 1, in general a useful
review of the development of studies of the first millennium), and Everson
and Williamson (1998, esp. chapter 1). Hingley (1989) and Dark and

Dark (1997) for the earlier half of the millennium, and Graham-Campbell and Batey (1998, esp. chapter 3), Hooke (1998) and Reynolds (1999) for the later, contain bibliographies currently among the most useful and up-to-date for farming and landscape. On 'reading the landscape', see Hoskins (1955), Aston and Rowley (1974) and Muir (1981); for the use of place-names, see Gelling (1978; 1984) and, reflecting on their cultural significance, Fellows-Jensen (1990). Sawyer (1998a, 156–66) provides an excellent short discussion of place-names.

Transhumance features strongly in Hooke (1998). Fowler (2000c, chapter 16) remarks on the time depth but not the global incidence, while Woodside and Crow (1999, 62–6), in an excellent transhumant cameo, relate Northumbrian medieval transhumance to present-day practice 'in parts of Mediterranean Europe and Turkey' but nothing earlier. Beresford (1988) takes it aboard in a medieval Dartmoor context.

Environmental evidence and methodologies of acquiring and interpreting it are discussed in Bayley (1998), Bell and Dark (1998), Bell and Walker (1992), Dark (2000), Dincauze (2000), Fulford (1990) and Lowe and Walker (1997). Processes of deposition are discussed by Needham and Macklin (1992), and in Bell and Boardman (1992), *passim* and specifically pp. 5–6. Good modern examples of research into and interpretation of deposition in palaeoenvironmental landscape terms are Evans *et al.* (1993) and Tipping (1998b). Specific examples are in Evans (1999); in Bell (1992, Figs. 3.4 and 3.8), photographically illustrating the first millennium AD in stratified sequences at Bascombe, Hampshire, and Brean Down, Somerset; and in Allen (1992, Figs. 4.2 and 4.3).

As well as Miket and Burgess (1984), the development of archaeology in north-east England is illustrated by Chapman and Mytum (1983), Clack and Hazelgrove (1982), Cramp (1969), Fowler (1997b), Harding and Johnston (2000), Hope-Taylor (1977), Jobey (1966; 1982a; 1982b) and Topping (1989).

The quotation about discoveries on the Channel Tunnel Rail Link comes from *British Archaeology* 44, May 1999, 4. The topic was subsequently covered much more fully, giving details of sites mentioned here, in *Current Archaeology* 168, May 2000, Special Issue – Kent.

Metal-detecting and the use of its results, where known, underlie an important study by Ulmschneider (2000).

Chapter 3 Environment

Dark (1996) was a key paper in early drafts of this chapter, soon superceded by Dark (2000), now the prime synthesis to consult for Britain, for its summaries, original work and excellent bibliography. It has been used to an extent here but only became available immediately before submission of this text, so it has not been properly subsumed. Its bibliography renders redundant any attempt to provide more than introductory points to environmental matters here. One of them is Jones (1988a), a prime source with key contents on woodlands, grasslands, coastland, moorlands, and disturbed habitats in arable field and towns. Evans (1999) is another; its relevance here is in particular case studies, notably those of 'Roman towns' and 'Dark-earth and Anglian and Anglo-Scandinavian York' (chapters 9, 10). His chapter 7, 'The River Tyne and Hadrian's Wall', independently chose an earlier and more southerly aspect of our 'Roman impact' case study. Fortunately, although the issues are the same, his sources are different, namely Dumayne and Barber (1994), McCarthy (1995), Tipping (1997) and Manning *et al.* (1997). Smout (1993), though mainly post-AD 1000 in topic, is stimulating, with implications wider than its Scottish remit.

Earlier key palaeoenvironmental works are, for prehistory, Simmons and Tooley (1981); and for the first millennium AD, Jones and Dimbleby (1981) and Rackham (1994). The last is currently the best collective summary of relevant original scientific research, though its predecessor over a longer time-span, Jones and Dimbleby (1981), is, in several respects, not yet superseded, e.g. Jones (1981), Maltby (1981) and Turner (1981). Keeley (1984), because of advances it may well have encouraged, is curiously more dated in some of its discussion but remains a basic source for soils, geomorphology, research trajectories and regional characterisation. Climate is a controversial specialism. Best general reviews of the changing British situation are Lamb (1995) and Harding (1982), with the works of Parry (1978 *et seq.*) (Tipping (1998a) references Parry's works) directed particularly to consideration of climatic change and agriculture. Mills and Coles (1998) contains some relevant studies of marginality in the first millennium.

For coastline, see Coles and Coles (1986), Williams (1970), Hall and Coles (1994), Fulford *et al.* (1994), Dark (2000, chapter 2 and bibliography). For a marshy alternative to the Fens, see now Eddison (2000). Gates (1999) comments further on vegetation and Hadrian's Wall.

Chapter 4 Land

Coppock (1964; 1971), Dodgshon and Butlin (1978) and Thirsk (1984b) are useful general discussions of land in, respectively, its agricultural, geographical and regional dimensions. Good archaeological bibliographies exist in Salway (1981), Millett (1990) and Dark and Dark (1997). The tenurial and proprietorial framework of the landscape is discussed learnedly and comprehensively, largely from personal research, in Hooke (1998, chapters 3–5), with excellent references. Similar ideas about power and territory underlie much of Alcock's (1988) discussion of land in mid-millennium Northumbria and can be compared with Higham (1992, chapter 5).

Roman villa estates in southern England have been frequently discussed but see in particular Stevens (1966), Applebaum (1972), Salway (1981), Hingley (1989, 100–10) and Hall and Coles (1994). The river gravels, and in particular the Thames valley, are where much of the recent archaeological work on rural land-use and settlement has been conducted. Syntheses of recent work have recently been prepared by Fulford, Lambrick, Hamerow and Robinson in Fulford and Nichols (1992). Here we use Fulford (1992) and Hamerow (1992), concentrating on land organisation and settlement patterns. Henig and Booth (2000), writing of Roman Oxfordshire but including later prehistory too, synthesise Thames valley material more fully, and after the preparation of our text. Welch (1985) produced a useful assessment of settlement patterns slightly later in the millennium. Dyer (1990) provides a helpful case study across the millennium and beyond in Midland England, with wide implications. Raths and rounds are best accessed through Wainwright (1967; 1971) and Todd (1987), with reports and notes on more recent investigations in the periodical literature of Wales and Cornwall.

My section on ecclesiastical estates is brief because they are a subject of study in their own right, with much written on them elsewhere (reflecting the huge amount of primary documentation). Holdsworth (1995) addresses the topic squarely, with a useful bibliography including some of the older, major studies, and Morris (1989) contains much of relevance and percipience, particularly in landscape terms. Blair (1988; 1995) and Dumville (1992, 29–54) are recent scholarly additions to the topic which runs through Hooke (1998, chapters 3–5). Hall (1993) provides our opening quotation in her conclusion to an illuminating study of a large county with material we might well have used instead of our chosen examples. Similarly, Brown and Foard's (1998) review of the Saxon landscape in Northamptonshire is among the very best of such modern writing at county level. Fig. 4.2 is derived from Williamson (1987), showing an area of Suffolk which the author 'revisited' (Williamson 1998) after criticisms of his proposal that the basic pattern of the existing countryside is 'old'. His slightly modified conclusion was that, while the pattern is probably the result of organic development rather than a single act of landscape planning, the framework is essentially late prehistoric in origin. This author would agree.

Chapter 5 Settlements

Hingley (1989) provides many comparative plans for the earlier centuries, his concern being specifically settlements, physically, spatially and morphologically, while Johnson (1996) reviews similar material from an architectural angle. Smith (1997) also applies morphological analysis to villas, with a view to social elucidation with potentially significant agrarian implications. Keevil (1996) provides an illuminating example of how a villa with a field system began as a mill. Crucial publications in the reappraisal of Anglo-Saxon 'settlement shift' lie in Hooke (1985b) and Hamerow (1987; 1991; 1992; 1995). Much Scottish evidence is embraced within Graham-Campbell and Batey (1998, chapters 9 and 10); see also Amorosi *et al.* (1998) for the far north and islands beyond. Later English settlements are summarised in Reynolds (1999), and dispersed settlement in Austin (1989).

Towns are obviously a huge subject, and currently a dynamic one for the first millennium. Best overall introductions are Ottaway (1992) and, for post-Roman, Dyer (1988), Vince (1994), Scull (1997) and Reynolds (1999). Students could well find, once again, that quarrying under appropriate entries by topic and individual towns in *EASE* is a better source than most, e.g. 'Towns', *EASE* (451–3). The 'dark earth' debate, and related environmental matters, can be accessed in Ottaway (1992), *EASE* (396, 451–3), and Evans (1999, chapters 9 and 10).

Chapter 6 Farms

Farms, mainly after the first millennium AD, are discussed generically in, for example, Fowler (1983b) and Harvey (1984). Modern surveys of extant farms include Barnwell and Giles (1997), Mercer (1979) and Wade-Martins (1991). Hingley (1989, chapters 4 and 5) discusses aspects of farms earlier in the millennium, but the fullest discussions, though now overtaken by many new discoveries and excavations, remain Applebaum (1972), Salway (1981) and Taylor (1983). A Classical view of villas is in Percival (1976), while Branigan and Miles (nd) contains much that in general informs our discussions here. Numerous examples in their western British context were discussed in Branigan and Fowler (1976) and Burnham and Davies (1990); see also Wainwright (1967; 1971) for two of the best-excavated enclosed sites, Coygan Camp, Carmarthenshire, and

Walesland Rath, Pembrokeshire. Examples of more recent archaeological work are found in, for the earlier first millennium, Dark and Dark (1997) and, for the later first millennium, Graham-Campbell and Batey (1998) and Reynolds (1999).

For discussions of settlement and settlement pattern, with plentiful local examples, see e.g. Aston *et al.* (1989), Aston and Lewis (1994), Dyer (1991), Everitt (1986), Taylor (1992), Warner (1987). Such studies contain much on farms, hamlets and dispersed settlement, mainly after the first millennium AD but not necessarily therefore irrelevant, as is demonstrated *par excellence* by Roberts and Wrathmell (1998, 2000).

For Green Shiel, Lindisfarne, in addition to Brown *et al.* (1998), an interpretative essay used here, see also the fuller accounts in O'Sullivan and Young (1991; 1995, chapter 7). Ribblehead is not fully published, but see King (1978) and Reynolds (1999, Fig. 70); for Simy Folds, see Coggins *et al.* (1983) and Reynolds (1999, Figs. 67–9).

Chapter 7 Fields

The Continental background is illustrated, at the start of the millennium, for Holland in Brongers' (1976) original study and for Denmark in Nielsen and Clemmenson (1995), both with specialist bibliographies, and more generally in for example Harsema (1992); and, at its end, by Steensberg (1968). Evidence specifically on fields in between is in very short supply and Muller-Wille's (1965) review needs to be both updated and extended to include the first millennium AD. Kelly (1998) literarily, Norman and St. Joseph (1969) aerially, and Edwards (1996) graphically, present the material for pre-Anglo-Norman fields in Ireland. For Britain, no major study of farming in the first half of the millennium has yet replaced Applebaum (1972) at the level of scholarship and detail of himself and his colleagues; Jones (1972) stands similarly for western Britain, supplemented by later considerations by the same scholar. Both illustrate and discuss numerous field systems. More up-to-date detail on Roman aspects of the topic was included by Salway (1981) in his illuminating discussion within a more general study. Dark and Dark (1997, 93–103) is a useful, recent résumé, but a modern, academic synthesis of the large amount of evidence acquired since the 1970s is seriously needed.

For the second half of the millennium and later, the major works, tending to obsession with 'open field systems', are Baker and Butlin (1973, with an excellent 'Select Bibliography', generally and by region), Barger (1938), Barker and Lawson (1971), Bowen (1961), Dodgshon (1980), Finberg

(1972), Fowler (1976a; 1981b; 2000a), Fowler and Thomas (1962), Hall (1981; 1988), Muir and Muir (1989) and Rowley (1981a).

Williamson's work (especially 1988; 1998; 1999) raises basic issues of fields and fieldwork through the millennium; Fleming's work (notably 1985 and 1998 for present purposes) contains important correctives, both in anthropologically based theory and in practical, local application. Dodgshon (1980, chapter 4) is particularly good on 'infield–outfield', and (chapter 7, 155) proposes that there was 'but one type of British field system, articulated into different regional variants, rather than different regional types', an interesting idea to set beside the models based on processes and chronology in, respectively, chapters 7 and 14 here. Taylor's (1975, chapters 2 and 3) discussion of 'Roman' and 'Saxon' fields, though now overtaken by new information in some respects (as reflected in the second edition, 2000), remains an interesting review of interpretative possibilities; his, and the papers by Hall, Hooke, Fox and Campbell, together forming the first five chapters of Rowley (1981a), remain the academic, bibliographically rich starting point for modern appraisal of open field origins. Harvey, in the same book (pp. 184–201), opted at that stage of her work in Holderness for 'the decades following the Norman Conquest of 1066' as the only period 'when the conditions thought to have been necessary for planning were present'.

Higham (1990), usefully, and Kerridge (1992), learnedly and controversially, provide subsequent discussions. The latter's basic thesis that 'common fields' were exported from England to Europe is somewhat questionable; and his provocative text, albeit of reducing credibility, is ensured by arresting statements such as 'the sull and the ridge-and-furrow system of ploughing were invented by the Germanic peoples', 'these same inventions were introduced in England by the English during the Dark Ages', and 'it is futile to try to explain the differences between various types of these [common] fields by reference to peoples other than the English' (p. 46). Kerridge flatly rejects the idea, tentatively suggested here, of 'supposed Danish or Friesian influences' in these matters. Hooke (1998) has now brought forward a sensible discussion of changes in field types and systems, giving, for example, a key role to 'hamlets and their associated field systems in the less intensively developed parts of Anglo-Saxon England' (p. 193). Consideration of other field matters would now need to include much new material and assessment from northern Britain too, indicated in, for example, Smout (1993), Foster and Smout (1994), Carter (1993–94) and, in detail, RCAHMS (1994).

Tools and Tillage and *Agricultural History Review* are the main specialist academic journals, though the latter contains little on the first millennium

AD; but relevant material is as likely to have been published in period journals like *Britannia* and *Medieval Archaeology*.

Specific references in this chapter

Excavation of fields, Fyfield and Overton Downs, Wiltshire, together with reference to relevant material: Fowler (2000a; 2000b; 2000c; 2000d). Heathrow airport, late Roman field system: excavated 1999, publication in prep., information from Framework Ltd, courtesy of Gill Andrews. Housesteads and the surrounding area in the National Trust estate: Crow (1995), Woodside and Crow (1999), the latter with a wider context without adding significantly to the information specifically on fields. Ingram: following Cameron (1977, 220). 'Cord rig' is best discussed by Topping (1989) and Halliday (1993), with the radiocarbon dating evidence clearly, if not yet entirely convincingly, deployed by Carter (1993–94). Smith (1992) summarises much eastern North American experimental data by Gallagher and others behind the bald assertion here about ridging producing warmer soil. The topic has now been further advanced, with a good bibliography, in Gartner (1999).

Chapter 8 Technology

The basic publications about pre-medieval agricultural implements are Steensberg (1943), Singer *et al.* (1954–78, esp. vols. I–III), White (1967; 1975), Rees (1979a) and Manning (1985). A useful 'horizon' for ironwork of the first–fourth centuries AD is provided by Manning (1974) who catalogues virtually all the material from the Gadebridge Park Roman villa, Hertfordshire. It makes an interesting comparison with our two case studies in the text, Gorhambury and Overton Down. A most interesting bar-chart placing Roman agrarian technological innovations in a time perspective from the ninth century BC to the eleventh century AD appears in Salway (1983, 452).

Water supply, one major aspect of the technology applied to a limited extent in Britain in the early centuries AD, is covered by Hodge (1995). Manning (1985) provides a wide-ranging review of contemporary iron tools and implements. Edwards (1996, Fig. 22) illustrates a range of implements from Ireland including shares, spades and bill-hooks; and Kelly (1998) discusses the extensive contemporary Irish literature about such implements, with some illustrations. Evans (1957) provides twentieth-century ethnographic comparanda. Our paragraphs on 'The basic tools' draw heavily on Jenkins' (1965) study of tools largely from the nineteenth and twentieth centuries. Sculptural and/or decorative material is used in Rees (1979a), White (1967; 1975) and Carver (1986). Langdon (1986) is authoritative on yokes, van der Veen (1989) on corn-dryers which she sees as both roasting germinated grain for malt-production and parching grain for storage. Earwood's (1993) survey of wooden artefacts includes some tools and utensils as well as numerous containers used in the agricultural life. Modern tools and techniques, including some argued here to be relevant to the unmechanised farming of the first millennium, are discussed by Fussell (1981) and illustrated photographically in Brown (1993).

The quotation about and description of Danish peasant farming come from Michelsen and Rasmussen (1955, 11–16). White (1962), though partly discredited, continues to be stimulating. The manuscript illustrating threshing and a range of tools is Cotton Tiberius B.V fols. 3–8.v 1025–50 (Carver 1986, table 9; Temple 1976, no. 87). The value of such manuscripts for agrarian purposes was hinted at rather than exploited in a brief, pioneering consideration of Anglo-Saxon agriculture and its implements (Wilson 1960, 74–80). Ohlgren (1986; 1992) published the basic material on illuminated Anglo-Saxon manuscripts; Hill (1998) discusses them and farming work: see chapter 9 notes below. Holt (1988) provided a standard academic text on mills, beginning with Domesday.

Another mill in Mercia, from near Wellington a few miles north of Hereford, was reported in *British Archaeology*, February 2001, 5. Dated to *c.* 700, it is a vertical type, contrasting with the one we illustrate from Tamworth. The Corbridge Anglo-Saxon horizontal mill and its context in north-east England are now discussed in Hutt (2001).

Chapter 9 Ards and ploughs

This topic as a field of academic study in its own right was firmly established in the second half of the twentieth century with the basic studies of Glob (1951) for ards and Haudricourt and Delamarre (1955) for ploughs. The former's work was new and archaeological; the latter built on a long tradition, part ethnographic, part anthropological and part antiquarian, scholastically located by Gow (1914) and then subsumed into Leser's (1931) great compilation. Ards and ploughs are comprehensively discussed in their wider technological contexts in Singer *et al.* (1954–78) and Parain (1966). The European tradition of cataloguing, ethnography and experiment in these matters was continued above all in the life's work of Steensberg (1943 onwards), of Lerche, and in the journal *Tools and Tillage* (1968–). Šach (1968) on tilling implements in that journal exemplifies the continuing tradition of classification. Lerche (1994, esp.

chapters 2 and 9) looks at plough technology in Denmark and elsewhere in the first millennium AD and her Appendix IV lists the evidence for a continuing use of ards in north-west Europe. Her (1995) catalogue and review of the radiocarbon dating of agricultural implements, including many parts of ards, is fundamental.

Key references for Britain are: Passmore (1930), Payne (1948; 1957), Bowen (1961), Manning (1964; 1966; 1971; and 1985, esp. Section F, 'Agricultural tools'), Fenton (1962–63; 1968), Fowler (1978a) and Rees (1979a). For the Box shares (in Devizes Museum), see Manning (1964, Pl. VIII, 6, 7); and for the Great Witcombe coulter (in BM), see Payne (1948, 111) and Manning (1985, F6). The excavations at Odell, summarised in Dix (1981), have not yet been published in full, and the note here on the possible ard is based on a consequently unpublished short specialist report provided to the excavator (Fowler 1983c).

Leser's (1931) great compilation included some archaeological material, for example both Danish ards and Swedish rock-carvings of aratral scenes; but the implications took almost a generation to be assimilated, at least in Britain. Archaeological information about ards in general only became available as a body of knowledge with Glob (1951), so was not known to Passmore (1930) or Barger (1938) nor really taken on board by Payne (1948; 1957). In the specialist British literature, Bowen (1961) and then Fenton (1962–63; 1968) were among the first to try to build on the new dimensions provided by Singer *et al.* (1954–78) and Haudricourt and Delamarre (1955), a lead followed each successive decade on a narrow front, e.g. Fowler (1976a; 1981b; 1997a), while others advanced the subject in studies both of great detail, e.g. White (1967), Bentzien (1968), Manning (1971; 1985), Lerche (1994), and in broader contexts, e.g. Langdon (1986), Dark and Dark (1997) and Kelly (1998, massively referenced). Rees (1979a) covers the British archaeological material up to mid-first millennium, but there is no comparable study for its second half. Indeed, not even a basic catalogue of (parts of) ards and ploughs, AD 500–1000, seems to have been assembled. The apparently scant evidence then is exemplified by an ard claimed at York (info. P.V. Addyman) and another possibility, now dismissed, at Sutton Hoo (info. Professor M. Carver). Ploughshares from late in the period have been noted from Thetford (Norwich Museum), St Neots, Huntingdon, and Westley Waterless, Cambridgeshire (Fowler 1981b). Almost certainly, others have now been found but have not come to this author's attention. Pl. XXV here is often reproduced, e.g. Passmore Pl. I, top; outside front cover of Faull (1984). Hill (1998) discusses illuminated manuscripts and farming work: see chapter 13 notes below. Ohlgren (1992) illustrates all the relevant material: see under 'plowing' in his index, p. 119; similarly in his catalogue (1986). The plough in the Bayeux Tapestry is shown as an enlargement in Stenton (1957), 'Detail from no. 12'.

Of the specific pieces mentioned and/or illustrated, the following are in the British Museum: Sussex model ard (PRB 1854.12), discussed in Manning (1966, Fig. 1) (Fig. 9.2); the Piercebridge model ard-team (PRB 1879.7–10.1), discussed in Manning (1971), here frontispiece and Fig. 9.2; the Great Witcombe plough coulter; five ard-shares from various places, including Great Chesterford, Essex, catalogued in Manning (1985, 43–4, Pls. 17–18); and the Camerton and Stantonbury Hill ard-tips, catalogued in Jackson (1990, nos. 255–58 and 308). Four of the last five examples (the exception is no. 255, flanged) are socketed; all are asymmetrical to some extent, showing wear on the right-hand ('landward') side. What could be a very close analogy for the ard in the Piercebridge group is illustrated by Isager and Skydsgaard (1995, Pl. 3.2) in an ethnographically useful chapter 3 on 'Agricultural implements' in ancient and modern Greece.

Chapter 10 Arable

Russell (1961) remains the classic text on soil conditions and plant growth, though the subject has now attracted a huge literature, e.g. Bell and Boardman (1992), with references. Courty *et al.* (1989) remains very useful, particularly Parts I and II, 'Basic principles' and 'Processes and features'. Applebaum (1972) continues to be the single fullest, most scholarly discussion of farming in general, arable farming in particular, for Roman Britain; Rackham (1994) is the key to the second half of the millennium, preceded chronologically by the basic Baker and Butlin (1973) and now followed by Dark (2000). For modern crops, Barker (1985, Fig. 18) followed Shackleton (1964, Fig. 12). Greig (1991) first collated modern palaeobotanical evidence for the first millennium, van der Veen (1992) pioneered regional study, Rackham (1994, chapters 4 and 6–8 for rural sites, and 9, 12 and 13 for towns) brought forward new evidence, and now Dark (2000, 173–4) has helpfully synthesised the current situation. The work of M. Jones and Robinson during the 1970s–1990s stands out (see Bibliography).

Evans (1999, 93) on the Tyne valley was using several sources he quotes on his p. 155; Lambrick and Robinson (1979, 124) is the prime source for the Thames valley alluvium; see also generally Bell and Boardman (1992). Manuring is a crucial sub-topic with a scattered literature. The index entries under 'manuring' in Barker (1985) provide prehistoric European examples; the equivalent in White (1970b, four 'manure' entries) for Roman farming and Spurr (1986, esp. 126–32) do likewise for Italy in the three centuries up to *c*. AD 100; manuring from domestic/farmyard middens is believed to be evidenced by potsherds in the plough-soils of fields of the early centuries AD, as, generally, in Bowen (1961, 6, 31) and, in detail, in Bowden *et al.* (1993) and Fowler (1976b; 2000a); and in early medieval times, in Europe (van Bath 1963, esp. 9–11 and index), in Ireland (Kelly 1998, indexed under 'dung'), and in Cornwall for key chronological contexts in Fowler and Thomas (1962). Barber's observations on *plaggen* soil on Iona were followed up by further discoveries, commented on by Sheil in Haggerty (1988, 207–8). Evans (1957, chapter XVI) deals with seaweed as fertiliser. Brongers (1976), a major pioneering agrarian study in European archaeology, discusses regeneration of soil fertility (pp. 60–2), *essen* (pp. 70–2) and radiocarbon dates (Appendix V).

The downland succession of arable to pasture in late Roman times is only one interpretation of Bowden *et al.* (1993), though similar evidence is similarly independently interpreted in Fowler (2000c). Topping (1989) is the most comprehensive appraisal of cord rig, but see also Halliday (1993). Hill, D. 1995, 'A Frontier note', *Newsletter*, Soc. Landscape Studies, Spring 1995, 5–6, replied to Everson (1991) about possible rig earlier than Offa's Dyke. Lambrick (1992) and Robinson (1992) are discussed in chapter 9 as well as 10.

Chapter 11 Livestock

Payne supplies a very convenient summary of animal husbandry (*EASE*, 38–9). The generality of provisioning towns that lies behind our discussion of some particulars at *Hamwic* was initially illuminated by O'Connor at Lincoln, data seized upon and discussed by Hinton (1998, 95–6).

Evans (1957) discusses many aspects of recent, essentially pastoral societies in Ireland; Fenton (1980) describes a traditional model of wider relevance than Scotland. Pastoralism is often a major element of 'marginality', so is present *passim* in Mills and Coles (1998); Halliday (1993) usefully illustrates aspects of upland pastoralism on the Anglo-Scottish border in the light of (then) new archaeological discovery. The 'Grasslands' section in Jones (1988a, 39–85) is a significant help in understanding this habitat and its uses, with a discussion of floodplain grassland in one of the areas we discuss, the Upper Thames valley. Wide-ranging models concerning fodder, some directly relevant to Britain in the first millennium AD, e.g. Amorosi *et al.* (1998), are in Charles *et al.* (1998). Rees (1979b) covers scythes. Higham (1990) discusses the subject of our opening remarks, numbers of oxen.

Chapter 12 Food and diet

The subject of food has been admirably covered in several modern studies, and there is really nothing new that can be said in a brief survey
such as this chapter. We nod in the direction of Hartley (1954), a remarkable eclectic culinary ensemble which undoubtedly contains much
of relevance, most of it not immediately recognisable in that guise; but,
more seriously, we refer to three books in particular which we happily acknowledge as our principal sources: Renfrew's (1993) culinary overview
of Roman Britain in a book which does not cover the second part of our
millennium; and the two excellent *compendia* by Hagen (1992; 1995) which
fortunately do.

Farrar (1998) provides a broad survey of Roman gardens; Ryley (1998)
is helpful on Roman gardens and plants, as is Roach (1985) on cultivated
fruits. In addition to indigenous hazel nuts, walnut and sweet chestnut
may have been available in the early centuries AD as introductions, see
Godwin (1975, 248, 277).

For the second half of the millennium, 'Diseases', 'Fishing', 'Food and
drink', 'Hawking and wildfowling', 'Hunting', 'Magic' and 'Medical literature and medicine' in *EASE* (141–3, 185–6, 190–1, 230–1, 244–5, 298–9
and 304–5) provide well-researched summaries with good references. Our
all-too-brief use of Bald's *Leechbook* can be supplemented by Cameron's
(1983; 1990) original research. Pearson's (1997) authoritative study, which
we follow assiduously, is a bonus, innovative if somewhat controversial in
some respects, e.g. her basic hypothesis for an increased reliance on cereals.
Kelly (1998, chapter 10, 'Diet and cooking') is an excellent, rather different discussion of the topic in general from an Irish viewpoint. Salisbury's
(1981) Anglo-Saxon fish-weir indicated rather more than a simple barrier
across the Trent (cf. *EASE*, Fig. 7) and could be taken to hint, like the
Tamworth mill, at seigneurial estate development. Collins' (2000) herbal
overview for AD 600–1450 arrived too late to be assimilated.

Chapter 13 Agrarian society in the first millennium AD

Randsborg (1991) embraces Europe, the Mediterranean and the whole of
the first millennium, preceded by his earlier (1985) study of European
agrarian subsistence and settlement throughout the millennium; but for
neither Britain nor England is there a study of society over the thousand
years, an illuminating comment on how the period has been thought
about by British scholars. For more rounded, conventional appreciations
of first-millennium societies than this chapter, see discussions nevertheless

specific to either the first or second halves of the millennium such as Salway (1981), Whitelock (1952; 1972), Dyer (1980) and Loyn (1991). Sawyer (1998a) and Higham (1992) are bold and stimulating attempts to address societal issues in a historical framework across the mid-millennial divide; Smith (1976) provides in contrast one example of a more theoretical, almost time-free geographical model. Faith (1999) authoritatively and more conventionally now embraces England late in the millennium and ranges more widely too.

For Wales, M.L. Jones (1984) is detailed, and Owen (1989) contains an excellent bibliography as well as good discussion germane to this book in chapters 2–7. G.R.J. Jones (1972; 1989 is a later summary of much of his work) and Morris (1973) are particularly valuable on British social affairs but, sooner or later, one always returns to Maitland (1897). For examples of embryonic regional diversity, see Blair (1991) for Surrey, Davies (1989), Edwards (1997) and Owen (1989) for Wales, Everitt (1986) for Kent, Gelling (1992) and Stafford (1985) for the Midlands, and Fenton-Thomas (1992) for north-east England.

For the economy itself, in the absence of a book covering the whole millennium in Britain, the first centuries AD are best considered in the wider contexts provided by Jones (1964) and Postan (1966). Roymans (1996), at one and the same time both a theoretical and a detailed consideration of northern Gaul and the Rhineland, is a timely example of how established thinking about socio-economic change can be challenged by the eruption of new archaeological evidence interpreted in different parameters, in this case 'an increasing relativisation of the role of the Roman authorities' (p. 10) in the process of Romanisation. With an equivalent caveat, van Bath (1963) remains an authoritative study for western Europe. Aspects of economy in western Britain are discussed by Campbell (1996). An excellent modern review of the *Vikings in Scotland* (Graham-Campbell and Batey 1998) includes a chapter on 'The Norse economy' covering livestock, crop production, natural resources and trade.

Wilson (1962) can be acknowledged as a brave, early attempt to consider the rural economy in England in the light of new sorts of archaeological evidence then beginning to emerge, though long superseded now by such as Loyn (1991) and, head-on and in detail in respect of manuscript evidence, by Hill (1998). The latter provides a learnedly vivid verbal and graphic picture of farming at the end of our period, overlapping with my overview here and detail in chapters 8 and 9; but since my passages were written before I saw his paper, I let them stand, encourage diversity and link the two more or less synchronous but independent discussions by creating my Table 13.1 from his Table 1, 'The labours of the months' (with his permission). Finberg (1972b, 512–16) provides more detail on *Rectitudines Singularum Personarum* and *gerefa* than our summary; Harvey (1993) provides a detailed bibliography on both.

An important paper by Ulmschneider (2000) discusses the rapidly changing picture of the Middle Anglo-Saxon rural economy in Lincolnshire, significantly advancing my text. Hadley (1996) is an important paper, excellently referenced, on the Scandinavian settlement of England. The most comprehensive survey of the topic is now Hadley and Richards (2000).

For folklore collected geographically, see Westwood (1987); for pagan survivals, Ross (1967); for Christianity, Frend (1999) and Thomas (1981); for Teutonic and Scandinavian beliefs, Davidson (1993). The passage on All Saints' Day/All-Hallows was inspired by Stephen Moss, 'Weatherwatch', *The Guardian*, 29 October 1999. For an excellent summary of fasting, see *EASE*, 414–15, a volume sadly without a contrapuntal entry on 'feasting'. Pearsall and Salter (1973) explore the medieval centuries but some of their research is relevant here.

Weathercocks: Carver 1986, Table 1: Hand IA: weathercock Harley 603, fols. 3.v, 4, not in Utrecht Temple Fig. 91; weathercock 1000 fol. 3.v Harley 603, Temple 1976, no. 64.

Chapter 14 Farming in the first millennium AD

Since this chapter attempts to subsume main points from the previous chapters, little new bibliographical source material is needed; but it is important to remember Finberg (1972a) and note John (1960; 1973; 1996), a scholarly *corpus* full of wise and pertinent insights.

To help any student wishing to enter (or revise!) the specifically agrarian field, the following titles are the author's choice, in the light of experience writing this book, of the thirteen most useful, basic texts in print: Baker and Butlin (1973), Dark (2000), *EASE*, *EHD*, Finberg (1972a), Hines (1997), Hooke (1998), Manning (1985), Rackham (1994), Reynolds (1999), Rowley (1981a), Salway (1981), Taylor (2000).

Appendix 2

Relevant glossaries exist in several of the main books already quoted, e.g. Hallam (1981, 265–9), Orwin and Orwin (1967, 189–91).

Appendix 3

Currently the best book covering a range of approaches and examples of 'reconstruction' world-wide is Stone and Planel (1999).

Appendix 4

For herbs, see Bown's (1995) *Encyclopedia*.

APPENDIX 2   **Glossary**

General

ard: see specialist glossary below.

ard-mark: a groove cut or etched into soil or bedrock by the share-head of an ard. Such grooves are typically fragmentary, about 30 cm apart and 5–10 cm deep, and are often asymmetrical in section, indicating that the ard was tilted to one side. Areas of ard-marks, now quite commonly found in archaeological excavation, e.g. at Whithorn (Hill 1997) and Overton Down (Fowler and Evans 1967, Fowler 2000c), also characteristically show a criss-cross pattern in plan, indicative of cross-ploughing, that is the cultivation of a field by ploughing backwards and forwards on one axis and then, as part of the same act, at right angles; detailed excavation can sometimes show which axis was ploughed first but, of course, a criss-cross pattern of itself may well be the product of separate ploughings in different years. Areas of ard-marks often show evidence of land-use change, e.g. from pasture to arable, and demonstrate successive cultivations. Such marks may have been produced accidentally during normal cultivation, accidentally or deliberately during occasionally deeper soil preparation, or as a 'ritual' act in preparing the ground, for example before a burial. Ard-marks are often associated with 'Celtic' fields (q.v.), with which in general they share a date-range though the earliest examples in Britain lie in the fourth millennium BC.

broch: a circular, stone-built structure, now often like (the stump of) an empty round tower but originally fitted with wooden floor, partitions and furniture and often surrounded by less ostentatious settlement structures in the early centuries AD in northern and eastern Scotland.

carucate: as much land as could be ploughed by an ox in one year. It is roughly twice the area of a virgate.

'**Celtic' fields**: a misnomer but still the name in general academic use for rectangular, arable fields characteristically about 50 m square, in use in 'Celtic' field systems over much of north-west Europe from early in the second millennium BC to at least the middle centuries of the first millennium AD.

centuriation: 'a highly individual type of landscape formed by the Roman method of land partition for settling a farming population ... The component-unit most commonly used by the Roman surveyors [*agrimensores*] as the basis of the grid was a convenient square (the *centuria quadrata*) with a side of 20 *actus* (776 yards, 710 metres) and an area of 200 *jugera*' (Bradford 1974, 145). No 'pure' Roman centuriation is proven in Britain, but various patterns of axial and symmetrical, rectilinear field systems of the first century AD and later (e.g. Fig. 4.2) seem to reflect an Imperial desire for efficient landscape order.

common land ('land held in common'): land owned by one or more proprietors but used, under specified conditions, as a communal resource by those entitled to exercise rights over it such as pasturage.

cord rig: cultivation ridges created by an ard and/or a spade – a narrow version of the generic 'ridge and furrow' (q.v.) – characteristically with rounded ridges slight in elevation and furrows about 1–1.5 m apart, surviving over extensive areas of north Britain in blocks ranging from a few square metres to hectares, often in arrangements like furlongs in an 'open field' (q.v.). Not closely dated in many places but seems to represent a common method of cultivation through the first millennium BC, beginning in the second and perhaps earlier, and continuing into the first/second centuries AD (Topping 1989, Halliday 1993). Some ard-marks (q.v.) may well have been created in cord rig cultivation.

crannog: a small artificial island usually supporting one large timber building to provide a semi-defensive habitation during the last centuries BC and the first millennium AD.

demesne: the lord's land farmed directly by him (technically 'in hand').

diplomatic (noun): written historical evidence.

estate: an area or areas of land constituting a tenurial whole, as in 'villa estate' or 'manorial estate'.

flume: an artificial channel, or leet, to carry water for use; in this book to drive a water-mill.

furlong: a subdivision of an open field (q.v.), divided into parallel strips of cultivated land characteristically about 200 m (220 yards) long.

gluten: 'nitrogenous part of flour remaining as viscous substance when starch is washed out'. *Concise Oxford Dictionary*, 7th edn, 1985.

hide: a unit of land, roughly estimated as being enough for a household to live on (and therefore changing in area from place to place, so not an absolute value like 'acre').

hoe: throughout this book in the sense 'mattock-hoe' or 'digging hoe', an extremely useful, multi-purpose implement used like a mattock or pick-axe for hitting the soil from above to break it up or to remove weeds, and also to draw through the soil in a prepared seed-bed to make furrows for planting or mounding-up around plants. Quite different from the modern garden hoe or 'Dutch hoe', a much later invention.

lynchet: a purely descriptive term (locally 'linches' etc.) usually for an accumulation of plough-soil at the downhill side of a field ('positive lynchet'); but the term can also be applied to the scarp at the upper side of a field from which plough-loosened soil has moved downhill under the forces of gravity and erosion ('negative lynchet'). Within a field system, therefore, many boundaries with a field on either side are composed of both positive and negative elements making up a lynchet. Despite the impressive size and steep scarps of some lynchets, there is little evidence that they were deliberately built, though some may have formed around walls or against the back of revetments. Lynchets are created by a field edge being fixed along the same line for some time, allowing the edge to become defined by downhill soil movement. The process continues today, especially on light soils. By definition a lynchet is a consequence of cultivation; 'field lynchet' or 'plough lynchet' and similar phrases are tautologous. Lynchets as such can be of any date, though their description is often qualified with a morphological or chronological phrase as in 'Celtic field lynchet' or 'Roman lynchet'. The word comes from OE *hlinc*, often used in Anglo-Saxon land charters, perhaps of remains of former field systems rather than the boundaries of fields in contemporary use.

marl: a natural mixture of clay and lime, valuable as a fertiliser, usually dug out of pits into chalk subsoil.

open field: a cultivated area divided into strips of land farmed by in-dividuals holding their strips under communal arrangements. Such a field was, by medieval times, characteristically part of a village or estate open field system of three or four fields, an arrangement common in Midland England and, locally, elsewhere in Britain. This method of cultivating the land developed in the tenth century and usually lasted until Enclosure in the decades either side of AD 1800.

pannage: food scavenged for by pigs, notably in woodland and charac-teristically beech mast.

plough-mark: as **ard-mark** above, but produced by a plough.

ridge and furrow ('rig and furrow'): now commonly used to describe the fossilised, undulating remains of cultivation with a one-way plough in long, thin strips of land, characteristically some 70 × 8 m and of late medieval date in Midland England and other places where land was farmed in common; but also used as a general term to describe the undulating effect left on the ground by former cultivation in adjacent rectilinear blocks of land. The remains may represent a technique of cultivation, permanent or marginal cultivation, and/or tenure and, though characteristically of sixteenth- to eighteenth-century date, may be of any period from the fourth or third millennium BC to nineteenth century AD.

serf: a largely post-Norman Conquest term indicating 'a peasant with a holding, which, however small, supported him and his family and provided a surplus which was transferred to the lord in rent paid in cash, kind or labour' (Faith 1997, 69–70).

settlement: here, unless otherwise indicated, used specifically of a place where people lived, as in 'West Stow is an Anglo-Saxon settlement' and 'their characteristic settlement-type was a village'; but see settlement pattern.

settlement pattern: the pattern of human activity on the landscape, either as an expression of contemporary activity at any one moment in time, or as a composite pattern including relics of former activity.

souterrain: an underground passage or (series of) chamber(s) associated with a building or buildings in settlements, particularly in the centuries either side of AD 1 in western Britain and eastern Scotland.

strip field: either a general description of a field much longer than wide or, more technically and properly, a strip of land making up with other strips a furlong (q.v.) in an open field (q.v.).

strip lynchet: long, often curving or sinuous lynchet (q.v.), typically defining the forward (or outer or downhill) edge of a more or less horizontal medieval strip field (q.v.) laid out along the contours across a slope.

tithing: an area of land, often the whole or part of a manor which subsequently became a parish, obliged to pay part, originally and often theoretically one tenth, of its income to a specific church.

villa: as in 'Roman villa' in Britain, meaning a building or group of buildings in relatively prosperous mode designed on or aspiring to Classical models as the domestic and functional centre of an estate (q.v.). Such sites were concentrated in southern Britain, their distribution petering out in Yorkshire and Devon, with examples of, in effect, palaces and great houses notably in Gloucestershire/Somerset and Kent/Sussex.

Some were built as villas *de novo*; most developed from economically and apparently socially humble beginnings into architectural complexes fitted with the trappings of success such as mosaics and central heating. The earliest villas were being built from mid-first century AD onwards; many were not being maintained by the later fourth century and all were effectively abandoned for their intended purposes by mid-fifth century. The sites of some, nevertheless, remained settlement nodes, and a few persisted as religious places where later a church was built.

virgate: an old land measurement of approximately 30 acres.

wag: local name for a particular type of stone-built house in northern Scotland in the earlier centuries AD.

wergild: a man's 'worth' or value, expressed in cash terms and used for calculating both compensation and fines in Anglo-Saxon England. See throughout the royal Laws.

yoke: the link between two draught animals, characteristically oxen pulling an ard or plough in the first millennium, it is usually a heavy piece of wood carved with recesses along one edge to fit across the oxen's necks, keeping the animals apart but making them work as one; and the link between the traction power and beam which is lashed to or suspended from the yoke's underside (Pl. XXII; see chapter 8).

Specialist: parts and types of ards and ploughs

ard (Latin *aratrum*; Fr. *araire*): the characteristic principal cultivating implement of prehistoric and first-millennium AD Europe, still in use in the twenty-first century around the Mediterranean and in much of those parts of the world involved in arable cultivation. It consists basically of an often small and light arrangement of wooden parts designed to enable usually two animals, in Europe oxen, to drag a pointed share (q.v.) through the ground (see Fig. 9.1). Critically it lacks a mouldboard. It basically makes a groove through the soil, and in its simplest form, certainly in north-west Europe, had to criss-cross the area being cultivated along axes at right angles to each other in order sufficiently to disturb the soil to create a seed-bed (Pls. XXIV and XXVII).

ard-head: the forward end of the sole when it is not also the share (Pl. XXVIII). It is often protected, e.g. by an iron cap.

beam: where it existed, the wooden attachment between the cultivating implement and the (ox)-team. It was attached to the yoke, but sometimes, particularly as ploughs became heavier and plough-teams became larger, fore-beams had to be added to the beam to carry the line of traction back from the yoke to the cultivating implement, sometimes via a wheel-carriage (Pl. XXVI).

carriage: probably did not much concern the first millennium AD, merely the technical term for a wheeled link between the beam and the fore-beam. It is not essential to a plough and denotes neither a technical breakthrough nor the heaviness of the plough. As Passmore noted (1930, 5), 'the use of wheels depends on local fashion and local soil requirements'.

coulter: a knife-like blade with a leading, cutting edge, suspended vertically on or through the frame of an ard or plough immediately in front of the share-tip and in front of the mouldboard if such exists. Its purpose is to cut a vertical slice through the plough-soil. Its presence does not demand a mouldboard, but a mouldboard requires a coulter.

mouldboard: a curved attachment on either or both sides of a plough designed to turn the soil completely over after it has been sliced vertically by the coulter and horizontally by the share. A relatively broad piece of wood or metal fixed to the sole at an acute angle to the longitudinal axis through the base of the implement, it is the crucial part of a cultivating implement which makes the difference between an ard and a plough (Pl. XXVIII).

plough (Fr. *charrue*): cultivating implement with a share, coulter and, crucially, mouldboard pulled frontwards by a team of animals, typically by two or more oxen. It turns the soil over, making furrows (Pl. XXVI). The principal cultivating implement in medieval and later times, known in the Classical world and, to some, in southern Britain in the early centuries AD and at the end of the first millennium AD. (See ard for named parts.)

share: as in 'plough-share', the leading point of an ard or plough in contact with the ground, designed to disturb and break up the soil during its preparation as a seed-bed; the share first makes contact with the soil below ground level, either forcing its way through the soil on its own, or undercutting the vertical slice cut by the coulter, or doing both in preparing the way for the mouldboard to turn the soil over. The depth at which a share operates can be adjusted to soil conditions and the ploughman's intentions, cf. ard-marks. A share takes the full brunt of abrasion as the implement moves forward, so early shares were sometimes, perhaps even characteristically, of stone or burnt to harden the wooden point. In late prehistory and the earlier first millennium AD, the share, or the fore-share if the ard was a composite one, was often tipped with an iron cap or sheath. The idea of an all-metal share, well established in the fourth century AD, probably developed from this or may have been imported from the Mediterranean world; such shares survived in some places in Britain later than AD 400.

sole: the base of the ard or plough which slides along in the groove or furrow made by the 'working parts' in front. Sometimes its front edge is the share; when it is not, the same point is called the ard-head. The rest of the implement is built up from or on the sole.

stilt: the handle at the back of the cultivating implement held in one hand by the ploughman to do two things: guide the ard's direction and keep the share of the implement at the appropriate angle into the soil. The word tends to be reserved for ards.

APPENDIX 3   **Select list of sites and museums specifically relevant to farming in the first millennium AD**

First-millennium 'farms' and 'buildings' out of doors

England

Ancient Technology Centre, Cranborne, Dorset (cf. Butser below: Stone and Planel 1999, 229–44)

Bede's World, Jarrow, near Newcastle upon Tyne (including *Gyrwe* – an 'Anglo-Saxon' landscape: Stone and Planel 1999, 245–57)

Butser Ancient Farm, near Petersfield, Hampshire (essentially 'late pre-historic', but with 'Roman' components and technologically relevant to the first millennium AD: Stone and Planel 1999, 124–35)

Cotswold Wildlife Park, near Cirencester, Gloucestershire (good range of unimproved animals and fowl)

Danelaw Viking Village, Murton Road, York ('living history', with the emphasis on the 'living')

Fishbourne Roman villa, near Chichester, Sussex (especially for its garden)

Romano-British farm, with reconstructed buildings, Upton Country Park, Poole, Dorset

Weald and Downland Open Air Museum, Singleton, West Dean, Sussex (reconstructions of medieval and later buildings removed from their original sites, but with examples of earlier buildings 'reconstructed' in another sense using excavated evidence and imagination)

West Stow Anglo-Saxon Village, Suffolk (buildings recreated *in situ* after excavation)

Wales

Castell Henllys, Dyfed, Wales (reconstructions of buildings in late prehistoric/early first-millennium settlement: Stone and Planel 1999, 181–93)

National Folk Life Museum, St Fagan's, near Cardiff

323

Numerous 'historic' farms now exist around Britain, a few of them excellent in presenting what they claim to be, e.g. Acton Scott Working
Farm, Wenlock Edge, Church Stretton, Shropshire; but two caveats
must be entered:

i. most relate to farming in the twentieth and nineteenth centuries
    and, however authentic they may be for the recent past, the prac-
    tices and implements they demonstrate cannot be taken uncritically
    as representing what may have been happening in the first millen-
    nium AD, e.g. neither horses nor machines were in common use
    then;
ii. many such places are primarily commercial/entertainment ventures
    not necessarily based on properly researched or understood agrar-
    ian knowledge and somewhat prone to the perpetuation of rustic
    stereotypes, e.g. in their portrayal of 'villages' and 'peasants'.

Other farms and similar establishments open to the public maintain
stocks of officially recognised 'rare breeds', some of which are relevant
to the first millennium AD, e.g. the farm at Wimpole Hall, Cambridge
(National Trust). 'The Chillingham herd' of unimproved long-horn cattle which can be visited with a guide in its medieval parkland habitat at
Chillingham Castle, Northumberland, is correctly claimed to have originated only in medieval times, but is helpful in envisaging the appearance
and behaviour of *bos longifrons* in earlier times.

Several villas and other Roman sites relevant to the agrarian theme
are open to the public, e.g. Bignor villa and museum, Pulborough, West
Sussex, and Chedworth villa and museum, Yarnworth, near Cheltenham,
Gloucestershire, both of which give a good idea of the scale and layout
of large villas as the centres of agricultural estates; and *Arbeia* fort and
museum, Baring Street South Shields, Tyne and Wear, Corbridge military site and museum, Northumberland, and Housesteads fort in the
central section of Hadrian's Wall, all of which display impressive arrays
of granaries.

Indoor museums

England

Bede's World, Jarrow ('Life of Bede' exhibition, opened 2000, includes
    aspects of farming and monastic life)
British Museum, London (for Romano-British and Anglo-Saxon models,
    implements, etc.)

Cambridge University Museum (for Romano-British metalwork, esp. scythes)

Cirencester Museum (Romano-British farming)

Folk Museum, Gloucester (good collection of post-medieval ploughs)

Museum of Antiquities, University of Newcastle upon Tyne (aspects of life in the Hadrian's Wall area)

Museum of English Rural Life, Reading University (with library, mainly post-medieval)

Ryedale Folk Museum, North Yorkshire (good local collection, post-medieval)

West Stow Visitor Centre (the excavated material plus good interpretation of Anglo-Saxon life)

Yorvik Viking Centre, York (urban environment in ninth–tenth centuries, emphasising trading connection: Stone and Planel 1999, 258–68; newly displayed 2001)

Scotland
Dumfries Museum, The Observatory, Dumfries (for ards)
National Museum of Scotland, Edinburgh

Wales
National Museum of Wales, Cardiff

Note: White (1967, Appendix B) provides a list of museums in Europe (plus the Museum of Natural History, Chicago) 'containing important collections or individual items' discussed in his text.

APPENDIX 4　**Herbs and medicinal plants**

We list some herbs and herb gardens. First is a list alphabetically by common name of some of the main herbs and medicinal plants, with their properties and uses, which were available in the countryside – not everywhere, of course – and are likely to have been used in first-millennium Britain:

Agrimony – digestive tonic, wound treatment (scientifically has been found to increase blood coagulation)

Black mustard – antibiotic, condiment

Broom – cardiac treatment, strong diuretic

Chickweed – vitamin C, salad or as vegetable; or as ointment for inflamed skin, ulcers, etc.

Common sorrel – vitamin C, salad and pot herb

Cowslip – sedative, expectorant; anti-whooping cough, bronchitis and arthritis; flowers in drinks

Dog rose – petals for perfume, leaves as laxative and antiseptic; hips for vitamin C (more than any other plant) and rose-hip syrup

Elder – multi-purpose: infusion anti-catarrh, etc.; as eyewash; flowers and berries as wine; berries as fruit; but all rest of plant poisonous

Eyebright – eyewash

Fennel – ingredient of many proprietary cough medicines; base as vegetable

Garlic mustard – antiseptic; substitute for garlic in salads and sauces

Greater plantain – multi-purpose: styptic, and anti-stings, bites, etc.; as infusion to relieve bronchitis, coughs and lung problems

Hawthorn – flowers and fruit as infusion; *contra* high blood pressure, heart problems, etc.

Hop – mild sedative, anti-insomnia

Juniper – antiseptic; berries delicious with meat

Lady's mantle – *contra* internal and external bleeding

Lime tree – tea from flowers for nervous disorders, colds, bronchial complaints; inner bark for kidney disorders and coronary disease

Marsh-mallow – *contra* stomach inflammation, mouth infections, stick for teething troubles

Meadowsweet – as per aspirin (which is named after it: *Spiraea*)

Nettle – multi-purpose for many complaints from dandruff to gout; relieves arthritis and rheumatism when rubbed in (ouch!); rich in vitamins A and C, iron and other minerals (though that was not known in the first millennium); can be added to soups and salads, or made into nettle pudding, beer and tea (only the last is personally recommended!)

Perforate St John's-wort – antibacterial for deep wounds; induces euphoria

Raspberry – leaf-tea for chills and fevers, and later pregnancy; fruits treat kidney problems and anaemia

Salad burnett – salads

Sweet violet – as aspirin *contra* migraines, headaches and hangovers; as a wine

Water-cress – high mineral and vitamin content: soups and salads

White mustard – antibiotic, condiment, laxative; seedlings used with cress in salads

White willow – painkiller (basis of aspirin)

Wood avens – antiseptic; digestive aid; substitute for quinine; worn as charm *contra* evil spirits

Woodruff – contains coumarin which treats haemorrhoids and prevents thrombosis; tea from leaves and flowers

Other herbs with medicinal/edible uses include borage, burdock, chamomile, chicory, cleavers, comfrey, couch grass, deadly nightshade, dandelion, goldenrod, great mullein, lady's bedstraw, lily-of-the-valley, lungwort, motherwort, pennyroyal, vervain, wood betony and yarrow.

Herb gardens

Herb gardens are now much more common than even a few years ago. The following are particularly helpful, not least in their range and/or labelling, and have contributed in a general sense to chapter 12:

Chelsea Physick Garden, Royal Hospital Road, London SW3 (founded 1673; now with new Garden of World Medicine and, opened in 2000, a Pharmaceutical Garden)

Hardwick Hall, Derbyshire (National Trust)
Sissinghurst Castle, Kent (National Trust)
University Botanical Gardens, Oxford (Physic garden founded 1621, the
    earliest in Britain)

Among many commercial/garden-centre-type places open to the public are two of particular interest with National Collections, of lavender
and rosemary at Downderry Nursery, near Tonbridge, Kent, and of
thyme and marjoram (plus a Roman herb garden) at Chesters Walled
Garden, Chollerford, next to Chesters Roman fort on Hadrian's Wall,
Northumberland. The Herb Garden, Hardstoft, near Chesterfield (and
Hardwick Hall above), Derbyshire, and Norfolk Lavender, near Hunstan-
ton, are good examples of well-displayed establishments, with lavender
and physic/herb gardens.

Bibliography

This bibliography is weighted towards recent, in many cases the most recent, publications, many of which themselves reference earlier sources not listed here. It includes some items not cited in the text; these may appear in Appendix 1, giving a guide to their significance. Overall, while this bibliography does not attempt to be comprehensive for the first millennium, it provides a serviceable list of material as published by late 2000.

For abbreviations, see p. xviii above

Aberg, F.A. and Bowen, H.C. 1960, 'Ploughing experiments with a reconstructed Donneruplund ard', *Antiquity* 34, 144–7

Addyman, P.V. 1976, 'Archaeology and Anglo-Saxon society', in G. de G. Sieveking, J.H. Longworth and K.E. Wilson, *Problems in Economic and Social Archaeology*, Duckworth, London, 309–22

Alcock, L. 1963, *Dinas Powys: An Iron Age, Dark Age and Early Medieval Settlement in Glamorgan*, University of Wales Press, Cardiff

1971, *Arthur's Britain: History and Archaeology AD 367–634*, Penguin, London

1972, *'By South Cadbury is that Camelot . . .': The Excavation of Cadbury Castle 1966–1970*, Thames and Hudson, London

1982, 'Cadbury Camelot: a fifteen year perspective', *Proc. Brit. Acad.* 68, 355–88

1987, *Economy, Society and Warfare among the Britons and Saxons*, University of Wales Press, Cardiff

1988, *Bede, Eddius and the Forts of the North Britons* (Jarrow Lecture), St Paul's Church, Jarrow

1993, *The Neighbours of the Picts: Angles, Britons and Scots at War and at Home*, Groam House Museum Trust, Dornoch

1995, *Cadbury Castle, Somerset: The Early Medieval Archaeology*, Cardiff, University of Wales Press

Allen, J.R.L. and Fulford, M.G. 1986, 'The Wentlooge Level: a Romano-British saltmarsh reclamation in southeast Wales', *Britannia* 17, 91–117

1987, 'Romano-British settlement and industry on the westlands of the Severn Estuary', *Antiq. J.* 67, 237–74

Allen, M.J. 1992, 'Products of erosion and the prehistoric land-use of the Wessex chalk', in Bell and Boardman, 37–52

Allen, T.G. 1990, *An Iron Age and Romano-British Enclosed Settlement at Watkins Farm, Northmoor, Oxon. Thames Valley Landscapes: The Windrush Valley*, vol. I, Oxford University Committee for Archaeology, Oxford

Allen, T.G., Darvill, T.C., Green, L.S. and Jones, M.U. 1993, *Excavations at Roughground Farm, Lechlade, Gloucestershire: A Prehistoric and Roman Landscape*, Oxford University Committee for Archaeology, Oxford

Amorosi, T. *et al.* 1998, 'They did not live by grass alone: the politics and palaeo-ecology of animal fodder in the North Atlantic region', in Charles *et al.*, 41–54

Anderson, A.O. and Anderson, M.O. 1961, *Adomnan's Life of St. Columba*, Nelson, London

Anderton, M. 1999, *Anglo-Saxon Trading Centres: Beyond the Emporia*, Cruithne Press, Glasgow

Andrews, D.D. and Milne, G. (eds.) 1979, *Wharram: A Study of Settlement on the Yorkshire Wolds* I, *Domestic Settlement I: Areas 10 and 6*, Monograph 8, Society for Medieval Archaeology, London

Applebaum, S. 1972, 'Roman Britain', in Finberg 1972a, 3–270

Armit, I. and Ralston, I.B.M. 1997, 'The Iron Age', in Edwards and Ralston, 169–93

Arnold, C. 1982, 'The end of Roman Britain; some discussion', in Miles, 451–9

Arnold, C.J. and Davies, J.L. 2000, *Roman and Early Medieval Wales*, Sutton, Stroud

Ashbee, P. 1972, 'Field archaeology: its origins and development', in Fowler, 38–74

Astill, G.G. and Lobb, S.J. 1989, 'Excavation of prehistoric, Roman and Saxon deposits at Wraysbury, Berkshire', *Archaeol. J.* 146, 68–134

Aston, M. 1985, *Interpreting the Landscape: Landscape Archaeology and Local History*, Routledge, London

(ed.) 1988, *Medieval Fish, Fisheries and Fishponds in England*, BAR Brit. Ser. 182, Oxford

Aston, M., Austin, D. and Dyer, C. (eds.) 1989, *The Rural Settlements of Medieval England: Studies in Honour of Maurice Beresford and John Hurst*, Blackwell, Oxford

Aston, M. and Gerrard, C. 1999, ' "Unique, traditional and charming". The Shapwick Project, Somerset', *Antiq. J.* 79, 1–58

Aston, M. and Lewis, C. (eds.) 1994, *The Medieval Landscape of Wessex*, Oxbow Monograph 46, Oxford

Aston, M. and Rowley, T. 1974, *Landscape Archaeology*, David and Charles, Newton Abbott

Atkin, M. 1985, 'The Anglo-Saxon urban landscape in East Anglia', *Landscape Hist.* 7, 27–40

Austin, D. 1989, 'The excavation of dispersed settlement in medieval Britain', in Aston *et al.*, 231–46

Avery, B.W. 1990, *Soils of the British Isles*, CAB International, Wallingford

Backhouse, J., Turner, D.H. and Webster, L. (eds.), 1984, *The Golden Age of Anglo-Saxon Art*, British Museum Publications, London

Baillie, M.G.L. 1994, *A Slice through Time*, Batsford, London

Baker, R.H. and Butlin, R.A. (eds.) 1973, *Studies of Field Systems in the British Isles*, Cambridge University Press, Cambridge

Barber, J.W. 1981, 'Excavations on Iona, 1979', *Proc. Soc. Antiq. Scot.* 111, 282–380

Barger, E. 1938, 'The present position of studies in English field-systems', *Eng. Hist. Rev.* 53, 385–411

Barker, G. 1985, *Prehistoric Farming in Europe*, Cambridge University Press, Cambridge

   1995, *A Mediterranean Valley: Landscape Archaeology and Annales History in the Biferno Valley*, Leicester University Press, Leicester

Barker, G. and Gamble, C. (eds.) 1985, *Beyond Domestication in Prehistoric Europe: Investigations in Subsistence Archaeology and Social Complexity*, Academic Press, London

Barker, K. 1988, 'Aelfric the Mass-Priest and the Anglo-Saxon estates of Cerne Abbey', in K. Barker (ed.), *The Cerne Abbey Millennium Lectures*, Cerne Abbey Millennium Committee, Cerne Abbas, Dorset

Barker, K. and Darvill, T. (eds.) 1997, *Making English Landscapes*, Oxbow Monograph 93, Oxford

Barker, P. and Lawson, J. 1971, 'A pre-Norman field system at Hen Domen, Montgomery', *Med. Archaeol.* 15, 58–72

Barnwell, P.S. and Giles, C. 1997, *English Farmsteads, 1750–1914*, RCHME, Swindon

Bayley, J. (ed.) 1998, *Science in Archaeology: An Agenda for the Future*, English Heritage, London

Bede, *HE*, see Sherley-Price

Bell, M. 1981, 'Valley sediments and environmental change', in Jones, M., 75–91

   1990, *Brean Down Excavations 1983–1987*, English Heritage Archaeological Report 15, London

   1992, 'The prehistory of soil erosion', in Bell and Boardman, 21–35

Bell, M. and Boardman, J. (eds.) 1992, *Past and Present Soil Erosion: Archaeological and Geographical Perspectives*, Oxbow Monograph 22, Oxford

Bell, M. and Dark, P. 1998, 'Continuity and change: environmental archaeology in historic periods', in Bayley, 179–93

Bell, M., Fowler, P.J. and Hillson, S. (eds.) 1995, *The Experimental Earthwork Project, 1960–1992*, CBA Research Report 100, York

Bell, M. and Limbrey, S. (eds.) 1982, *Archaeological Aspects of Woodland Ecology*, BAR Int. Ser. 146, Oxford

Bell, M. and Walker, M.J.C. 1992, *Late Quarternary Environmental Change: Physical and Human Perspectives*, Longman, London

Benson, D.G., Evans, J.G. and Williams, G.H. 1990, 'Excavations at Stackpole Warren, Dyfed', *Proc. Prehist. Soc.* 59, 179–246

Bentzien, U. 1968, 'Der Haken von Dabergotz', *Tools and Tillage* 1, 50–5

Beresford, G. 1987, *Goltho: The Development of an Early Medieval Manor*, English Heritage Archaeological Report 4, London

    1988, 'Three deserted medieval settlements on Dartmoor', *Med. Archaeol.* 32, 175–83

Beresford, M. and Hurst, J.G. 1990, *Wharram Percy: Deserted Medieval Village*, Batsford/English Heritage, London

Bewley, R.H. 1994, *Prehistoric and Romano-British Settlement in the Solway Plain, Cumbria*, Oxbow Monograph 36, Oxford

Bidwell, P.T. and Speak, S. 1994, *Excavations at South Shields Roman Fort*, vol. 1, Society of Antiquaries, Newcastle upon Tyne

Bidwell, P.T. and Watson, M. 1996, 'Excavations on Hadrian's Wall at Denton, Newcastle upon Tyne, 1986–89', *Archaeol. Aeliana* 5th ser, 24, 1–56

Bintliff, J. and Hamerow, H. (eds.) 1995, *Europe between Late Antiquity and the Middle Ages*, BAR Int. Ser. 617, Oxford

Birch, W. de G. (ed.) 1885–93, *Cartularium Saxonicum*, Oxford

Black, E.W. 1987, *The Roman Villas of South-East England*, BAR Brit. Ser. 171, Oxford

    1995, *Cursus Publicus: The Infrastructure of Government in Roman Britain*, BAR Brit. Ser. 241, Oxford

Blackford, J.J. and Chambers, F.M. 1991, 'Proxy records of climate from blanket mires: evidence for a Dark Age (1400 BP) climatic deterioration in the British Isles', *The Holocene* 1, 63–7

Blair, J. (ed.) 1988, *Minsters and Parish Churches: The Local Church in Transition 950–1200*, Oxford Committee for Archaeology, Oxford

    1991, *Early Medieval Surrey: Landholding, Church and Settlement before 1300*, Alan Sutton and Surrey Archaeological Society, Stroud

1995, 'Ecclesiastical organisation and pastoral care in England', *Early Medieval Europe* 4, 193–212

1996a, 'Churches in the early English landscape: social and cultural contexts', in J. Blair and C. Pyrah (eds.), *Church Archaeology: Research Directions for the Future*, CBA Research Report 104, York, 6–18

1996b, 'Palaces or minsters? Northampton and Cheddar reconsidered', *Anglo-Saxon England* 25, 97–121

Blair, P.H. 1956, *An Introduction to Anglo-Saxon England*, Cambridge University Press, Cambridge

1970, *The World of Bede*, Cambridge University Press, Cambridge

1976, *Northumbria in the Days of Bede*, Gollancz, London

Bonney, D.J. 1966, 'Pagan Saxon burials and boundaries in Wiltshire', *Wiltshire Archaeological and Natural History Magazine* 61, 25–30

1972, 'Early boundaries in Wessex', in Fowler, 168–86

1976, 'Early boundaries and estates in southern England', in Sawyer, 72–82

Bonser, W. 1964, *A Romano-British Bibliography (55 B.C. – A.D. 449)*, Blackwell, Oxford

Boserup, E. 1994, *The Conditions of Agricultural Growth*, 2nd edn, Earthscan, London

Bourdillon, J. 1988, 'Countryside and town: the animal resources of Southampton', in Hooke, 177–95

Bourdillon, J. and Coy, J. 1980, 'The animal bones', in Holdsworth, 79–120

Bowden, M., Ford, S. and Mees, G. 1993, 'The date of the ancient fields on the Berkshire Downs', *Berkshire Archaeol. J.* 71 (1991–3), 109–33

Bowen, H.C. 1961, *Ancient Fields: A Tentative Analysis of Vanishing Earthworks and Landscapes*, British Association for the Advancement of Science, London

1978, ' "Celtic" fields and "ranch" boundaries in Wessex', in Limbrey and Evans, 115–23

1991, *The Archaeology of Bokerley Dyke*, RCHME, London

Bowen, H.C. and Fowler, P. J. 1966, 'Romano-British rural settlements in Dorset and Wiltshire', in Thomas, 43–67

Bowen, H.C. and Fowler, P.J. (eds.) 1978, *Early Land Allotment in the British Isles*, BAR Brit. Ser. 48, Oxford

Bown, D. 1995, *Encyclopedia of Herbs and Their Uses*, Royal Horticultural Society, Dorling Kindersley, London

Boyd, W.E. 1985, 'Palaeobotanical report' [in report on Bar Hill excavations), *Glasgow Archaeol. J.* 12, 79–81

1988, 'Cereals in Scottish antiquity', *Circaea* 5, 101–10

Bradford, J. 1974, *Ancient Landscapes: Studies in Field Archaeology*, Chivers, Bath

Branigan, K. 1977a, *Gatcombe: The Excavation and Study of a Romano-British Villa Estate, 1967–1976*, BAR Brit. Ser. 44, Oxford

1977b, *The Roman Villa in South-West England*, Adams and Dart, Bradford-on-Avon

1982, 'Celtic farm to Roman villa', in Miles, 81–96

Branigan, K. and Fowler, P.J. (eds.) 1976, *The Roman West Country*, David and Charles, Newton Abbot

Branigan, K. and Miles, D. (eds.) nd [*c.* 1990], *The Economies of Romano-British Villas*, J.R. Collis, University of Sheffield, Department of Archaeology and Prehistory, Sheffield

Breeze, D. 1984, 'Demand and supply on the Northern Frontier', in Miket and Burgess, 264–86

1998, *Roman Scotland: Frontier Country*, Batsford/Historic Scotland, London

Breeze, D.J. and Dobson, B. 1987 *Hadrian's Wall*, 3rd edn, Penguin, Harmondsworth

Brodribb, A.C.C., Hands, A.R. and Walker, D.R. 1968–78, *Excavations at Shakenoak Farm, near Wilcote, Oxfordshire Parts I–V*, I–IV privately published, Oxford; V, BAR, Oxford

Brongers, J.A. 1976, *Air Photography and Celtic Field Research in the Netherlands*, Nederlandse Ouheden 6, ROB, Amersfoort

Brown, A.E. 1977, 'Some Anglo-Saxon estates and their boundaries', *Northants. Archaeol.* 12, 155–67

Brown, A.E. and Foard, G. 1998, 'The Saxon landscape: a regional perspective', in Everson and Williamson, 67–94

Brown, J. 1993, *Farm Tools and Techniques: A Pictorial History*, Batsford, London

Brown, T. *et al.* 1998, 'Marginality, multiple estates and environmental change; the case of Lindisfarne', in Mills and Coles, 139–48

Burnham, B.C. and Davies, J.L. (eds.) 1990, *Conquest, Co-Existence and Change: Recent Work in Roman Wales*, Trivium 25, St David's University College, Lampeter

Cadman, G. and Foard, G. 1984, 'Raunds: manorial and village origins', in Faull, 81–100

Cameron, K. 1977, *English Place-Names*, 3rd edn, BCA/Batsford, London

Cameron, M.L. 1983, 'Bald's *Leechbook*: its sources and their use in its compilation', *Anglo-Saxon England* 12, 153–82

1990, 'Bald's *Leechbook* and cultural interactions in Anglo-Saxon England', *Anglo-Saxon England* 19, 5–12

1993, *Anglo-Saxon Medicine*, Cambridge University Press, Cambridge

Campbell, E. 1996, 'The archaeological evidence for external contacts: imports, trade and economy in Celtic Britain A.D. 400–800', in Dark, 83–96

Campbell, J. (ed.) 1991, *The Anglo-Saxons*, Penguin, London

Campey, L.H. 1989, 'Medieval village plans in County Durham: an analysis of reconstructed plans based on medieval documentary sources', *Northern History* 25, 60–87.

Carpocino, J. 1956, *Daily Life in Ancient Rome: The People and the City at the Height of Empire*, Penguin, Harmondsworth

Carr, E.H. 1990, *What is History?*, 2nd edn, Penguin, London

Carr, R.D., Tester, A. and Murphy, P. 1988, 'The Middle Saxon settlement at Staunch Meadow, Brandon', *Antiquity* 62, 371–7

Carter, S.P. 1993–94, 'Radiocarbon dating evidence for the age of narrow cultivation ridges in Scotland', *Tools and Tillage* 7, 83–91

Carver, M.O.H. 1986, 'Contemporary artefacts illustrated in late Saxon manuscripts', *Archaeologia* 108, 117–45

 (ed.) 1992, *The Age of Sutton Hoo: The Seventh Century in North-Western Europe*, Boydell Press, Woodbridge

Chadwick, H.M. 1907, *The Origins of the English Nation*, Cambridge University Press, Cambridge

Chambers, F.M. and Jones, M.K. 1984, 'Antiquity of rye in Britain', *Antiquity* 58, 219–24

Chapman, J.C. and Mytum, H.C. (eds.) 1983, *Settlement in North Britain 1000 BC–AD 1000*, BAR Brit. Ser. 118, Oxford

Charles, M., Halstead, P. and Jones, G. (eds.) 1998, *Environmental Archaeology (The Journal of Human Palaeoecology)* 1, *Fodder: Archaeological, Historical and Ethnographic Studies*, Oxbow, Oxford

Charles-Edwards, T.M. 1972, 'Kinship, status and the origin of the hide', *Past and Present* 56, 3–33

Clack, P.A.G. and Haselgrove, S. 1982, *Rural Settlement in the Roman North*, CBA Research Report 3, Durham

Clark, A. 1993, *Excavations at Mucking*, vol. I, *The Site Atlas*, English Heritage/ British Museum Press, London

Clarke, H. and Ambrosiani, B. 1991, *Towns in the Viking Age*, Leicester University Press, Leicester

Cleary, S.E. 1995, 'Changing constraints on the landscape AD 400–600', in Hooke and Burnell, 11–26

Clemoes, P. and Dodwell, C.R. 1974, *The Old English Illustrated Hexateuch*, Early English Texts in Facsimile 18

Close-Brooks, J. 1986, 'Excavations at Clatchard Craig, Fife', *Proc. Soc. Antiq. Scot.* 116, 117–84

Clutton-Brock, J. 1987, *A Natural History of Domesticated Animals*, British Museum (Natural History), London, and Cambridge University Press, Cambridge

1992, *Horse Power: A History of the Horse and the Donkey in Human Societies*, Natural History Museum Publications, London

Coggins, D., Fairless, K.J. and Batey, C.E. 1983, 'Simy Folds: an early medieval settlement in Upper Teesdale, Co. Durham', *Med. Archaeol.* 27, 1–26

Coles, B. and Coles, J. 1986, *Sweet Track to Glastonbury: The Somerset Levels in Prehistory*, Thames and Hudson, London

Coles, J. 1990, *Images of the Past: A Guide to the Rock Carvings . . . of Northern Bohuslän*, Hällristningsmuseet Vitlycke, Uddevalla, Sweden

Coles, J. and Hall, D. 1998, *Changing Landscapes: The Ancient Fenland*, Cambridgeshire County Council and Wetland Archaeology Research Project, Cambridge and Exeter

Collingwood, R.G. 1989. *The Idea of History*, Oxford

Collingwood, R.G. and Myres, J.N.L. 1936, *Roman Britain and the English Settlements*, Clarendon Press, Oxford

Collins, M. 2000, *Medieval Herbals: The Illustrative Traditions*, British Library, London

Collis, J. 1984, *Oppida: Earliest Towns North of the Alps*, University of Sheffield, Sheffield

Collis, J.S. 1975, *The Worm Forgives the Plough*, Penguin, Harmondsworth

Columella 1955, *De Re Rustica*, Loeb, London

Cook, H. and Williamson, T. (eds.) 1999, *Water Management in the English Landscape: Field, Marsh and Meadow* Edinburgh University Press Edinburgh

Coppock, J.T. 1964, *An Agricultural Atlas of England and Wales*, Faber and Faber, London

1971, *An Agricultural Geography of Great Britain*, Bell, London

Cosgrove, D. and Daniels, S. (eds.) 1988, *The Iconography of Landscape: Essays on the Symbolic Representation, Design and Use of Past Environments*, Cambridge University Press, Cambridge

Courty, M.A., Goldberg, P. and Macphail, R. 1989, *Soils and Micromorphology in Archaeology*, Cambridge University Press, Cambridge

Cowley, D.C. 1997, 'Archaeological landscapes in Strathbraan, Perthshire', *Tayside and Fife Archaeol. J.* 3, 161–75

1999, 'Squaring the circle: domestic architecture in later prehistoric Sutherland and Caithness', in Frodsham *et al.*, 67–75

Crabtree, P. 1985, 'The faunal remains', in West, 85–96

1989, *West Stow, Suffolk: Early Anglo-Saxon Animal Husbandry*, East Anglian Archaeology Report 47, Suffolk County Planning Department, Ipswich

1994, 'Animal exploitation in East Anglian villages', in Rackham, 40–54

Cramp, R. 1969, 'Excavations at the Saxon monastic sites of Wearmouth and Jarrow, Co. Durham: an interim report', *Med. Archaeol.* 13, 21–66

1983, 'Anglo-Saxon settlement', in Chapman and Mytum, 263–97

1993, 'A reconsideration of the monastic site of Whitby', in R.M. Spearman and J. Higgitt (eds.), *The Age of Migrating Ideas: Early Medieval Art in Northern Britain and Ireland*, Sutton, Edinburgh and Stroud

Crawford, B.E. 1987, *Scandinavian Scotland*, Leicester University Press, Leicester

Crawford, O.G.S. 1924, *Air Survey and Archaeology*, OS Professional Papers, NS 7, Southampton

1953, *Archaeology in the Field*, Phoenix House, London

Crawford, O.G.S. and Keiller, A. 1928, *Wessex from the Air*, Clarendon Press, Oxford

Cronon, W. 1983, *Changes in the Land: Indians, Colonists and the Ecology of New England*, Hill and Wang, New York

Crossley-Holland, K. (ed.) 1999, *The Anglo-Saxon World: An Anthology*, Oxford University Press, Oxford

Crow, J. 1995, *Housesteads*, Batsford/English Heritage, London

Crummy, P., Hillam, J. and Crossan, C. 1982, 'Mersea Island: the Anglo-Saxon causeway', *Essex Archaeol. Hist.* 14, 77–93

Cunliffe, B. 1971, *Excavations at Fishbourne I, II*, Research Reports of the Society of Antiquaries, London

1973, 'Chalton, Hants: the evolution of a landscape', *Antiq. J.* 53, 173–90

1976, 'The origins of urbanisation in Britain', in B. Cunliffe and T. Rowley (eds.), *Oppida: The Beginnings of Urbanisation in Barbarian Europe*, BAR Suppl. Ser. 2, Oxford

1977, 'The Romano-British village at Chalton, Hants.', *Procs. Hants. Field Club Archaeol. Soc.* 33, 45–67

1978, 'Settlement and population in the British Iron Age: some facts, figures and fantasies', in B.W. Cunliffe and T. Rowley (eds.), *Lowland Iron Age Communities in Europe*, Oxford, 3–24

1991, *Iron Age Communities in Britain*, Routledge, London

Dark, K. 1994, *Civitas to Kingdom: British Political Continuity 300–800*, Leicester University Press, Leicester

(ed.) 1996, *External Contacts and the Economy of Late Roman and Post-Roman Britain*, Boydell Press, Woodbridge

Dark, K. and Dark, P. 1997, *The Landscape of Roman Britain*, Sutton, Stroud

Dark, S.P. 1996, 'Palaeoecological evidence for landscape continuity and change in Britain *ca* A.D. 400–800', in Dark, K., 23–51

2000, *The Environment of Britain in the First Millennium AD*, Duckworth, London

Darlington, R.R. 1955, 'Anglo-Saxon Wiltshire', in *VCH Wiltshire*, vol. 2, Oxford University Press, London, 1–34

Daubeny, C. 1857, *Lectures on Roman Husbandry delivered before the University of Oxford . . .*, Oxford University Press, Oxford

Davidson, H.E. 1993, *The Lost Beliefs of Northern Europe*, Routledge, London

Davies, J.L., Hague, D.B. and Hogg, A.H.A. 1971, 'The hut settlement on Gate-holm, Pembrokeshire', *Archaeol. Cambrensis* 120, 102–10

Davies, N. 1999, *The Isles: A History*, Macmillan, London

Davies, W. 1979, *Llandaff Charters*, National Library of Wales, Cardiff

   1989, *Wales in the Early Middle Ages*, Leicester University Press, Leicester

de la Bédoyère, G. 1993, *Roman Villas and the Countryside*, English Heritage/Batsford, London

Dickson, A. 1798, *The Husbandry of the Ancients*, Edinburgh

Dimbleby, G.W. 1962, *The Development of British Heathlands and Their Soils*, Clarendon Press, Oxford

   1977, *Ecology and Archaeology* (Studies in Biology 77, Institute of Biology), Arnold, London

   1985, *The Palynology of Archaeological Sites*, Academic Press, London

Dincauze, D.F. 2000, *Environmental Archaeology: Principles and Practice*, Cambridge University Press, Cambridge

Dix, B. 1981, 'The Romano-British farmstead at Odell and its setting', *Landscape Hist.* 3, 17–26

Dixon, P.J. 1994, 'Field systems, rig and other cultivation remains in Scotland: the field evidence', in Foster and Smout, 26–52

Dodgshon, R.A. 1980, *The Origin of British Field Systems: An Interpretation*, Academic Press, London

Dodgshon, R.A. and Butlin, R.A. (eds.) 1978, *An Historical Geography of England and Wales*, Academic Press, London

Donaldson, G. 1960–61, 'Sources for Scottish agrarian history before the eighteenth century', *Agric. Hist. Rev.* 8, 82–90

Duignan, M. 1944, 'Irish agriculture in Early Historic times', *J. Roy. Soc. Antiq. Ireland* 74, 124–45

Dumayne, L. 1993, 'Invader or native? – vegetation clearance in northern Britain during Roman-British times', *Vegetation History and Archaeobotany* 2, 29–36

Dumayne, L. and Barber, K.E. (1994), 'The impact of the Romans on the environment of northern England', *The Holocene* 4, 165–73

Dumville, D. N. 1992, *Wessex and England from Alfred to Edgar: Six Essays on Political, Cultural and Ecclesiastical Revival*, Boydell, Woodbridge

Dyer, C. 1980, *Lords and Peasants in a Changing Society: The Estates of the Bishopric of Worcester 680–1540*, Cambridge University Press, Cambridge

   1988, 'Recent developments in early medieval urban history and archaeology in England', in D. Denecke and G. Shaw (eds.), *Urban Historical Geography*, Cambridge University Press, Cambridge

   1990, 'Dispersed settlements in medieval England. A case study of Pendock, Worcestershire', *Med. Archaeol.* 34, 97–121

1991, *Hanbury: Settlement and Society in a Woodland Landscape*, Leicester University Press, Leicester

Dymond, D. 1974, *Archaeology and History: A Plea for Reconciliation*, Thames and Hudson, London

Earwood, C. 1993, *Domestic Wooden Artefacts in Britain and Ireland from Neolithic to Viking Times*, University of Exeter Press, Exeter

Eddison, J. 2000, *Romney Marsh: Survival on a Frontier*, Tempus, Stroud

Edwards, K.J. and Ralston, I.B.M. (eds.) 1997, *Scotland: Environment and Archaeology, 8000 BC – AD 1000*, John Wiley, Chichester

Edwards, K.J. and Whittington, G. 1997, 'Vegetation change', in Edwards and Ralston, 63–82

Edwards, N. 1996, *The Archaeology of Early Medieval Ireland*, Batsford, London
(ed.) 1997, *Landscape and Settlement in Medieval Wales*, Oxbow Monograph 81, Oxford

Evans, E.E. 1957, *Irish Folk Ways*, Routledge and Kegan Paul, London
1958, *Irish Heritage: The Landscape, the People and Their Work*, Dundalgan Press, Dundalk

Evans, G.E. 1967, *The Horse in the Furrow*, Faber and Faber, London
1987, *Spoken History*, Faber and Faber, London

Evans, J.G. 1972, *Land Snails in Archaeology*, Seminar Press, London
1999, *Land and Archaeology: Histories of Human Environment in the British Isles*, Tempus, Stroud

Evans, J.G., Limbrey, S., Máté, A. and Mount, R. 1993, 'An environmental history of the Upper Kennet Valley, Wiltshire, for the last 10,000 years', *Proc. Prehist. Soc.* 59, 139–95

Evans, J. and O'Connor, T. 1999, *Environmental Archaeology: Principles and Methods*, Sutton, Stroud

Everitt, A. 1986, *Continuity and Colonization: The Evolution of Kentish Settlement*, Leicester University Press, Leicester

Everson, P. 1991, 'Offa's Dyke at Dudston in Chirbury, Shropshire. A pre-Offan field system?', *Landscape Hist.* 13, 53–63

Everson, P. and Williamson, T. (eds.) 1998, *The Archaeology of Landscape*, Manchester University Press, Manchester

Everton, A. and Fowler, P.J. 1978, 'Pre-Roman ard-marks at Lodge Farm, Falfield, Avon: a method of analysis', in Bowen and Fowler, 179–85

Faith, R. 1999, *The English Peasantry and the Growth of Lordship*, Leicester University Press, London

Farmer, D.H. (ed.) 1988, *The Age of Bede*, Penguin, London

Farrar, L. 1998, *Ancient Roman Gardens*, Sutton, Stroud

Fasham, P. and Hanworth, R. 1978, 'Ploughmarks, Roman roads and motorways', in Bowen and Fowler, 175–7

Faull, M.L. (ed.) 1984, *Studies in Late Anglo-Saxon Settlement*, Department for External Studies, Oxford University, Oxford

Fellows-Jensen, G. 1990, 'Place-names as a reflection of cultural interaction', *Anglo-Saxon England* 19, 13–21

Fenland Survey Reports 1987–, various authors, mainly published in *East Anglian Archaeology*

Fenton, A. 1962–63, 'Early and traditional cultivating implements in Scotland', *Proc. Soc. Antiq. Scot.* 94, 264–317

1968, 'Plough and spade in Dumfries and Galloway', *Trans. Dumfries and Galloway Natur. Hist. Antiq. Soc.* 45, 147–83

1970, 'The plough-song, a Scottish source for medieval plough history', *Tools and Tillage* 1(3), 175–91

1971–72, 'Early yoke types in Britain', *Proc. Hungarian Agric. Mus.* 69–75

1978, *The Northern Isles: Orkney and Shetland*, John Donald, Edinburgh

1980, 'The traditional pastoral economy', in M.L. Parry and T.R. Slater (eds.), *The Making of the Scottish Countryside*, Croom Helm, London

Fenton-Thomas, C. 1992, 'Pollen analysis as an aid to the reconstruction of patterns of land-use and settlement in the Tyne-Tees region during the first-millennia BC and AD', *Durham Archaeol. J.* 8, 51–62

Ferrell, G. (1997), 'Space and society in the Iron Age of north-east England', in Gwilt and Haselgrove, 228–38

Field, J. 1972, *English Field Names: A Dictionary*, David and Charles, Newton Abbott

Finberg, H.P.R. 1957, *Roman and Saxon Withington*, Occasional Paper, Department of English Local History, University of Leicester, Leicester

(ed.) 1972a, *The Agrarian History of England and Wales I.2 A.D. 43–1042*, Cambridge University Press, Cambridge

1972b, 'Anglo-Saxon England to 1042', in Finberg 1972a, 383–525

Fleming, A. 1985, 'Land tenure, productivity, and field systems', in Barker and Gamble, 129–46

1987, *The Dartmoor Reaves*, Batsford, London

1990, 'Landscape archaeology, prehistory and rural studies', *Rural Hist.* 1, 5–15

1998, *Swaledale: Valley of the Wild River*, Edinburgh University Press, Edinburgh

Forbes, H. 1998, 'European agriculture viewed bottom-side upwards: fodder- and forage-provision in a traditional Greek community', in Charles *et al.*, 19–34

Foster, S. 1996, *Picts, Gaels and Scots*, Batsford/Historic Scotland, London

Foster, S. and Smout, T.C. (eds.) 1994, *The History of Soils and Field Systems*, Scottish Cultural Press, Edinburgh

Fowler, E. (ed.) 1972, *Field Survey in British Archaeology*, CBA, London

Fowler, E. and Fowler, P.J. 1988, 'Excavations on Tor Abb, Iona', *Proc. Soc. Antiq. Scot.* 118, 181–201

Fowler, P.J. 1962, 'A native homestead of the Roman period at Porth Godrevy, Gwithian', *Cornish Archaeol.* 1, 17–60

    1968, 'Excavations of a Romano-British settlement at Row of Ashes Farm, Butcombe, North Somerset, Interim Report, 1966–7', *Proc. Univ. Bristol Spelaeol. Soc.* 11(3), 209–36

    1970, 'Fieldwork and excavation in the Butcombe area, north Somerset', *Proc Univ. Bristol Spelaeol. Soc.*, 169–94

    (ed.) 1972, *Archaeology and the Landscape: Essays in Honour of L.V. Grinsell*, John Baker, London

    (ed.) 1975a, *Recent Work in Rural Archaeology*, Moonraker Press, Bradford-on-Avon

    1975b, 'Continuity in the landscape? . . .', in Fowler 1975a, 121–36

    1976a, 'Agriculture and rural settlement', in Wilson, 23–48

    1976b, 'Farms and fields in the Roman West Country', in Branigan and Fowler, 162–82

    1978a, 'The Abingdon ard share', in Parrington, 83–8

    1978b, 'Lowland landscapes: culture, time and personality', in S. Limbrey and J.G. Evans (eds.), *The Effect of Man on the Landscape: The Lowland Zone*, CBA, London, 1–11

    1979, 'Archaeology and the M4 and M5 motorways 1965–78', *Archaeol. J.* 136, 12–26

    1981a, 'Later prehistory', in Piggott, 61–298

    1981b, 'Farming in the Anglo-Saxon landscape: an archaeologist's review', *Anglo-Saxon England* 9, 263–80

    1981c, 'Wildscape to landscape: "enclosure" in prehistoric Britain', in Mercer, 9–54

    1983a, *The Farming of Prehistoric Britain*, Cambridge University Press, Cambridge

    1983b, *Farms in England*, HMSO, London

    1983c, 'A note on a wooden object, possibly from an ard' [from Odell, Bedfordshire], unpublished note for the excavation report, with the object in Bedford Museum

    1985, 'The Roman field system in Barnsley Park', *Trans. Bristol and Gloucester Archaeol. Soc.* 103, 77–82

    1997a, 'Farming in early medieval England: some fields for thought', in Hines, 25–41

    1997b, ' "A trifle historical": making landscapes in Northumbria', in Barker and Darvill, 55–69

    1998, 'Moving through the landscape', in Everson and Williamson, 25–41

1999, 'Bede's World UK: the monk who made history', in Stone and Planel, 245–57

2000a, *Seven Small Excavations on Fyfield and Overton Downs, with Summaries of Eighteen Other Excavations in and near Fyfield and West Overton Parishes, Wiltshire*, Fyfod Working Paper 66, ADS, York (Fowler 2000 a-b and d available at www.ads.ahds.ac.uk/catalogue/)

2000b, *The excavation of a settlement of the fourth and fifth centuries AD on Overton Down, West Overton, Wilts*, Fyfod Working Paper 64, ADS, York

2000c, *Landscape Plotted and Pieced: Landscape History and Local Archaeology in Fyfield and Overton, Wiltshire*, Society of Antiquaries Research Report 64, London

2000d, *Excavation within a Later Prehistoric Field System on Overton Down, West Overton, Wilts: Land-Use over 4,000 Years*, Fyfod Working Paper 63, ADS, York.

2001, 'Wansdyke in the woods. An unfinished Roman military earthwork for a non-event?', in P.J. Ellis (ed.), *Roman Wiltshire*, Wiltshire Archaeological Society, Devizes, 179–98

Fowler, P.J. and Blackwell, I.W. 1998, *The Land of Lettice Sweetapple: An English Countryside Explored*, Tempus, Stroud (pb, with title and subtitle reversed, 2000)

Fowler, P.J. and Evans, J.G. 1967, 'Plough-marks, lynchets and early fields', *Antiquity* 41, 289–301

Fowler, P.J. and Mills, S.A. forthcoming, 'An early medieval landscape at Bede's World, Jarrow', in J.H. Jameson (ed.), *The Reconstructed Past: The Value of Reconstruction in the Public Interpretation of Archaeology and History*, Altamira Press, Walnut Grove, CA

Fowler, P.J. and Sharp, M. 1990, *Images of Prehistory*, Cambridge University Press, Cambridge

Fowler, P.J. and Thomas, A.C. 1962, 'Arable fields of the pre-Norman period at Gwithian', *Cornish Archaeol.* 1, 61–84

Fox, C. 1932, *Personality of Britain*, National Museum of Wales, Cardiff

1955, *Offa's Dyke: A Field Survey of the Western Frontier-Works of Mercia in the 7th and 8th centuries AD*, British Academy, London

Frend, W.H.C. 1996, *The Archaeology of Early Christianity: A History*, Geoffrey Chapman, London

Frere, S.S. 1967, *Britannia*, Routledge and Kegan Paul, London

1972, 1983, *Verulamium Excavations I, II*, Society of Antiquaries Research Reports 28, 41, London

1987, *Britannia: A History of Roman Britain*, 3rd edn, RKP, London

Frere, S.S. and St. Joseph, J.K.S. 1983, *Roman Britain from the Air*, Cambridge: Cambridge University Press.

Frodsham, P. 1999, 'Forgetting *Gefrin*: elements of the past in the past at Yeavering', in Frodsham *et al.*, 191–207

Frodsham, P., Cowley, D.C. and Topping, P. (eds.) 1999, *We Were Always Chasing Time*, special edition of *Northern Archaeol.* 17/18, Newcastle upon Tyne

Fulford, M. 1989, 'The economy of Roman Britain', in Todd, 175–201

    1990, 'The landscape of Roman Britain: a review', *Landscape Hist.* 12, 25–31

    1992, 'Iron Age to Roman: a period of radical change on the gravels', in Fulford and Nichols, 23–38

Fulford, M.G., Allen, J.R.L. and Rippon, S.J. 1994, 'The settlement and drainage of the Wentlooge Level, Gwent: excavation and survey at Rumney Great Wharf 1992', *Britannia* 25, 175–211

Fulford, M. and Nichols, E. (eds.) 1992, *Developing Landscapes of Lowland Britain. The Archaeology of the British Gravels: A Review*, Occasional Paper 14, Society of Antiquaries of London, London

Fussell, G.E. 1972, *The Classical Tradition in West European Farming*, David and Charles, Newton Abbot

    1981, *The Farmer's Tools: The History of British Farm Implements, Tools and Machinery AD 1500–1900*, Orbis, London

Gailey, A. and Fenton, A. (eds.) 1970, *The Spade in Northern and Atlantic Europe*, Ulster Folk Museum/Institute of Irish Studies, Queen's University, Belfast

Gameson, R. (ed.) 1997, *The Study of the Bayeux Tapestry*, Boydell, Woodbridge

Gardner, W. and Savory, H.N. 1964, *Dinorben, a Hill-Fort Occupied in Early Iron Age and Roman Times*, University of Wales Press, Cardiff

Gartner, W.G. 1999, 'Late Woodland landscape of Wisconsin: ridged fields, effigy mounds and territoriality', *Antiquity* 73, 671–83

Gates, T. 1999, 'Hadrian's Wall amid fields of corn', *British Archaeol.* 49, 6–7

Gates, T. and O'Brien, C. 1988, 'Crop marks at Milfield and New Bewick and the recognition of Grubenhaüser in Northumberland', *Archaeol. Aeliana*, 5th series, 16, 1–9

Gelling, M. 1978, *Signposts to the Past: Place-Names and the History of England*, Dent, London

    1992a, *Place-Names in the Landscape: The Geographical Roots of Britain's Place-Names*, Dent, London

    1992b, *The West Midlands in the Early Middle Ages*, Leicester University Press, Leicester

Giraldus Cambrensis, *The Description of Wales*, see Thorpe (trans.) 1978

Glob, P.V. 1951, *Ard og Plog i Nordens Oldtid*, Aarhus University Press, Jysk Arkaeologisk Selskab Skrifter Bind 1, Aarhus

Godwin, H. 1975, *The History of the British Flora*, Cambridge University Press, Cambridge

Gollancz, I. 1927, *The Caedmon Manuscript of Anglo-Saxon Biblical Poetry. Junius XI in the Bodleian Library*, British Academy, Oxford

Goodier, A. 1984, 'The formation of boundaries in Anglo-Saxon England: a statistical study', *Med. Archaeol.* 28, 1–21

Gow, A.S.F. 1914, 'The ancient plough', *J. Hellenic Stud.* 34, 249–75

Graham-Campbell, J. and Batey, C.E. (eds.) 1998, *Vikings in Scotland: An Archaeological Survey*, Edinburgh University Press, Edinburgh

Grant, A. 1989 'Animals in Roman Britain', in Todd, 135–46

Gray, H.L. 1915, *English Field Systems*, Harvard University Press, Cambridge, MA

Green, F.J. 1994, 'Cereals and plant food: a reassessment of the Saxon economic evidence from Wessex', in Rackham, 83–8

Greig, J. 1988, 'Some evidence of the development of grassland plant communities', in Jones, M., 39–54

1991, 'The British Isles', in W. van Zeist, K. Waslikowa and K.-E. Behre (eds.), *Progress in Old World Palaeoethnobotany*, Balkema, Rotterdam, 299–334

Grigg, D.B. 1974, *The Agricultural Systems of the World: An Evolutionary Approach*, Cambridge University Press, Cambridge

1980, *Population Growth and Agrarian Change: An Historical Perspective*, Cambridge University Press, Cambridge

Griggs, B. 1981, *Green Pharmacy: A History of Herbal Medicine*, Robert Hale, London

Gwilt, A. and Haselgrove, C. (eds.) 1997, *Reconstructing Iron Age Societies: New Approaches to the British Iron Age*, Oxbow Books, Oxford

Hadley, D.M. 1996, '"And they proceeded to plough and to support themselves": the Scandinavian settlement of England', *Anglo-Norman Studies* 19, 69–96

Hadley, D.M. and Richards, J.D. (eds.) 2000, *Cultures in Contact: Scandinavian Settlement in England in the Ninth and Tenth Centuries*, Brepols (University of York, Centre for Medieval Studies, Studies in the Early Middle Ages 2), Turnhout, Belgium

Hagen, A. 1992, *A Handbook of Anglo-Saxon Food: Processing and Consumption*, Anglo-Saxon Books, Pinner, Middlesex

1995, *A Second Handbook of Anglo-Saxon Food and Drink: Production and Distribution*, Anglo-Saxon Books, Frithgarth, Hockwold-cum-Wilton, Norfolk

Haggerty, A.M. 1988, 'Iona: some results from recent work', *Proc. Soc. Antiq. Scot.* 118, 203–13

Hall, D. 1981, *Medieval Fields*, Shire, Aylesbury

1988, 'The late Saxon countryside: villages and their fields', in Hooke, 99–122

Hall, D. and Chippendale, C. 1988, 'Introduction' to 'Survey, environment and excavation in the English Fenland', *Antiquity* 62, 305–10

Hall, D. and Coles, J. 1994, *Fenland Survey: An Essay in Landscape and Persistence*, English Heritage Archaeological Report 1, London

Hall, K.M. 1993, 'Pre-conquest estates in Yorkshire', in H.E.J. le Patourel, M.H. Long and M.F. Pickles, *Yorkshire Boundaries*, Yorkshire Archaeological Society, Leeds, 25–38

Hall, R. 1984, *Viking Age York*, Batsford, London

Hallam, H.E. 1981, *Rural England 1066–1348*, Fontana, London

    1988, 'England before the Norman Conquest', in H.E. Hallam (ed.), *The Agrarian History of England and Wales II 1042–1350*, Cambridge University Press, Cambridge, 1–44

Hallam, S.J. 1964, 'Villages in Roman Britain: some evidence', *Antiq. J.* 44, 19–32

Halliday, S.P. 1986, 'Cord rig and early cultivation in the Borders', *Proc. Soc. Antiq. Scot.* 116, 584–5

    1993, 'Marginal agriculture in Scotland', in Smout, 64–78

Halliday, S.P., Hill, P.J. and Stevenson, J.B. 1981, 'Early agriculture in Scotland', in Mercer, 55–65

Hamerow, H. 1987, 'Anglo-Saxon settlement pottery and spatial development at Mucking, Essex', *Berichten van de Rijksdienst voor het Oudheidkundig Bodemonderzoek Jaargang* 37, 245–73

    1991, 'Settlement mobility and the "Middle Saxon Shift": rural settlements and settlement patterns in Anglo-Saxon England', *Anglo-Saxon England* 20, 1–17

    1992, 'Settlement on the gravels in the Anglo-Saxon period', in Fulford and Nichols, 39–46

    1993, *Excavations at Mucking*, vol. 2, *The Anglo-Saxon Settlement*, English Heritage/British Museum Press, London

    1995, 'Shaping settlements: early medieval communities in Northwest Europe', in Bintliff and Hamerow, 8–37

Hamilton, J.R.C. 1956, *Excavations at Jarlshof, Shetland*, Ministry of Works Archaeological Report 1, HMSO, Edinburgh

Hammond, P.W. 1995, *Food and Feast in Medieval England*, Sutton, Stroud

Hanson, W.S. 1996, 'Forest clearance and the Roman army', *Britannia* 27, 354–8

Harden, D.B (ed.) 1956, *Dark Age Britain*, Methuen, London

Harding, A.F. (ed.) 1982, *Climatic Change in Later Prehistory*, Edinburgh University Press, Edinburgh

Harding, J. and Johnston, R. (eds.) 2000, *Northern Pasts: Interpretations of the Later Prehistory of Northern England and Southern Scotland*, BAR Brit. Ser. 302, Oxford

Härke, H. 1997, 'Early Anglo-Saxon social structure', in Hines, 125–60

Harris, D.R. (ed.) 1996, *The Origins and Spread of Agriculture and Pastoralism in Eurasia*, UCL Press, London

Harsema, O.H. 1992, *Geschiedenis in het landschap*, Drents Museum, Drenthe

Hartley, D. 1999 [1954], *Food in England*, Little, Brown and Co., London

Harvey, M. 1983, 'Planned field systems in Eastern Yorkshire: some thoughts on their origin', *Agric. Hist. Rev.* 31, 91–103

Harvey, N. 1984 (2nd edn), *A History of Farm Buildings in England and Wales*, David and Charles, Newton Abbott

Haudricourt, A.G. and Delamarre, M.J.-B. 1955, *L'Homme et la charrue à travers les âges*, Paris

Hawkes, J. 1996, *The Golden Age of Northumbria*, Sandhill Press, Warkworth, Northumberland

Hawkes, J. and Mills, S. (eds.) 1999, *Northumbria's Golden Age*, Sutton, Stroud

Hayfield, C. 1987, *An Archaeological Survey of the Parish of Wharram Percy, East Yorkshire I, The Evolution of the Roman Landscape. Wharram: A Study of Settlement in the Yorkshire Wolds Volume V*, BAR Brit. Ser. 172, Oxford

   1988, 'The origins of the Roman landscape around Wharram Percy, East Yorkshire', in J. Price and P.R. Wilson (eds.), *Recent Research in Roman Yorkshire: Studies in Honour of Mary Kitson Clark*, BAR Brit. Ser. 193, Oxford, 99–122

Hedley, W.P. 1931, 'Ancient cultivations at Housesteads', *Antiquity* 5, 351–4

Hencken, H. O'Neill 1933, 'An excavation by H.M. Office of Works at Chysauster, Cornwall, 1931', *Archaeologia* 83, 237–84

Henig, M. and Booth, P. 2000, *Roman Oxfordshire*, Sutton, Stroud

Herbert, K. 1994, *Looking for the Lost Gods of England*, Anglo-Saxon Books, Hockwold-cum-Wilton, Norfolk

Herring, P. 1993, 'Examining a Romano-British boundary at Foage, Zennor', *Cornish Archaeol.* 32, 17–28

Highham, N.J. 1986, *The Northern Counties to AD 1000*, Longman, London

   1990, 'Settlement, land use and Domesday ploughlands', *Landscape Hist.* 12, 33–44

   1992, *Rome, Britain and the Anglo-Saxons*, Seaby, London

   1993, *The Kingdom of Northumbria, AD 350–1100*, Sutton, Stroud

Higham, N.J. and Jones, G.D.B. 1975, 'Frontier, forts and farmers: Cumbrian aerial survey 1974–5', *Archaeol. J.* 132, 16–53

   1983, 'The excavation of two Romano-British farm sites in North Cumbria', *Britannia* 14, 45–72

Higham, R. and Barker, P. 2000, *Hen Domen, Montgomery. A Timber Castle on the English–Welsh Border. A Final Report*, University of Exeter Press, Exeter

Hill, D. 1981, *An Atlas of Anglo-Saxon England*, Blackwell, London

  1998, 'Eleventh century labours of the months in prose and pictures', *Landscape Hist.* 20, 29–39

Hill, D. and Rumble, A.R. (eds.), 1996, *The Defence of Wessex: The Burghal Hidage and Anglo-Saxon Fortification*, Manchester University Press, Manchester

Hill, P. 1997, *Whithorn and St Ninian: The Excavation of a Monastic Town, 1984–91*, The Whithorn Trust/Sutton, Stroud

Hines, J. 1992, 'The Scandinavian character of Anglian England: an update', in Carver, 315–29

  1994, 'The Anglo-Saxons reviewed', *Med. Archaeol.* 37, 314–18

Hines J. (ed.) 1997, *The Anglo-Saxons from the Migration Period to the Eighth Century: An Ethnographic Perspective*, Boydell, Woodbridge

Hingley, R. 1989, *Rural Settlement in Roman Britain*, Seaby, London

Hinton, D.A. 1998, *Archaeology, Economy and Society: England from the Fifth to the Fifteenth Century*, Routledge, London

Hoare, R.C. 1821, *The Ancient History of North Wiltshire*, London

Hodge, A.T. 1995, *Roman Aqueducts and Water Supply*, Duckworth, London

Hodges, R. 1989, *The Anglo-Saxon Achievement*, Duckworth, London

  1991, *Wall-to-Wall History: The Story of Roystone Grange*, Duckworth, London

  undated, *Roystone Grange Archaeological Trail*, University of Sheffield and Peak District National Park

Hodges, R. and Hobley, B. (eds.) 1988, *The Rebirth of Towns in the West, AD 700–1050*, Research Report 68, CBA, London

Hodgkin, R.H. 1935, *A History of the Anglo-Saxons*, 2 vols., Clarendon Press, Oxford

Holdsworth, C. 1995, 'Bishoprics, monasteries and their landscape, *c.* AD 600–1066', in Hooke and Burnell, 27–49

Holdsworth, C. and Wiseman, T.P. (eds.) 1986, *The Inheritance of Historiography, 350–900*, Exeter Studies in History, University of Exeter Press, Exeter

Holdsworth, P. 1980, *Excavations at Melbourne Street, Southampton 1971–76*, Research Report 33, CBA, London

Hole, F. 1996, 'The context of caprine domestication in the Zagros region', in Harris, 263–81

Holt, R. 1988, *The Mills of Medieval England*, Oxford

Hooke, D. 1981a, *Anglo-Saxon Landscapes of the West Midlands: The Charter Evidence*, BAR Brit. Ser. 95, Oxford

  1981b, 'Open field agriculture – the evidence from the pre-Conquest charters of the West Midlands', in Rowley 1981a, 39–63

1985a, *The Anglo-Saxon Landscape: The Kingdom of the Hwicce*, Manchester University Press, Manchester

(ed.) 1985b, *Medieval Villages: A Review of Current Work*, Monograph 5, Oxford University Committee for Archaeology, Oxford

(ed.) 1988a, *Anglo-Saxon Settlements*, Blackwell, Oxford

1988b, 'Regional variation in southern and central England in the Anglo-Saxon period and its relationship to land units and settlement, in Hooke 1988a, 123–52

1989, 'Pre-Conquest woodland: its distribution and usage', *Agric. Hist. Rev.* 37, 113–29

1990, *Worcestershire Anglo-Saxon Charter-Bounds*, The Boydell Press, Woodbridge

1995, 'The mid-late Saxon period: settlement and land use', in Hooke and Burnell, 95–114

1997, '*Lamberde leie, dillameres dic*: a lost or living landscape?', in Barker and Darvill, 26–45

1998, *The Landscape of Anglo-Saxon England*, Leicester University Press, Leicester

Hooke, D. and Burnell, S. (eds.) 1995, *Landscape and Settlement in Britain AD 400–1066*, University of Exeter Press, Exeter

Hope-Taylor, B. 1977, *Yeavering: An Anglo-British Centre of Early Northumbria*, HMSO, London

Hoskins, W.G. 1955, *The Making of the English Landscape*, Hodder and Stoughton, London

Hostetter, E. and Howe, T.N. (eds.) 1997, *The Romano-British Villa at Castle Copse, Great Bedwyn*, Indiana University Press, Bloomington and Indianapolis

Houston, J.M. 1953, *A Social Geography of England*, Duckworth, London

Hunter, J.R. 1986, *Rescue Excavations on the Brough of Birsay 1974–82*, Monograph Series 4, Society of Antiquaries of Scotland, Edinburgh

Huntley, J.P. and Stallibrass, S. 1995, *Plant and Vertebrate Remains from Archaeological Sites in Northern England*, Architectural and Archaeological Society of Durham and Northumberland, Durham

Hutt, D. (ed.) 2001, *Northumbrian Mills with Horizontal Waterwheels*, North East Mills Group, Newcastle upon Tyne

Isager, S. and Skydsgaard, J.E. 1995, *Ancient Greek Agriculture: An Introduction*, Routledge, London

Jackson, K. 1953, *Language and History in Early Britain*, Edinburgh University Press, Edinburgh

Jackson, R. 1990, *Camerton: The Late Iron Age and Early Roman Metalwork*, British Museum Publications, London

James, E. 2000, *Britain in the First Millennium: From Romans to Normans*, Arnold, London

James, S., Marshall, A. and Millett, M. 1984, 'An early medieval building tradition', *Archaeol. J.* 140, 182–215

Jarman, M.R., Bailey, G.N. and Jarman, H.N. (eds.) 1982, *Early European Agriculture: Its Foundation and Development*, Cambridge University Press, Cambridge

Jarrett, M.G. and Wrathmell, S., 1981, *Whitton: An Iron Age and Roman Farmstead in South Glamorgan*, University of Wales Press, Cardiff

Jenkins, J.G. 1965, *Traditional Country Craftsmen*, Routledge and Kegan Paul, London

Jewell, P.A., Milner, C. and Morton-Boyd, J. 1974, *Island Survivors: The Ecology of the Soay Sheep of St. Kilda*, Athlone Press, London

Jobey, G. 1966, 'Homesteads and settlements of the frontier area', in Thomas, 1–14

1982a, 'Between Tyne and Forth: some problems', in Clack and Haselgrove, 7–20

1982b, 'The settlement at Doubstead and Romano-British settlement on the coastal plain between Tyne and Forth', *Archaeol. Aeliana* 5th ser., 10, 1–23

John, E. 1960, *Land Tenure in Early England*, Leicester University Press, Leicester

1973, 'The Agrarian History of England and Wales Volume 1', *Agric. Hist. Rev.* 21, 135–9

1996, *Reassessing Anglo-Saxon England*, Manchester University Press, Manchester

Johnson, N. and Rose, P. 1994, *Bodmin Moor, An Archaeological Survey*, vol. 1, *The Human Landscape to 1800*, English Heritage and RCHME, London

Johnson, P. (ed.) 1996, *Architecture in Roman Britain*, Research Report 94, CBA, York

Jones, A.H.M. 1964, *The Late Roman Empire*, 2 vols., Blackwell, Oxford

Jones, G.R.J. 1972, 'Post-Roman Wales', in Finberg 1972a, 283–382

1976, 'Multiple estates and early settlement', in Sawyer, 15–40

1989, 'The Dark Ages', in Owen, 172–97

Jones, M. 1978, 'The plant remains', in Parrington, 93–110

1981, 'The development of crop husbandry', in Jones and Dimbleby, 95–127

1982, 'Crop production in Roman Britain', in Miles, 97–107

(ed.) 1988a, *Archaeology and the Flora of the British Isles*, Oxford University Committee for Archaeology, Oxford

1988b, 'The arable field: a botanical battleground', in Jones 1988a, 86–92

1989, 'Agriculture in Roman Britain: the dynamics of change', in Todd, 127–34

1991, 'Food consumption and production – plants', in Jones, R. F. J., 21–8

Jones, M., Brown, T. and Allaby, R. 1996, 'Tracking early crops and early farmers: the potential of biomolecular archaeology', in Harris, 93–100

Jones, M. and Dimbleby, G.W. (eds.) 1981, *The Environment of Man: The Iron Age to the Anglo-Saxon Period*, BAR Brit. Ser. 87, Oxford

Jones, M. and Robinson, M. 1986, 'The crop plants', in Miles, chapter 9 microfiche

Jones, M.E. 1996, *The End of Roman Britain*, Cornell University Press, Ithaca and London

Jones, M.L. 1984, *Society and Settlement in Wales and the Marches 500 B.C. to A.D. 1100*, 2 vols., BAR Brit. Ser. 121, Oxford

Jones, R.F.J. (ed.) 1991, *Britain in the Roman Period: Recent Trends*, J.R. Collis Publications, Department of Archaeology and Prehistory, University of Sheffield, Sheffield

Jones, R.F.J., Bloemers, J.H.F., Dyson, S.I. and Biddle, M. (eds.) 1988, *First Millennium Papers: Western Europe in the First Millennium AD*, BAR Int. Ser. 401, Oxford

Karslake, J.P.B. 1933, 'Plough coulters from Silchester', *Antiq. J.* 13, 455–63

Keeley, H.C.M. (ed.) 1984, *Environmental Archaeology: A Regional Review*, Occasional Papers 6, Directorate of Ancient Monuments and Historic Buildings, Department of the Environment, London

Keevil, G.D. 1996, 'The reconstruction of the Romano-British villa at Redlands Farm, Northamptonshire', in Johnson, 44–55

Kelly, F. 1998, *Early Irish Farming: A Study Based Mainly on the Law-Texts of the 7th and 8th Centuries AD*, Early Irish Law Series 4, Dublin Institute for Advanced Studies, Dublin

Kelly, R.S. 1991, 'Recent research on the hut-group settlements of north west Wales', in Burnham and Davies, 102–11

Kemble, J.M. 1839–48, *Codex Diplomaticus Aevi Saxonici*, 6 vols., London

Ker, W.P. 1958 [1904], *The Dark Ages*, Mentor Books, New York

Kerridge, E. 1973, *The Farmers of Old England*, Allen and Unwin, London
1992, *The Common Fields of England*, Manchester University Press, Manchester

Killion, T.W. (ed.) 1992, *Gardens of Prehistory: The Archaeology of Settlement Agriculture in Greater Mesoamerica*, University of Alabama Press, Tuscaloosa and London

King, A. 1984, 'Gauber High Pasture, Ribblehead', in Hall, 21–5

King, A.C. 1991, 'Food production and consumption – meat', in Jones, 15–20

Knight, J.K. 1999, *The End of Antiquity: Archaeology, Society and Religion AD 235–700*, Tempus, Stroud

Kooistra, L.I. 1996, *Borderland Farming: Possibilities and Limitations of Farming in the Roman Period and Early Middle Ages between the Rhine and Meuse*, Rijksdienst vor het Oudheidkundig Bodemonderzoek, Amersfoort

Lamb, H.H. 1995, *Climate, History and the Modern World*, 2nd edn, Routledge, London

Lambrick, G. 1992, 'The development of late prehistoric and Roman farming on the Thames gravels', in Fulford and Nichols, 78–105

Lambrick, G. and Robinson, M. 1979, *Iron Age and Roman Riverside Settlements at Farmoor, Oxfordshire*, Research Report 32, CBA, London

1988, 'The development of floodplain grassland in the Upper Thames Valley', in Jones, 55–75

Langdon, J. 1986, *Horses, Oxen and Technical Innovation: The Use of Draught Animals in English Farming from 1066 to 1500*, Cambridge University Press, Cambridge

Lapidge, M., Blair, J., Keynes, S. and Scragg, D. (eds.) 1999 (pb 2000), *The Blackwell Encyclopedia of Anglo-Saxon England*, Blackwell, Oxford (= *EASE*)

Latouche, R. 1961, *The Birth of the Western Economy: Economic Aspects of the Dark Ages*, Methuen, London (2nd edn, University Paperbacks 1967)

Lawson, A.J. 2000, *Potterne 1982–5: Animal Husbandry in Later Prehistoric Wiltshire*, Wessex Archaeology Report 17, Salisbury

Leech, R. 1981, 'The excavation of a Romano-British farmstead and cemetery on Bradley Hill, Somerton, Somerset', *Britannia* 12, 177–252

1982, *Excavations at Catsgore, 1970–3*, Western Archaeological Trust, Excavation Monographs 2, Bristol

Leeds, E.T. 1913, *The Archaeology of the Anglo-Saxon Settlements*, Clarendon Press, Oxford

1936, *Early Anglo-Saxon Art and Archaeology*, Clarendon Press, Oxford

Leighton, A.C. 1972, *Transport and Communications in Early Medieval Europe AD 500–1100*, David and Charles, Newton Abbot

Lennard, R. 1959, *Rural England, 1086–1135*, Clarendon Press, Oxford

Lerche, G. (ed.) 1994, *Ploughing Implements and Tillage Practices in Denmark from the Viking Period to about 1800: Experimentally Substantiated*, Commission for Research on the History of Agricultural Implements and Field Structures 8, Royal Danish Academy of Sciences and Letters, Poul Kristensen, Herning

1995, 'Radiocarbon datings of agricultural implements in "Tools and Tillage" 1868–1995. Revised calibrations and recent additions', *Tools and Tillage* 4, 172–205

Lerche, G. and Steensberg, A. 1980, *Agricultural Tools and Field Shapes*, International Secretariat for Research on the History of Agricultural Implements Publication 3, National Museum of Denmark, Copenhagen

Leser, P. 1931, *Entstehung und Verbreitung des Pfluges*, Anthropos-Bibliothek III, 3, originally published Münster I.W., republished as a photographic reprint by the International Secretariat for Research on the History of Agricultural Implements, Special-Trykkeriet, Viborg, 1971

Limbrey, S. and Evans, J.G. (eds.) 1978, *The Effect of Man on the Landscape: The Lowland Zone*, Research Report 21, CBA, London

Longworth, I. and Cherry, J. (eds.) 1986, *Archaeology in Britain since 1945: New Directions*, British Museum Publications, London

Loveluck, C.P. 1998, 'A high-status Anglo-Saxon settlement at Flixborough, Lincolnshire', *Antiquity* 72, 146–61

  2001, 'Wealth, waste and conspicuous consumption. Flixborough and its importance for mid and late Saxon settlement studies', in H. Hamerow and A. MacGregor (eds.), *Image and Power in the Archaeology of Early Medieval Britain: Essays in Honour of Rosemary Cramp*, Oxbow Books, Oxford

Lowe, C. 1998, *St. Boniface Church, Orkney: Coastal Erosion and the Archaeological Assessment of an Eroding Shoreline*, Sutton, Stroud, and Historic Scotland, Edinburgh

Lowe, J.J. and Walker, M.J.C. 1997, *Reconstructing Quaternary Environments*, Longman, London

Loyd Jones, M. 1984, *Settlement and Society in Wales and the Marches 500 B.C. to A.D. 1100*, BAR Brit. Ser. 121, Oxford

Loyn, H.R. 1962 (2nd edn 1991), *Anglo-Saxon England and the Norman Conquest*, Longman, London

Lucas, A.T. 1972–75, 'Irish ploughing practices', Parts 1–4, *Tools and Tillage* 2(1–4), 52–62, 67–83, 149–60, 195–210

Luff, R.M. 1982, *A Zooarchaeological Study of the Roman Northwestern Provinces*, BAR Int. Ser. 137, Oxford

McCarthy, M.R. (1995), 'Archaeological and environmental evidence for the Roman impact on vegetation near Carlisle, Cumbria', *The Holocene* 5, 491–5

McClure, J. and Collins, R. (eds.) 1999, *Bede: The Ecclesiastical History of the English People*, Oxford University Press, Oxford

McCullagh, R.P.J. and Tipping, R. (eds.) 1998, *The Lairg Project 1988–1996: The Evolution of an Archaeological Landscape in Northern Scotland*, Star Monograph 3, Edinburgh

McDonnell, J. 1988, 'The role of transhumance in northern England', *Northern History* 24, 1–17

  1990, 'Upland Pennine hamlets', *Northern History*, 26, 20–39

Mackreth, D. 1978, 'Orton Hall Farm, Peterborough: a Roman and Saxon settlement', in Todd, 209–28

McLean, T. 1989, *Medieval English Gardens*, Barrie and Jenkins, London

McOmish, D. 1998, 'Landscape preserved by the men of war', *Brit. Archaeol.* 34, 12–13

Maitland, F.W. 1897, *Domesday Book and Beyond*, Cambridge University Press, Cambridge. Revised edn 1960

Maltby, M. 1981, 'Iron Age, Romano-British and Anglo-Saxon animal husbandry: a review of the faunal evidence', in Jones and Dimbleby, 155–203

Manning, W.H. 1964, 'The plough in Roman Britain', *J. Rom. Stud.* 54, 54–65

   1966, 'A group of bronze models from Sussex in the British Museum', *Antiq. J.* 46, 50–9

   1971, 'The Piercebridge plough group', *Brit. Mus. Quarterly* 35, 125–36

   1974, 'Objects of iron', in Neal, 157–87

   1985, *Catalogue of the Romano-British Iron Tools, Weapons and Fittings in the British Museum*, British Museum, London

Manning, W.H. *et al.* 1997, 'Roman impact on the environment at Hadrian's Wall', *The Holocene* 7, 175–86

Marchandiau, J.N. 1984, *Outillage agricole de la Provence d'autrefois*, Edisud, Aix-en-Provence

Marsh, D. nd, 'A handlist of herbs in Jarrow Hall herb garden', duplicated leaflet on sale at Bede's World, Jarrow

Marshall, A. and Marshall, G. 1991, 'A survey and analysis of the buildings of Early and Middle Anglo-Saxon England', *Med. Archaeol.* 35, 29–43

Marshall, J.D. 1971, *Old Lakeland*, David and Charles, Newton Abbot

Marwick, A. 1989, *The Nature of History*, 3rd edn, Macmillan, London

Maxwell, G.S. (ed.) 1983, *The Impact of Aerial Reconnaissance on Archaeology*, CBA, Res. Rep. 49, London

Maynard, D. 1994, 'Archaeological discoveries in the dune system at Brighouse Bay', *Trans. Dumfries and Galloway Natur. Hist. Antiq. Soc.* 69, 13–33

Meadows, I. 1996, 'Wollaston: the Nene valley, a British Moselle?', *Current Archaeol.* 150, 212–15

Mercer, E. 1979 (2nd imp.), *English Vernacular Houses: A Study of Traditional Farmhouses and Cottages*, HMSO, London

Mercer, R. (ed.) 1981, *Farming Practice in British Prehistory*, Edinburgh University Press, Edinburgh

Michelsen, P. and Rasmussen, H. 1955, *Danish Peasant Culture*, Danish National Museum, Copenhagen

Miket, R. and Burgess, C. (eds.) 1984, *Between and Beyond the Walls: Essays on the Prehistory and History of North Britain in Honour of George Jobey*, John Donald, Edinburgh

Miles, D. (ed.) 1982, *The Romano-British Countryside: Studies in Rural Settlement and Economy*, 2 vols., BAR Brit. Ser. 103, Oxford

   1984, *Archaeology at Barton Court Farm, Abingdon, Oxon*, Research Report 50, CBA, London

   1989, 'The Romano-British countryside', in Todd, 115–26

Miles, D. and Palmer, S. 1982, *Archaeological Investigations at Claydon Pike, Fairford/Lechlade: An Interim Report 1979–1982*, Oxford

Millet, M.J. 1983, 'Excavations at Cowdery's Down, Basingstoke, 1978–81', *Archaeol. J.* 140, 151–279

1987, 'The question of continuity: Rivenhall reviewed', *Archaeol. J.* 144, 434–8

1990, *The Romanization of Britain: An Essay in Archaeological Interpretation*, Cambridge University Press, Cambridge

1995, *Roman Britain*, English Heritage/Batsford, London

Millet, M.J. and Hodder, I. 1978, 'The human geography of Roman Britain', in Dodgshon and Butlin, 24–44

Millet, M.J., James, S.T. and Marshall, A. 1984, 'An early medieval building tradition', *Archaeol. J.* 141, 182–215

Mills, C.M. and Coles, G. (eds.) (1998), *Life on the Edge: Human Settlement and Marginality*, Symposia of the Association for Environmental Archaeology 13, Oxbow Monograph 100, Oxford

Milne, G. and Richards, J.D. 1992, *Wharram: A Study of Settlement on the Yorkshire Wolds, VII. Two Anglo-Saxon Buildings and Associated Finds*, York University Archaeology Publications 9, York

Mitcheson, M.M. 1984, 'Bibliography of the published works of George Jobey', in Miket and Burgess, 410–14

Moffett, L. 1988, 'The archaeobotanical evidence for Saxon and Medieval agriculture in central England circa 500 AD to 1500 AD', M.Phil. thesis, University of Birmingham

Monk, M. 1991, 'The archaeobotanical evidence for field crop plants in early historic Ireland', in Renfrew, 315–28

Moritz, L.A. 1958, *Grain-Mills and Flour in Classical Antiquity*, Clarendon Press, Oxford

Morris, C.D. 1977, 'Northumbria and the Viking settlement: the evidence of landholding', *Archaeol. Aeliana* 5th ser., 5, 81–103

1981, 'Viking and native in northern England: a case study', *Proc. Eighth Viking Congress* (Odense), 233–44

1984, 'Aspects of Scandinavian settlement in northern England: a review', *Northern Hist.* 20, 1–22

1996, *The Birsay Bay Project*, vol. 2, *Sites in Birsay Village [Beachview] and on the Brough of Birsay, Orkney*, Monograph Series 2, Department of Archaeology, University of Durham, Durham

Morris, J. 1973, *The Age of Arthur: A History of the British Isles from 350 to 650*, Weidenfeld and Nicolson, London

Morris, P. 1979, *Agricultural Buildings in Roman Britain*, BAR Brit. Ser. 70, Oxford

Morris, R. 1989, *Churches in the Landscape*, Dent, London

Muir, R. 1981, *Shell Guide to Reading the Landscape*, Michael Joseph, London

2001, 'Editorial', *Landscapes* 2(1), 1–2

Muir, R. and Muir, N. 1989, *Fields*, Macmillan, London

Müller-Wille, M. 1965, *Eisenzeitliche Fluren in den festländischen Nordseegebieten*, Siedlung und Landschaft in Westfalen, Geographischen Kommission für Westfalen, Münster

Murphy, P. 1985, 'The cereals and crop weeds', in West, 100–8

    1994, 'The Anglo-Saxon landscape and rural economy: some results from sites in East Anglia and Essex', in Rackham, 23–39

Musson, C. 1994, *Wales from the Air: Patterns of Past and Present*, RCAMW, Aberystwyth

Myres, J.N.L. 1986, *The English Settlements*, Oxford University Press, Oxford

Neal, D.S. 1974, *The Excavation of the Roman Villa in Gadebridge Park, Hemel Hempstead 1963–8*, Research Report 31, Society of Antiquaries, London

Neal, D.S., Wardle, A. and Hunn, J. 1990, *Excavation of the Iron Age, Roman and Medieval Settlement at Gorhambury, St. Albans*, Archaeological Report 14, Historic Buildings and Monuments Commission for England, London

Needham, S.P. and Macklin, M.G. (eds.) 1992, *Archaeology under Alluvium: Archaeology and the River Environment in Britain*, Oxbow, Oxford

Nees, L. 1997, 'Introduction', *Speculum* 72, 959–69

Neville, R.C. 1856, 'Description of a remarkable deposit of Roman antiquities of iron, discovered at Great Chesterford, Essex, in 1854', *Archaeol. J.* 13, 1–13

Newman, J. 1992, 'The late-Roman and Anglo-Saxon settlement pattern in the sandlings of Suffolk', in Carver, 25–38

Nielsen, V. and Clemmenson, N.-C. 1995, 'Surveying of ancient field systems. Danish experiences', *Tools and Tillage* 7, 147–71

Norman, E.R. and St. Joseph, J.K.S. 1969, *The Early Development of Irish Society: The Evidence of Aerial Photography*, Cambridge University Press, Cambridge

O'Brien, C. and Miket, R. 1991, 'The Early Medieval settlement of Thirlings, Northumberland', *Durham Archaeol. J.* 7, 57–91

Ohlgren, T.H. 1986, *Insular and Anglo-Saxon Illuminated Manuscripts: An Iconographic Catalogue c A.D. 625–1100*, Garland Publishing, New York and London

    1992, *Anglo-Saxon Textual Illustration: Photographs of Sixteen Manuscripts . . .* , Western Michigan University, Medieval Institute Publications, Kalamazoo

O'Neill, B. St. J. 1933, 'The Roman villa at Magor farm, near Camborne, Cornwall', *J. Brit. Archaeol. Assoc.* 39, 116–75

Orwin, C.S. and Orwin, C.S. 1938 (3rd edn 1967), *The Open Fields*, Clarendon Press, Oxford

OS 1994, *Historical Map and Guide: Roman Britain*, Ordnance Survey, Southampton

O'Sullivan, D. and Young, R. 1991, 'The early medieval settlement at Green Shiel, Northumberland', *Archaeol. Aeliana* 5th ser., 19, 55–70

    1995, *Book of Lindisfarne: Holy Island*, Batsford/English Heritage, London

Ottaway, P. 1992, *Archaeology in British Towns: From the Emperor Claudius to the Black Death*, Routledge, London

Owen, D. 1976, 'Chapelries and rural settlement: an examination of some of the Kesteven evidence', in Sawyer, 66–71

Owen, D.H. (ed.) 1989, *Settlement and Society in Wales*, University of Wales Press, Cardiff

Pals, J.P. 1987, 'Reconstruction of landscape and plant husbandry', in W. Groenman-van Waateringe and L.H. van Wijngaarden-Bakker (eds.), *Farm Life in a Carolingian Village: A Model Based on Botanical and Zoological Data from an Excavated Site*, University of Amsterdam, A.E. van Giffen Instituut voor Prae- en Protohistorie, Studies in Prae- and Protohistorie 1, Amsterdam

Parain, C. 1966, 'The evolution of agricultural technique', in Postan, 125–79

Parrington, M. 1978, *The Excavation of an Iron Age Settlement, Bronze Age Ring Ditches and Roman Features at Ashville Trading Estate, Abingdon, Oxfordshire, 1974–76*, Research Report 28, CBA, London

Parry, M.L. 1978, *Climate Change, Agriculture and Settlement*, Dawson, Folkestone

Passmore, J.B. 1930, *The English Plough*, Oxford University Press, London

Payne, F.G. 1948, 'The plough in Ancient Britain', *Archaeol. J.* 104, 82–111

1957, 'The British plough: some stages in its development', *Agric. Hist. Rev.* 5, 74–84

Pearce, S.M. 1982, 'Estates and church sites in Dorset and Gloucestershire: the emergence of a Christian society', in S.M. Pearce (ed.), *The Early Church in Western Britain and Ireland: Studies Presented to C.A. Ralegh Radford*, BAR Brit. Ser. 102, Oxford, 117–38

Pearsall, D. and Salter, E. 1973, *Landscapes and Seasons of the Medieval World*, Elek, London

Pearson, K.L. 1997, 'Nutrition and the early-medieval diet', *Speculum* 72, 1–32

Percival, J. 1976, *The Roman Villa: An Historical Introduction*, Batsford, London

Phillips, A. 1997, *The Hallowing of England: A Guide to the Saints of Old England and Their Places of Pilgrimage*, Anglo-Saxon Books, Hockwold-cum-Wilton, Norfolk

Phillips, C.W. (ed.) 1970, *The Fenland in Roman Times: Studies of a Major Area of Peasant Colonization*, Research Series 5, Royal Geographical Society, London

Piggott, S. (ed.) 1981, *The Agrarian History of England and Wales* I.1 *Prehistory*, Cambridge University Press, Cambridge

Pliny the Elder 1952, *Historia Naturalis*, Loeb, London

Plog, P.V. 1951, *Plov og Ard i nordens oldtid*, Aarhus University Press, Jysk Arkaeologisk Selskab Skrifter Bind I, Aarhus

Plummer, C. (ed.) 1896, *Venerabilis Baedae Opera Historica*, Clarendon Press, Oxford

Postan, M.M. (ed.) 1966, *The Cambridge Economic History of Europe* I, *The Agrarian Life of the Middle Ages*, 2nd edn, Cambridge University Press, Cambridge

　1972, *The Medieval Economy and Society: An Economic History of Britain in the Middle Ages*, Penguin, Harmondsworth

　1973, *Essays on Medieval Agriculture and General Problems of the Medieval Economy*, Cambridge University Press, Cambridge

Potter, T.W. 1989, 'The Roman Fenland: a review of recent work', in Todd, 147–173

Powlesland, D. 1997, 'Early Anglo-Saxon settlements, structures, form and layout', in Hines, 101–24

　1999, 'The Anglo-Saxon settlement at West Heslerton, North Yorkshire', in Hawkes and Mills, 55–65

Powlesland, D., Houghton, C.A. and Hanson, J.H. 1986, 'Excavations at Heslerton, North Yorkshire, 1978–82', *Archaeol. J.* 143, 53–173

Price, L. 1982, *The Plan of St. Gall in Brief*, University of California Press, Berkeley

Pritchard, J. 1969, *The Ancient Near East: An Anthology of Texts and Pictures*, Princeton University Press, Princeton, NJ

Pryor, F. 1998, *Farmers in Prehistoric Britain*, Tempus, Stroud

Rackham, J. (ed.) 1994, *Environment and Economy in Anglo-Saxon England*, Research Report 89, CBA, York

Rackham, O. 1986, *The History of the Countryside*, Dent, London

　1990, *Trees and Woodland in the British Landscape*, Dent, London

Rahtz, P. 1974, *Rescue Archaeology*, Penguin, Harmondsworth

　1979, *The Saxon and Medieval Palaces at Cheddar, Excavations 1960–62*, BAR Brit. Ser. 65, Oxford

Rahtz, P. *et al.* 1992, *Cadbury Congresbury 1968–73: A Late/Post-Roman Hilltop Settlement in Somerset*, BAR Brit. Ser. 223, Oxford

Rahtz, P. and Bullough, D. 1977, 'The parts of an Anglo-Saxon mill', *Anglo-Saxon England* 6, 15–37

Rahtz, P. and Meeson, R. 1992, *An Anglo-Saxon Watermill at Tamworth: Excavations in the Bolebridge Street Area of Tamworth, Staffordshire, in 1971 and 1978*, Research Report 83, CBA, London

Ralston, I.B.M. 1997, 'Pictish homes', in D. Henry (ed.), *The Worm, the Germ and the Thorn: Pictish and Related Studies Presented to Isobel Henderson*, The Pinkfoot Press, 19–33

Randsborg, K. 1985, 'Subsistence and settlement in Northern Temperate Europe in the First Millennium A.D.', in Barker and Gamble, 233–65

　1991, *The First Millennium A.D. in Europe and the Mediterranean*, Cambridge University Press, Cambridge

RCAHMS 1994, *South-East Perth: An Archaeological Landscape*, HMSO, Edinburgh

RCHME 1970, *An Inventory ... Dorset III, pt 2*, HMSO, London

Rees, S.E. 1978, 'Tools available for cultivation in prehistoric Britain', in Limbrey and Evans, 103–14

1979a, *Agricultural Implements in Prehistoric and Roman Britain*, 2 vols., BAR Brit. Ser. 69, Oxford

1979b, 'The Roman scythe blade', in Lambrick and Robinson, 61–4

1981, 'Agricultural tools: function and use', in Mercer, 66–84

Renfrew, C. and Bahn, P. 2000, *Archaeology: Theories, Methods and Practice*, 3rd edn, Thames and Hudson, London

Renfrew, J.M. (ed.) 1991, *New Light on Early Farming: Recent Developments in Palaeoethnobotany*, Edinburgh University Press, Edinburgh

1993, 'Roman Britain', in P. Brears, M. Black, G. Corbishley, J. Renfrew and J. Stead (eds.), *A Taste of Honey: 10,000 Years of Food in Britain*, English Heritage/British Museum Press, London, 51–92

Reynolds, A. 1999, *Later Anglo-Saxon England: Life and Landscape*, Tempus, Stroud

Reynolds, P.J. 1979, *Iron Age Farm: The Butser Experiment*, British Museum Publications, London

1981, 'Deadstock and livestock', in Mercer, 97–122

Richards, J.D. 1991, *Viking Age England*, Batsford, London

1999, 'Anglo-Saxon settlements of the Golden Age', in Hawkes and Mills, 44–54

2000, *Viking Age England* (rev. edn), Tempus, Stroud

Richards, J.D. with contributions from T. Austin *et al.* 1999, 'Cottam: an Anglo-Scandinavian settlement on the Yorkshire Wolds', *Archaeol. J.* 156, 1–111

Richardson, H.G. 1942, 'The medieval plough team', *History* 26, 287–94

Richmond, I.A. 1955, *Roman Britain*, Penguin, Harmondsworth

Rickman, G. 1980, *The Corn Supply of Ancient Rome*, Oxford University Press, Oxford

Riley, D. 1980, *Early Landscape from the Air: Studies of Crop Marks in South Yorkshire and North Nottinghamshire*, Department of Prehistory and Archaeology, University of Sheffield, Sheffield

Rippon, S. 1997, *The Severn Estuary: Landscape Evolution and Wetland Reclamation*, Leicester University Press, Leicester

1999, 'Romano-British reclamation of coastal wetland', in Cook and Williamson, 101–21

Ritchie, A. 1993, *Viking Scotland*, Batsford/Historic Scotland, London

Rivet, A.L.F. 1958, *Town and Country in Roman Britain*, Hutchinson, London

(ed.) 1969, *The Roman Villa in Britain*, Routledge and Kegan Paul, London

Rivet, A.L.F. and Smith, C. 1979, *The Place-Names of Roman Britain*, Batsford, London

Roach, F.A. 1985, *The Cultivated Fruits of Britain*, Blackwell, Oxford

Roberts, B.K. 1977, *Rural Settlement in Britain*, Hutchinson, London

1987, *The Making of the English Village: A Study in Historical Geography*, Longman, Harlow

Roberts, B.K. and Wrathmell, S. 1998, 'Dispersed settlement in England: a national view', in Everson and Williamson, 95–116

Roberts, B. and Wrathmell, S. 2000, *An Atlas of Rural Settlement in England*, English Heritage, London

Robertson, A.J. 1925, *The Laws of the Kings of England from Edmund to Henry I*, Cambridge University Press, Cambridge

Robinson, M. 1979, 'Plants and invertebrates: methods and results', in Lambrick and Robinson, 77–103

1992, 'Environmental archaeology of the river gravels: past achievements and future directions', in Fulford and Nichols, 47–62

Rodwell, W.J. and Rodwell, K.A. 1985, *Rivenhall: Investigations of a Villa, Church and Village 1950–1977*, Research Report 55, CBA, London

Ross, A. 1967, *Pagan Celtic Britain*, Routledge and Kegan Paul, London

Rowley, T. (ed.) 1974, *Anglo-Saxon Settlement and Landscape*, BAR Brit. Ser. 6, Oxford

(ed.) 1981a, *The Origins of Open-Field Agriculture*, Croom Helm, London

(ed.) 1981b, *The Evolution of Marshland Landscapes*, Oxford University Department for External Studies, Oxford

Roymans, N. (ed.) 1996, *From the Sword to the Plough: Three Studies on the Earliest Romanisation of Northern Gaul*, Amsterdam Archaeological Studies, Amsterdam University Press, Amsterdam

Russell, E.W. 1961, *Soil Conditions and Plant Growth*, 9th edn, Longmans, London

Russell, R.C. 1974, *The Logic of Open Field Systems*, Standing Conference on Local History, Bedford Square Press, London

Russell-White, C.J. 1995, 'The excavation of a cairnfield at Kildonan, Sutherland', *Northern Stud.* 31, 25–35

Ryley, C. 1998, *Roman Gardens and Their Plants*, Sussex Archaeological Society, Lewes

Rynne, C. 1989, 'The introduction of the vertical watermill into Ireland: some recent archaeological evidence', *Med. Archaeol.* 33, 21–31

Šach, F. 1968, 'Proposal for a classification of pre-industrial tilling implements', *Tools and Tillage* 1, 3–27

St. Joseph, J.K.S. (ed.) 1977, *The Uses of Air Photography*, 2nd edn, John Baker, London

Salisbury, C. 1981, 'An Anglo-Saxon fish-weir at Colwick, Nottinghamshire', *Trans. Thoroton Soc.* 85, 26–36

Salway, P. 1981, *Roman Britain*, Clarendon Press, Oxford

1993, *A History of Roman Britain*, Oxford: Oxford University Press

Salway, P. and Blair, J. 1992, *Roman and Anglo-Saxon Britain*, Oxford: Oxford University Press, Oxford History of Britain vol. 1

Sawyer, P.H. 1968, *Anglo-Saxon Charters: An Annotated List and Bibliography*, Royal Historical Society, Guides and Handbooks 8, London

(ed.) 1976, *Medieval Settlement: Continuity and Change*, Edward Arnold, London

1998a, *From Roman Britain to Norman England*, 2nd edn, Routledge, London

1998b, *Anglo-Saxon Lincolnshire*, History of Lincolnshire Committee, Lincoln

Scull, C. 1992, 'Before Sutton Hoo: structures of power and society in early East Anglia', in Carver, 3–22

1995, 'Approaches to material culture and social dynamics of the Migration period of eastern England', in Bintliff and Hamerow, 71–83

1997, 'Urban centres in pre-Viking England?', in Hines, 269–98

Seebohm, F. 1890 (4th edn 1905), *The English Village Community Examined in Its Relations to the Manorial and Tribal Systems and to the Common or Open Field System of Husbandry*, Longmans, Green and Co., London

1914, *Customary Acres and Their Historical Importance*, Longmans, Green and Co., London

Seymour, W.A. (ed.) 1980, *A History of the Ordnance Survey*, Dawson and Sons, Folkestone

Shackleton, M.R. 1964, *Europe: A Regional Geography*, 7th edn, Longman, London

Shephard, J. 1979, 'The social identity of the individual in isolated barrows and barrow cemeteries in Anglo-Saxon England', in B.C. Burnham and J. Kingsbury (eds.), *Space, Hierarchy and Society*, BAR Brit. Ser. 73, Oxford, 47–79

Sherley-Price, L. 1955, *Bede: A History of the English Church and People*, Penguin, Harmondsworth

Simmons, I.G. 1997, *Humanity and Environment: A Cultural Ecology*, Longman, Harlow

Simmons, I.G. and Tooley, M.J. 1981, *Environment in British Prehistory*, Duckworth, London

Singer, C., Holmyard, E.J., Hall, A.R. and Williams, T.I. (eds.) 1954–78, *A History of Technology*, 7 vols., Oxford University Press, Oxford

Smith, B.D. 1992, *Rivers of Change: Essays on Early Agriculture in Eastern North America*, Smithsonian Institution Press, Washington, DC

1995, *The Emergence of Agriculture*, Scientific American Library, New York

Smith, C.A. 1976, 'Exchange systems and the spatial distribution of élites: the organisation of stratification in agrarian societies', in C.A. Smith (ed.), *Regional Analysis* 2, 309–74

Smith, G. 1996, 'Archaeology and environment of a Bronze Age cairn and prehistoric and Romano-British field system at Chysauster, Gulval, near Penzance, Cornwall', *Proc. Prehist. Soc.* 62, 167–219

Smith, I.M. 1991, 'Sprouston, Roxburghshire: an early Anglian centre of the eastern Tweed Basin', *Proc. Soc. Antiq. Scot.* 121, 264–91

Smith, J.T. 1997, *Roman Villas: A Study in Social Structure*, Routledge, London

Smout, T.C. (ed.) 1993, *Scotland since Prehistory: Natural Change and Human Impact*, Scottish Cultural Press, Aberdeen

Smout, T.C. and Foster, S. (eds.) 1994, *The History of Soils and Field Systems*, Scottish Cultural Press, Aberdeen

Smyth, A.P. 1984, *Warlords and Holy Men: Scotland AD 80–1000*, Edward Arnold, London

Snape, M.E. 1997, 'An Anglo-Saxon watermill at Corbridge', in T. Corfe (ed.), *Before Wilfrid. Hexham Historian* 7, 40–56

Spurr, M.S. 1986, *Arable Cultivation in Roman Italy c.200 B.C. – c.A.D. 100*, Monograph 3, Society for the Promotion of Roman Studies, London

Stafford, P. 1985, *The East Midlands in the Early Middle Ages*, Leicester University Press, Leicester

Stallibras, S. 1998, 'On the outside looking in: a view of animal bones in Roman Britain from the North West Frontier', in Mills and Coles, 53–9

Stamper, P.A. and Croft, R. 2000, *Wharram: A Study of Settlement on the Yorkshire Wolds* VIII, *The South Manor Area Excavations*, York University Archaeology Publications 10, York

Stead, I. 1980, *Rudston Roman Villa*, Yorkshire Archaeological Society, Leeds

Steensberg, A. 1943, *Ancient Harvesting Implements: A Study in Archaeology and Human Geography*, I Kommission Hos Gyldendalske Boghandel, Nordisk Forlag, Copenhagen

Steensberg A., Østergaard Christensen, J.L. and Neilsen, S. 1968, *Atlas over en del af Middelalderlandsbyen Borups Agre i Borup Ris Skov ved Tystrup So, Sjælland*, Det Kongelige Danske Videnskabernes Selskabs Kommission til Udforskning af Landbrugsredskabernes og Agerstrukturnes Historie, Publikation Nr. 1, Copenhagen

Stenton, D. 1952, *The Beginnings of English Society*, Penguin, Harmondsworth

Stenton, F. 1943, 1947, 1971 (1st, 2nd and 3rd edn), *Anglo-Saxon England*, (*Oxford History of England* II), Clarendon Press, Oxford

(ed.) 1957, *The Bayeux Tapestry: A Comprehensive Survey*, Phaidon Press, London

Stevens, C.E. 1966, 'Agriculture and rural life in the later Empire', in Postan, 92–129

Stoertz, C. 1997, *Ancient Landscapes of the Yorkshire Wolds: Aerial Photographic Transcription and Analysis*, RCHME, Swindon

Stone, P.G. and Planel, P.G. (eds.) 1999, *The Constructed Past: Experimental Archaeology, Education and the Public*, Routledge, London

Street, A.G. 1932, *Farmer's Glory*, Faber and Faber, London

Sturt, G. 1923, *The Wheelwright's Shop*, Cambridge University Press, Cambridge

Swanton, M. (ed.) 1993, *Anglo-Saxon Prose*, Dent (Everyman), London

Taylor, C.C. 1966, 'Strip lynchets', *Antiquity* 40, 277

1972, 'The study of settlement patterns in pre-Saxon England', in P.J. Ucko, R. Tringham and G.W. Dimbleby (eds.), *Man, Settlement and Urbanism*, Duckworth, London, 109–13

1975, *Fields in the English Landscape*, Dent, London

1977, 'Polyfocal settlement and the English village', *Med. Archaeol.* 21, 189–93

1983, *Village and Farmstead: A History of Rural Settlement in England*, George Philip, London

1992, 'Medieval rural settlement: changing perceptions', *Landscape Hist.* 14, 5–17

2000, *Fields in the English Landscape*, 2nd edn, Sutton, Stroud

Taylor, C.C. and Fowler, P.J. 1978, 'Roman fields into medieval furlongs', in Bowen and Fowler, 159–62

Taylor, H.M. and Taylor, J. 1965, *Anglo-Saxon Architecture*, Cambridge University Press, Cambridge

Temple, E. 1976, *Anglo-Saxon Manuscripts 900–1066*, Harvey Miller, London

Thirsk, J. 1964, 'The common fields', *Past and Present* 29, 3–29

1967, 'The farming regions of England', in J. Thirsk (ed.), *The Agrarian History of England and Wales* IV, *1500–1640*, Cambridge University Press, Cambridge, 1–112

1984a, *The Rural Economy of England*, Hambledon Press, London

(ed.) 1984b, *The Agrarian History of England and Wales* V, *1640–1750*, 1, *Regional Farming Systems*, Cambridge University Press, Cambridge

1997, *Alternative Agriculture: A History from the Black Death to the Present Day*, Oxford University Press, Oxford

Thomas, C. (ed.) 1966, *Rural Settlement in Roman Britain*, Research Report 7, CBA, London

1981, *Christianity in Roman Britain to AD 500*, Batsford, London

1998, *Christian Celts: Messages and Images*, Tempus, Stroud

Thorpe, I.J. 1996, *The Origins of Agriculture in Europe*, Routledge, London

Thorpe, L. (trans.) 1978, Gerald of Wales, *The Journey through Wales and The Description of Wales*, Penguin, Harmondsworth

Tilley, C. 1994, *A Phenomenology of Landscape: Places, Paths and Monuments*, Berg, Oxford

Tipping, R. 1997, 'Pollen analysis and the impact of Rome on native agriculture around Hadrian's Wall', in Gwilt and Haselgrove, 239–47

1998a, 'Cereal cultivation on the Anglo-Scottish border during the "Little Ice Age"', in Mills and Coles, 1–11

1998b, 'Towards an environmental history of the Bowmont Valley and the northern Cheviot Hills', *Landscape Hist.* 20, 41–50

Todd, M. 1978, *Studies in the Romano-British Villa*, Leicester University Press, Leicester

1987, *The South West to AD 1000*, Longmans, London

(ed.) 1989, *Research on Roman Britain: 1960–89*, Britannia Monograph 11, London

Topping, P. 1989, 'Early cultivation in Northumberland and the Borders', *Proc. Prehist. Soc.* 40, 161–79

Toulson, S. 1993, *The Celtic Year*, Element, Shaftesbury

Trochet, J.-R. 1993, *Aux Origines de la France rurale: outils, pays et paysages*, CNRS, Paris

Trow-Smith, R. 1953, *Society and the Land*, Cresset Press, London

1957, *A History of British Livestock Husbandry to 1700*, Routledge and Kegan Paul, London

Turner, J. 1981, 'The vegetation', in Jones and Dimbleby, 67–73

Tusser, T. 1573 [1984], *Five Hundred Points of Good Husbandry*, Oxford University Press, Oxford

Ulmschneider, K. 2000, 'Settlement, economy and the "Productive" Site: Middle Anglo-Saxon Lincolnshire A.D. 650–780', *Med. Archaeol.* 44, 53–79

van Bath, B.H. Slicher 1963, *The Agrarian History of Western Europe A.D. 500–1850*, Arnold, London

van der Veen, M. 1989, 'Charred grain assemblages from Roman period corn driers in Britain', *Archaeol. J.* 146, 302–19

1991, 'Consumption or production? Agriculture in the Cambridgeshire Fens?', in Renfrew, 349–61

1992, *Crop Husbandry Regimes: An Archaeobotanical Study of Farming in Northern England 1000 BC–AD 500*, Sheffield Archaeological Monograph 3, J.R. Collis Publications, University of Sheffield, Sheffield van der Veen, M. and Palmer, C. 1997, 'Environmental factors and the yield potential of ancient wheat crops', *J. Archaeol. Sci.* 24, 163–82

Vince, A. 1994, 'Saxon urban economies', in Rackham, 108–19

Vinogradoff, P. 1892, *Villeinage in England*, Clarendon Press, Oxford

    1905 (2nd edn 1911), *The Growth of the Manor*, Swann Sonnenschein, London

    1908, *English Society in the Eleventh Century*, Clarendon Press, Oxford

Wacher, J. 1995, *The Towns of Roman Britain*, 2nd edn, Batsford, London

Wade, K. 1988, 'Ipswich', in Hodges and Hobley, 93–100

Wade-Martins, P. 1975, 'The origins of rural settlement in East Anglia', in Fowler, 137–57

    1980, *Excavations in North Elmham Park, 1967–1972*, 2 vols., East Anglian Archaeology, Report 9, Norfolk Museums Service, Gressenhall

Wainwright, F.T. 1962, *Archaeology and Placenames and History: An Essay on the Problems of Co-ordination*, Routledge and Kegan Paul, London

Wainwright, G.J. 1967, *Coygan Camp: A Prehistoric, Romano-British and Dark Age Settlement in Carmarthenshire*, Cambrian Archaeological Association, Cardiff

    1968, 'The excavation of a Durotrigian farmstead near Tollard Royal in Cranbourne Chase, Southern England', *Proc. Prehist. Soc.* 34, 102–47

    1971, 'The excavation of a fortified settlement at Walesland Rath, Pembrokeshire', *Britannia* 2, 48–116

Wardle, A. 1990, 'The artefacts . . . ' [from Gorhambury] in Neal *et al.*, 113–69

Warner, P. 1987, *Greens, Commons and Clayland Colonization: The Origins and Development of Green-Side Settlement in East Suffolk*, Occasional Papers 4th ser. 2, Department of English Local History, Leicester University Press

    1988, 'Pre-Conquest territorial and administrative organization in East Suffolk', in Hooke, 9–34

    1996, *The Origins of Suffolk*, Manchester University Press, Manchester

Watson, M. 1986, 'Common Irish plough types and tillage techniques', *Tools and Tillage* 5, 85–98

    1998, 'The facts don't speak for themselves', in Mills and Coles, 45–8

Watts, L. and Leach, P. 1996, *Henley Wood, Temples and Cemetery Excavations 1962–69*, Research Report 99, CBA, York

Welch, M. 1985, 'Rural settlement patterns in the early and middle Anglo-Saxon periods', *Landscape Hist.* 7, 13–25

    1992, *English Heritage Book of Anglo-Saxon England*, BCA/Batsford, London

West, S. 1985, *West Stow: The Anglo-Saxon Village*, 2 vols., East Anglian Archaeology Report 24, Ipswich

Westwood, J. 1987, *Albion: A Guide to Legendary Britain*, Paladin, London

Whimster, R. 1989, *The Emerging Past: Air Photography and the Buried Landscape*, RCHME, London

White, K.D. 1967, *Agricultural Implements of the Roman World*, Cambridge University Press, Cambridge

1970a, *Roman Farming*, Thames and Hudson, London

1970b, *A Bibliography of Roman Agriculture*, Institute of Agricultural History, Reading

1975, *Farm Equipment of the Roman World*, Cambridge University Press, Cambridge

1977, *Country Life in Classical Times*, Elek, London

1984, *Greek and Roman Technology*, Thames and Hudson, London

White, L. 1962, *Medieval Technology and Social Change*, Oxford University Press, Oxford

1972, 'The expansion of technology 500–1500', in C.M. Cipolla (ed.), *The Middle Ages*, Fontana Economic History of Europe I, London

Whitelock, D. 1952, *The Beginnings of English Society*, Penguin, Harmondsworth

(ed.) 1955 (2nd edn 1979), *English Historical Documents* I, *c AD 500–1042*, Oxford University Press, Oxford

(ed.) 1961, *The Anglo-Saxon Chronicle*, London

Whittington, G. 1973, 'Field Systems of Scotland', in Baker and Butlin, 530–79

1974–75, 'Place-names and the settlement pattern of dark-age Scotland', *Proc. Soc. Antiq. Scot.* 106, 99–110

Whittington, G. and Edwards, K.J. 1993, '*Ubi solitudinem faciunt pacem appellant:* the Romans in Scotland, a palaeoenviromental contribution', *Britannia* 24, 13–25

Whittington, G. and McManus, J. 1998, 'Dark Age agricultural practices and environmental change: evidence from Tentsmuir, Fife, eastern Scotland', in Mills and Coles, 111–19

Whittle, A. 1982, 'Climate, grazing and man: notes towards the definition of a relationship', in Harding, 192–203

Wild, J.P. 1968, 'Clothing in the north-west provinces of the Roman Empire', *Bonner Jahrbücher* 168, 166–240

Wilkinson, L.P. 1997, *The Georgics of Virgil: A Critical Survey*, new edn, Bristol Classical Press (Duckworth), London

Williams, D. 1977, 'A consideration of the sub-fossil remains of *Vitis vinifera* L., as evidence for viticulture in Roman Britain', *Britannia* 8, 327–34

Williams, J.H. 1984, 'A review of some aspects of late Saxon urban origins and development', in Faull, 255–34

Williams, J.H., Shaw, M. and Denham, V. 1985, *Middle Saxon Palaces at Northampton*, Northampton Development Corporation, Northampton

Williams, M. 1970, *The Draining of the Somerset Levels*, Cambridge University Press, Cambridge

Williamson, T. 1984, 'The Roman countryside: settlement and agriculture in North West Essex', *Britannia* 15, 225–30

1986, 'Parish boundaries and early fields: continuity and discontinuity', *J. Hist. Geog.* 12, 241–8

1987, 'Early co-axial field systems on the East Anglian boulder clays', *Proc. Prehist. Soc.* 53, 419–31

1988, 'Settlement chronology and regional landscapes: the evidence from the claylands of East Anglia', in Hooke, 153–75

1998, 'The "Scole-Dickleburgh field system" revisited', *Landscape Hist.* 20, 19–28

1999, 'Field systems', in *EASE*, 183–5

Wilson, D.M. 1960, *The Anglo-Saxons*, Thames and Hudson, London

1962, 'Anglo-Saxon rural economy', *Agric. Hist. Rev.* 10, 65–79

(ed.) 1976, *The Archaeology of Anglo-Saxon England*, Methuen, London

Wilson, D.R. (ed.) 1975, *Aerial Reconnaissance for Archaeology*, Research Report 12, CBA, London

1982, *Air Photo Interpretation for Archaeologists*, Batsford, London (2nd edn, 2000, Tempus, Stroud)

Wilson, P.R., Jones, R.F.J. and Evans, D.M. 1984, *Settlement and Society in the Roman North*, School of Archaeological Sciences, University of Bradford, and Yorkshire Archaeological Society, Bradford and Leeds

Winchester, A.J.L. 1987, *Landscape and Society in Medieval Cumbria*, Donald, Edinburgh

Woodiwise, S. (ed.) 1992, *Iron Age and Roman Salt Production and the Medieval Town of Droitwich: Excavations at the Old Bowling Green and Friar Street*, Research Report 81, CBA, London

Woodside, R. and Crow, J. 1999, *Hadrian's Wall: An Historic Landscape*, The National Trust, London

Woolf, G. 1993, 'Rethinking the oppida', *Oxford J. Archaeol.* 12, 223–34

Wright, R. 1991, *Anglo-Norman Studies: Index to Volumes I–IX, 1978–87*, The Boydell Press, Woodbridge

Yorke, B. 1995, *Wessex in the Early Middle Ages*, Leicester University Press, Leicester

Index

Page numbers in *italics* refer to illustrations. County names are as given in the text.